D1606768

NEGOTIATION
AS A
SOCIAL
PROCESS

NEGOTIATION AS A SOCIAL PROCESS

Roderick M. Kramer
David M. Messick
Editors

SAGE Publications
International Educational and Professional Publisher
Thousand Oaks   London   New Delhi

For information address:

SAGE Publications, Inc.
2455 Teller Road
Thousand Oaks, California 91320

SAGE Publications Ltd.
6 Bonhill Street
London EC2A 4PU
United Kingdom

SAGE Publications India Pvt. Ltd.
M-32 Market
Greater Kailash I
New Delhi 110 048 India

Printed in the United States of America

Library of Congress Cataloging-in-Publication Data

Negotiation as a social process : New trends in theory and research /
    edited by Roderick M. Kramer, David M. Messick.
        p. cm.
    Includes bibliographical references and index.
        ISBN 0-8039-5737-8 (alk. paper). — ISBN 0-8039-5738-6 (pbk.
    alk. paper)
    1. Negotiation. 2. Negotiation—Social aspects. I. Kramer,
Roderick Moreland, 1950–   II. Messick, David M.
BF637.N4N425 1995
302.3—dc20   95-5106

This book is printed on acid-free paper.

95 96 97 98 99 10 9 8 7 6 5 4 3 2 1

Sage Production Editor: Yvonne Könneker

Contents

Preface

Few areas of conflict research have enjoyed as much vogue over the past decade, or can claim as much substantive progress, as negotiation theory. Scholarly research on negotiation has proliferated, and progress is evident not only with respect to the number of studies published, but in the impressive array of conceptual perspectives evident in those studies. For example, important new frameworks from anthropology, behavioral economics, game theory, political science, social psychology, and sociology have infused empirical research and inspired new and deeper understanding of the negotiation process.

In a recent and thoughtful assessment of this rapidly accumulating body of theory and research, Carroll and Payne (1991) note that most negotiation studies have taken one of four approaches: a *normative* or prescriptive approach derived from economic and game-theoretic perspectives, an *individual differences* approach that focuses primarily on personality factors, a *structural* approach grounded in sociological conceptions of bargaining, or a *cognitive* or information-processing approach that highlights the role of judgmental heuristics and biases in negotiations. From the standpoint of the present volume, what is most striking about Carroll and Payne's list is not how much it includes, but what it leaves out. Somehow, as the cognitive revolution swept its way from psychology to conflict theory, the social dimension of negotiation became minimized and marginalized. This neglect of the social is evident not only in much of the recent experimental literature on bargaining, but also, and conspicuously, in the theoretical frameworks that have provided the springboard for this empirical work.

The demotion of the social in negotiation theory and research, to be sure, was largely unintended and resulted from a number of factors. The first was the sheer success of the cognitive paradigm, which quickly absorbed researchers' attention and dominated inquiry across much of behavioral negotiation theory. Over the space of only a few years, powerful new cognitive theories (e.g., Kahneman and Tversky's prospect theory) emerged that significantly advanced our understanding of the cognitive dimensions of judgment and decision making. These conceptual strides were accompanied by a rapid evolution of laboratory paradigms to be used in the study of these cognitive dimensions of choice. Not surprisingly, negotiation researchers were quick to recognize, and seize upon, the opportunities these developments provided. In exploiting and extending cognitive theory and method so energetically, unfortunately, researchers have largely pushed the social dimensions of judgment and decision processes to the sidelines. As a result, the literature on negotiation "lost sight of negotiation as a form of social action, given meaning by certain structural contexts" (Morley, Webb, & Stephenson, 1988, p. 117). At most, social factors were deemed irrelevant. At worst, they constituted annoying sources of extraneous and uncontrolled variation in empirical investigations. Thus the ascendancy of the cognitive led to an unintended degradation of the social.

Barley (1991) has provided one of the most articulate chronicles of this trend. He notes: "Consciously or unconsciously, both researchers and laypersons [came] to speak as if negotiation, bargaining, and mediation occur during experiential 'time outs.' That is, we portray such activities as bounded encounters into which actors knowingly enter and during which they employ behaviors calculated for those situations alone" (p. 166). He goes on to observe that negotiation, as well as other conflict resolution processes, have become increasingly "bracketed" from ordinary forms of social and organizational experience. In many respects, such bracketing is exemplified most clearly in recent experimental paradigms in which individuals who are linked by computer terminals negotiate in isolated cubicles, their range of responses limited to relaying fixed, predetermined, and discrete choices that correspond to an experimenter's preassigned options, which, in turn, correspond to a matrixlike payoff schedule. In some instances, individuals do not even interact with real persons, but merely "simulated others" provided by a computer program. Thus, intentionally or not, negotiation has come to be treated increasingly as a form of rational, strategic, and calculative activity. The present volume is intended to remedy this tacit derogation and neglect of social context in negotiation theory and research.

To defend our claim that social context matters, and to provide a preamble to the chapters that follow, it might be helpful if we say something briefly about what we mean by *social context,* and how we think an understanding of social context contributes to the study of negotiation. First, we would like to suggest that a social contextualist perspective encompasses a set of core ideas about negotiation processes and outcomes. Among the most central of these ideas is the assumption that in order to understand bargaining phenomena, one needs to take into account the impact of the social and organizational environments within which such phenomena are not occasionally, but inevitably, embedded. Second, a social contextualist perspective articulates a set of values about the importance of conceptualizing individuals as fundamentally and essentially social decision makers. This emphasis distinguishes it from most economic and game-theoretic formulations of decision making, which have generally advanced what Granovetter (1985) aptly characterizes as an "undersocialized" conception of human action. In sharp contrast with such a view, the social contextualist paradigm assumes at the outset that individuals are inherently social actors. It construes sociability as a given, but notes that the levels of sociability negotiators display vary across different contexts. Self-interest is thus construed not as an assumption or a baseline condition, but as a dependent variable like any other.

Third, and significantly, research emerging from a social contextualist perspective encompasses a set of methodological convictions regarding how to approach the study of conflict behavior. It argues, first and foremost, that laboratory experiments need to afford more systematic attention to the effects of social context on negotiation behavior. Although negotiations sometimes involve strangers, they are more commonly embedded in ongoing interpersonal and intergroup relationships. And even when they involve strangers, negotiations occur against a backdrop of social and cultural expectations about norms, roles, duties, obligations, and so on. Thus at the heart of the social contextualist critique of laboratory research is the fact that such research has not very consistently or faithfully kept its eye on matters relating to ecological validity.

Relatedly, and obviously, no one method can adequately capture all of the social dimensions along which negotiations vary. Although this is not a profound or controversial observation, it merits making. We feel that, in overlooking the social, researchers have also sometimes overlooked interesting ways of studying the social. If the notion of social context, in all of its multivariate complexity, is taken seriously, then it is necessary to use a variety of methods of empirical inquiry, some rather new and relatively exotic, in attempting to study it. These include deconstruction, experience sampling, unobtrusive observation, and autobiographical narratives, to name just a few.

This articulation of what the social contextualist paradigm entails implies, of course, a discontent with the status quo in negotiation theory and research. One pragmatic consequence of that discontent was our recognition of an opportunity. We believed that the skew away from the social should provide a unique chance for negotiation scholars to elaborate more systematically on some of the social contextual processes that shape negotiation processes and outcomes. In keeping with the spirit of our claim that social context really matters, we decided to convene a conference; for several days, we met, discussed works in progress, and ruminated collectively about the process of negotiation in various social contexts. The following chapters reflect our collective efforts not only to redeem some past sins, but to suggest some exciting emerging trends and future prospects.

The authors invited to the conference were given a simple charge: Think about how social context affects negotiation. The chapters that ultimately emerged reflect the realization of the conference participants' different goals of theory development and empirical documentation. Accordingly, we decided to divide the book into sections along these same lines. Parts I and II document primarily conceptual trends and prospects: The chapters in Part I focus on the cognitive processes and structures that represent or are influenced by social context, and those in Part II deal with the nature and impact of relationships on negotiations. In Part III, we present some recent experimental advances that probe the mechanisms through which social context influences negotiation processes and outcomes.

RODERICK M. KRAMER
DAVID M. MESSICK

References

Barley, S. R. (1991). Contextualizing conflict: Notes on the anthropology of disputes and negotiations. In M. H. Bazerman, R. J. Lewicki, & B. H. Sheppard (Eds.), *Research on negotiation in organizations: Vol. 3. Handbook of negotiation research.* Greenwich, CT: JAI.

Carroll, J. S., & Payne, J. W. (1991). An information-processing approach to two-party negotiations. In M. H. Bazerman, R. J. Lewicki, & B. H. Sheppard (Eds.), *Research on negotiation in organizations: Vol. 3. Handbook of negotiation research* (pp. 3-34). Greenwich, CT: JAI.

Granovetter, M. (1985). Economic action and social structure: The problem of embeddedness. *American Journal of Sociology, 91,* 481-510.

Morley, I. E., Webb, J., & Stephenson, G. M. (1988). Bargaining and arbitration in the resolution of conflict. In W. Stroebe, A. W. Kruglanski, D. Bar-Tal, & M. Hewstone (Eds.), *The social psychology of intergroup conflict.* New York: Springer-Verlag.

Acknowledgments

Throughout this book, we repeatedly draw attention to the importance of thinking about social context when trying to understand how negotiations happen. It seems fitting, therefore, that we acknowledge the social context in which this book evolved. When we first started looking for a publisher for our book, several people whose judgment we trusted suggested Harry Briggs at Sage. We contacted Harry and, from that first meeting, he has been an enthusiastic and wonderful editor with whom to work. From its inception, he has championed and skillfully guided this project through the publication process. His advice has been timely and constructive, and the book has progressed smoothly largely owing to his steady helmsmanship. We are grateful as well to the many other professional staff members at Sage who helped move this book along the way to publication, including Wendy Appleby, Joe Cribben, Gillian Dickens, Yvonne Könneker, and Abby Nelson. They were all extraordinary. We also owe a special debt to a number of other individuals whose labor contributed to this volume, including Lupe Winans and Benjamin Hanna at the Stanford Graduate School of Business. We thank Joanne Martin for her help in securing funding for this project, as well as the Miller Foundation, Stanford Graduate School of Business, and Northwestern University Kellogg Graduate School of Management for their support. We also thank Judy and Maureen, Chris and Andy, and Matthew and Catherine simply for being there when needed and for making work worthwhile.

Negotiator Cognition in Social Contexts

The five chapters that make up Part I deal with some of the cognitive processes that are involved, for better or worse, in negotiation. The contributions vary from a comprehensive overview to an insightful case study of the failure of Lyndon Johnson's presidency. Understanding the complexity of the interaction between the social context and negotiator cognition stands as a challenge for the next generation of researchers.

The overview offered in Chapter 1 by Thompson, Peterson, and Kray is an excellent place to begin. In developing their information-processing approach, the authors marshal concepts and theories from the area of social cognition to create a framework that can help to identify fruitful areas of research and relate different research themes to one another. The framework provides a definition of the social context in terms of relationships, configuration of the parties, social norms and values, and communication structures. Thompson et al. then explore the traditional stages of information-processing theories— information distribution, encoding, representation, retrieval, and judgment—at three levels. The first level is the bread and butter of experimental social psychologists, namely, that of an isolated person dealing with social information. The second level, contextualized social cognition, places the individual in specified social context and examines the impact of the context on the processing of social information. The third level is that of socially shared cognition, in which the unit of analysis becomes the negotiation team, organization, or group. The focus on socially shared cognition, such as language, norms, and customs, has the potential to stimulate new and exciting ways of thinking about negotiation.

This theme is echoed in the idea of socially shared scripts discussed by Pruitt in Chapter 2. His proposal that negotiations be viewed in terms of dynamic systems, rather than cause-and-effect relationships, makes the system itself the unit of analysis. This being so, it becomes crucial to understand some of the system's rules. Pruitt suggests that there are scripts that characterize working relationships, rules that guide or coordinate the interactions among the participants. Although scripts generally have been viewed as characteristics of individuals, they become system properties when they are shared, and the aggregate consequences of the scripts can be measured.

In Chapter 3, Samuelson and Messick focus on the individual cognitive processes that are involved when problems arise in the use of a shared resource. Rules evolve for the sharing of common resources through negotiation and other processes. Simply detecting that there are problems is not sufficient for new rules to be instituted, however, because feasible alternatives that may plausibly solve the problems may not be available. Samuelson and Messick outline a model of a cognitive sequence, not unlike a script, that speculates about the mental processes required for persons in this type of social arrangement to be willing to institute new rules that constrain and govern the collective access to the resource. Their chapter may be seen as sketching the psychological processes that lead to the motivation for and acceptance of new institutions and norms that regulate interaction.

Cognitive processes may be disruptive and maladaptive, as the last two chapters in Part I point out in very different ways. In Chapter 4, Harrison and Bazerman describe three related phenomena that create cognitive problems for negotiators and other decision makers. Regression to the mean, a purely statistical phenomenon, is often misconstrued and forms the basis for erroneous judgments. When students who have been selected because of their outstanding performance are retested, they generally fail to do as well as they did in previous testing, so it appears that they are doing more poorly. To the extent that expectations are formed on the basis of the original performance, the expectations are inflated because they do not account for any random or noisy elements that could not be counted on in a later performance. Finally, Harrison and Bazerman discuss the winner's curse, which afflicts those who win commodities in bidding situations, such as auctions, in which there are many bidders and some uncertainty about the true value of the commodities. The curse is that the winner will often have paid too much for the commodity, and the cause may be that the winner failed to account sufficiently for uncertainty about the commodity's worth. Whereas all of these phenomena are caused by people's failure to understand and deal adequately with randomness, a quality that is not inherently social, many manifestations of this deficiency have social outcomes and implications, which the authors explore.

The cognitive representation of the negotiator's world may be distorted by more than just a misunderstanding of randomness, however, as Kramer describes in the final chapter in this section. Kramer paints a dramatic portrait of Lyndon Johnson's failing presidency and probes the cognitive processes that underlay Johnson's gnawing paranoia. The fascinating puzzle Kramer addresses is to reconcile the wheeling-dealing reputation of Johnson through most of his career, his image as the consummate negotiator, with his failure once he gained the White House, the ultimate goal of his political ambition. The model that Kramer offers stresses the interplay of a number of factors, including intense public scrutiny of the president's decisions and Johnson's tendency toward rumination, as well as Johnson's distrust of, but dependence on, Kennedy's White House appointees. For Johnson, the social context led to a downward spiral of self-defeating negotiation strategies.

Social Context in Negotiation

An Information-Processing Perspective

LEIGH THOMPSON
ERIKA PETERSON
LAURA KRAY

Decades of research attest to the importance of information for reaching effective negotiation agreements. Walton and McKersie (1965), in their seminal book on negotiations, state: "When information is low, the result will be a less adequate definition of the problem; fewer alternatives will be generated; and the potential consequences of these alternatives will be less explored. . . . when the information is relatively low, the parties will produce relatively low-grade solutions" (p. 140). Similarly, Rubin and Brown (1975) note the importance of information for distributive bargaining: "To the extent that the other party knows both what the first wants as well as the least that he will accept, he (the other) will be able to develop a more effective, more precise bargaining position than would be possible in the absence of this information" (p. 14).

Given the importance of information for effective negotiation, it is little surprise that theoretical development in the area of conflict and negotiation has been guided by cognitive information-processing models (see Bazerman & Carroll, 1987; Carroll & Payne, 1991; Neale & Bazerman, 1991; Neale &

AUTHORS' NOTE: This chapter is based on research supported by grants from the National Science Foundation: SES-8921926, SES-9210298, and PYI-9157447. Many of the research studies reported in this chapter were developed while Leigh Thompson was a summer scholar at the Center for Advanced Study in the Behavioral Sciences.

Northcraft, 1990; Thompson, 1990). Information-processing models offer a number of important advantages for the negotiation theorist. First, information-processing theory is truly a general theory of the mind that accounts for most of the mind's characteristics and functions. Like other general theories, it includes conceptual links to other theories at different levels of scientific analysis as well as applications to naturally occurring practical problems. For example, information-processing models provide an important conceptual link between the fields of decision making and negotiations (Carnevale & Pruitt, 1992; Neale & Bazerman, 1991; Neale & Northcraft, 1990). Second, information-processing approaches account for the variety of cognitive heuristics and short-comings that pervade human judgment (see Fiske & Taylor, 1991; Markus & Zajonc, 1985); similar judgment errors and biases extend to the negotiation domain (see Neale & Bazerman, 1991; Thompson & Hastie, 1990). Finally, information-processing models bring with them methods that have proven useful in identifying constructs, measuring variables, and exploring implications (Fiske & Taylor, 1991).

Whereas the information-processing approach provides a compelling account of how the individual negotiator processes information, from the initial stages of encoding to retrieval and judgment, the model is largely asocial (Greenhalgh, 1987; Kramer, Pommerenke, & Newton, 1993; Neale & Northcraft, 1990). That is, the model effectively describes the flow of information from acquisition to retrieval inside the head of the individual negotiator, but does not consider how the social context may influence information processing. Kramer et al. (1993) note the importance of considering social context in negotiation research. The purpose of this chapter is to develop and describe a social context information-processing model of negotiator judgment and behavior that may serve as an organizing structure for theorizing about social context in negotiation.

In this chapter, we first describe how social context is examined in information-processing models and then describe what is meant by social context in negotiation. The body of the chapter is organized around a general information-processing paradigm. Our coverage is not exhaustive, but rather selective, provocative, and speculative. We supplement our analysis with representative research examples, many drawn from our own laboratory. Finally, we consider limitations of our approach and future directions for theoretical and empirical research.

Types of Social Context Research

We distinguish three types of social context research in negotiation: Type I, or *social cognition,* research examines how the individual perceiver *processes* social information. Studies of person memory (Hastie, 1981), scripts (Abelson, 1976), and schemata (Markus, 1977) are classic examples of Type I research that also have applications in negotiation (Bazerman & Carroll, 1987; Carroll & Payne, 1991; Neale & Northcraft, 1990; Thompson, 1990; Thompson & Hastie, 1990). Type II, or *contextualized social cognition,* research examines how the individual perceiver, embedded in a particular social context, processes information (see Levine, Resnick, & Higgins, 1993). Type II research examines how social context *stimulates* cognition. In Type I research, perceivers cognize about social contexts; in Type II research, perceivers *in a particular social context* cognize about social actors and situations. Studies of accountability (Tetlock, 1985) and interaction goals (Devine, Sedikides, & Fuhrman, 1989) are examples of Type II research that have been applied to negotiation (Carnevale, Pruitt, & Seilheimer, 1981). Type III, or *socially shared cognition,* research examines how the social context in which the individual interacts with others *produces* cognition. In Type III research, the social context, or interaction, constitutes cognition (Larson & Christensen, 1993; Levine et al., 1993). The unit of analysis is no longer the individual information processor (as in Type I and Type II research); rather, it is the interacting dyad or group. The fundamental elements of Type III research are the individual information-processing systems of individuals and the communication between individuals.

We believe that Type II and Type III research provides the most fruitful contributions to the body of negotiation knowledge. Because the basis of Type II and Type III research is the fundamental information-processing model in Type I models, we present and briefly describe the essential elements of the information-processing approach (for more extensive treatments, see Anderson, 1990; Bazerman & Carroll, 1987; Hastie & Park, 1986). We then present a social context information-processing model of negotiation. Before we launch into the description of the model, we present a framework for conceptualizing social context in negotiation.

A Social Context Framework

Social context here refers to the broad constellation of social factors in negotiations. As a way of organizing the constellation of factors that fall under the large umbrella of social context, we identify four key social context factors: negotiation parties, social knowledge and goals, social norms of the institution or organization, and communication.

Negotiation Parties

Probably the most common conceptualization of social context in negotiation concerns the relationship among the parties. This general category includes the configuration of the parties, relationships among negotiators, and the relationships between negotiators and their constituents.

Party configuration. The most basic negotiation configuration is the simple dyad. Several more complex configurations exist, including multiparty negotiation, wherein groups of three or more individuals, each representing their own interests, are at the bargaining table (see Bazerman, Mannix, & Thompson, 1988; Kramer, 1991); team negotiation, wherein two or more individuals unite as one party (see Keenan & Carnevale, 1992; Thompson, Brodt, & Peterson, 1993); intergroup negotiation, wherein individuals who represent different collectives or social groups negotiate with members of other groups (Klar, Bar-Tal, & Kruglanski, 1988; Thompson, 1993); agent negotiation, wherein individuals negotiate through agents (Valley, White, Neale, & Bazerman, in press); and coalitions (Mannix, 1993).

Negotiator relationships. The relationship of the negotiators at the bargaining table is considered to be the primary relationship in negotiation. Relationships among negotiators may be characterized in terms of the type of relationship, such as friend/stranger/spouse (see Fry, Firestone, & Williams, 1983; Greenhalgh & Gilkey, 1993; Schoeninger & Wood, 1969; Shah & Jehn, 1993; Thompson & DeHarpport, 1993); expectations of future interaction (Ben-Yoav & Pruitt, 1984; Shapiro, 1975; Thompson, 1990); affect (Kramer et al., 1993; Loewenstein, Thompson, & Bazerman, 1989); similarity (Thompson, Valley, & Kramer, in press; Valley, Moag, & Bazerman, 1994); and outcome dependence (Kelley, 1979).

Constituent relationships. Negotiator-constituent relationships are also known as the "second table" (Ancona, Friedman, & Kolb, 1991). Whereas constituents may not be physically present at the negotiation table, their presence is often strongly felt (Kramer et al., 1993; Pruitt & Carnevale, 1993; Tetlock, 1985). For example, negotiators who are accountable to their constituents are more likely to make higher demands and are less willing to compromise in negotiations than are those not accountable to constituents (Ben-Yoav & Pruitt, 1984; Carnevale, Pruitt, & Britton, 1979).

Social Knowledge and Goals

Knowledge and *goals* refer to information that negotiators have about others in the negotiation. This information may concern another person's preference structure (preferences and priorities), alternatives to agreement, and strategies. Social goals may include fairness, competition, altruism, and the like. Information about other parties may be based on previous experience, reputation, or direct disclosure. In addition to such explicit forms of information, negotiators may have implicit information about parties derived from stereotypes and role and group schemata. Information stores may be used to fill in missing information about a particular target person, and may contain or prescribe certain goals or motivations for the perceiver who interacts with parties.

Social Norms

Social norms are the beliefs held by members of a particular culture, organization, group, or institution that define acceptable and unacceptable behavior (Bettenhausen & Murnighan, 1985). Our framework considers three broad types of norms: social interaction norms, decision-making norms, and negotiation norms. *Social interaction* norms prescribe appropriate behavior in social interactions, such as politeness rituals, reciprocity in disclosure, and turn taking. *Decision-making* norms prescribe how decisions should be reached by groups (e.g., majority rule, consensus). *Negotiation* norms prescribe appropriate behavior and the conduct of bargaining (e.g., agendas, reciprocity, good faith bargaining, symmetric concessions; see Lindskold, 1978; Schelling, 1960) and appropriate outcomes (e.g., focal points, compromises; Schelling, 1960).

Communication

Communication refers to the mechanisms by which negotiators interact with one another. Probably the most common form of communication is unrestricted, face-to-face negotiation. However, other forms of communication are possible, such as telephone interaction, written correspondence, electronic mail, and communication through messenger. Different forms of communication may affect the way information is perceived, remembered, and acted upon (Bazerman, Gibbons, Thompson, & Valley, in press; Carnevale et al., 1981; Valley et al., 1994).

A Social Context Approach to Information Processing

We organize our analysis of social context in negotiations in term of five major subprocesses of information processing: information distribution, encoding, representation, retrieval, and judgment. In a simplistic sense, the subprocesses represent a linear chain of cognitive events (Pryor & Ostrom, 1987), however, we believe that information processing in negotiation is more complex than a simple linear model.

Information Distribution

The first step toward reaching a negotiated agreement is getting the necessary information onto the bargaining table. In Type I models, information often emanates from some unspecified source. However, in Type II and III models, information is embedded in the social context. We examine two kinds of social context effects that may influence the provision of information during negotiation: the initial distribution of information among participants and negotiators' beliefs about the appropriateness of sharing information.

Initial Information Distribution

The information distribution of a decision-making group consists of the number of pieces of decision-relevant information held by group members and who holds them. *Shared information* is held by all members of the group; *unshared information* is held by only one group member. Information may also be partly shared, held by some percentage of the group members. Effective use of unshared information is often an advantage in group decision making; each member has a different knowledge base, and if all members pool their unique knowledge, together they have more decision-relevant information than any single individual. Multiparty negotiation is a good example of a situation in which information is distributed among individuals, but, more likely than not, is unshared. To the extent that parties divulge information about their preferences and priorities, the probability of finding a mutually beneficial joint agreement increases. Of course, strategic considerations affect the likelihood that a particular negotiator will share information with the larger group. However, factors other than pure strategic concerns affect the likelihood that information will be shared in decision-making groups. Below, we discuss six principles that characterize the exchange of information in groups, as well as some implications of the exchange of information for negotiation.

Common knowledge effect. The common knowledge effect is the tendency for groups to discuss shared information more often than unshared information (Gigone & Hastie, 1993; Stasser, Taylor, & Hanna, 1989). Stasser et al. (1989) use an information-sampling model (Stasser & Titus, 1985) to account for this finding and suggest that discussion is biased toward shared information because it is more probable that any given piece of shared information will be recalled by one of the members who holds it.

Group size and information load. In general, the common knowledge effect is exacerbated as group size increases (Stasser et al., 1989) and as the overall information load increases (Stasser & Titus, 1987).

Demonstrable tasks. Decision makers discuss unshared information more often when they believe the task has a demonstrably correct solution than when they believe it is a matter of judgment (Stasser & Stewart, 1992). When group members believe the task has a correct solution, they risk being proved wrong if they fail to consider all of the necessary information; however, when they believe the task is a matter of judgment, group consensus is the only way to determine if their answer is accurate, so they focus on reaching consensus. Some outcomes are clearly better than others in negotiation; however, individuals use persuasive arguments to justify their most preferred solutions. Further, negotiation tasks contain potential for creative agreements and innovative problem solving. For these reasons, we should expect that negotiators will be less likely to discuss information that is not shared. This may hinder the likelihood of reaching an integrative agreement.

Decision weight. Shared information is given greater weight in group decision making than is unshared information (Gigone & Hastie, 1993; Stasser & Stewart, 1992). Shared information exerts more influence, through both greater presence in group discussion (Stasser et al., 1989) and greater influence on the individual members' prediscussion judgments (Gigone & Hastie, 1993). For example, Gigone and Hastie (1993) examined individual judgments, pooling of information, and group judgments in three-person groups, with information cues that were shared, partly shared, or unshared. In the task, group members predicted the grade of a student on the basis of several cues, such as high school GPA. Even when the researchers controlled for pooling of information in discussion, the initial distribution of information still had an impact on the group judgments, with shared information accorded greater weight in final judgments than unshared information. Furthermore, individual members' judgments predicted the group judgments; when individual judgments were controlled for, the information cues had no additional impact on the group judgments. Below, we discuss two applications of principles of information distribution in negotiation: intraparty information distribution and interparty information distribution.

Intraparty implications. Prior to negotiation, team or coalition members must pool their ideas about their interests and reach consensus about what they want. Teams and coalitions are likely to concentrate on information that is known to all members, rather than pool unique, unshared information. This will probably enhance feelings of solidarity and cohesion. Under many circumstances, the consensus may accurately reflect the group's underlying interests. For example, we might expect members of a team or coalition to be apprised about the most important issue or priority, and so members would discuss and heavily weight this information. However, in other circumstances, such as when information about priorities is unshared, or team and coalition members have highly specialized knowledge or expertise, groups may fail to reach agreements that maximize their interests because such interests were not apparent. Such nonobvious optimal solutions are known as "hidden profiles" (Stasser & Stewart, 1992). Indeed, the discovery of integrative agreements in negotiation may be conceptualized as the emergence of a hidden profile.

Interparty implications. In the interparty context of negotiation, however, the task structure is different. Typically, there is no single optimal solution to a negotiation. However, some agreements are demonstrably better than others for both parties. Because negotiators possess the criteria necessary to assess the quality of different solutions, unshared information may be more likely to be discussed in negotiations than in many judgment tasks. To the extent that consensus pressures operate in the group, the discussion of unshared information may be hindered. Further, to the extent that there is little initial overlap in negotiators' information, such as when parties have differential expertise and knowledge, this may also hinder information sharing and, consequently, produce low-quality agreements.

Under most circumstances, negotiators acquire knowledge about the other party during negotiation. Such information may be considered common knowledge, because both parties know that both parties have the information. In other circumstances, however, negotiators may acquire information about the other party without that party's knowledge. This is known as "inside information" (Brodt, 1994). In contrast to other kinds of shared information, inside information is unlikely to be emphasized during discussion; the negotiator who holds the inside information is typically reluctant to let the other party know about it. However, because inside information influences the pre-negotiation judgments of both parties, it may be quite influential in shaping the final agreement. Indeed, inside information about another party's payoffs (Roth & Murnighan, 1982) or deadlines (Brodt, 1994) sways the final agreement, relative to identical negotiations in which all information is unshared.

Beliefs About Information Sharing

In any decision-making group, members have beliefs about the appropriateness of discussing various pieces of information. Such beliefs may arise for two reasons. First, social norms may prescribe the discussion of certain kinds of information. Second, strategic considerations may lead negotiators to discuss or conceal particular information. For example, one reason members may hesitate to volunteer unshared information when their group faces a judgment task is that the members believe reaching consensus is more important than accuracy (Janis, 1982; Stasser & Stewart, 1992). The key information in negotiation concerns preferences; if negotiators want to obtain their pre-ferred outcomes, it usually becomes necessary for them to state their preferred outcomes or induce others to reveal their interests. However, negotiators may believe that they place themselves in a weak position by revealing this infor-mation (Raiffa, 1982). Also, when negotiators state their preferences they may have concerns about appearing impolite or greedy (Mikula & Schwinger, 1978). Such self-presentational concerns may be heightened when negotia-tions involve parties who are friends or who are in other long-term relation-ships (Cook & Hegtvedt, 1983). Close relationships may alleviate some concerns about providing information, but may exacerbate others (Valley, Neale, & Mannix, in press). For example, in negotiations between friends, negotiators may be less concerned about information weakening their position than they are about appearing demanding or greedy. In other words, trust between parties may increase information provision, but self-presentation concerns may de-crease it.

In summary, the amount and kind of information that negotiators provide each other is likely to be influenced by the structural aspects of the task and by negotiators' beliefs about the appropriateness of sharing information. Large group size and consensus pressures may reduce the extent to which negotia-tors discuss unique unshared information. Both strategic considerations and interpersonal considerations influence negotiators' provision of information.

Encoding

Encoding refers to how negotiators evaluate and interpret information. People interpret information in a manner that fits their initial expectations (Fiske & Taylor, 1991), and may ignore or discount information that is inconsistent with their expectations (Hastie, 1981). Below, we discuss how negotiators' processing objectives, knowledge, and involvement affect social information processing.

Processing Objectives

Processing objectives consist of the perceiver's immediate goals and influ-ence the extent to which he or she uses prior expectancies to interpret new information (Srull, 1981). Biased interpretation or construal of information occurs when people perceive the same stimuli but evaluate it differently (Ross & Nisbett, 1991). In the classic study "They Saw a Game," Hastorf and Cantril (1954) showed college student subjects a film of a football game between the students' school and a rival college. Although students from both opposing uni-versities saw the same film, their evaluations of the infractions and behaviors of actors in the film differed markedly. Princeton students saw the Dartmouth team make more than twice as many infractions as their own team made. Although a third of the Dartmouth students felt that Dartmouth was to blame for starting the rough play, the majority of Dartmouth students thought both sides were to blame. The Dartmouth students felt that the charges being made were not true, and most of them thought the reason for the charges was Princeton's concern for its football star. In sum, the students on each side saw a game in which their team were the good guys and the other team were the bad guys. Lord, Lepper, and Ross (1979; also Nisbett & Ross, 1980; Ross & Lepper, 1980) showed that two opposing partisan groups responded to the same body of mixed and inconclusive evidence by increasing the strength and polarization of their respective beliefs. Further, the same biases that affect partisans' assimilation of evidence influence the reactions that partisan groups have to third parties who offer evaluations or summary reports of evidence (Vallone, Ross, & Lepper, 1985). For example, partisans perceive objective and evenhanded evaluations and those who offer them to be unfairly biased and hostile. Thus there is a clear tendency for the partisan perceiver to view the other side's interests as more opposed to his or her own than is actually the case.

Perspective

Construal processes also distort individuals' perceptions of information in negotiation. For example, partisan perspectives lead individuals to devalue proposals offered by the other party (Oskamp, 1965; Stillinger, Epelbaum, Keltner, & Ross, 1990). Partisan perceptions promote an "us versus them" viewpoint in which individuals believe that what is good for the other party must be bad for themselves, and vice versa.

To examine how partisanship affects perception in negotiation, Thompson (in press) created a methodology in which individuals observed a negotiation between two people and then made judgments about the interests of the parties in the bargaining situation. Observers were instructed to view the negotiation from either a partisan standpoint or a neutral, nonpartisan standpoint. Specifically, observers in the partisan set were instructed to adopt the point of view of one of the parties in the negotiation; nonpartisan observers adopted an objective, balanced point of view. The key analysis examined the judgment accuracy of three groups: the actual participants, partisan observers, and nonpartisan observers. The key prediction was that nonpartisans, compared with partisan observers and the actual participants, should be more likely to make accurate judgments about the negotiators' interests in the negotiation situation and less likely to succumb to the incompatibility perception. As predicted, nonpartisan observers were more likely to make accurate judgments (that is, to avoid the incompatibility perception) than were the actual participants. Further, the judgments of partisan observers were correlated with those of the actual participants, but not with the nonpartisan observers.

Involvement

In this context, *involvement* refers to the extent to which a negotiator cares about a particular situation. Involvement may be produced by several factors, such as accountability, when the perceiver must explain his or her judgments (see Tetlock, 1985); outcome dependence, when the perceiver's outcomes are determined by others (Erber & Fiske, 1984); and when the perceiver expects to interact with another party in the future (Ben-Yoav & Pruitt, 1984). Outcome dependence increases attention to inconsistent information, which leads to more accurate judgment (Erber & Fiske, 1984). Similarly, outcome-dependent individuals who expect to have to work with someone in the future ask more diagnostic questions that are less likely to confirm their prior expectations (Darley, Fleming, Hilton, & Swann, 1988). Individuals recall more information and are more accurate about individuals with whom they expect to interact again (Devine et al., 1989). And, competing individuals attend more to their opponents than do individuals who are independent (Ruscher & Fiske, 1990).

Although involvement is typically thought to eliminate bias by increasing attention to information and thoughtful information processing, Thompson (in press) reasoned that involvement may in fact increase bias, depending upon the *motivations* of the perceiver. The impact of involvement on judgment accuracy depends upon the perceiver's goals (Baumeister & Newman, 1994; Kruglanski, 1989, 1990; Kunda, 1990). Kruglanski's (1989, 1990) lay epistemological process model suggests that people can be highly motivated (or not) either to reach a specific conclusion or to reach whatever conclusion is appropriate and correct. Thus motivation increases effort, which may increase or decrease bias.

Two broad motivational mechanisms may be invoked to understand the social perceiver in negotiation: the intuitive scientist and the intuitive lawyer (see Baumeister & Newman, 1994). The intuitive scientist wants to find the correct or optimal conclusion. In contrast, the intuitive lawyer wants to make the best case for a particular preselected conclusion. In negotiations, participants and partisans may have preferences for particular outcomes. To the extent that the perceiver has a partisan perspective, greater involvement or motivation should induce the perceiver to find support for that conclusion (Baumeister & Newman, 1994; Kruglanski, 1989). In other circumstances, however, perceivers may not seek predetermined conclusions. Nonpartisan perceivers should be equally willing to accept any outcome that evidence suggests (Baumeister & Newman, 1994). When perceivers have a nonpartisan perspective, greater involvement or motivation should improve judgment accuracy (see Neuberg, 1989; Neuberg & Fiske, 1987). Thompson (in press) found that partisan perceivers in negotiation who were highly involved (or made accountable for their judgments) made less accurate judgments than did partisans who were less involved (or not accountable). In contrast, the opposite pattern emerged for nonpartisan perceivers: Nonpartisans were more accurate in their perceptions when they were highly involved (or accountable for their judgments) than when they were less involved. In conclusion, perceivers often see what they expect to see in negotiation as a consequence of their social context.

Social Inference Mechanisms

Social inference refers to the process of collecting and combining information into a judgment (Fiske & Taylor, 1991). A negotiator may use various processes to assimilate and evaluate information about the other party. Certainly, it is not always the case that the negotiator assimilates information about the other party in an objective fashion. Rather, evaluation of information is influenced by negotiators' social context or existing information stores and expectancies. Below, we outline four inference mechanisms that negotiators may invoke to encode information about another party in a negotiation. The mechanism invoked by the negotiator depends upon the information the negotiator has about the target, characteristics of the target, the negotiator's goals, and other social factors.

Structural balance principles. Sometimes, a negotiator makes assumptions about another party on the basis of very little information, using primitive relations among the elements in a social system. For example, one may make inferences about the target based on the mere observation that one is in a bargaining situation and the other party is an opponent. The terms *bargaining, negotiation, conflict,* and *opponent* all imply opposition. Such beliefs are rooted in social norms that lead individuals to interpret competitive situations as win/lose (Neale & Bazerman, 1991). Individuals hold a core belief is that people in conflict situations have incompatible goals (Kruglanski, 1989). Individuals tend to generalize from such win/lose situations and create similar expectations for other situations that are not necessarily win/lose.

Role-based inference mechanisms. In other situations, negotiators rely on stereotypes or category-based information to evaluate targets (Fiske & Neuberg, 1990). When a negotiator has no information about an opponent, he or she may rely on stereotype utility functions (Harsanyi, 1962). As Harsanyi (1962) notes: "In a given society with well-established cultural traditions, people tend to enter bargaining situations with more or less consistent expectations about each other's utility functions. . . . Persons of a given sex, age, social position, education, etc. are expected to have similar utility functions of a specified sort" (p. 13). For example, many people have a stereotype utility function for used-car salesmen. As an illustration of this, we provided some subjects with a description of a "typical" used-car salesman (e.g., wears leisure suits and smokes cigars); we gave other subjects a description of a counterstereotypical used-car salesman (health fanatic). Subjects in both conditions were given identical information about the negotiation situation (e.g., price of the car they were interested in buying) and asked how they thought the situation could be resolved. Those who were exposed to the counterstereotypical car salesman were more likely to believe that a mutually beneficial solution could be reached than were those who dealt with the stereotypical salesman.

Correspondent inference processes. In other instances, negotiators may make inferences through correspondence inference processes, whereby they infer unobservable dispositions or interests on the basis of observable acts. For example, negotiators' positions are different from their underlying interests (*positions* here refers to the negotiator's specific statement of wants; *interests* refers to the values and needs that underlie the negotiator's position) (Fisher & Ury, 1981; Pruitt & Rubin, 1986). This suggests that although negotiators' stated positions may differ, their underlying interests may not be opposed. Just as the social perceiver erroneously assumes that an actor's behavior reflects his or her underlying disposition (Jones & Davis, 1965), perceivers may draw unwarranted correspondent inferences between a negotiator's stated position and his or her underlying interests.

Individuated target impression. Sometimes negotiators will form individuated impressions of a target and not rely on role-based correspondent inference or structural balance principles. Individuated target impressions involve the use of a target's particular attributes, to the relative exclusion of role and membership categories. Individuated target impressions may be instigated by target characteristics (i.e., the target is not readily classifiable; Fiske & Neuberg, 1990), encoding operations (i.e., accuracy goal; Neuberg & Fiske, 1987), or may be developed through experience. In general, individuated target impressions may be achieved through direct questioning (Thompson, 1991) and are more likely to result in accurate judgment than theory-driven processes.

Representation

Representation refers to the structuring of information about a concept or type of stimulus, including attributions and relations among attributions (Fiske & Taylor, 1991). Mental representations are created during encoding, providing a structure for key features and processes of negotiation. Below, we discuss Type I and Type II conceptualizations of social representation in negotiation, along with two Type III models of social representation: shared mental models and group situation awareness.

Social Representation in Negotiation

Cognitive schemata, or organized relations between attributes, are used to structure information (Fiske & Taylor, 1991). Below, we discuss four different conceptualizations of social representation in negotiation: Bazerman and Carroll's (1987) implicit theories, Pinkley's (1990) conflict frames, Thompson and Hastie's (1990) judgment model, and Klar et al.'s (1988) conflict schema model.

Implicit theories. According to Bazerman and Carroll (1987), individuals represent negotiations in terms of implicit theories about situations, people, and causality. A script is an implicit theory of a situation that specifies a coherent sequence of social activities. Individuals may have several scripts relevant to negotiation. For example, a script about selling cars may evoke the familiar used-car lot scenario, or a script of a luxury automobile car dealership, or a script of a college student selling her car through the local classified ads. Each script calls for different behaviors from the actors in the negotiation.

Implicit theories of people are also important in negotiations. A prototype is an image that typifies a particular group of individuals (Rosch, 1978). Individuals who strongly resemble a prototype tend to be categorized quickly, whereas individuals not resembling a prototype take longer to categorize, and the categorization is done with less certainty (Bazerman & Carroll, 1987). For example, a manager in a labor dispute who wears a coat and tie and carries a briefcase would be easier to categorize than an individual in a sport shirt and jeans. Another type of implicit theory affecting negotiation concerns causality (Hastie & Carlston, 1980). Causes are inferred about behaviors throughout a negotiation. For example, a surprisingly high opening offer from the other party may evoke dispositional attributions, or the negotiator may assume that it is a strategic ploy. Finally, throughout negotiation, people may seek confirmatory evidence to support their implicit theories of events, people, and causality (Lord et al., 1979; Schneider, Hastorf, & Ellsworth, 1979).

Conflict frames. Pinkley (1990) suggests that negotiators mentally represent negotiations in terms of three dimensions, or conflict frames: relationship/task, emotional/intellectual, and compromise/win. The relationship/task dimension distinguishes between interpersonal issues and nonrelationship issues. For example, a conflict between the members of a dating couple is distinguished from a conflict between a customer and a store employee. The emotional/

intellectual dimension differentiates between feelings and thoughts or facts. For example, a negotiation between a teenager and her parents about her curfew is likely to be conceptualized in terms of emotional responses, whereas a negotiation between a teenager and her teacher about a book report may be conceived in terms of factual information. The win/compromise dimension differentiates between purely distributive negotiations and those that have integrative potential. Pinkley's (1990) empirical investigation of these dimensions in negotiations indicates that mediators tend to focus more on relationship and compromise issues than do disputants.

Judgment tasks. Thompson and Hastie (1990) suggest that negotiators' mental representations may be represented by several judgments about negotiations: judgments about other party, self, utilities, sequence of events, outcomes, and procedural fairness. Judgments of the other party involve inferences about strength, competitiveness, fairness, similarity in beliefs, attributions, and traits. Judgments of the self include aspiration levels, reservation prices, and a strategy for achieving goals. Another judgment made during negotiation focuses on the utilities of all parties concerned, along with the division of scarce resources. Judgments regarding the sequence of events are made during the negotiation, and involve expected offers and counteroffers. For example, a negotiator may expect the other party to start with an extremely low offer on the most important dimension, yet make a reasonable offer on peripheral issues. In this case, the negotiator has already planned to reject both offers in favor of a counterproposal that weighs more evenly on both dimensions. After negotiation, parties make outcome judgments, which include evaluations of equity and overall success to both parties (Loewenstein et al., 1989; Thompson et al., 1994). A procedural judgment is also made at the termination of a negotiation regarding the fairness of the process (Tyler & Lind, 1992). For example, a negotiator may be dissatisfied with personal outcomes but have no objections about the fairness of the procedure.

Conflict schemata. Klar et al. (1988) suggest that individuals mentally represent certain situations that involve incompatible goals between parties with conflict schemata. A negotiation is a situation that frequently invokes win/lose beliefs. Kruglanski (1988) argues that beyond a core belief in incompatible goals, disputants' conflict schemata differ substantially. Klar et al. (1988) propose a two-stage process of hypothesis generation and validation, based upon both cognitive and motivational factors. The cognitive factors proposed to affect hypothesis generation are the availability of ideas and their accessibility. Motivational factors affecting hypothesis generation include a need for cognitive structure, which stems from an intolerance for ambiguity. In negotiation, a hypothesis may be formed about the procedure that satisfies this need. Further, the fear of invalidity is a motivational factor disposing negotiators to uphold self-serving views rather than confront the objective reality. Another motivational factor is the need for conclusion.

Socially Shared Representations

Up to this point, our analysis of mental representations in negotiation has focused on Type I and Type II research. We now describe two examples of socially shared cognition (Type III) research. These models focus on the interaction of multiple individuals in creating social cognition.

Shared mental model. A shared mental model is a concept that explains how people effectively interact with each other in the presence of complex environmental factors. Formally, Rouse and Morris (1986) define a shared mental model as "a mechanism whereby humans generate descriptions of system purpose and form, explanations of system functioning and observed system states, and predictions of future system states" (p. 360). Shared mental models increase speed, accuracy, and flexibility in the retrieval of information by emphasizing the most salient and important features of a given system (Cannon-Bowers, Salas, & Converse, 1993). Mental models are dynamic, and may account for a constantly changing environment.

Efficient and effective performance in many complex systems depends on the mutual efforts of teams of individuals (Cannon-Bowers et al., 1993). Implicit in this assumption is the distinction between a team and a group. According to Klaus and Glaser (1968), teams are individuals with heterogeneous information, whereas groups possess homogeneous information. Although information in a team is heterogeneous, shared mental models rely on an overlap of implicit information regarding the procedure and environment. For example, a team of negotiators may have different areas of expertise and/or knowledge about the other party, but share similar models of how to resolve conflict. Shared mental models explain how negotiators assess the situation to determine their goals and strategies and to predict future outcomes.

Empirical studies suggest that teams do not share a single mental model of a situation (Adelman, Zirk, Lehner, Moffett, & Hall, 1986; Brehmer, 1972); rather, multiple mental models of a situation exist within individuals (Rouse & Morris, 1986; Stevens & Collins, 1980; Wilson & Rutherford, 1989). Young (1983) proposes several models, including a surrogate model that represents relationships among components in a situation and a task-action mapping model that represents causality of outcomes. In negotiation, numerous simultaneous conceptions of the parties, their goals, and the task may be represented by multiple mental models. To the extent that success is dependent upon common expectations of party members, similarity and overlap of these multiple mental models within each individual is important (Cannon-Bowers & Salas, 1990; Orasanu & Salas, in press). For example, in negotiations in which individuals have different conceptualizations of the situation, effective conflict resolution may be hindered.

Several types of mental models have been identified in the literature (Cannon-Bowers et al., 1993). Probably the most important mental model in negotiation pertains to the *negotiation task*. Mental models of negotiation tasks encompass the procedures of the task, along with the norms associated with procedures. For example, the norms of a particular negotiation scenario may dictate that outcomes should be distributed equally or equitably or that concessions should be matched. Task-oriented mental models organize information regarding task strategies and the environmental constraints imposed on these strategies. A person buying a new house may know that she wants to live in Seattle with a scenic view and hardwood floors and pay no more than $120,000, but finds environmental constraints: Such a house may not exist in the market. This type of mental model also considers possible contingencies and scenarios that play a part in the negotiation and its outcomes.

Team interaction mental models specify methods of interparty and intraparty communication (Cannon-Bowers et al., 1993). Implicit in this model are the roles and responsibilities associated with the negotiation task. For example, an individual serving as the leader of a negotiation team may have responsibilities specific to that position. Further, this mental model takes into account the interdependencies of certain roles, such as a negotiation in which two experts are dependent upon each other because of their complex area of specialization. Particular patterns of team interaction are also important. Team interaction mental models account for the sources of transmitted information in a negotiation, in addition to the exact channels of communication. An accurate perception of this mental model requires constant monitoring and revising of the current scenario because each factor within the model is only moderately stable across situations.

The *team* model represents the manner in which information about the teammates' knowledge, skills, abilities, preferences, and tendencies is organized (Cannon-Bowers et al., 1993). Because the team model is a socially shared cognition, a conceptualization of the content of negotiation teammates' minds is essential if integrative agreements are to be reached. For example, a group striving for maximum hours of paid vacation for its constituents will more easily attain this goal if group members have an understanding of the group's abilities. This mental model has the least stability across situations, presumably because it relies more heavily on the intuitions of individuals than on machinery or situations (Cannon-Bowers et al., 1993).

Group situation awareness. Situation awareness is "the perception of the elements in the environment within a volume of time and space, the comprehension of their meaning, and the projection of their status in the near future" (Endsley, 1988, p. 792). Originally conceptualized in the designing of military and other emergency scenarios, situation awareness is an information-processing perspective that considers the individual to be in a constant dynamic state in which complexity is high. Wellens (1987) expanded the definition of individual situation awareness to group situation awareness, or "the sharing of a common perspective between two or more individuals regarding current environmental events, their meaning and projected future status" (p. 6). In negotiation, both individual and group situation awareness are important.

Group situation awareness involves several key elements (Wellens, 1993). A holistic image is formed based on a perception of the current situation. This image is projected into the future, and several units of time, referred to as zones, are considered in the development of an understanding of individual decision making. These zones are subjective interpretations of reality in the context of some temporal cue. An immediate zone includes the environmental factors requiring immediate attention. In its original model, situation awareness research focused on flight pilots interacting in the immediate zone, or at the control panel in the cockpit. In negotiation, the immediate zone may take into account social context factors such as the presence of constituencies, salient social norms, and communication networks and channels in an organization. The intermediate zone encompasses moderating information that does not directly affect the negotiation situation. For example, the dispute settlement history of the opponent's company would be relevant to the negotiation situation, but it would not be the focal point of interest. The long-term zone encompasses future projections of the current situation. Along with the wide-ranging goals of a negotiator, this zone includes the potential threats that may inhibit the attainment of these goals. This zone is useful for placing the current situation into the big picture of a negotiator's long-range activities. For example, a negotiator may make concessions to an opponent with whom he or she expects to have long-term future relations.

Empirical tests of the group situation awareness model measure the extent to which subjects report an awareness of details in a simulated emergency situation (Wellens, 1987, 1990; Wellens, Grant, & Brown, 1990). At the group level, subjects are required to communicate effectively to make the necessary information connections for successful decisions under varying time pressures. Whereas individuals under pressure are situationally aware, groups do not report joint awareness (Wellens, 1987). In other experiments, a computer program simulated the human decision-making aspect of the task to allow the groups to focus on information exchange during the scenario (Wellens, 1990). Under these conditions, information exchange increased systematically with increasing intensity of communication channels. With the concerns of the immediate zone alleviated, subjects were able to concentrate on intermediate and long-term zones.

Socially shared cognitions are important to the understanding of intra-group representations, such as in the case of group situation awareness, and also in the intergroup context. The attributions and stereotypes held by a group of individuals regarding another group are also important to the under-standing of negotiations (Hewstone, 1989). Shared mental models can also be thought of at the organizational or societal level, as in Hewstone's (1989) concept of societal attributions, which proposes that members of a society share certain causal attributions for societal events.

We have described several types of mental representations that are created during encoding, which provide a structure for organizing important features and processes of negotiation. We have discussed Type I and Type II concep-tualizations of social representation in negotiation, along with shared mental models and group situation awareness, which are Type III models of social representation. After encoding and representation, retrieval is the next step in an information-processing model of negotiations.

Retrieval

Retrieval refers to the acquisition of previously stored information. We will not review retrieval processes that characterize individual cognition, but focus instead on retrieval processes that occur at the group or dyadic level, and also at the intergroup level with respect to retrieval of information between parties to negotiation. At these levels, the organization of social information is broader than the individual information processor.

Transactive Memory

Transactive memory is a shared system for encoding, storing, and retriev-ing information (Wegner, Erber, & Raymond, 1991). Intersubjectivity is the understanding that develops in a transactive memory system and leads to coordinated cognitive activity (Levine et al., 1993). The fundamental compo-nent in a group memory system is information processing at the individual level, or Type I cognition. Yet the system is socially shared, or Type III, because it requires links between the individual systems, or communication among members, to produce a larger information-processing system.

Storage. In the transactive system, an important distinction is drawn between internal and external information stores. Internal information is stored within the memory of an individual. External information is stored outside of the memory of an individual. In a transactive memory system, individuals rely on two pieces of knowledge when they retrieve external information: a label and a location. A label is a retrieval cue that identifies the piece of information to be called from memory. For example, *preference structure* may be the label an individual assigns to the preferences that the other party earns for each possible outcome in a negotiation. A location must also be identified for an item to be successfully retrieved. For example, the location may be another team member who stores the information. By employing a label and a location for stored information, an individual need not internally store the information itself.

Groups of individuals structure information storage to facilitate retrieval much as individuals do (Wegner, 1986). The key aspect of successful group information exchange is that group members have an understanding of the memory systems of the individuals within the group. In other words, the individuals within the negotiation team, coalition, or group become the location for the labeled information. Without an understanding of others' knowledge, retrieval is difficult. Modification of information during storage is more likely to occur in group memory storage than in the individual case because the information is less concentrated and more likely to be replaced by misinformation (Loftus, Miller, & Burns, 1978). In negotiation, multiple members of a party may witness the same sequence of events, yet their memories may be distorted by the differing labels they attach to the situation. One member's recall of a heated debate may distort another member's memory of the event. Further, members who did not witness the event pass along the information, altering the story to resolve inconsistencies. Finally, a new story may emerge that is significantly different from the original, relatively mild, negotiation. We may expect to find greater retrieval inconsistencies between negotiation parties who selectively recall different pieces of information regarding past situations. Similarly, transactive memory retrieval is subject to imperfections because it involves the interplay of multiple items coming from various sources (Wegner, 1986). For example, a group of negotiators responsible for retrieving information about their constituents' financial status may bring inaccurate figures to the bargaining table if the information is spread among group members, or if group members use different labels to represent similar information. The greatest discrepancies between information sources may occur across negotiation parties, who may begin with conflicting goals and interests that partly guide their retrieval of information.

Responsibility. We identify four key determinants of knowledge acquisition, or how a group decides which member will be responsible for given information. In some cases, *personal expertise* determines who will be responsible for encoding, representing, and retrieving information regarding a certain domain. For example, in a negotiation involving complex legal issues, the person with legal expertise may store and retrieve information regarding legal matters. In other cases, *social roles* determine information responsibility. A person who holds a particular role may not necessarily be an expert, but may nevertheless be expected to store and retrieve information. When a clear candidate is not apparent, groups may appoint or assign members to assume responsibility for information through *election* or *assignment.* Finally, *circumstances* determine storage responsibility. For example, circumstantial knowledge responsibility would be assigned to a particular negotiator who has overheard the other negotiating party state a reservation price if the negotiator's partners did not hear this information.

It is relatively straightforward to see how transactive memory systems may develop within negotiating parties such as coalitions, teams, or constituencies. Transactive memory systems may also develop across the bargaining table. This may be especially true when a negotiation involves highly specialized expertise and parties must pool information to resolve conflict. For example, consider a negotiation between two managers of different departments in a company. Each manager may rely on the other party as a source of information concerning a particular area (e.g., the sales manager may seek information about the marketing department's knowledge of product viability).

We draw a distinction between focal and peripheral memory stores in negotiation contexts. *Focal* transactive memory systems pertain to information that is directly relevant to the particular negotiation context, such as issues, alternatives, and preferences. In contrast, *peripheral* transactive memory pertains to information that is less pertinent to a particular negotiation. For example, in a negotiation between union and management representatives, negotiators may discover that both parties have stored knowledge of sports information. In conversations, the representatives can reconstruct or construct sporting events on the basis of each other's knowledge. One question is whether only focal stores improve the quality of negotiated agreements or whether peripheral information stores may enhance (or possibly) hinder effectiveness.

Negotiation Implications

Relationships. People in relationships may have the special information retrieval advantage that accrues to well-established transactive memory stores. For example, Wegner et al. (1991) hypothesize that couples in close relationships have established transactive memory systems that assist in memory storage and retrieval. In their research, Wegner et al. presented couples with numerous sentences containing an underlined category label and associated word or phrase that they were instructed to remember. After all words had been presented, the couples were separated and each member was asked to recall as many underlined words as possible. For example, a category label may be *alcohol,* and the associated phrase would be, "*Midori* is a Japanese melon liqueur" (Wegner et al., 1991). Dating couples were more successful in storing and retrieving information than were stranger dyads when the pairs were not forced to adhere to a specific structure or routine. In contrast, pairs of strangers performed better on a structured memory task (e.g., one person was instructed to remember food items, another to remember history items, and so on) than did dating couples. Apparently, transactive memory is a natural process within dating dyads, and when it is interrupted by imposed structure, the memory functions of the dyad are disrupted. In negotiation contexts, we might expect that natural pairs or groups may develop efficient transactive memory systems (Peterson & Thompson, 1995). The advantages of greater recall in negotiation are important in judgmental accuracy and effective performance.

Disruption. Transactive memory structures are not without their disadvantages. The tendency for the memory system to wander during retrieval opens up an avenue of opportunities for memory distortion (Wegner, 1986). Internal cues associated with various labels may distort the initial label to the extent that the new information is unrecognizable in relation to the original information. For example, an ambiguous label such as *attractiveness of offer* may trigger vastly different information for negotiators (such as cost and date of acquisition) to the extent that the negotiators neglect their constituent's chief concern, which is that the deal provides an opportunity for future growth. As shown in the Wegner et al. (1991) study, groups with established memory structures suffer from interference when new structures are imposed on them (Peterson & Thompson, 1995). In negotiation contexts, an intact negotiation team may represent a new set of constituents who place new constraints on the team's memory structure by assigning different tasks to team members, thus causing inferior memory retrieval and performance.

Improving Transactive Memory

The advantages of a transactive memory system in negotiation are numerous. In most circumstances, negotiators would be allowed to form their own memory structures for information rather than have memory schemes imposed on them. As Wegner et al.'s (1991) work has shown, groups with already established memory systems benefit by greater recall. For example, each member of an established negotiation team should be fairly certain of what information he or she will be expected to bring forth during the negotiation. This allows for a more efficient group that is more likely to attain its goals. Furthermore, the tendency for transactive memory systems to wander from one memory label to another during the retrieval process could prove to be beneficial to a negotiation team (Wegner, 1986). Useful items that were not initially sought may be discovered in transactive retrieval. For example, a party member who questions the rest of the group about another party's bidding status may discover information about the other party's financial history and current debts.

Wegner et al. (1991) suggest several ways in which a dyad may improve transactive memory. Essentially, an updating of information about each person's knowledge base improves group memory structures. Wegner et al. discuss three different strategies for accomplishing this goal. Primarily, agreement about the actual knowledge for which each person is responsible is necessary. A trade-off of information responsibility makes explicit the duties of each negotiator. Another way to update directories of knowledge to improve transactive memory is by evaluating potential areas of expertise of negotiators. For example, a negotiator may realize that she is the most knowledgeable member about financial matters while another member is superior in administrative matters. A similar way to improve transactive memory is by considering each member's access to knowledge. For example, the acknowledgment that a team or coalition member has a working relationship with a member of the other party's team would be beneficial.

Retrieval of stored mental representations created during the encoding stage of information processing is important because it influences how negotiators form judgments and strategies during negotiation. At the group level, the retrieval of information includes the information itself as well as the communication link between negotiators.

Judgment

The goal of information processing is the formation of judgments that can be used to guide behavior. Judgments can either be made on-line, as the relevant information is processed, or derived from memory (Hastie & Park, 1986). For example, a negotiator may assess the other party's preferred alternative on an issue as the other party makes an offer; both the judgment and the offer could then be stored in memory for later use. Alternatively, if the negotiator does not make a judgment as the offer is made and later finds such a judgment to be necessary, the offer must be retrieved from memory and used as a basis for the judgment. The goals and expectations most important or salient to negotiators are likely to affect what judgments are made on-line. To the extent that the social context influences negotiators' goals and expectations, it will also influence what judgments are made. For example, as we have discussed, close relationships in negotiation tend to increase negotiators' concerns about self-presentation and relationship maintenance. Two friends negotiating are likely to make a series of on-line judgments about each other's emotions and reactions that two strangers in a similar negotiation would not make. The social context may influence the type or number of memory-based judgments as well. Negotiators in teams or coalitions may prompt each other, through discussion, to make memory-based judgments that would not have occurred to a solo negotiator in a similar negotiation.

Using the framework derived above, we examine four broad issues related to judgment in negotiation for which social context is particularly relevant: accuracy of judgments about the other party, coordination of judgments among negotiators, judgments about the negotiator's own performance, and the link between judgment and behavior.

Judgment Accuracy

Judgments about other parties' preferences and priorities are typically considered the most important judgments negotiators make. The accuracy of such judgments is greatly enhanced by increased provision of relevant information (Thompson, 1991). However, accurate judgment depends not only on sufficient transmission of information, but also on accurate, unbiased reception (Thompson, in press). In other words, the provision and evaluation stages of information processing are key to developing accurate judgments in negotiation; if a judgment needs to be made from memory, rather than on-line, the representation and retrieval stages would be equally important.

Social contexts that enhance either the transmission or reception of information should improve accuracy. In an investigation of team and solo negotiators, Thompson et al. (1993) found that participants in negotiations that included at least one team were more accurate in their judgments than participants in dyadic (solo versus solo) negotiations. It was reasoned that negotiators provide more information in the team negotiations. The team negotiation advantage in accuracy can also plausibly be explained by a reception hypothesis; that is, the more people involved in a negotiation, the greater the probability that a given piece of information will be accurately received by someone. Our earlier discussion of transactive memory suggests this is true.

We speculate that individuals in multiparty negotiations, on the other hand, will show decreased judgment accuracy. Negotiators in this context may have difficulty with both transmission and reception of information. As the number of parties increases, communication will become more complex and each party will find it more difficult to voice preferences. Similarly, the task structure will become increasingly complex (Bazerman et al., 1988), and, working under this greater cognitive load, negotiators are less likely to receive a given piece of information.

Judgment Coordination

Some social contexts, such as team negotiations, demand coordination of judgments between negotiators. Coordination of behavior between members is often a concern in teams or coalitions (Ancona et al., 1991); given that members share the same interests, difficulties in coordinating behavior are likely to stem from differences in judgments about the other party or the negotiation situation. However, coordination may not be as problematic as it is often considered to be. Thompson et al. (1993) allowed some teams, but not others, to caucus privately midway through negotiations with another party, reasoning that teams given an opportunity to caucus privately during the negotiation would be at an advantage because they would be able to compare and coordinate their judgments and plan their behavior. However, teams that received caucusing breaks did not perform differently from teams that did not. This suggests that the teams already possessed shared mental models of the situation and needed no breaks to coordinate their judgments or behavior.

Performance Judgments

In every negotiation, negotiators make judgments about the quality of their own performance and their satisfaction with their outcomes. The social context has been shown to have dramatic impacts on such judgments. Thompson et al. (in press) have demonstrated the judgment process of inverse affect, whereby negotiators' subjective evaluations of their performance are inversely related to the affect displayed by their opponents. Negotiators who perceived their opponents to be happy with the outcomes of negotiation felt less successful than negotiators who perceived their opponents to be disappointed with the outcomes. The effect was moderated by the relationship between the parties; when both parties were members of the same in-group, inverse affect did not hold. That is, negotiators did not feel successful after negotiating with an in-group member who expressed disappointment. The feelings of success generated through inverse affect are bittersweet; negotiators who felt successful also regarded themselves as less honest, less sincere, less generous, and less fair. Opponent affect also affected negotiators' allocations in a subsequent task: They allocated substantially more resources to in-group members who had expressed disappointment than to out-group members who expressed the same disappointment.

Judgment and Behavior

Judgments are used to guide behavior, but to what extent do they predict behavior directly? In the case of judgments about the other party's preferences, judgment accuracy predicts behavior quite well. Negotiators who make accurate judgments are more successful at crafting integrative agreements (Thompson & Hastie, 1990). However, the relation between judgment and behavior is not perfect. Occasionally, negotiators make accurate judgments but do not reach optimal outcomes (Thompson & Hrebec, 1994). It is puzzling that negotiators would pass up opportunities to improve the profits of all parties. One explanation for this seeming contradiction lies in the distinction between on-line and memory-based judgments. Typically, judgment accuracy is assessed after the negotiation, in response to prompts from an experimenter. Negotiators who show accurate judgment without integrative outcomes may possess the information necessary for accurate judgment, but do not spontaneously make the necessary judgments until questioning prompts them to derive the judgments from memory. We would expect this pattern of judgment to occur only rarely in contexts that emphasize the importance of judging the other party's interests from the outset, or in contexts where others (such as team or coalition members) can prompt negotiators to return to the relevant information and make the necessary judgments. However, it is still possible that a negotiator could make accurate on-line judgments about the other party during negotiation and not carry those judgments through to the final agreement. Whereas economic considerations would dictate that a negotiator who sees a possibility for integration should pursue it, social considerations may dictate otherwise. For example, toward the end of a contentious, drawn-out multiparty negotiation, all the parties have finally reached a satisfactory agreement; one negotiator suddenly realizes that a more efficient solution exists, but, reluctant to disturb the peace, says nothing.

Ultimately, the information-processing mechanisms outlined in this chapter may allow negotiators to craft coherent, strategic sequences of behavior. Complex behaviors may be coordinated by teams, as in the well-known good cop/bad cop routine, and between parties, as in coalitions in multiparty negotiations.

Conclusion

Our goal in this chapter has been to develop a framework for theorizing about social context in negotiations. The basis of our model is the information-processing approach, which we believe offers the negotiation theorist many advantages. However, our cognitive model, like others, has limitations. For example, the information-processing model does not offer well-developed treatments of motivational factors and goals. In addition, the derivation of novel predictions is difficult because of the absence of clear specification of information-processing systems in negotiation.

Negotiation research has for a long time focused strongly on the outcomes or products of negotiations, whereas the process has been the focus of relatively less interest. Part of the reason for this is that outcome measures provide such compelling measures of behavior in negotiation. Another reason is that processes are difficult to measure and capture. And there is little consensus across research studies in the critical components. We suggest that Type II and especially Type III models of the sort discussed in this chapter may provide a mechanism for understanding the process of negotiation.

One criticism that may be leveled at Type III models is that they are really no different from task specialization among group members. However, we believe that socially shared cognition of the type discussed here is different from task specialization in groups. First, socially shared cognition is an implicit system developed within groups of individuals over time, rather than explicitly defined by task roles. Second, socially shared cognition is not simply task specific; it implicates a number of processes and judgments other than simply who does what. Third, socially shared cognition is a mental representation and retrieval system that operates independent of task-related problems facing groups. Our ultimate goal is to understand the mind of the negotiator in the context of negotiation. We believe that an understanding of socially shared cognitions in negotiations will allow researchers to study much of the art of negotiation empirically while preserving its richness.

References

Abelson, R. (1976). Script processing in attitude formation and decision making. In J. S. Carroll & J. W. Payne (Eds.), *Cognition and social behavior* (pp. 33-46). Hillsdale, NJ: Lawrence Erlbaum.

Adelman, L., Zirk, D., Lehner, P., Moffett, R., & Hall, R. (1986). Distributed tactical decision making: Conceptual framework and empirical results. *IEEE Transactions on Systems, Man, and Cybernetics, 16,* 794-805.

Ancona, D. G., Friedman, R. A., & Kolb, D. M. (1991). The group and what happens on the way to yes. *Negotiation Journal, 2,* 155-173.

Anderson, J. (1990). *Cognitive psychology and its implications.* New York: W. H. Freeman.

Baumeister, R., & Newman, L. (1994). Self-regulation of cognitive inference and decision processes. *Personality and Social Psychology Bulletin, 20,* 3-19.

Bazerman, M. H., & Carroll, J. (1987). Negotiator cognition. In B. M. Staw & L. L. Cummings (Eds.), *Research in organizational behavior* (Vol. 9, pp. 247-288). Greenwich, CT: JAI.

Bazerman, M. H., Gibbons, R., Thompson, L., & Valley, K. (in press). When and why do negotiators outperform game theory? In R. N. Stern & J. Halpern (Eds.), *Nonrational elements of organizational decision making.* Ithaca, NY: ILR.

Bazerman, M. H., Mannix, E., & Thompson, L. (1988). Groups as mixed-motive negotiations. In E. J. Lawler & B. Markovsky (Eds.), *Advances in group processes: Theory and research.* Greenwich, CT: JAI.

Ben-Yoav, O., & Pruitt, D. G. (1984). Resistance to yielding and the expectation of cooperative future interaction in negotiation. *Journal of Experimental Social Psychology, 20,* 323-353.

Bettenhausen, K., & Murnighan, K. (1985). The emergence of norms in competitive decision-making groups. *Administrative Science Quarterly, 30,* 350-372.

Brehmer, B. (1972). Policy conflict as a function of policy similarity and policy complexity. *Scandinavian Journal of Psychology, 13,* 208-221.

Brodt, S. (1994). Inside information and negotiator decision behavior. *Organizational Behavior and Human Decision Processes, 58,* 172-202.

Cannon-Bowers, J., & Salas, E. (1990). Cognitive psychology and team training: Shared mental models in complex systems. *Human Factors Society Bulletin, 33,* 1-4.

Cannon-Bowers, J., Salas, E., & Converse, S. (1993). Shared mental models in expert team decision making. In N. J. Castellan, Jr. (Ed.), *Individual and group decision making* (pp. 221-246). Hillsdale, NJ: Lawrence Erlbaum

Carnevale, P. J., & Pruitt, D. G. (1992). Negotiation and mediation. *Annual Review of Psychology, 43,* 531-582.

Carnevale, P. J., Pruitt, D. G., & Britton, S. (1979). Looking tough: The negotiator under constituent surveillance. *Personality and Social Psychology Bulletin, 5,* 118-121.

Carnevale, P. J., Pruitt, D., & Seilheimer, S. (1981). Looking and competing: Accountability and visual access in integrative bargaining. *Journal of Personality and Social Psychology, 40,* 111-120.

Carroll, J. S., & Payne, J. W. (1991). An information-processing approach to two-party negotiations. In M. H. Bazerman, R. J. Lewicki, & B. H. Sheppard (Eds.), *Research on negotiation in organizations: Handbook of negotiation research* (pp. 3-34). Greenwich, CT: JAI.

Cook, K., & Hegtvedt, K. (1983). Distributive justice, equity, and equality. *Annual Review of Sociology, 9,* 217-241.

Darley, J. M., Fleming, J. H., Hilton, J. L., & Swann, W. B. (1988). Dispelling negative expectancies: The impact of interaction goals and target characteristics on the expectancy confirmation process. *Journal of Experimental Social Psychology, 24,* 19-36.

Devine, P. G., Sedikides, C., & Furhman, R. W. (1989). Goals in social information processing: A case of anticipated interaction. *Journal of Personality and Social Psychology, 56,* 680-690.

Endsley, M. (1988). Situation awareness global assessment techniques (SAGAT). *Proceedings of the IEEE Aerospace Electronic Conference, 3,* 789-795.

Erber, R., & Fiske, S. T. (1984). Outcome dependency and attention to inconsistent information. *Journal of Personality and Social Psychology, 47,* 709-726.

Fisher, R., & Ury, W. (1981). *Getting to yes: Negotiating agreement without giving in.* Boston: Houghton Mifflin.

Fiske, S. T., & Neuberg, S. L. (1990). A continuum of impression formation, from category-based to individuating processes: Influences of information and motivation on attention and interpretation. In M. P. Zanna (Ed.), *Advances in experimental social psychology* (pp. 1-74). New York: Academic Press.

Fiske, S. T., & Taylor, S. E. (1991). *Social cognition.* New York: McGraw-Hill.

Fry, W. R., Firestone, I., & Williams, D. (1983). Negotiation process and outcome of stranger dyads and dating couples: Do lovers lose? *Basic and Applied Social Psychology, 4,* 1-16.

Gigone, D., & Hastie, R. (1993). The common knowledge effect: Information sharing and group judgment. *Journal of Personality and Social Psychology, 65,* 959-974.

Greenhalgh, L. (1987). Relationships in negotiations. *Negotiation Journal, 3,* 325-343.

Greenhalgh, L., & Gilkey, R. (1993). The effect of relationship orientation on negotiators' cognitions and tactics. *Group Decision and Negotiation, 2,* 167-183.

Harsanyi, J. (1962). Bargaining in ignorance of the opponent's utility function. *Journal of Conflict Resolution, 6,* 29-38.

Hastie, R. (1981). Schematic principles in human memory. In E. T. Higgins, C. P. Herman, & M. P. Zanna (Eds.), *Social cognition: The Ontario Symposium* (pp. 39-88). Hillsdale, NJ: Lawrence Erlbaum.

Hastie, R., & Carlston, D. (1980). Theoretical issues in person memory. In R. Hastie, T. M. Ostrom, E. B. Ebbesen, R. S. Wyer, D. L. Hamilton, & D. E. Carlston (Eds.), *Person memory: The cognitive basis of social perception* (pp. 1-53). Hillsdale, NJ: Lawrence Erlbaum.

Hastie, R., & Park, B. (1986). The relationship between memory and judgment depends on whether the judgment task is memory-based or on-line. *Psychological Review, 93,* 258-268.

Hastorf, A., & Cantril, H. (1954). They saw a game: A case study. *Journal of Abnormal and Social Psychology, 49,* 129-134.

Hewstone, M. (1989). *Causal attribution: From cognitive processes to collective beliefs.* Cambridge, MA: Basil Blackwell.

Janis, I. (1982). *Groupthink: Psychological studies of policy decisions and fiascos.* Boston: Houghton Mifflin.

Jones, E. E., & Davis, K. E. (1965). From acts to dispositions: The attribution process in person perception. In L. Berkowitz (Ed.), *Advances in experimental social psychology* (pp. 220-266). New York: Academic Press.

Keenan, P. A., & Carnevale, P. J. (1992). *Negotiation teams: Within-group and between-group negotiation.* Unpublished manuscript, University of Illinois, Urbana-Champaign.

Kelley, H. (1979). *Personal relationships.* Hillsdale, NJ: Lawrence Erlbaum.

Klar, Y., Bar-Tal, D., & Kruglanski, A. W. (1988). Conflict as a cognitive schema: Toward a social cognitive analysis of conflict and conflict termination. In W. Stroebe, A. W. Kruglanski, D. Bar-Tal, & M. Hewstone (Eds.), *The social psychology of intergroup conflict.* New York: Springer-Verlag.

Klaus, D., & Glaser, R. (1968). *Increasing team proficiency through training: 8* (AIR E 1-6/68FR). Springfield, VA: Clearinghouse for Federal Scientific & Technical Information.

Kramer, R. M. (1991). The more the merrier? Social psychological aspects of multiparty negotiations. In M. H. Bazerman, R. J. Lewicki, & B. H. Sheppard (Eds.), *Research on negotiation in organizations: Vol. 3. Handbook of negotiation research* (pp. 307-332). Greenwich, CT: JAI.

Kramer, R. M., Pommerenke, P. L., & Newton, E. (1993). The social context of negotiation: Effects of social identity and accountability on negotiator judgment and decision making. *Journal of Conflict Resolution, 37,* 633-656.

Kruglanski, A. W. (1988). On the epistemology of conflicts: Toward a social cognitive analysis of conflict resolution. In W. Stroebe, A. W. Kruglanski, D. Bar-Tal, & M. Hewstone (Eds.), *The social psychology of intergroup conflict.* New York: Springer-Verlag.

Kruglanski, A. W. (1989). *Lay-epistemics and human knowledge: Cognitive and motivational bases.* New York: Plenum.

Kruglanski, A. W. (1990). Lay-epistemic theory in social-cognitive psychology. *Psychological Inquiry, 1,* 181-197.

Kunda, Z. (1990). The case for motivated reasoning. *Psychological Bulletin, 108,* 480-498.

Larson, J. R., & Christensen, C. (1993). Groups as problem-solving units: Toward a new meaning of social cognition. *British Journal of Social Psychology, 32,* 5-30.

Levine, J., Resnick, L., & Higgins, E. (1993). Social foundations of cognition. *Annual Review of Psychology, 44,* 585-612.

Lindskold, S. (1978). Trust development, the GRIT proposal, and the effects of conciliatory acts on conflict and cooperation. *Psychological Bulletin, 85,* 772-793.

Loewenstein, G., Thompson, L., & Bazerman, M. H. (1989). Social utility and decision making in interpersonal contexts. *Journal of Personality and Social Psychology, 57,* 426-441.

Loftus, E., Miller, D., & Burns, H. (1978). Semantic integration of verbal information into a visual memory. *Journal of Experimental Psychology: Human Learning and Memory, 4,* 19-31.

Lord, C. G., Lepper, M. R., & Ross, L. (1979). Biased assimilation and attitude polarization: The effects of prior theories on subsequently considered evidence. *Journal of Personality and Social Psychology, 37,* 2098-2109.

Mannix, E. (1993). Organizations as resource dilemmas: The effects of power balance on coalition formation in small groups. *Organizational Behavior and Human Decision Processes, 55,* 1-22.

Markus, H. (1977). Self-schemata and processing information about the self. *Journal of Personality and Social Psychology, 42,* 38-50.

Markus, H., & Zajonc, R. (1985). The cognitive perspective in social psychology. In G. Lindzey & E. Aronson (Eds.), *Handbook of social psychology.* New York: Random House.

Mikula, G., & Schwinger, T. (1978). Intermember relations and reward allocation: Theoretical considerations of affects. In H. Brandstatter, H. Davis, & H. Schuler (Eds.), *Dynamics of group decisions.* Beverly Hills, CA: Sage.

Neale, M. A., & Bazerman, M. H. (1991). *Cognition and rationality in negotiation.* New York: Free Press.

Neale, M. A., & Northcraft, G. (1990). Behavioral negotiation theory: A framework for conceptualizing dyadic bargaining. In L. L. Cummings & B. M. Staw (Eds.), *Research on organizational behavior.* Greenwich, CT: JAI.

Neuberg, S. L. (1989). The goal of forming accurate impressions during social interactions: Attenuating the impact of negative expectancies. *Journal of Personality and Social Psychology, 56,* 374-386.

Neuberg, S. L., & Fiske, S. T. (1987). Motivational influences on impression formation: Outcome dependency, accuracy-driven attention, and individuating processes. *Journal of Personality and Social Psychology, 53,* 431-444.

Nisbett, R. E., & Ross, L. (1980). *Human inference: Strategies and shortcomings of social judgment.* Englewood Cliffs, NJ: Prentice Hall.

Orasanu, J., & Salas, E. (in press). Team decision making in complex environments. In G. Klein, J. Orasanu, R. Calderwood, & C. Zsambok (Eds.), *Decision making in action: Models and methods.* Norwood, NJ: Ablex.

Oskamp, S. (1965). Attitudes toward U.S. and Russian actions: A double standard. *Psychological Reports, 16,* 43-46.

Peterson, E. & Thompson, L. (1995). *Negotiation teamwork: Personal relationships and shared mental nodels.* Working paper, University of Washington.

Pinkley, R. (1990). Dimensions of conflict frame: Disputant interpretations of conflict. *Journal of Applied Psychology, 75,* 117-126.

Pruitt, D. G., & Carnevale, P. J. (1993). *Negotiation in social conflict.* Pacific Grove, CA: Brooks/Cole.

Pruitt, D. G., & Rubin, J. (1986). *Social conflict: Escalation, stalemate, and settlement.* New York: Random House.

Pryor, J., & Ostrom, T. (1987). Social cognition theory of group processes. In B. Mullen & G. Goethals (Eds.), *Theories of group behavior.* New York: Springer-Verlag.

Raiffa, H. (1982). *The art and science of negotiation.* Cambridge, MA: Belknap.

Rosch, E. (1978). Principles of categorization. In E. Rosch & B. Lloyd (Eds.), *Cognition and categorization* (pp. 27-48). Hillsdale, NJ: Lawrence Erlbaum.

Ross, L., & Lepper, M. R. (1980). The perseverance of beliefs: Empirical and normative considerations. In R. A. Shweder (Ed.), *New directions for methodology of behavioral science: Fallible judgment in behavioral research.* San Francisco: Jossey-Bass.

Ross, L., & Nisbett, R. (1991). *The person and the situation.* New York: McGraw-Hill.

Roth, A., & Murnighan, K. (1982). The role of information in bargaining: An experimental study. *Econometrica, 50,* 1123-1142.

Rouse, W., & Morris, N. (1986). On looking into the black box: Prospects and limits in the search for mental models. *Psychological Bulletin, 100,* 359-363.

Rubin, J. Z., & Brown, B. (1975). *The social psychology of bargaining and negotiations.* New York: Academic Press.

Ruscher, J. B., & Fiske, S. T. (1990). Interpersonal competition can cause an individuating impression formation. *Journal of Personality and Social Psychology, 58,* 832-842.

Schelling, T. (1960). *The strategy of conflict.* Cambridge, MA: Harvard University Press.

Schneider, D., Hastorf, A., & Ellsworth, P. (1979). *Person perception.* Reading, MA: Addison-Wesley.

Schoeninger, D., & Wood, W. (1969). Comparison of married and ad hoc mixed-sex dyads negotiating the division of a reward. *Journal of Experimental Social Psychology, 5,* 483-499.

Shah, P. P., & Jehn, K. A. (1993). Do friends perform better than acquaintances? The interaction of friendship, conflict, and task. *Group Decision and Negotiation, 2,* 149-166.

Shapiro, E. (1975). Effects of expectations of future interaction on reward allocations in dyads: Equity or equality? *Journal of Personality and Social Psychology, 31,* 873-880.

Srull, T. (1981). Person memory: Some tests of associative storage and retrieval models. *Journal of Experimental Psychology: Human Learning and Memory, 7,* 440-463.

Stasser, G., & Stewart, D. (1992). Discovery of hidden profiles by decision-making groups: Solving a problem versus making a judgment. *Journal of Personality and Social Psychology, 63,* 426-434.

Stasser, G., Taylor, L., & Hanna, C. (1989). Information sampling in structured and nonstructured discussions of three- and six-person groups. *Journal of Personality and Social Psychology, 53,* 81-93.

Stasser, G., & Titus, W. (1985). Pooling of unshared information in group decision making: Biased information sampling during discussion. *Journal of Personality and Social Psychology, 48,* 1467-1478.

Stasser, G., & Titus, W. (1987). Effects of information load and percentage of shared information on the dissemination of unshared information in group discussion. *Journal of Personality and Social Psychology, 53,* 81-93.

Stevens, A., & Collins, A. (1980). Multiple conceptual models of complex system. In R. Snow, P. Federico, & W. Montague (Eds.), *Aptitude, learning and instruction* (pp. 177-197). Hillsdale, NJ: Lawrence Erlbaum.

Stillinger, C., Epelbaum, M., Keltner, D., & Ross, L. (1990). *The reactive devaluation barrier to conflict resolution.* Unpublished manuscript, Stanford University.

Tetlock, P. (1985). Accountability: A social check on the fundamental attribution error. *Social Psychology Quarterly, 48,* 227-236.

Thompson, L. (1990). Negotiation behavior and outcomes: Empirical evidence and theoretical issues. *Psychological Bulletin, 108,* 515-532.

Thompson, L. (1991). Information exchange in negotiation. *Journal of Experimental Social Psychology, 27,* 161-179.

Thompson, L. (1993). The impact of negotiation on intergroup relations. *Journal of Experimental Social Psychology, 29,* 304-325.

Thompson, L. (in press). They saw a negotiation: Partisan and nonpartisan perspectives. *Journal of Personality and Social Psychology.*

Thompson, L., Brodt, S., & Peterson, E. (1993, August). *Teams versus solo negotiations: Are two heads better than one?* Paper presented at the annual meeting of the Academy of Management, Atlanta, GA.

Thompson, L., & DeHarpport, T. (1993). *Relationships, task construal, and communal orientation in negotiations.* Working paper, University of Washington, Seattle, WA.

Thompson, L., & Hastie, R. (1990). Judgment tasks and biases in negotiation. In B. H. Sheppard, M. H. Bazerman, & R. J. Lewicki (Eds.), *Research on negotiation in organizations* (Vol. 2, pp. 31-54). Greenwich, CT: JAI Press.

Thompson, L., & Hrebec, D. (1994). *The incompatibility effect in interdependent decision making.* Unpublished manuscript, University of Washington.

Thompson, L., Valley, K., & Kramer, R. (in press). *The bittersweet feeling of success in negotiations. Journal of Experimental Social Psychology.*

Tyler, T., & Lind, A. (1992). A relational model of authority in groups. *Advances in Experimental Social Psychology, 25,* 115-191.

Valley, K., Moag, J., & Bazerman, M. H. (1994). *Avoiding the curse: Relationships and communication in dyadic bargaining* (Working paper). Ithaca, NY: Cornell University.

Valley, K., Neale, M., & Mannix, E. (in press). Friends, lovers, colleagues, strangers: The effects of relationship on the process and outcome of negotiation. In R. J. Lewicki, B. H. Sheppard, & R. Bies (Eds.), *Research on negotiation in organizations* (Vol. 5). Hillsdale, NJ: Lawrence Erlbaum.

Valley, K., White, S., Neale, M., & Bazerman, M. H. (in press). The effect of agent's knowledge on negotiator performance in simulated real estate negotiations. *Organizational Behavior and Human Decision Processes.*

Vallone, R. P., Ross, L., & Lepper, M. (1985). The hostile media phenomenon: Biased perception and perceptions of media bias in coverage of the Beirut massacre. *Journal of Personality and Social Psychology, 49,* 577-585.

Walton, R. E., & McKersie, R. B. (1965). *A behavioral theory of labor relations.* New York: McGraw-Hill.

Wegner, D. (1986). Transactive memory: A contemporary analysis of the group mind. In B. Mullen & G. Goethals (Eds.), *Theories of group behavior* (pp. 185-208). New York: Springer-Verlag.

Wegner, D., Erber, R., & Raymond, P. (1991). Transactive memory in close relationships. *Journal of Personality and Social Psychology, 61,* 923-929.

Wellens, A. (1987). *Effects of communication bandwidth upon group and human-machine situation awareness and performance* (AFOSR Final Report No. P.O. S-760-6MG-085). Coral Gables, FL: University of Miami.

Wellens, A. (1990). *Assessing multi-person and person-machine distributed decision making using an extended psychological distancing model* (AAMRL-TR-90-006). Dayton, OH: Wright-Patterson Air Force Base.

Wellens, A. (1993). Group situation awareness and distributed decision making: From military to civilian applications. In N. J. Castellan, Jr. (Ed.), *Individual and group decision making* (pp. 267-292). Hillsdale, NJ: Lawrence Erlbaum.

Wellens, A., Grant, B., & Brown, C. (1990). *Effects of time stress upon human and machine operators of a simulated response system.* Paper presented at the annual meeting of the Human Factors Society, Orlando, FL.

Wilson, J., & Rutherford, A. (1989). Mental models: Theory and application in human factors. *Human Factors, 31,* 617-634.

Young, R. M. (1983). Surrogates and mappings: Two kinds of conceptual models for interactive devices. In D. Genter & A. L. Stevens (Eds.), *Mental Models* (pp. 35-52). Hillsdale, NJ: Lawrence Erlbaum.

2

Networks and Collective Scripts
Paying Attention to Structure in Bargaining Theory

DEAN G. PRUITT

Most theories in the social sciences concern causal relationships. Causal theories surely have their place in a field like ours, which strives for prediction and control. We must be careful, however, not to overemphasize their value, because they are quite limited in the forms they can take. The only entities allowed in causal theories are variables. Furthermore, the relationships allowed among these entities all reduce to the rather simplistic formulation that variable A has a causal effect on variable B, sometimes mediated or moderated by variable C. These limitations mean that causal theories are not overly successful at handling complex phenomena. When they try to do so, they usually end up making laundry lists of variables that are in positions A, B, or C in the above formulation. This is a rather crude approach to complexity.

Theories about noncausal relationships underlie many of the most important developments in the physical and biological sciences. Some of these theories describe physical relationships—for instance, the periodic table in chemistry, the Bohr atom in physics, and all anatomical descriptions of living organisms. Other noncausal theories describe developmental sequences—either rigid series of stages, such as the early theories of human development, or contingent developmental paths with choice points along the way. Still other noncausal theories describe systems in equilibrium, such as theories about steady states in the regulation of various bodily functions. Finally, there are theories that consist of transitive mathematical relationships—for example, $E = mc^2$.

For want of a better term, I call all noncausal theories *structural accounts* or *structural models*. Structural accounts *make order out of complexity,* and thus compensate for the deficiency in causal theory. Yet they are quite useful as a basis for deriving causal hypotheses. Knowing how things are structured allows us to make educated guesses about how they function.

Two sophisticated structural models underlie most theory and research about bargaining. One is the game in normal form, which displays the value to each party of each pair of choices they make. The other is the joint utility space, which shows the value of the options available to bargainers in two-dimensional space. Both models have been extremely useful, but they cannot fill all needs.

Bargaining theory clearly needs more structural models in order to handle the complexity of the phenomena under study. In this chapter I propose two such models, one designed to deal with the complexities of *negotiation between organizations* and the other to illuminate the role of *working relationships* in negotiation. These models have in common that they help to specify some of the processes and conditions that lead to *integrative agreements,* that is, agreements that produce high joint benefit for the parties involved. But the two models do so in very different ways. In the organizational model, integrative agreements are achieved by reconciling the interests held by many parties at a given point in time. In the relationship model, integrative agreements are achieved by reconciling the interests held by two parties in a series of issues that unfold over time.

A Network Model of Negotiation Between Organizations

Prior thinking about negotiation between organizations (e.g., Benton & Druckman, 1974; Wall, 1975; Walton & McKersie, 1965) has been dominated by a simplistic model of communication structure: the constituent-representative model (see Figure 2.1). This assumes that negotiators ("representatives") communicate with each other and with policy makers in their organizations (their "constituents"). Representatives are assumed to engage in "negotiation," whereas constituents engage in "preparation for negotiation," often in consultation with their negotiators.

An implication of the constituent-representative model is that negotiators act as boundary role occupants or intermediaries (Colosi, 1983). This means that they are Janus-faced, each presenting constituents' views to the other negotiator and the other negotiator's views to constituents. Because negotiators have access to both sides' perspectives, they are often in a unique position to devise creative solutions to the issues under discussion (Ben-Yoav & Pruitt, 1984).

A   B   C
Constituent 1◄—►Negotiator 1 ◄—► Negotiator 2 ◄—► Constituent 2

Figure 2.1. The Constituent-Representative Model
SOURCE: Pruitt (1994). Reprinted by permission.

Though it has some useful features, the constituent-representative model is deficient in two main ways. First, the model treats constituents as a black box, failing to acknowledge that they usually are parts of complex organizations involving many individuals and groups who communicate and negotiate with each other about the issues under discussion (Winham, 1979). Second, the model draws a misleading distinction between *inter*organizational negotiation, taking place in arena B, and *intra*organizational *preparation* for negotiation, taking place in arenas A and C. In reality, negotiation is found in all three of these arenas, and usually many more, within the organizations. Furthermore, preparation for negotiation *within* organizations is often found in discussions *between* the organizations. For example, negotiators from two organizations sometimes meet privately to discuss how to deal with a particular constituent in one of their organizations. Indeed, the main resistance to agreement, and hence the main focus of preparation for negotiation, may lie deep in one organization, at a considerable distance from the boundary between the organizations.

The Branching Chain Model

I have developed a preliminary communication network model to correct the deficiencies just described, which I call the *branching chain model* (Pruitt, 1994; Pruitt & Carnevale, 1993). It was inspired by some case material I gathered in interviews with State Department officers more than 30 years ago (Pruitt, 1964). The model is an extension of the constituent-representative model. It assumes that the communication chain shown in that model extends in either direction into the two organizations, linking the various departments that are involved in the negotiation in one grand chain. Most individuals within the organizations are viewed as negotiators who behave toward each other in the same way as the representatives who meet at the boundary between the organizations. In other words, most members of the chain are Janus-faced intermediaries.

An example of a branching chain is shown in Figure 2.2, which is based on one of the cases in my study. The intermediaries are shown by the letter I. There are also stakeholders[1] at the ends of the branches on both sides of the chain, who are represented by the letter S. Though they may not always recognize it, the job of the intermediaries is to reconcile the interests of as many of the important stakeholders as possible. This means that *bilateral* negotiation is usually better understood as *multilateral* negotiation.

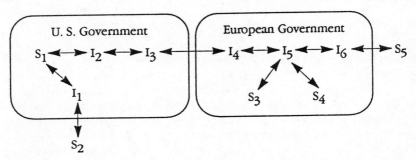

Figure 2.2. Example of the Branching Chain Model Involving Negotiation Between the Governments of the United States and a European Country
SOURCE: Pruitt (1994). Reprinted by permission.

Each intermediary provides a link between at least two other chain members. Normal communication is from person to person along the chain, with intermediaries presenting the views of the parties on both sides of them to each other. Adjacent members of the chain are "counterparts" who often work with each other on more than one issue.

The case shown in Figure 2.2 began when the U.S. Air Force decided that it needed some tracking equipment installed in a colonial area that was developing a measure of self-government. There was an initial negotiation between Air Force technical officers (S_1) and a Defense Department official (I_1) who felt responsible for representing the interests of the American industry that usually made and installed this equipment (S_2). The Air Force wanted the equipment to be under Air Force control, and the Defense Department wanted it to be under commercial control. The Air Force won this initial round.

Next, the Air Force technical people sent the request to install the equipment to the office of the Air Force General Counsel (I_2), which was their liaison with the State Department. It was sent on from there to a State Department desk officer (I_3) who handled contacts with the West European country that controlled the colony in question, which I shall call country X. This officer transmitted the request to his counterpart (I_4), a first secretary in the embassy of country X, who transmitted it to an officer in his home office (I_5). The U.S. request was approved by stakeholders in X's foreign ministry (S_3) and defense department (S_4) and then sent to someone in X's colonial office (I_6) to check with the local government in the colonial area (S_5). More intermediaries were probably involved at this point, but my informant did not have precise information about them. At any rate, the local government rejected the proposal, also arguing that the equipment should be installed commercially, and this information was transmitted back to the Air Force through the same channels. This was the beginning of a protracted process that eventually led to agreement, but let us stop at this point for some theoretical analysis.

Why Are There Intermediaries and Why So Many?

The chain of five intermediaries shown in Figure 2.2 was not atypical in length for this sample. Of the 13 international negotiations that I learned about in my interviews, 5 had chains of four, 4 had chains of five, 2 had chains of six, and 2 had chains of seven intermediaries. Furthermore, some of these chain lengths are probably underestimated, because my informants did not always know exactly what had happened in other departments or governments.

This raises several related questions. Chains of this length seem like an awkward way to communicate and make decisions. Why not dispense with the intermediaries and have direct communication between the stakeholders? And if intermediaries are needed, why so many?

There are two main answers to these questions. First, intermediaries become involved because stakeholders usually do not have sufficient knowledge, access, or resources to deal directly with each other. For example, in the case just given, the Air Force technical officers (S_1) and the local officials in the colonial area (S_5) were from totally different worlds. Hence it seems almost certain that the former did not have enough knowledge to locate the latter and deal effectively with them. Nor did they have the resources (e.g., the time or the travel funds) to develop the necessary knowledge. Their job was engineering, not foreign contacts. What they did was turn over the foreign contact job to their liaison with the State Department, the office of the Air Force General Counsel (I_2).

The same points explain why intermediaries often deal with other intermediaries, adding links to the chain. For example, the Air Force General Counsel turned to the State Department specialist on country X (I_3), a greater expert, and the latter turned to the first secretary in the embassy of country X (I_4), who had even more knowledge of and access to the relevant stakeholders. Thus the chain grew longer and longer.

Second, intermediaries can become involved because of the need to introduce *extraneous policy considerations* into most decisions. The issue raised by the Air Force potentially touched on a variety of State Department policies regarding country X and its colonies—policies based on past treaties, current negotiations, and future plans of all sorts. Hence government regulations required that the State Department serve as an intermediary—this was the *proper channel.* If the State Department had let other government agencies make direct contact with foreign countries, U.S. foreign policy would have consisted of thousands of loose ends.

Many of the policies introduced by intermediaries reflect the interests of stakeholders outside the primary chain. For example, I_1 represented the interests of American industry in early discussion of the case, and I_5 intruded European military considerations at a later stage. Such outside interests account for the branching at either end of the negotiation chain.

Achieving a Meeting of Minds

Long, branching chains of the kind just described seem to be a standard and necessary part of negotiation between organizations. But how is it possible to reach a meaningful meeting of minds in such a system? What happens when there is a weak link in the chain—a chain member who fails to transmit messages or to interpret them accurately? And how does one avoid the distortions that inevitably occur as messages travel along chains (Bartlett, 1932)?

One answer to these questions lies in the fact that the issues are usually *important* to the participants. Hence they are trying to influence thinking and action down the line rather than simply passing along what they have heard. This motivates them to check to be sure that their messages are transmitted accurately and taken seriously. An *initialing procedure* is used by the U.S. government as an aid to this checking. For the government to adopt a policy or negotiation position, all officials who have legitimate interest in the issues must affix their initials to a written document. This procedure also, of course, commits the officers to the decision, making them more likely to participate in its implementation and to accept responsibility if it fails.

A second answer lies in the availability of *alternative channels* of communication at most junctures in the chain. For example, if U.S. officials had not been satisfied with the way I_4 handled their request, they could have resubmitted it through the American embassy in country X, or sent a high State Department official to see the Washington ambassador of that country, a superior of I_4.

A third answer lies in *meetings* that often occur between people from several points along the chain. Such meetings reduce reliance on intermediaries and, hence, help to solve the problem of weak links. When disagreements arose in the cases in my sample, meetings were almost always organized; these meetings sometimes involved large segments of the chain, reaching across national boundaries. An example is a meeting that involved an Air Force technical officer (S_1), an official from the Defense Department (I_1), a representative of the Air Force General Counsel (I_2), the State Department area specialist (I_3), and the first secretary from X's Washington embassy (I_4). The aim of that meeting was to decide how to approach the recalcitrant party, the local government in the colonial area (S_5). This was followed by an even larger meeting, in which the officers just listed met with an official from the local government. This last meeting produced a creative agreement that served the interests of both S_1 and S_5.

The existence of such meetings drives another nail into the coffin of the constituent-representative model (Figure 2.1). According to this model, all contacts across organizational boundaries are handled by specialists, the "negotiators"; "constituents" do not become involved in such contacts. Yet, assuming that I$_3$ and I$_4$ were the negotiators in this case, constituents were involved in both meetings just described. Furthermore, the first meeting casts doubt on the traditional distinction between *inter*organizational negotiation and *intra*organizational preparation for negotiation. This meeting was an *international* discussion to decide how to deal with a recalcitrant party *associated with one of the countries.*

Successful Negotiation in Branching Chains

A possible measure of success in interorganizational negotiations is the extent to which they produce integrative agreements that speak to the interests of as many important stakeholders as possible. This criterion may seem odd to people who view negotiation as an essentially competitive enterprise, but integrative agreements are important for at least three reasons: They are especially likely to endure, they tend to strengthen the relationship between the parties to the negotiation, and they foster joint enterprises involving these parties. As an example of the last point, consider the United States and its ally, country X, at the time of the case just described. Their joint enterprise was the Cold War, a vast struggle. Integrative agreements allowed both of them to pursue this struggle more effectively.

Under what circumstances can systems of the kind just described produce integrative agreements? There are three answers to this question:

- Success is partly a function of the *quality of the relationships* between people who are adjacent to each other along the communication chain. These people serve as buffers between the stakeholders, bridging the gaps that inevitably develop because of different languages, meanings, customs, and values (see Friedman, 1992). This buffering will be effective to the extent that cultural understanding develops between counterparts along the chain, so that they can accurately portray the viewpoints of the parties on either side of them to each other. Proper buffering also requires that sympathy and trust develop between counterparts, so that they can talk freely to each other and take each other's interests seriously enough to devise integrative agreements.
- Success is a function of *optimal chain length.* It is clear that chains can be too long, producing troublesome failures of communication from one end to the other. But they can also be *too short.* Chains of considerable length are usually needed when there are large differences in worldviews and values between stakeholders at either end. This ensures that there will be sufficient cultural understanding and adequate sympathy and trust *at every point along the chain.* Remove one intermediary from such a chain, and a troublesome gap in understanding or appreciation may develop.[2]
- Success is a function of *organizational flexibility*—the availability of alternative channels of communication and the capacity to hold large meetings that cut

across significant organizational boundaries. Such flexibility becomes particularly important when chains are long, increasing the likelihood of miscommunication and inadequate counterpart relationships. Systems that make it easy to communicate around weak parts of the chain and to organize meetings of diverse interests are more likely to solve their interorganizational problems than those that do not.

Collective Scripts in Working Relationships Between Negotiators

My second illustration of structural analysis is designed to deal with some of the complexities of working relationships between people. In working relationships, the parties help each other for instrumental reasons, because they are interdependent and want to encourage each other to be helpful in the future. Working relationships can be contrasted with communal relationships (Clark & Mills, 1979): In the former, help is given for instrumental reasons; in the latter, for genuine reasons. Most relationships are a combination of both types.

The structure I propose is a *collective script,* which, I argue, is universal in working relationships around the world and may well contain some instinctive features. This script ensures that the parties will help each other on a continuing basis and makes it likely that they will achieve high joint benefit in doing so.

Scripts are, of course, basically the property of individuals. However, some scripts are best understood as collective, or the property of a group as well as the individuals in the group. Such scripts are enacted only if other people are also enacting them, and they involve interlocking roles and/or substitutability (i.e., if one person fails to perform an element of the script, others fill in). Collective scripts belong to the class of contingent-path developmental models.

The working-relationship script involves a four-part routine. The first three procedures in this routine are ready to be enacted whenever there is a divergence of interest between the parties. They are as follows:

- *Inquiry:* Ascertain the value to each party of the available options.
- *Problem solving:* If the parties prefer different options, engage in problem solving to seek a win/win solution.
- *Mutual responsiveness:* If problem solving is unsuccessful, choose the option that satisfies the party with the stronger feelings about the issue. This part of the routine involves interpersonal comparisons of utility. Economists typically deny that such comparisons are possible, but they are often observed in everyday life.

These procedures will tend to produce high joint benefit in a *sequential agenda,* in other words, when a series of issues is encountered over a period of time, as is usually the case in relationships. They will also provide roughly *equal* benefit if one party feels strongly about some issues and the other party feels strongly about others.

But what happens when there is a run of issues on which one party feels more strongly than the other? For example, today we are deciding whether or not to see your favorite client, tomorrow you are tired and want me to finish your work, the next day you need my advice, and so on. The problem with such runs is that your benefit is likely to pull ahead of my benefit, endangering the working relationship. A fourth part of the routine applies to such runs:

- *Reciprocity:* Reward a party who falls "seriously" behind in benefit.

There are two ways to do this. One is to grant the other party's wishes on the next issue, *even if the party who is ahead in benefit feels more strongly about the issue.* The other is to devise a way to benefit the lagging party—for example, by buying the party an unexpected gift. It should be noted that reciprocity often involves a temporary departure from mutual responsiveness that is designed to shore up one party's commitment to the relationship.

The four procedures just described are affected by the *strength* of the working relationship, that is, the extent to which the people have something to offer each other on a continuing basis and trust each other to enact the script. When relationships are stronger, the first three components are enacted more vigorously. The people work harder at ascertaining needs and at problem solving, and are willing to incur more costs in order to be responsive to each other's needs. But the fourth component, reciprocity, becomes *less* prominent when there is a strong working relationship that is expected to endure. This is because the two parties' benefits can be expected to even out in the long run. One party's benefits must be way ahead of the other's for either party to see the situation as serious enough to warrant reciprocity. Reciprocity is a hallmark of shallow relationships, where there is little time perspective, commitment, or trust.

As with all joint enterprises, the working relationship script is accompanied by norms that guard against standard temptations. The three most important norms are as follows:

- There is always a temptation to act selfishly even though the other's feelings about the issue are stronger than one's own. Hence a *norm of responsiveness* tends to develop, which requires that one yield in this circumstance.
- There is also a temptation to ignore the fact that the other has fallen behind in a one-sided run of issues. Hence we find a *norm of reciprocity.*

- In addition, we find a *norm of truth in signaling* (Pruitt & Carnevale, 1993, p. 137). This requires that one give an honest account of the depth of one's feelings on an issue, despite the temptation to overstate in an effort to win.

In the absence of these three norms, the entire collective procedure is likely to collapse.

When parties have a lot to offer each other, the collective script just described, with its accompanying norms, produces high individual and joint benefit. This means that the capacity to enact such a script should be selected by evolutionary processes, because it contributes to the success and survival of the individuals who employ it (and their blood relatives as well). This also means that the script should be favored by culture and endorsed by each new generation as applicable to situations in which parties have something to offer each other. Such endorsement is even more certain because this script also satisfies the most important canons of distributive justice (equal outcomes and responsiveness to needs) and of procedural justice (equal rights and voice).

Conclusion

Two structural models have been presented in this chapter: a branching chain model of negotiation between organizations and a collective script for working relationships. They are put forward here as a challenge to the field of bargaining research, which is greatly in need of new structural models to account for the complexities of the phenomena under study.

Notes

1. The term *stakeholder* is borrowed from Gray (1989).
2. Kraslow and Loory (1968) report that during the Vietnam War, a mediation chain went from the U.S. government through officials in Great Britain to officials in Eastern Europe and finally to the government of North Vietnam. This analysis suggests that a chain of such unusual length (most mediation efforts involve only one intermediary) was needed so that there would be people who understood and trusted each other at every point along the way. When there is a high level of distrust between organizations, representatives may lose influence with their constituents because they consort with the "enemy." Friedman and Podolny (1992) present evidence that some negotiation teams solve this problem by further lengthening the communication chain, assigning the roles of coordinating with constituents and coordinating with the adversary to different team members. Because of their common team membership, these coordinators presumably trust each other enough to establish effective communication.

References

Bartlett, F. C. (1932). *Remembering.* Cambridge: Cambridge University Press.

Benton, A. A., & Druckman, D. (1974). Constituent's bargaining orientation and intergroup negotiations. *Journal of Applied Social Psychology, 4,* 141-150.

Ben-Yoav, O., & Pruitt, D. G. (1984). Accountability to constituents: A two-edged sword. *Organizational Behavior and Human Performance, 34,* 282-295.

Clark, M. S., & Mills, J. (1979). Interpersonal attraction in exchange and communal relationships. *Journal of Personality and Social Psychology, 37,* 12-24.

Colosi, T. (1983). Negotiation in the public and private sectors: A core model. *American Behavioral Scientist, 27,* 229-253.

Friedman, R. A. (1992). The culture of mediation: Private understandings in the context of public conflict. In D. M. Kolb & J. M. Bartunek (Eds.), *Hidden conflict in organizations: Uncovering behind-the-scenes disputes.* Newbury Park, CA: Sage.

Friedman, R. A., & Podolny, J. (1992). Differentiation of boundary spanning roles: Labor negotiations and implications for role conflict. *Administrative Science Quarterly, 37,* 28-47.

Gray, B. (1989). *Collaborating: Finding common ground for multiparty problems.* San Francisco: Jossey-Bass.

Kraslow, D., & Loory, S. H. (1968). *The secret search for peace in Vietnam.* New York: Vintage.

Pruitt, D. G. (1964). *Problem solving in the Department of State.* Denver: University of Denver Press.

Pruitt, D. G. (1994). Negotiation between organizations: A branching chain model. *Negotiation Journal, 10,* 217-230.

Pruitt, D. G., & Carnevale, P. J. (1993). *Negotiation in social conflict.* Pacific Grove, CA: Brooks/Cole.

Wall, J. A., Jr. (1975). Effects of constituent trust and representative bargaining orientation on intergroup bargaining. *Journal of Personality and Social Psychology, 31,* 1004-1012.

Walton, R. E., & McKersie, R. B. (1965). *A behavioral theory of labor negotiations.* New York: McGraw-Hill.

Winham, G. R. (1979). Practitioners' views of international negotiation. *World Politics, 32,* 111-135.

3

Let's Make Some New Rules
Social Factors That Make Freedom Unattractive

CHARLES D. SAMUELSON
DAVID M. MESSICK

The sharing of common resources is one of the most social of human activities. It may be regulated by complex sets of rules and institutions (Ostrom, 1990) or by relatively free access to the common resources. Probably all common resources were originally unregulated, suggesting that rules and institutions evolved through the negotiation of concerned parties in efforts to achieve benefits superior to those enjoyed through unbridled freedom. In this chapter we present a theory of the social conditions that stimulate the search for rules that would replace free access for everyone to a shared resource. The theory we outline is less a theory of negotiation than a theory of psychological processes that lead to the belief that negotiation is desirable. The theory also suggests social factors that contribute to the preference for one type of rule over others. To illustrate our topic, consider the following examples.

1. In 1983, because of rapidly declining crab stocks owing to overfishing, the state of Alaska took action and closed the red king crab fishery in western Alaska. The state prohibited further fishing for red king crab and provided aid to affected fishermen to refit their boats for groundfish operations (Borrego & Burns, 1985).

2. In 1975, in response to overfishing of its cod banks by fleets from Great Britain, Soviet Union, Norway, and Denmark, the nation of Iceland extended its "zone of economic interest" boundary out to 200 miles from its coastline. This unilateral political action prevented neighboring nations from depleting the economically

valuable cod population in this region by establishing Iceland as "conservator" of this territory.

3. In 1986, the U.S. Congress passed the Gramm-Rudman Bill. This legislation was designed to reduce the national debt by placing restrictions on the amount of money that could be spent by the U.S. government each year. Advocates of this bill argued that the law would discourage members of Congress from proposing costly government programs that benefit their own constituencies at the expense of the nation's collective debt, which will ultimately be borne by future generations of Americans.

The above three examples share several important features. First, each illustrates a social dilemma involving shared resources—red king crab, cod banks, and federal government funds. In all three situations, self-interested choices by individual users resulted in poorer collective outcomes than if all had made cooperative choices favoring the group interest. Second, a solution to the problem in each case necessitated collective action either by the group members themselves or by a superordinate authority. Third, the solution adopted in all three examples required a structural change in the rules for allocating and managing the shared resource.

In this chapter we present an overview of the theoretical approach and major empirical results from our research program, which began more than 10 years ago to investigate institutional solutions to social dilemmas involving shared resources. We began this research with the goal of understanding the conditions under which people will decide to change the rules for allocating shared resources among group members. We attempt here to provide the reader with a chronology of the developmental phases through which this research has progressed, from the early experiments to our most recent work. Our thinking about this problem has changed during the course of our studies, and it is our hope that this chapter will reveal some of the unexpected twists and turns of this research project.

Messick and Brewer (1983), in a review of the social dilemma literature, have made a distinction between individual and structural solutions to social dilemmas. *Individual solutions* are voluntary changes in the behavior of individual group members made to achieve higher levels of cooperation. These solutions can be implemented on a decentralized basis. That is, appeals for greater cooperation are directed toward individuals in the hope of achieving voluntary compliance from group members. In contrast, *structural solutions* typically involve collective action among group members to either modify or eliminate the social dilemma incentive structure facing the group. The bulk of experimental social dilemma research has examined individual solutions (e.g., What factors influence individual cooperation in groups?). The focus of the research reported in this chapter, however, is on structural solutions to social dilemmas, particularly those involving shared resources.

The individual/structural distinction made by Messick and Brewer (1983), aside from its taxonomic merits, has important implications for research. Individual solutions depend on choices made by group members within a given pattern of interdependence. Structural solutions, on the other hand, depend on group members' choices about the rules or structure that determines their pattern of social interdependence. Simply put, research on individual solutions focuses on the effects of structure on members' choices, whereas research on structural solutions examines preferences for certain types of interdependence structures. Decisions to implement structural changes are, in essence, metadecisions by group members about the decision environment in which individual choices will be made. Because of this crucial difference, decisions about structural change are likely to be influenced by a different set of psychological factors from those that have been found to affect members' choices within a given interdependence structure. Recent empirical evidence from several of our experiments confirms this point (Messick et al., 1983; Samuelson & Messick, 1986a; Samuelson, Messick, Rutte, & Wilke, 1984).

It is important, however, to recognize the interrelationship between individual and structural approaches to solving social dilemmas. Recent theory and research by Yamagishi (1986b) makes this point clear. His structural goal/expectation theory of cooperation in social dilemmas emphasizes the close interdependence between structural and psychological factors. Structural factors help shape group members' perceptions and expectations about others' behavior. These psychological variables (e.g., expectations of trust/reciprocity), however, can influence members' preferences to change the structure itself. For example, Yamagishi (1986a) found that low-trust subjects contributed more money to maintain a punishment fund (i.e., sanctioning system for noncooperators) than did high-trust subjects in a public goods task. In addition, the sanctioning system produced higher rates of cooperation among low-trust subjects than among high-trust subjects. These data suggest that structural changes can have indirect effects on members' expectations and perceptions of others' behavior in addition to the direct effects on the payoff structure. Consequently, because of this reciprocal relationship, it is important to understand how people make decisions about various forms of structural change.

This chapter is organized into four sections. First, we describe the general experimental method employed in our research. We next review and analyze results from an earlier series of experiments on structural change, and then present an elaborated version of our model of the decision processes involved in structural change, along with empirical data that bear on the model. Finally, we conclude with some general observations on what has been learned from this program of research on institutional solutions to social dilemmas.

Experimental Task

Most of the experiments reviewed here were conducted in the computer-controlled laboratory described by Parker et al. (1983). Subjects were recruited and participated in groups of six. Upon arrival at the laboratory, each subject was seated in one of six semiprivate cubicles that prevented visual contact with other group members. On a desk in each cubicle were a computer monitor and keyboard. All experimental instructions were presented to subjects through visual display on the computer screens, and subjects typed all responses to experimental questions on their computer keyboards.

The subjects' instructions stated that the experiment involved decision making in an environment involving shared resources. The analogy to the use of real natural resources was stressed, as well as the conflict between short-term use and long-term health of the common resource. The subjects were instructed that their goals in this task were to (a) accumulate as much of the available resource as possible, and (b) preserve the shared resource so that it would be available for use over a long period of time.

Each subject was told that he or she would be sharing a renewable resource with five other subjects. On each of a series of trials, the subject would be given the chance to harvest from this common resource pool. The amount harvested per trial would then become the private property of each subject. Subjects were informed that their private resources could potentially be exchanged for cash (i.e., $.05 per unit) at the conclusion of the study. Subjects typically appeared to be motivated to perform well at the task.

The instructions further explained that the resource was capable of replenishing itself. After all group members had made their harvests for a given trial, a new pool size was calculated that was proportional to the size of the postharvest pool. The rate of replenishment could be varied experimentally. At the end of each trial, the subjects were given feedback about the five other subjects and the amount of resources remaining in the common pool. In most of the studies described here, this feedback information was preprogrammed and did not reflect the actual decisions of the other group members. This part of the experiment continued for 10 trials. On each of these trials, we recorded the harvest size requested by each subject. Thus harvest size constituted the first dependent variable measured in our studies.

Following the first session, subjects were told that they would be given an opportunity to repeat the experiment a second time. We explained to them that some groups in the past had expressed a preference to change the way the experiment was conducted. Although the specific details of how this was accomplished varied from study to study, the general goal was to provide subjects with a chance to decide whether or not to change the rules for allocating the shared resource. Subjects were always given a choice between performing the second session of the experiment according to the same rules used in the first session (i.e., free access to the common resource pool) or changing to a different allocation system. This expressed preference for either the status quo or a structural change was the second dependent variable of importance in our research.

Initial Theory and Experiments

The research question with which we began was as follows: Under what conditions will people want to bring about a structural change in the way they share resources? Our initial answer to this question was that they would do so only when they were dissatisfied with the status quo (Messick et al., 1983). This prediction turned out to be as incorrect as it was simplistic. We hypothesized that subjects would express dissatisfaction with the group when (a) the resource pool was being poorly managed (i.e., rapid depletion of resources), and (b) large inequalities among group members emerged in the distribution of the common resource.

In our first test of these hypotheses, Messick et al. (1983) manipulated efficiency of resource use by exposing some subjects to a pool that was shrinking rapidly, whereas others observed a resource pool that stayed at or close to the maximum capacity. The only structural change alternative available to subjects was to elect a leader from the group to manage the common resource. The role of this leader would be to make a single harvest on each trial for the entire group and then allocate the total amount among the group members. Thus the leader would have both exclusive access to the resource and the right to determine how much of it each group member would receive. The results of this study showed that subjects who witnessed their resource pool dropping did feel more dissatisfied and did vote for a leader more frequently than did subjects in the other conditions.

Our second hypothesis was that subjects experiencing gross inequities in the harvests of others would express dissatisfaction because of the perceived inequity in the allocation of resources. Based on Adams's (1965) equity theory, we expected that these subjects, compared with others who saw a more egalitarian resource distribution, would express their dissatisfaction by voting to elect a leader for the second session. Presumably, electing a leader might be perceived by these subjects as a means of restoring equity in the group. This did not occur. Although the high-inequity subjects did feel more dissatisfied than the low-inequity subjects, they did not vote in favor of electing a leader significantly more often.

In a follow-up study, Samuelson et al. (1984) made a second attempt to obtain this inequity effect. In this experiment, we performed a conceptual replication of the Messick et al. (1983) study in two locations, one in the United States and the other in the Netherlands. To our surprise, we found an interesting cultural difference. Although the American subjects did not show the predicted preference for structural change in response to perceived inequity, the Dutch subjects did. In addition, replicating earlier results, both American and Dutch subjects voted for a leader more often when they saw the declining resource pool compared with an optimal or underuse condition.

These studies suggested two conclusions that we have not had to change in light of subsequent data. First, people want to change the rules and bring about structural change when they observe that the common resource is being depleted. They seem to feel that it is better to relinquish one's private access to the shared resource and depend on someone else—a leader—than to lose access to the resource permanently because it has been exhausted.

A second conclusion is that the effects of perceived inequity in harvest outcomes are much more complex and fragile than the effects of resource overuse. In these studies, we found no evidence for an inequity effect with American subjects, but we did find this effect with Dutch subjects, suggesting a cultural difference in subjects' responses to inequality. This difference between cultures is further supported by the fact that Dutch and American subjects' harvest behavior was also influenced differentially by the perceived inequity manipulation. Hence Dutch and American subjects appear to respond differently to inequality on both of our dependent measures.

Although we offer no convincing explanation for this cultural difference, the results of the Messick et al. (1983) and Samuelson et al. (1984) studies clearly demonstrate that dissatisfaction per se is not a sufficient condition to bring about structural change. Moreover, our subsequent experiments examining the relationship between harvest equality/inequality and subjects' preferences for changing the rules forced us to conclude that the decision-making process underlying such choices is far more complex than we originally had thought (Samuelson & Messick, 1986a, 1986b).

In retrospect, this result should not have come as a surprise. Thibaut and Kelley (1959), in their classic analysis of interdependence relations in groups, made the important distinction between the comparison level (CL) and the comparison level for alternatives (CLalt). The comparison level is the neutral point on the hedonic scale on which people evaluate experiences. It is the reference standard used to determine one's degree of satisfaction or dissatisfaction with the outcomes received in relationships. Outcomes that exceed the CL will be experienced as satisfying, whereas outcomes that fall below CL will be coded as unpleasant or affectively negative. The CLalt, in contrast, represents the level of outcomes that are attainable in one's best alternative relationship. According to Thibaut and Kelley (1959), it is this second standard, the CLalt, that determines whether a person will stay in or leave the current relationship. If the outcome level of the status quo exceeds the CLalt, people will remain in the current relationship; if the outcome level is below the CLalt, people will exit for the more attractive alternative. Thus there is no necessary correspondence between satisfaction or dissatisfaction (which depends on relative positions of current outcomes and CL) and the decision to remain in or leave the relationship. The latter choice depends on the relationship between the outcome level in the current situation (status quo) and the CLalt.

Recent empirical research and theory in the area of relative deprivation (RD) also point to similar conclusions regarding the relationship between dissatisfaction and collective action. It is now recognized that knowledge about what factors create dissatisfaction may not be helpful in predicting how people will respond behaviorally to the situation provoking the state of dissatisfaction (Martin, Brickman, & Murray, 1984). In other words, what makes people feel unhappy in social relationships does not necessarily tell us what they will do about their unsatisfactory situation. Moreover, as proposed by Mark and Folger (1984), responses to RD may take various forms, with the locus for action directed toward the self, the object one is deprived of, or the system responsible for allocating the object. In addition, responses can be either attitudinal or behavioral. System-directed, behavioral responses are most relevant to the studies described above, but they represent only one of several possible responses to RD. Thus Mark and Folger's multiple-response typology may explain the rather loose coupling between dissatisfaction (or RD) and behavior that is often observed in many laboratory and field experiments, including our own.

This analysis may shed some light on why subjects report being dissatisfied with the results of allowing free access to a resource but do not want to give up free access and change the allocation system. Subjects might view the alternative available, electing a group leader, as even worse. For instance, the person who is elected leader might be one of the most extreme overusers of the common resource. This risk may be magnified in the high-inequity conditions, where the feedback indicates the presence of several exceptionally greedy members. Subjects may recognize the need for change owing to unequal outcomes, but the risk of electing a leader may outweigh the benefits of such a change in the group's structure. The general question raised by this mode of analysis is, How do people evaluate the quality or attractiveness of one allocation system in comparison with another, particularly when one of the systems is the status quo?

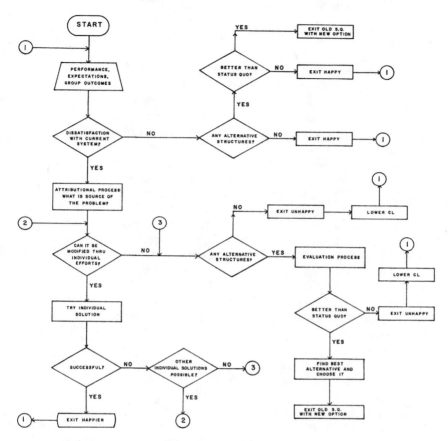

Figure 3.1. Flow Diagram for Model of Structural Change in Resource Dilemmas

Elaborated Model of Decision to Change Rules

Our current conceptualization of the decision processes involved in bringing about structural change is more complex than our earlier version. In this section, we describe the major features of this model and then review some empirical studies that bear on its validity.

Figure 3.1 summarizes the model in the form of a flowchart. The general structure of the model can be described as follows. First, following the group's performance in the resource dilemma, the group member evaluates the outcomes obtained. If the group outcomes are judged to be satisfactory, then the group member will consider changing the group's decision structure only if an alternative is available that is clearly better than the status quo. The upper right-hand portion of Figure 3.1 illustrates this decision process for satisfied group members.

If the group member is dissatisfied with the group outcomes, then the model proposes that an attributional process will be triggered (Weiner, 1985). This causal diagnosis is performed to locate the source of the group's problem. Depending on the perceived cause of the group's poor performance, the group member will initially attempt to remedy the problem through independent, individual efforts. These individual solutions could include actions such as changing one's own behavior, moral suasion, or increasing communication among group members. Thus the theory assumes that individual solutions will be tried first, primarily because these efforts are generally less costly than structural changes and can be enacted independently by all group members.

If these individual efforts are unsuccessful or not possible, then the group member will consider the possibility for structural change (Step 3 in Figure 3.1). The next decision point is whether or not alternative structures are available. If not, then the group member exits dissatisfied and lowers his or her comparison level (Thibaut & Kelley, 1959). By lowering the CL through various cognitive mechanisms (e.g., Adams, 1965, Thibaut & Kelley, 1959), the group member should reduce the gap between current outcomes and his or her reference point for evaluating outcomes, thus lessening his or her feelings of dissatisfaction.

When alternative decision structures are available, the model proposes that the group member will engage in an evaluation process. Several dimensions are hypothesized to be important in the evaluation of alternative decision structures. Among these are (a) efficiency (i.e., Will system improve group outcomes?), (b) fairness (i.e., Will system produce fair outcomes for all members?), (c) freedom (i.e., Will my personal freedom to make own choices be curtailed by system?), (d) self-interest (i.e., Will system produce better outcomes for me personally?), (e) relevance to perceived problem (i.e., Does system address perceived cause of group's problem?), and (f) transition costs (i.e., What are the costs of changing systems?).

The reference point for evaluating alternative structures is the status quo (e.g., free access), as indicated in Figure 3.1. Each alternative system will first be evaluated along the dimensions mentioned above, and this overall judgment will be compared with the outcome level under the status quo. If the group member perceives no alternative structures to be superior to the status quo, then he or she exits the evaluation process dissatisfied and can be expected to engage in cognitive activities directed toward lowering the CL, as discussed previously. If an alternative is available that is clearly better than the status quo, then the group member will compare this alternative structure with other available alternatives. If this option proves to be superior, then the group member will choose this alternative for structural change. It is important to remember, however, that the status quo system is not static. For example, if group members vote to elect a leader, then they will make any subsequent evaluation of structural changes by comparing anticipated benefits and costs of the new system with the outcome level under the leader system. Thus the model recognizes the iterative nature of most social dilemmas by assuming that the status quo system, and hence members' frame of reference, may change over time.

Our model highlights a number of important aspects of the decision-making process regarding structural change. In the following subsections we identify four such areas within the model that merit further discussion: complex causation of dissatisfaction, type of alternative structure, attributional processes, and evaluation processes.

Complex Causation of Dissatisfaction

The model outlined above implicitly assumes that group members will evaluate group performance and be either satisfied or dissatisfied with the resulting outcomes. It does not state, specifically, which factors cause dissatisfaction with the group's performance. Our earlier experimental work identified both inefficiency of resource use and inequity in resource allocation as potential causes of dissatisfaction in resource dilemmas (Messick et al., 1983; Samuelson et al., 1984). As noted earlier, inefficiency had rather straightforward effects on subjects' level of satisfaction and voting preferences, whereas the inequity variable did not. Following equity theory (Adams, 1965), we expected large inequalities in members' harvests to generate greater dissatisfaction with the group than small differences. Our manipulation check items supported this assumption. Nevertheless, the type and intensity of dissatisfaction generated by our variance manipulation was not sufficient to motivate subjects to vote for a leader to solve the problem. The question is why.

Data collected from a follow-up study suggest that the determinants of dissatisfaction in this group setting are more complex than the standard equity theory formulation would have us believe. We performed an experiment to test the notion that the decision to vote for or against a leader may depend on the source to which the inequity problem is attributed (Samuelson & Messick, 1986b). According to this approach, high-inequity subjects should vote for a leader when the inequalities in members' harvests are attributed to the system of free access rather than to the selfish behavior of a few unscrupulous individuals in the group. To provide a structural basis for inequity in the replenishable resource paradigm, we varied subjects' access to the resource (i.e., the maximum number of resource units that group members could harvest from the common pool on a single trial). Thus, in a six-person group, subjects were told that three members would be allowed to harvest from 0 to

10 units per trial (low access), and the other three members would be permitted to harvest from 0 to 30 units per trial (high access). No justifications for these access differences were provided. In addition to the access manipulation, we also included the use and variance variables employed in earlier experiments, resulting in a 2 × 2 × 2 factorial design.

The major hypothesis was that high-variance subjects, when placed in a situation where harvest inequities could easily be attributed to structural features of the free-access system (i.e., access differences), would demonstrate a stronger preference for equality-restoring decision structures (e.g., leader) than would low-variance subjects. In short, the elusive inequity main effect was expected to emerge in this study because of the structural manipulation of access. To our surprise, we found no evidence for the hypothesized inequity main effect. Instead, we obtained a significant three-way interaction among access, use, and variance on the vote to elect a leader. Only two of the eight cells in the design (high access/overuse/high variance and high access/overuse/low variance) produced the expected voting pattern. Among high-variance subjects in the overuse/high-access condition, the election of a leader was virtually unanimous (89%) compared with the low level of support for this option among low-variance subjects in the overuse/high-access condition (25%). It should be noted that this voting pattern was not observed in the optimal-use or low-access conditions.

This complex interaction was totally unexpected, yet quite intriguing. Why did the variance manipulation produce this pattern of preferences only in these two conditions? Our explanation for this result, although admittedly post hoc, focuses on the subject's relative position vis-à-vis the other group members in the final distribution of harvest outcomes. It is possible that a subject's level of satisfaction with the harvest inequities in the high-variance condition may be affected by his or her perceived self-restraint compared with other members. If we assume that subjects engage in social comparison to assess their own degree of self-restraint, the most salient members for comparison purposes would be those who are similar along some relevant dimension (Festinger, 1954)—those who shared the same access level to the common resource.

In this situation, subjects may feel more resentment when they have used self-restraint in harvesting from the pool but other similar members (high access) have not done so. This perception may lead to a feeling of moral superiority over one's fellow high-access members. Therefore, it is possible that voting to elect a leader may be an expression of moral outrage at the improper behavior of other group members. In contrast, if a subject observes other similar group members who have sacrificed more than him or her, he or she may experience less resentment when harvest inequities emerge, because subjects cannot blame others for the resource depletion when their own behavior also reflected a lack of self-restraint. These subjects may be less likely to vote to regulate access to the resource pool by electing a leader. The general point here is that subjects' evaluation of the harvest inequities and perhaps their voting behavior may be more a function of their own perception of self-restraint relative to the restraint of others in their peer group than of the absolute magnitude of the harvest differences among group members.

Careful examination of the harvest and satisfaction data in the appropriate cells of the design provided support for this conceptual interpretation. Subjects in the high-access/overuse/high-variance condition were harvesting considerably less than the two bogus high-access members. In contrast, high-access/overuse/low-variance subjects were harvesting a similar amount compared with the other two bogus high-access members. In addition, for the high-access/overuse conditions, high-variance subjects reported being less satisfied with the resource total differences than did low-variance subjects.

This interpretation of the three-way interaction also fits with Folger's (1986) referent cognitions theory (RCT) of relative deprivation. According to this model, feelings of resentment or moral outrage should be maximized when a high referent outcome (i.e., person easily imagines an outcome that is hedonically superior to the actual outcome) is combined with low likelihood of improvement in future and low justification (i.e., causal factors that produced actual outcomes are unjustified on moral grounds). The only cell in our experimental design in which high referent outcomes appear to be combined with low justification is the high-access/overuse/high-variance condition. High-access subjects in this condition are presented with a situation in which they can easily imagine better outcomes by observing the behavior of other high-access members, but in which these high outcomes may have been regarded by subjects as unjustified because of others' selfishness. Folger's model would predict the greatest degree of resentment and injustice in this condition because high-access subjects would compare their actual outcomes with those that could have been obtained if only the other group members had behaved in a morally responsible manner (high justification). The fairness ratings of subjects in this condition are consistent with this interpretation.

In summary, Folger's (1986) RCT framework appears to provide a good account of the dissatisfaction and resentment data from the Samuelson and Messick (1986b) experiment. It does not, however, seem as convincing in its explanations for the observed voting behavior. It may be that this model is more useful for predicting the causes of dissatisfaction with inequities in groups (Step 1 in Figure 3.1). In this context, Folger's theory emphasizes the importance of cognitive processes as well as moral evaluations of own and others' behavior in resource dilemma situations.

Type of Alternative Structure

The model represented in Figure 3.1 proposes that dissatisfied group members will search for alternative decision-making structures when faced with poor group performance. Thus far, we have considered only one type of structural change—the election of a group leader. Subsequent experiments, however, have examined subjects' preferences for other types of structural solutions to resource dilemmas (Samuelson, 1993; Samuelson & Messick, 1986a, 1986b). It appears that the nature of the alternative itself is an important variable in decisions to institute structural change.

The first experiment to investigate alternative structural solutions (Samuelson & Messick, 1986a) followed a design that was conceptually similar to those used by Messick et al. (1983) and Samuelson et al. (1984). In addition to the manipulations of use and variance, a third variable was introduced by systematically varying the type of alternative offered to subjects. Subjects were given the following options for conducting the second session: (a) free access, (b) group leader, (c) equal territorial division, and (d) proportional territorial division. The last two alternatives solved the resource dilemma by "privatizing" the common resource pool such that each subject would have a private resource to harvest units from during the session. Equal division provided a resource pool of equal size to each group member. Proportional division allocated the common resource based on prior consumption during the first session, such that larger resource pools would be assigned to members who collected more resource units in the initial session. This variable (type of alternative) was manipulated between subjects in this study. Thus each subject evaluated only one of the three alternatives to free access.

Our predictions were twofold: First, overuse subjects should vote for any type of structural change more frequently than optimal-use subjects, and second, a variance by alternative interaction should occur such that high variance should increase subjects' preferences for structural change in the leader and equal division conditions while decreasing preferences for change in the proportional division condition. The rationale for the latter hypothesis was that under conditions of high inequity among group members, the leader and equal-division options would be viewed as alternatives that could restore equality to the distribution of resources in the second session. The proportional-division option, on the other hand, would actually perpetuate any inequities that emerged among members in the first session. Consequently, it was expected that high-variance subjects, compared with low-variance subjects, would vote against proportional division to prevent the inequities from becoming institutionalized in the second session.

The results were in agreement with these predictions. Overall, 56% of the subjects in the high-variance conditions voted for leader or equal division, compared with 42% of the low-variance subjects. For the proportional-division option, the percentages were reversed, with 41% of the high-variance subjects in favor of this change versus 68% of the subjects in the low-variance conditions. In addition, the main effect for the use manipulation was obtained, with 59% of the overuse subjects voting for structural change, compared with 42% in the optimal use condition. The important finding in this study concerns the interaction between variance and type of alternative. The effect of the inequity variable on subjects' preferences depended on the particular type of decision structure available to subjects. In contrast, the effects of efficiency of resource use were uninfluenced by the nature of the alternative system.

In a subsequent study, we allowed subjects to evaluate all four alternatives (free access included) by asking them to rank order the options, from most preferred to least preferred (Samuelson & Messick, 1986b). We classified free access and proportional division as decision structures that allow for individual differences in harvest outcomes, whereas the election of a group leader and equal division were considered to be equality-restoring structures. This binary cross-classification analysis found main effects for both access and use. Low-access (and overuse) subjects preferred equality-restoring structures (69%) more often than did high-access (and optimal-use) subjects (31%) as their first choice for structural change. In addition, the three-way interaction on the binary votes (e.g., free access versus leader) discussed earlier was found for both the leader and equal-division alternatives, but was not obtained for the proportional-division option. These findings reinforce the conclusion that certain environmental and social variables have different effects on structural change decisions, depending on the specific alternative at issue.

Attributional Processes

One key assumption in our model is that dissatisfaction will trigger an attributional process to determine the cause of the group's poor performance. Although we have no available data from studies on resource dilemmas to substantiate this claim, a recent review of the literature on spontaneous attribution lends some support to this assumption. In that review, Weiner (1985) concludes that two conditions that tend to produce spontaneous attributional activity are failure and unexpected events. In our experiments, when subjects receive feedback on the group's performance, information suggesting that the group is depleting the resource pool is likely to be viewed as a failure at the task and probably an unexpected outcome as well.

Given the existence of an attributional process, how might these processes mediate decisions to institute structural change in resource dilemmas? One important distinction in this problem-diagnosis phase is likely to be whether the problem with the group's performance is caused by group-related factors or task-related ones. Examples of group-related factors might be problems such as personal greed or selfishness, poor understanding of task, and lack of effort. Task-related features might include task difficulty, unpredictable nature of environment, and inability of group members to communicate.

The general argument proposed here is that the perceived cause for the group's performance—group versus task—should have systematic effects on subjects' preferences for structural solutions. The basic assumption is that any given structural change will be more preferred to the extent that it promises to solve the diagnosed cause of the group's problem. This implies that some structural solutions may be more effective in dealing with group-related causes and others may be more appropriate for task-related problems. In short, a matching process is predicted in which the group member evaluates and chooses among the available structural solutions based on the perceived "fit" with the diagnosed cause.

Although we have few data bearing on the nature of this attributional process, Samuelson (1991) has conducted a study that demonstrates its importance. In our standard experimental paradigm, subjects' causal attributions for group performance were manipulated experimentally through an instructional induction. Half of the subjects were told prior to the task that the resource management task was very easy, whereas the other half of the subjects were led to believe that the task would be very difficult. All subjects were then exposed to a rapidly declining resource pool, suggesting that the group was overusing the resource.

The task difficulty manipulation was designed to produce systematic differences in subjects' attributions for the group's poor performance. In the easy task condition, subjects were expected to attribute the resource depletion to other members' unwillingness to reduce their harvests—a group-related cause. The rationale here is that if the task is simple, then people's behavior must be the source of the problem. In the difficult task condition, the subjects were expected to attribute the declining pool size to a difficult and unpredictable environment—a task-related factor. In this case, it is the difficulty of the task, not the people in the group, that is seen to be causing the poor performance.

Following the trials, subjects were asked to vote on the leader option. Samuelson (1991) predicted that subjects would be more likely to support a group leader when the task was perceived as difficult than when it was viewed as easy. The logic behind this hypothesis was that if subjects believe that the group's failure at the task was caused by a difficult task environment, then an intelligent, responsible leader may be more effective in solving the resource allocation problem than six individuals operating in an uncoordinated group (Messick, Allison, & Samuelson, 1988). On the other hand, if subjects attribute the group's poor performance to the selfish behavior of other members, then electing a leader from among these individuals could be risky and could possibly lead to worse outcomes for all if the elected leader behaves in an unethical or self-interested manner (Messick, 1984; Rutte, Wilke, & Messick, 1987).

The leader vote results from this study supported this prediction nicely. Overall, 57% of the subjects in the difficult task condition voted for a leader, compared with only 30% in the easy task condition. Given the fact that these two groups of subjects received identical pool feedback, it is striking that the subtle manipulation of expectations regarding task difficulty exerted such a strong effect on subjects' preferences for a leader. This finding is intriguing and suggests that attributional processes may play an important role in decisions to change the rules in social dilemmas.

Evaluation Processes

Having abandoned the simplistic idea that people will accept any structural change in preference to an unsatisfactory status quo, we are forced to consider the processes that are involved when a current allocation system is compared with possible alternatives. Our approach to this problem has been detailed by Samuelson (1993); we will roughly sketch it here.

A system for allocating resources to members of a group is a social institution that can be evaluated on a number of dimensions. We assume that when people consider an allocation system, they think about its various features, its advantages and disadvantages, along a number of dimensions, with special emphasis on those dimensions that are most important to them. Before discussing what those dimensions might be in the kinds of situations with which we are concerned, there are two prior issues that would tend to render people's preferences conservative (i.e., favoring the status quo) that are distinct from unique features of different systems.

First, any change in a social institution will entail transition costs. Replacing the status quo with any alternative system will generally involve costs that simply maintaining the status quo avoids. Such transition costs tend to add to the attractiveness of what is relative to what might be. Second, people are generally familiar with the properties of the status quo, whereas the qualities of an alternative system may only be guessed at. There is, in short, less uncertainty about the status quo than about rival systems. Risk aversion would therefore cause one to view competing systems somewhat less favorably, even if the status quo's deficiencies were clear. Better to have a system whose flaws are known than one that might bring unpleasant surprises.

Transition costs and risks of unfamiliarity will have to be compensated for if structural change is to occur. Other dimensions of evaluation must promise sufficient benefits to make the change worthwhile. We propose that the dimensions of evaluation will include at least the following four: efficiency, fairness, freedom, and self-interest. *Efficiency* refers to the extent to which an allocation system can provide satisfactory levels of a resource to the members of a group without depleting the resource. *Fairness*, of course, refers to the degree to which distribution of the resource satisfies the principles of equality or equity. *Freedom* reflects the extent to which a system permits individuals to make resource use decisions for themselves. *Self-interest* refers simply to one's view of how one's own resource status would be affected by an allocation system.

There is no reason to believe that these dimensions will always be correlated. Electing a leader who will have exclusive access to a resource might be viewed as a way to establish an efficient system, but a system of questionable fairness and self-interest (unless one is elected leader). It would certainly not provide much individual harvest freedom to the group members.

The two crucial features of the evaluation process, from our perspective, are the perceived positions of the various allocation structures on these dimensions and the relative importance attached to the different dimensions. Someone for whom freedom is very important might well find the leader option mentioned above highly disagreeable, whereas a person who values efficiency above all might find it quite appealing. Someone whose primary value is fairness might not be able to make a confident evaluation without further information about how the resources will be distributed by the leader. The uncertainty about this issue might make the option relatively unattractive.

We assume that the overall attractiveness of an allocation system is some weighted function of the system's attributes, where the weights are related to the importance of the dimensions. There are many ways in which this assessment can be made, but the simplest is to assume that the overall attractiveness is a weighted average of the values of the system on the four dimensions described above. Thus we assume that the attractiveness of each allocation system is represented by its weighted average, and group members compare overall attractiveness measures of the different systems in order to make choices or comparative evaluations of two or more systems.

There are two systematic factors that should influence subjects' perceptions of the attributes of an allocation system, as well as the importance of those attributes. The first of these is the experience subjects have had with the system. Subjects who have witnessed a shared pool rapidly decreasing in size should conclude that free access is a less efficient system than should subjects whose pool has been optimally used. Subjects seeing high variances in the distributions of resources would probably conclude that free access is less fair as an allocation system than would subjects witnessing low variances. In short, different experiences should lead to different perceptions and, hence, to different evaluations.

Systematic individual differences among subjects in the relative importance attached to the dimensions should also lead to predictably different evaluations. For instance, Samuelson (1993) found that cooperative subjects ranked fairness higher in importance than did noncooperators, and that non-cooperative subjects ranked self-interest higher in importance than did coop-erators. Consequently, even if the two groups of subjects perceive different allocation structures as having the same attributes, they might be expected to have different preferences for them. In fact, Samuelson (1993) reports that noncooperators ranked the free-access system higher in attractiveness than did cooperators. This result could be caused by dispositional differences in cooperators, or possibly by differences in dimensional importance.

To summarize, we view the final evaluation process as a multiattribute utility problem (Edwards & Newman, 1982) in which the relevant dimensions include at least efficiency, fairness, freedom, and self-interest. The relative attractiveness of allocation systems will thus depend on the extent to which a person views the systems as being efficient, fair, permitting individual freedom, and promoting his or her interests, and also on the importance that the individual attaches to each of these attributes. This view is much more complex than our original approach, but it is surely more realistic.

Conclusions

Several general conclusions about the nature of the decision processes in-volved in changing allocation rules in resource dilemmas have emerged from our research program. In this final section, we summarize what we believe to be some of the more important lessons to be learned from this work.

The first point is that dissatisfaction with group outcomes does not appear to be a sufficient condition for structural change. Our data strongly suggest that dissatisfied group members do not always prefer changing the allocation rules and, in certain cases, satisfied members actually vote for structural changes in preference to the status quo (Messick et al., 1983; Samuelson & Messick, 1986a; Samuelson et al., 1984). Thus structural change may occur in the absence of dissatisfaction, as indicated in the upper right-hand portion of Figure 3.1. Our model also hypothesizes that dissatisfaction may trigger an attributional process, which in turn may influence group members' responses to the dissat-isfying situation (Step 2 in Figure 3.1). This suggests that causal attributions may mediate between affective responses to poor group performance and behavioral responses to the situation. In addition, the nature and availability of alternative allocation structures may be another variable that intervenes between dissatisfaction and decisions to change the rules (Step 3 in Figure 3.1).

A second observation is that attributional processes may influence the evaluation of alternative allocation rules in systematic ways. First, the causal diagnosis for the group's performance may guide the search for solutions. If group performance is attributed to members' behavior, then individual solutions may be appropriate for solving the problem through such means as moral suasion or modeling cooperative behavior. On the other hand, if the group's problem is attributed to task or environmental factors, then structural changes may be perceived as more effective in improving the group's performance. Second, there is some preliminary evidence that alternative allocation structures are evaluated, in part, based on the extent to which the alternative is expected to solve the group's problem, as diagnosed by the attributional analysis (Samuelson, 1991).

Finally, it is clear from our experiments that the evaluation process regarding structural changes is strongly influenced by the specific reference points adopted by subjects. In particular, the level of satisfaction with the status quo allocation system appears to set the comparison standard for evaluating whether an alternative system is preferable or not. Thus our data are consistent with other theories of outcome evaluation that emphasize the importance of the individual's "frame of reference" (Kahneman & Tversky, 1979; Thibaut & Kelley, 1959). Perhaps evaluations of social institutions for allocating resources may operate according to similar psychological principles. It is also evident that the evaluation process is more accurately modeled as a multiattribute utility problem in which allocation structures are judged along a set of distinct dimensions. The overall evaluation is assumed to be a weighted average of the ratings of the attributes multiplied by their respective importance weights. This conceptualization also recognizes that factors such as experience with various allocation systems and individual differences in the relative importance of various attributes will moderate the judgments of group members regarding the attractiveness of alternative allocation systems.

It should be noted here that the decision-making model outlined in this chapter has a number of features in common with Yamagishi's (1986b) structural goal/expectation approach to structural change in social dilemmas. He establishes several conditions that must be satisfied for structural change to occur voluntarily in small groups. First, the necessary condition is that group members develop the goal of mutual cooperation by recognizing their mutual interdependence and the fact that noncooperation cannot continue for an extended period (e.g., experience of poor group outcomes caused by defecting behavior). Second, the sufficient conditions are that members realize the futility of voluntarily based, "elementary" cooperation (i.e., individual solutions) and that members recognize the importance and effectiveness of the structural change.

Inspection of Figure 3.1 reveals that three decision nodes in our model correspond roughly to Yamagishi's (1986b) three preconditions: (a) Am I dissatisfied with the current system? (b) Can I modify the problem through individual efforts? and (c) Are alternative structural changes available that are better than the status quo? Although the parallels between the two models are not exact, it does appear that basic ideas implicit in Yamagishi's theory are similar to the series of choice points postulated in our model of structural change. Yamagishi's theory has been tested in several empirical studies, with supportive results obtained thus far (e.g., Sato, 1987; Yamagishi, 1986a, 1988). The conceptual overlap between Yamagishi's formulation and our approach is encouraging, and builds confidence in the proposed model.

In this chapter we have sketched a model of the decision processes involved in structural change that has emerged from our research program. Perhaps this model will have heuristic value in stimulating future social psychological research on this important problem. We have barely scratched the surface, however, in delineating the details of these complex decision processes. Future research should help uncover more of what we need to know.

References

Adams, J. S. (1965). Inequity in social exchange. In L. Berkowitz (Ed.), *Advances in experimental social psychology* (Vol. 2, pp. 267-299). New York: Academic Press.

Borrego, A., & Burns, D. (1985). Red king crab: A tragedy of the commons. *Alaska Fisherman's Journal, 8,* 38-39.

Edwards, W., & Newman, J. R. (1982). *Multiattribute evaluation.* Beverly Hills, CA: Sage.

Festinger, L. (1954). A theory of social comparison processes. *Human Relations, 7,* 117-140.

Folger, R. (1986). A referent cognitions theory of relative deprivation. In J. M. Olson, C. P. Herman, & M. P. Zanna (Eds.), *Relative deprivation and social comparison: The Ontario Symposium.* Hillsdale, NJ: Lawrence Erlbaum.

Kahneman, D., & Tversky, A. (1979). Prospect theory: A theory of decision under risk. *Econometrica, 47,* 263-291.

Mark, M. M., & Folger, R. (1984). Responses to relative deprivation: A conceptual framework. *Review of Personality and Social Psychology, 5,* 192-218.

Martin, J., Brickman, P., & Murray, A. (1984). Moral outrage and pragmatism: Explanations for collective action. *Journal of Experimental Social Psychology, 20,* 484-496.

Messick, D. M. (1984). Solving social dilemmas: Individual and collective approaches. *Representative Research in Social Psychology, 14,* 72-87.

Messick, D. M., Allison, S. T., & Samuelson, C. D. (1988). Framing and communication effects on group members' responses to environmental and social uncertainty. In S. Maital (Ed.), *Applied behavioral economics* (Vol. 2, pp. 677-700). New York: New York University Press.

Messick, D. M., & Brewer, M. B. (1983). Solving social dilemmas: A review. *Review of Personality and Social Psychology, 4,* 11-44.

Messick, D. M., Wilke, H., Brewer, M. B., Kramer, R. M., Zemke, P. E., & Lui, L. (1983). Individual adaptations and structural change as solutions to social dilemmas. *Journal of Personality and Social Psychology, 44,* 294-309.

Ostrom, E. (1990). *Governing the commons: The evolution of institutions for collective action.* New York: Cambridge University Press.

Parker, R., Lui, L., Messick, C., Messick, D. M., Brewer, M. B., Kramer, R., Samuelson, C., & Wilke, H. (1983). A computer laboratory for studying resource dilemmas. *Behavioral Science, 28,* 298-304.

Rutte, C. G., Wilke, H. A. M., & Messick, D. M. (1987). The effects of framing social dilemmas as give-some or take-some games. *British Journal of Social Psychology, 26,* 103-108.

Samuelson, C. D. (1991). Perceived task difficulty, causal attributions, and preferences for structural change in resource dilemmas. *Personality and Social Psychology Bulletin, 17,* 181-187.

Samuelson, C. D. (1993). A multiattribute evaluation approach to structural change in resource dilemmas. *Organizational Behavior and Human Decision Processes, 55,* 298-324.

Samuelson, C. D., & Messick, D. M. (1986a). Alternative structural solutions to resource dilemmas. *Organizational Behavior and Human Decision Processes, 37,* 139-155.

Samuelson, C. D., & Messick, D. M. (1986b). Inequities in access to and use of shared resources in social dilemmas. *Journal of Personality and Social Psychology, 51,* 960-967.

Samuelson, C. D., Messick, D. M., Rutte, C. G., & Wilke, H. (1984). Individual and structural solutions to resource dilemmas in two cultures. *Journal of Personality and Social Psychology, 47,* 94-104.

Sato, K. (1987). Distribution of the cost for maintaining common resources. *Journal of Experimental Social Psychology, 23,* 19-31.

Thibaut, J. W., & Kelley, H. H. (1959). *The social psychology of groups.* New York: John Wiley.

Weiner, B. (1985). "Spontaneous" causal thinking. *Psychological Bulletin, 97,* 74-84.

Yamagishi, T. (1986a). The provision of a sanctioning system as a public good. *Journal of Personality and Social Psychology, 51,* 110-116.

Yamagishi, T. (1986b). The structural goal/expectation theory of cooperation in social dilemmas. In E. J. Lawler & B. Markovsky (Eds.), *Advances in group processes* (Vol. 3). Greenwich, CT: JAI.

Yamagishi, T. (1988). The provision of a sanctioning system in the United States and Japan. *Social Psychology Quarterly, 51,* 265-271.

4

Regression to the Mean,
Expectation Inflation, and the
Winner's Curse in Organizational Contexts

J. RICHARD HARRISON
MAX H. BAZERMAN

In a simple decision model, several alternatives are identified and evaluated, and the best is chosen. The decision-making process can be biased because of common decision biases, such as framing or anchoring (e.g., Bazerman, 1990; Kahneman, Slovic, & Tversky, 1982), or organizational processes (e.g., Feldman & March, 1981). Most formulations of a rational decision process focus on the importance of examining a full set of alternatives—subject to search costs. In this chapter we explore biases that result from such a full consideration. Specifically, we examine the well-known regression-to-the-mean (RTTM) effect (Tversky & Kahneman, 1974) and show the role of RTTM in creating the asocial phenomenon of expectation inflation (Harrison & March, 1984) and the social phenomenon of the winner's curse (Bazerman & Samuelson, 1983; Capen, Clapp, & Campbell, 1971).

Imagine that your university has a position open for a new assistant professor. A committee carefully reviews 160 applications, including curricula vitae,

AUTHORS' NOTE: We would like to thank Joel Brockner and David Messick for comments on earlier drafts of this chapter. The second author was supported during the research reported here by the Dispute Resolution Research Center at Northwestern University.

letters of recommendation, and sample writings. The department brings four candidates to campus to meet with your faculty and present their research. You identify the preferred candidate and realize that your school will be facing stiff competition from other schools to hire this ideal choice. You convince the dean to make an unusually attractive offer, which the candidate accepts. After exerting all of this effort to make an optimal decision, why is it that such decisions so often lead to disappointment *and* investment in a candidate who is not worth it to the institution? This paper seeks to offer a systematic answer to this quandary.[1]

We believe that much of the answer lies in the RTTM concept. RTTM is the statistical tendency for extreme observations to be followed by less extreme observations—or to regress to the mean. Yet human intuition rarely accounts for this statistical tendency. Despite an awareness of the RTTM concept on the part of organizational researchers, they fail to generalize the concept to the related phenomena of expectation inflation and the winner's curse, or to their own decision problems. Expectation inflation argues that when a decision maker chooses an alternative from a large set of options in which there is a large error term in the assessment of the worth of alternatives, it is highly likely that the decision maker's expectation will exceed the true level of performance of the chosen alternative. The winner's curse argues that in an auction, when there are a large number of bidders and high variance in the estimates of the value of the commodity, it is highly likely that the winning bidder will pay more than the value of the commodity—or be cursed.

The expectation inflation phenomenon is a cognitive mistake with cognition at its root. In contrast, the winner's curse is a cognitive mistake with a social error at its root. That is, the winner's curse is somewhat different from typical applications of the RTTM phenomenon in that the critical error is not considering the actions of other *social* actors. In this chapter we cut across both asocial and social contexts to explore the adverse impact that the failure to consider the family of RTTM effects can have on individual and organizational decisions.

We will elaborate below on the overlap between these concepts, but it is useful to mention in the beginning that we have approached many colleagues, and have found that an understanding of RTTM does not inoculate against the adverse impact of expectation inflation or the winner's curse. We will clarify these three concepts, identify the number of alternatives and uncertainty as the key determinants of these effects, suggest why decision makers fail to recognize these influences, and assess the organizational influences that affect the magnitude of the expectation inflation and the winner's curse.

Regression to the Mean

Many effects predictably regress to the mean (Dawes, 1988; Gilovich, 1991; Kahneman & Tversky, 1973). Brilliant students frequently have less successful siblings. Short parents tend to have taller children. Great rookies have mediocre second years (the "sophomore jinx"). Firms having outstanding profits one year tend to have lesser performance the next. High-performing mutual funds in a specific year frequently recruit and disappoint new investors as a result of their earlier success. In each case, individuals typically are surprised when made aware of these predictable patterns of RTTM (Kahneman & Tversky, 1973). This lack of awareness of the RTTM concept is a bias in the intuition of virtually all decision makers. Kahneman and Tversky (1973) suggest that the representativeness heuristic accounts for this systematic bias in judgment. They argue that individuals typically assume that one child's intelligence is an excellent predictor of his or her siblings' intelligence, and ignore the systematic error in the predictability of their intelligence. Individuals tend to develop predictions naively that are based upon the assumption of perfect correlation with past data.

Bazerman (1990) presented a problem to subjects in which they were to act as sales forecasters for a department store chain with nine locations. Subjects were told that the main differences in their sales occurred because of location and random fluctuations. Sales for 1989 were as follows:

Store	1989	1991
1	$12,000,000	$_
2	11,500,000	_
3	11,000,000	_
4	10,500,000	_
5	10,000,000	_
6	9,500,000	_
7	9,000,000	_
8	8,500,000	_
9	8,000,000	_
Total	$90,000,000	$99,000,000

Subjects were further told that their economic forecasting service had convinced them that the best estimate of total sales increase between 1989 and 1991 was 10% (to $99,000,000). Their task was to predict 1991 sales for each store. Because the manager believes strongly in the economic forecasting service, subjects were told, it was imperative that their total sales equal $99,000,000.

Bazerman (1990) found that more than 70% of all subjects in M.B.A. programs who had previously taken statistics courses answered $13.2 million for Store 1 and $8.8 million for Store 9. The following quote clarifies their logic: "The overall increase in sales is predicted to be 10 percent ($99,000,000-$90,000,000/$90,000,000). Lacking any other specific information on the stores, it makes sense to simply add 10 percent to each 1989 sales figure to predict 1991 sales. This means that I predict sales of $13,200,000 for store 1, sales of $12,650,000 for store 2, etc." This logic is faulty because it ignores RTTM.

Proper analysis, in contrast, requires the assessment of the predicted correlation between 1989 and 1991 sales. If the correlation was zero, knowing 1989 sales would provide absolutely no information about 1991 sales, and the best estimates of 1991 sales would be equal to total sales divided by the number of stores ($99,000,000 divided by 9 equals $11,000,000). However, if the correlation between stores was 1.0, the logic of simply extrapolating from 1989 performance by adding 10% to each store's performance would be completely accurate. Obviously, 1989 sales are most likely to be *partially predictive* of 1991 sales—falling somewhere between independence and perfect correlation. Thus the best prediction for Store 1 should lie between $11,000,000 and $13,200,000, depending upon how predictive 1989 sales are of 1991 sales (Kahneman & Tversky, 1982).

In a study of sales forecasting, Cox and Summers (1987) examined the judgments of professional retail buyers. They examined the sales data from two department stores for six different apparel styles for a total of 12 different sales forecasts over a two-week period. They found that sales within the two weeks regressed to the mean. However, the judgment of 31 buyers from five different department stores failed to reflect the tendency for RTTM. As a result, Cox and Summers argue that a sales forecasting model that considers RTTM could outperform the judgments of all 31 professional buyers in their sample.

Kahneman and Tversky (1973) note that misconceptions surrounding regression can lead to overestimation of the effectiveness of punishment and underestimation of the power of reward. In a discussion about flight training, experienced instructors noted that praise for an exceptionally smooth landing is typically followed by a poorer landing on the next try, whereas harsh criticism after a rough landing is usually followed by improvement on the next try. The instructors then concluded that verbal rewards are detrimental to learning, and verbal punishments are beneficial. Obviously, the tendency of performance to regress to the mean can account for the results without ever taking verbal feedback into account. However, to the extent that the instructors were prone to biased decision making, they were prone to reach the false conclusion that punishment is more effective than positive reinforcement in shaping behavior.

Before moving to the related concepts of expectation inflation and the winner's curse, it is critical that we identify the key variables that create error in intuitive judgment as a result of ignorance of the RTTM concept. First is the role of uncertainty. When prior data are perfectly correlated with future data, uncertainty is eliminated, and there is no error from the failure to consider RTTM. However, as the correlation decreases and uncertainty rises, RTTM increases the error of decision makers. Second, the error created because of the lack of awareness of RTTM will be affected by the extremity of the point that is assessed. For example, decision makers are likely to make larger errors in predicting the sales for Store 1 than for Store 4. As the distance between the point being estimated and the mean increases, more RTTM can be anticipated.

Expectation Inflation

Harrison and March (1984) use the RTTM concept to argue that the process of choosing the best alternative from a set, even when the alternative evaluations are unbiased, will lead to systematic disappointment. The decision maker's expectations will be inflated in comparison with a realistic assessment of the likely performance of the chosen outcome. The outcome value of a chosen alternative is likely to be overestimated—that is, the expected value of the choice is inflated—if the estimated values of the decision alternatives include uncertainty of future performance and if many alternatives are considered.

The expectation inflation argument is a direct application of the RTTM principle. If a decision maker uses all the available information concerning a set of options to identify the one that will perform the best in the future, the available information can be viewed as an integrated proxy for an assessment of past performance, which is being used to predict future performance. In most cases, there is considerable error in predicting future performance based on past indicators. Thus the performance of the choice with the highest indicator will tend to be the choice with the greatest regression to the mean. However, because naive human judgment does not fully recognize the concept of regression, the indicator is viewed as a more representative predictor of future performance, and selecting the best alternative leads to disappointment. As more alternatives are considered, the expected value of the past perform- ance indicator will increase (as will the expected value of future performance). However, as noted above, this indicator will include a true predictive compo- nent and a systematic error. The true predictive component will be above the mean, and the systematic error will make the indicator appear greater than that suggested by the true predictive component. Thus the likelihood and magnitude of the postdecision disappointment will tend to increase as more alternatives are considered.

Harrison and March (1984) formalize the argument that the magnitude of expectation inflation will be influenced by the number of alternatives considered and the uncertainty of the estimated values: Assume that the estimated value of a chosen alternative out of a set of possible alternatives, z_i, is the sum of the true value xi and an error or noise term y_i; that is, $z_i = x_i + y_i$. Because $z_i = x_i + y_i$, z is positively correlated with both x and y, with the magnitudes of the correlations depending on the signal-to-noise ratio w. From this relationship, it is clear that the larger the value of z_i, the larger the expected values of both x_i and y_i. In particular, the expected value of y_i as a percentage of z_i increases as w decreases (or as the noise level increases). For apparently "good" (above-average) alternatives, the estimated alternative values are inflated by the y_i term, which increases with the noise level.

Applying this formulation to the store forecasting problem, if the task is to select the store that will have the best future performance, Store 1 is still the best choice. However, x_i, y_i, and z_i are all likely to have the highest values for Store 1. Thus, although Store 1 is the best choice, our nonregressive intuition will also end up being most disappointed in the performance of Store 1. Similarly, the assistant professor that your department selects based on observing zi, although the best choice, is also likely to be the candidate whose later performance most disappoints the field.

In general, reducing the noise level reduces expectation inflation and increases the expected true value of a decision choice, whereas increasing the number of alternatives increases both the expected true choice value and its expected inflation. There are two ways, then, to reduce expectation inflation by manipulating these structural characteristics. One is to reduce the noise level, which also increases the expected true choice value, but perhaps not enough to cover the costs of lowering the noise. The other is to reduce the number of alternatives considered, which has the disadvantage of also lowering the expected true value of the choice. In other words, reducing expectation inflation can be costly. However, awareness of the expected inflation problem allows for better management of postdecision performance. The new hire who performs very well, but not spectacularly, should not be informed of the department's disappointment. Rather, that disappointment should be eliminated through an understanding of expectation inflation.

There are other kinds of costs, however, associated with ignoring expectation inflation. These include postdecision disappointment and poor predictability. In many situations, it is as important to have an accurate estimate of the value of a choice as it is to choose an alternative with a high value. For a firm making an investment decision, choosing the alternative with the highest positive expected net present value can be a serious error if the net present value is actually negative after correction for expectation inflation. A choice that is heavily promoted on the basis of its expected performance character-istics—such as a new computer system or 911 emergency telephone service—could prove embarrassing to organizational leaders if it does not perform as advertised, even though it represents substantial improvement. The choice of a more efficient engine for a spacecraft could lead to disaster if fuel efficiency is overestimated and the spacecraft runs out of fuel before its mission is completed. A fund-raising event that generates $50,000 could be perceived as a failure if expected proceeds of $100,000 have already been budgeted. Finally, politicians elected on a promise of "no new taxes," based on unrecognized inflation in expected benefits from cost-cutting plans, could encounter a political crisis when it becomes apparent that a budgetary shortfall is inevita-ble. Thus the actions necessary for the politician to undertake to rally the electorate may be the same actions that create predictable disappointment.

The Winner's Curse

When a bidder wins an auction in which there are a large number of bidders and high variance in the estimates of the value of the commodity, it is highly likely that the winning bidder will pay more than the value of the commodity (Bazerman & Samuelson, 1983; Capen et al., 1971; Kagel & Levin, 1986). In expectation inflation, the inflated choice estimates are produced not by biased alternative estimates, but by the process of choosing the best estimate. The statistical structure that leads to expectation inflation is analogous to the one that produces the winner's curse in competitive auctions (e.g., Bazerman & Samuelson, 1983; Harrison, 1990). In contrast to expectation inflation, where the decision maker is choosing the best of several different alternatives, the winner's curse results from the acceptance of the highest of several offers by *different bidders* for *the same item.* Thus the true value is assumed to be the same for all bidders.[2] The winner of the auction is typically the bidder who most overestimates the value of the auctioned item. In this case, if we assume that each bidder makes a bid (b) based on his or her assessment of the true value (z_i), z_i will include a true component of the value of the commodity (x_i) and an error (y_i). Note that x will be the same for all bidders in a common value auction. The winning bidder is likely to be a bidder with one of the highest, if not the highest, positive errors in the estimate (y_i).

Organizations frequently bid against competitors to obtain important resource inputs, such as qualified job applicants and reasonably priced raw materials. In addition, many firms (e.g., defense contractors and architectural firms) rely on competitive bidding as a basic source of revenue. Frequently,

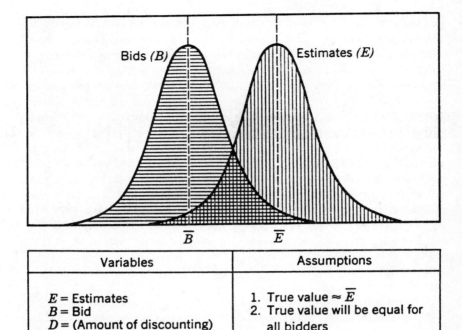

Figure 4.1. The Winner's Curse

there is little opportunity for communication between competing parties. We argue that these are prime conditions for observing the winner's curse. The winner's curse occurs when the winning bidder fails to consider the implications of having bid higher than a large number of other bidders—all of whom are at the same information disadvantage relative to the seller.

Bazerman and Samuelson (1983) argue that a possible reason an organization becomes the highest bidder is that it significantly overestimates the actual value of the commodity being sold. Figure 4.1 provides a graphic depiction of what may occur. Curve E shows the distribution of bidder estimates for the true value of the commodity, and Curve B depicts the distribution of bids. The depiction assumes (a) that the mean of the distribution is equal to the true value of the commodity (i.e., no aggregate under- or overestimation is expected), and (b) that bidders discount their estimates a fixed amount in making bids—thus explaining the leftward shift of the estimate distribution to the bidding distribution. The figure suggests that a winning bid—that is, one from the right tail of the distribution—is likely to exceed the actual value of the commodity.

Paralleling the RTTM and expectation inflation discussions, the number of bidders (paralleling alternatives) and uncertainty drive the winner's curse effect. The highest bidder is likely to have been one of the highest estimators, and unless that bidder has reason to believe that he or she has better information than the other bidders, overpayment can be expected. With this framework in mind, Bazerman and Samuelson (1983) predicted and found in their research that the winning bidder in auctions of highly uncertain commodities with a large number of bidders commonly pays more than the commodity is worth.

Why does the winning bidder fall prey to the winner's curse? The answer lies in the failure of bidders to draw a key inference: If a particular bidder assumes that his or her bid will win the auction, this information should tell the bidder that he or she is likely to have overestimated the value of the commodity in comparison with other bidders. Based on this reasoning, bidders on highly uncertain commodities should adjust their estimates of the true value of the commodities downward, and lower their bids accordingly. Thus, if they do win, they are less likely to have overbid, or at least will have overbid by a smaller margin.

The importance of the winner's curse in competitive bidding can be seen in the context of corporate takeovers. Corporate takeovers in the 1980s provided ample evidence that acquiring companies often compete against each other and pay too much for what they get. As many as one-third of all acquisitions prove to be failures, and an additional one-third fail to live up to expectations (Bazerman & Neale, 1992). In addition, any financial synergy that is created by mergers usually goes to the target, not the acquirer. On average, the financial benefit goes exclusively to the shareholders of the acquired company. Bazerman and Samuelson's (1983) analysis suggests that potential acquirers should temper their optimism by recognizing that the winning bidder is likely to acquire a company that is worth far less than the winning bidder's estimate of the expected value. More specifically, Bazerman and Samuelson point out that competitive decision makers should be particularly concerned about the winner's curse when there are a large number of bidders and uncertainty of the true value of the commodity is high.

Experimental economists have given great attention to the winner's curse, in auctions and in other contexts. Much of their effort has focused on showing that "experimental subjects, as well as most bidders in 'real world' settings, would eventually learn to avoid the winner's curse in any particular set of circumstances. The winner's curse is a disequilibrium phenomenon that will correct itself given sufficient time and the right kind of information feedback" (Kagel & Levin, 1986, p. 917). However, after many attempts to discredit this disequilibrium effect, the winner's curse has stood up remarkably well (Kagel & Levin, 1986; Lind & Plott, 1991).

Returning to the hiring of an assistant professor: To the extent that a "bidding war" develops for the candidate, the university that will go to the greatest extreme to hire this individual may be the one that can best use his or her talents, or it may be the wealthiest school in the bidding group. Alternatively, the university that is most willing to go beyond its standard offer may be the university that most overestimates the value of the recruit. Thus both the numbers of candidates evaluated by the school and the number of schools bidding on the candidate can contribute to the candidate's not doing as well as the "winning" university anticipated.

In the assistant professor story, expectation inflation and the winner's curse are both working against the focal organization. Expectation inflation leads to the prediction of postdecision disappointment, and the winner's curse leads to the prediction of overcompensation and a poor use of the university's scarce resources. In contrast, in some cases, expectation inflation and the winner's curse could lead to conflicting effects. Consider a firm that obtains multiple fixed-price bids from consulting firms to provide a set of services. If the quality of consulting services from various firms is uncertain to the client organization, if the nature of the required work is uncertain to the consulting firms, and if the client firm evaluates proposals from many consulting firms, we would predict both the client's receiving a best bid (involving price and nature of the work) that is inappropriately low for the work required and eventual disappointment in the performance of the chosen consulting firm.

Failure to Recognize These Biases and Corrective Strategies

Expectation inflation and the winner's curse are natural consequences of decision making with noisy estimates for the values of alternatives, varying systematically with the number of options considered. Yet people seem to be largely unaware of these effects. How can people fail to recognize such pervasive phenomena?

Although regression effects have been widely discussed, people do not normally take regression into consideration when making predictions or when making judgments in situations characterized by uncertainty (Bazerman, 1990; Hogarth, 1980; Kahneman & Tversky, 1979a; Nisbett & Ross, 1980). People often fail to understand regression properly; they do not expect regression in many situations, contexts, and domains in which it is bound to occur; and they invent spurious causal explanations for regression when it is observed. Regression effects are often ignored or misunderstood even by people thoroughly trained in regression. In a study using a large sample of psychology graduate students who had been exposed to a thorough treatment of statistical regression, Kahneman and Tversky (1973) found that most subjects ignored regression when interpreting IQ scores, and that none of the subjects recognized regression in a story illustrating an instance of regression.

Kahneman and Tversky (1979a) recommend a five-step procedure to assist experts in correcting for regression in prediction. A reference class (a group of cases with similar characteristics) related to the case at hand is selected, for which the distribution of outcomes is known or can be assessed with confidence; the distribution of outcomes for this class is assessed; the expert makes an intuitive estimate for the case at hand; the expert estimates the likely accuracy, or predictability, of his or her estimate, based on past experience; and, finally, the intuitive estimate is regressed toward the average of the reference class on the basis of the predictability estimate.

A slightly different procedure is suggested by the Harrison and March (1984) approach. Rather than estimating the accuracy or predictability of his or her estimates, the expert would estimate the "noisiness" of the estimates or of the information, based on past experience. As in estimating accuracy, records of past predictions and outcomes could be used in a straightforward manner to estimate the signal/noise ratio. Lacking such data, subjective estimates of the noise level could be made. This method has the psychological advantage of being less ego involved for the expert—it is psychologically easier, and has less potential for bias, to estimate a relatively "objective" noise level than to estimate the inaccuracy of one's own predictions. An external attribution, noisy information, is substituted for an internal attribution, inaccurate judgment, with respect to the cause of the regression problem. If no data are available to estimate the noise level, knowledge of the noise level for estimates in other areas based on similar types of information could be used. There may be a cognitive advantage to framing the problem in terms of noisy information. The merits of this approach relative to the Kahneman and Tversky (1979a) approach could be directly tested.

Given that regression effects in general seem to defy recognition, it is perhaps not surprising that expectation inflation and the winner's curse are often not noticed. A number of perspectives, many of which are complementary, provide insight into why this failure might occur. Festinger (1957) has observed that people develop attitudes consistent with their behaviors, and in particular with choices they have made, so that expectation inflation and the recognition of the winner's curse can be obscured through dissonance reduction. Staw (1980) notes that people have a need to appear competent and rational; he interprets dissonance reduction as a process of self-justification or rationalization, which may involve reevaluating outcomes as well as reformulating expectations. Staw argues that organizations are also prone to rationalization and justification. Thus, when an organization selects an employee who does not perform to the organization's initial expectations, a variety of mechanisms inhibit recognition of this underperformance.

Salancik (1977) found that choice leads to commitment, especially to the degree that the choice is explicit, irrevocable, voluntary, and public, and that commitment leads to satisfaction with choice. Choices that are important and that have been made several times before are also more likely to lead to commitment (Kiesler, 1971), as are choices made by groups (Salancik, 1977). Staw (1974) showed in a field experiment that subjects committed to a chosen course of action reported increased satisfaction when the benefits prompting the choice proved lower than expected.

The hindsight bias (Fischhoff, 1975, 1977; Fischhoff & Beyth, 1975; Goitein, 1984; Slovic & Fischhoff, 1977) can also obscure expectation inflation and recognition of the winner's curse. The hindsight bias is the tendency to recall expectations as having been close to the outcomes actually experienced; outcomes are "remembered" as being expected, irrespective of what the expectations actually were when the choices were made.

Kuhn (1962) and Nisbett and Ross (1980) note the general tendency of beliefs to persevere when people are confronted with disconfirming evidence. Ross, Lepper, and Hubbard (1975) and Lepper, Ross, and Lau (1979) have shown that beliefs induced by experimental manipulations persist even after debriefing procedures have exposed and explained the manipulations. This tendency is the result of a variety of cognitive biases, including the biased assimilation of data into existing theories and the development of causal theories attributing the unexpected outcomes to extraneous causes. Tversky and Kahneman (1980) and Anderson, Lepper, and Ross (1980) have shown that when predictions are based on causal theories, people resist changing their causal theories, and sometimes even their predictions, when presented with disconfirming outcome information. The existence of causal theories, then, can obscure expectation inflation and recognition of the winner's curse and can prevent adjustments for these effects in the future.

Disconfirming evidence, or negative feedback, has also been found to lead to escalating commitment to a chosen course of action in a wide variety of situations (Brockner & Rubin, 1985; Festinger, Riecken, & Schachter, 1956; Ross & Staw, 1986; Staw, 1976). Festinger et al. (1956) found that members of a religious group intensified their proselytizing activities following disconfirmation of their predictions. Staw (1976) found that business students presented with evidence of investment failure decided to put even larger amounts of money into the same investments if they had personally made the original investment choices. Brockner and Rubin (1985) found that escalating commitment is even more likely when feedback is framed in a manner that highlights its negative aspects, as suggested by the work of Kahneman and Tversky (1979b; Tversky & Kahneman, 1981). Ross and Staw (1986) describe the steadfast commitment of the government of British Columbia to hold Expo 86 even though projected losses rose from $6 million to $311 million over a seven-year period leading up to the fair. If, as discussed earlier, commitment leads to increased satisfaction with decisions and contributes to the failure to recognize unmet expectations, then the tendency to escalate commitment in the face of failure is likely to make the recognition of expectation inflation and the winner's curse even more difficult.

Another factor that contributes to the persistence of beliefs and the failure to recognize the role of RTTM is overconfidence. People tend to be far more confident in their judgments, or certain of their assessments, than could possibly be justified by reasonable analysis (Einhorn & Hogarth, 1978; Fischhoff, Slovic, & Lichtenstein, 1977; Kahneman & Tversky, 1979a; Nisbett & Ross, 1980). For example, a number of studies have reported considerable overconfidence in the estimation of uncertain quantities (Lichtenstein, Fischhoff, & Phillips, 1977). Typically, when people estimate a 98% confidence interval, the actual value of the uncertain quantity falls outside this interval in more than 25% of the cases, compared with the 2% exceptions that would be expected if the estimated confidence interval were accurate. According to Nisbett and Ross (1980), one of the main reasons for overconfidence is the failure to recognize regression. As Kahneman and Tversky (1973) and Hogarth (1980) note, extreme estimates tend to produce overconfidence. Thus we should expect people making choices on the basis of noisy estimates, which tend to produce more extreme values, to exhibit overconfidence. So we have a vicious circle—RTTM leads to overconfidence, and overconfidence makes it difficult to recognize the effects of inflated expectation and the winner's curse.

Accurate feedback concerning decision outcomes may be necessary to increase the recognition of expectation inflation and the winner's curse. The lack of accurate feedback may be a major contributor to the persistence of these effects in organizational decision making. Organizations often do not have data collection, feedback, and analysis systems to evaluate decision outcomes (Staw, 1980). Organizations may avoid collecting outcome information in order to resist being evaluated (Meyer & Rowan, 1977). When feedback on outcomes is available, it frequently is ambiguous, involves a time lag, and is impressionistic rather than factual; Connolly (1977) calls this "feedback degradation." Decisions leading to actions directed toward the organization's environment may result in outcomes that are unclear and hard to evaluate (Staw, 1980). When decisions have political consequences for organizational actors, those actors may distort outcome information or conceal it (Pfeffer, 1977).

Even when clear outcome information is available, the choice of evaluation criteria may inhibit the recognition of expectation inflation and the winner's curse. For complex decisions, organizational tendencies to rationalize and justify decisions may lead to an emphasis on the positive aspects of outcomes. Staw (1980) notes that individual outcomes may be evaluated by comparison with realigned baselines and aspirations (based, for example, on past outcomes), rather than with predecision expectations; this tendency may also apply to the evaluation of organizational outcomes. Finding favorable reference frames for comparison is probably easier in large, complex organizations and in institutional organizations (Meyer & Rowan, 1977), where ambiguous, multiple, and conflicting goals offer opportunities for reinterpretation, redefinition, and selective focus.

These observations suggest that there are strong psychological and organizational forces working against the recognition of expectation inflation and the winner's curse. These forces are likely to be particularly potent when people are strongly committed to their decisions, as is often the case in organizational settings. However, people do eventually become dissatisfied and act when their expectations are repeatedly not met, as Vroom and Deci (1971) have shown in a longitudinal study of people's job choices. The psychology of such long-term processes has not been investigated systematically and is not well understood.

Organizational Influences on
Expectation Inflation and the Winner's Curse

We established earlier the number of options considered and uncertainty as the two key variables driving expectation inflation and the winner's curse. In this section, we examine how behavioral factors and organizational contexts can influence the number of alternatives and the noise level. This analysis leads to a set of conditions that are expected to determine the extent of expectation inflation and the winner's curse in organizational decisions.

We consider in sequence below the number of options under consideration and the level of uncertainty. Within each of the following subsections, we assume that the focal organization is evaluating one or more options to make a choice and is the potential victim of expectation inflation, and that the organization is one of a number of bidders in some competition and is the potential victim of the winner's curse. Obviously, we could put the focal organization in the role of receiving many bids (e.g., see our earlier consulting firm example) and make the appropriate transformation of our discussion of the winner's curse. Within each subsection, we focus primarily on expectation inflation, then turn to a shorter, parallel discussion of the winner's curse.

Factors Influencing the Number of Alternatives

In a wide variety of situations, decision making is characterized by *satisficing*—looking for a course of action, or decision, that is "good enough" (Simon, 1976). The satisficing concept has been applied to decision-making behavior in general and to organizational decision making in particular (Cyert & March, 1963; March & Simon, 1958; Simon, 1957, 1976). Essentially, rather than evaluating a number of alternatives and choosing the best, decision makers consider alternatives sequentially, one at a time, until an alternative is found that meets the "good enough" criterion. On the average, fewer alternatives will be considered in using this procedure than in using a decision-making procedure that involves evaluating all of the alternatives and choosing the best. Because considering fewer alternatives tends to lead to more accurate estimates for choices, satisficing behavior will tend to produce more realistic expectations, although it will also lower average outcome values.

On the other hand, factors such as previous experience (Cyert & March, 1963) and the formulation of the choice problem (Kahneman & Tversky, 1979b) may influence the order in which alternatives are considered, so that the first alternatives considered may be those about which the decision maker has the highest expectations. Because these expectations are probably biased by the regression effect, satisficing will tend to produce inflated expectations to the extent that prior expectations are biased and influence the order of alternative consideration.

A variety of other factors can influence the number of alternatives considered and, hence, the level of expectation inflation. The complexity of an individual's cognitive structure has been positively related to the number of alternatives considered in decision making (Driscoll & Lanzetta, 1965; Driscoll, Tognoli, & Lanzetta, 1966). Similarly, Downs (1967) argues that people with greater analytic skills and training will consider more alternatives. Given that there is no evidence of a tie between analytic ability and recognition of the concepts underlying RTTM, analytic ability may actually *increase* expectation inflation.

People may learn to consider fewer alternatives in order to avoid high levels of uncertainty. Driscoll and Lanzetta (1965) and Driscoll et al. (1966) found that subjective uncertainty increases with the number of alternatives considered. In organizations, Downs (1967) argues, fewer alternatives are considered for more complex decisions. Payne (1976) and Staelin and Payne (1976) found that people engage in strategies that limit or reduce the number of alternatives seriously considered.

Rather than strategically limiting the number of alternatives considered, organizational decision makers often find that this is a natural consequence of their job situations. They are subjected to alternative claims for their attention (Downs, 1967; March & Shapiro, 1982) and to distractions (O'Reilly, 1983), and these competing demands limit their capacity to consider all individual decisions in detail.

Another factor related to the number of alternatives considered is psychological stress (George, 1980; Janis & Mann, 1977). A decision maker under high stress—for example, time pressure—is likely to consider fewer alternatives in the decision-making process. According to Janis and Mann (1977), threatening decision situations, if accompanied by loss of hope, can lead to "defensive avoidance," or, if accompanied by time pressures, can lead to a paniclike state called "hypervigilance"; in either case, individuals in these states are likely to consider fewer alternatives. Staw, Sandelands, and Dutton (1981) argue that organizational decision makers consider fewer alternatives when facing perceived threats, and Hogarth (1980) notes that people under stress have more difficulty assimilating information and are more prone to "panic judgments." Of course, time pressures alone, even without stress, permit less opportunity to identify and consider alternatives (Downs, 1967).

The norms of a group or organization can also influence the number of alternatives that will be considered, and these norms may vary by type of decision. Sometimes norms are formalized as "standard operating procedures" (Cyert & March, 1963). For example, an organization hiring a file clerk may hire the first eligible candidate, or may consider at most two or three possibilities, whereas the same organization may consider a large number of candidates for a job such as president or general manager. More alternatives will probably be considered in acquisition or plant location decisions than in decisions concerning where to buy office furniture. The factors influencing norms are complex, but one major dimension is the importance of the decision. More alternatives are probably considered for more important decisions (Hogarth, 1980), leading to greater expectation inflation as the importance of the decision increases.

The number of alternatives considered is also limited by the availability of information. There are both external and internal aspects to availability. In the external sense, the number of alternatives considered may be limited because the decision maker has no knowledge of the existence of other alternatives or is unable to obtain the information necessary to evaluate other alternatives; this may be related to prohibitive information costs (O'Reilly, 1982). In the internal sense, availability concerns the ease with which information can be perceived, recalled, or thought about (Hogarth, 1980; Nisbett & Ross, 1980; Tversky & Kahneman, 1974). The decision maker's causal framework or schema guides his or her thinking about the decision problem, leading the individual to perceive the problem selectively. This constrains the consideration of alternatives that are inconsistent with the causal schema—that is, some alternatives are not conceptually available or accessible.

On the other hand, the structural complexity of modern organizations tends to increase the number of alternatives available to the decision maker. The information-generating function in organizations is typically separate from the information-using function, and organizations provide incentives for gathering more information than is necessary or desirable from the standpoint of the decision makers (Feldman & March, 1981). The existence of highly developed information systems and the implementation of features such as electronic mail are also likely to contribute to the number of alternatives available. O'Reilly (1983) suggests that the degree to which available alternatives are actually considered is related to the power of the source; alternatives offered by more powerful subunits are more likely to be considered. Powerful subunits also have access to more resources with which to generate information.

The level of accountability for decision makers is another factor influencing the number of alternatives considered. If decisions are formally evaluated, or if it is important that decisions appear legitimate, rational, and acceptable (Feldman & March, 1981; Staw, 1980; Tetlock, 1985), the decision maker is likely to consider more alternatives to provide procedural protection in terms of evaluation or to signal the legitimacy of the decision-making process. This is related to Simon's (1978) notion of "procedural rationality." This factor is especially important in situations where the decision must be justified to many people (Downs, 1967), or where decision criteria are ambiguous or the outcomes of decisions are hard to observe or to evaluate (Feldman & March, 1981). In many cases, the outcomes are relatively clear to the decision maker, but external groups evaluating the decisions have little or no access to outcome data. As suggested by Meyer and Rowan (1977), when clear outcome information is not available, the value and legitimacy of decisions are judged on the basis of the process and structure of decision making. This form of judging decisions encourages the appearance of considering more alternatives, but does not necessarily mean that they are actually considered. Of course, only the number of alternatives actually considered influences expectation inflation.

Group decision making has the potential to increase the number of alternatives considered. Several people with differing perspectives on the decision issues can generate more alternatives than a single decision maker. Group decision making could occur in the context of an informal work group or in the context of a formal committee. Committee decision making in an organization is more likely when there is a high level of conflict arising from resource scarcity, high uncertainty, high interdependence, heterogeneity of goals and interests, dispersion of power, and decision importance (Pfeffer, 1981). High conflict combined with multiple participants with differing interests and perspectives suggests that a large number of alternatives will be considered. However, when groups are characterized by high levels of cohesiveness, group-think symptoms will influence decision making (Janis, 1972). In this situation, fewer alternatives will probably be considered; in fact, Janis (1972) has noted that decisions involving groupthink are usually reached after consideration of only two alternatives.

It is interesting to note that, although expectation inflation increases with the number of alternatives considered, there is some behavioral evidence that increasing the number of alternatives considered actually decreases the post-decision dissatisfaction of individuals (O'Reilly & Caldwell, 1981). In this case, satisfaction with the thoroughness of the search process may outweigh dissatisfaction with outcomes that fall short of expectations.

Most of the arguments we have made in this subsection concerning expectation inflation can be generalized to the winner's curse. If the focal organization is one bidder among many, the behavioral and organizational factors discussed provide diagnostic information concerning the choice processes of the organization selecting among bidders. As the numbers are predicted to increase from these behavioral and organizational factors, the organization should exhibit increased concern about the existence of the winner's curse. And, to the extent that high uncertainty also exists, the organization should see these as cues to opt out of the auction. In contrast, intuition will often lead individuals and organizations to use the interest of the other bidders as a positive sign of the value of winning the auction.

Factors Influencing Uncertainty

In addition to the number of alternatives considered, expectation inflation and the winner's curse are also related to the uncertainty of the values of alternatives. Unlike the number-of-alternatives effect, which involves a trade-off between outcome values and the accuracy with which these values can be predicted, lower noise levels are always preferable in terms of both features. Reducing noise, however, can be costly.

Random fluctuations, or noise, in the estimated values of alternatives can arise in several ways. First, there may be random variations in the subject of evaluation, whether it is a pilot's performance or the Dow Jones average. Second, there may be random error in measurement or observation. Third, there may be random error in the channels through which the observations are communicated. Finally, there may be random variations in the calculation or computation of estimates.

There are many ways in which errors can be introduced at each stage of this process, but only random unbiased errors, or noise, are of concern here.

However, it is probably most often the case that errors have both biased and unbiased components. When studying biases in the expected values of choices, investigators must distinguish the effects of the biased components from the effects of unbiased components of the errors in the estimated values of alternatives.

The first source of uncertainty is the random variation associated with the subject of evaluation. *Natural* variation may be a more appropriate term, because the variation may not really be random. It may be a result of causes that are not understood, or that are so complex they cannot be predicted accurately, analogous to the physical phenomenon of Brownian movement (Einstein, 1905). In either case, it is probably safe to treat this variation as random, or uncertainty, for purposes of this discussion.

Random errors in observation or measurement have many sources. Measuring instruments may be crude, as early telescopes were. The subject of observation may not be accessible—for instance, oil reserves or the profits of a private firm—so that rough guesses or estimates based on poor indicators are used. Observations may also be influenced by a variety of random social or organizational factors, such as differences in accounting systems or in observers' skills and approaches.

Communication errors are common. The physical transmission of information may be imperfect—for example, a poor telephone connection or a very faint computer printout. Another factor is the number of links in the communications chain. In general, the more people through whom a message is relayed, or the more levels it must pass through in an organization, the more likely it is to become distorted (Downs, 1967; Tullock, 1965). According to O'Reilly (1983), unintentional distortion of information occurs when the information is communicated between groups with different vocabularies, with sensitivities to different goals and constituencies, and with different criteria for determining what is important.

Computational errors can be random in nature. Errors of carelessness may be made, including mistakes in data entry and programming. In some cases, information-processing biases such as the inclusion of irrelevant information can produce random computational error.

Multiple sources, or redundancy, can reduce the errors in observation or measurement, in communication, and in computation. If an estimate is the average of several observations or measurements, its random error decreases as the number of observations increases. Similarly, communication errors may be reduced through the averaging of the data communicated independently by several information sources. Information systems with features such as electronic mail may facilitate this process. Computational errors could be reduced through the averaging of the results of several independent computations.

The use of groups in decision making can affect the noise level. If each group member advocates a value for each alternative based on his or her noisy estimate, a dilution effect (Nisbett & Ross, 1980) could produce group estimates with less noise. This is analogous to the use of multiple sources. Other factors, however, militate against this effect for groups. In cohesive groups, groupthink symptoms such as self-censorship, pressure on dissenters, and "mindguarding," including the avoidance of outside expert opinion (Janis, 1972), may work against noise reduction. The conditions associated with committee decision making, noted earlier, also lead to the use of power (Pfeffer, 1981), so committee estimates may be influenced by the organization's power structure. Committee decision making, then, rather than reducing noise, may lead to biased estimates. A similar outcome may result from the tendency of groups in some situations to become polarized (see McGrath & Kravitz, 1982).

Several other factors could influence the noise level of estimates. Cost or time pressures may reduce accuracy at any stage of the estimation process. Random error may be introduced through a lack of consistency in applying rules or standards for evaluation or judgment. Lack of feedback may result in efforts to achieve greater accuracy being deemed unnecessary.

Three general techniques to reduce noise levels in organizations are advocated by Downs (1967): redundancy, the use of parties external to the organization, and overlapping responsibilities within the organization. All of these techniques involve costs to the organization.

Again, the above arguments can be easily applied to the winner's curse. To the extent that the factors discussed increase uncertainty, the likelihood of the winner's curse is also greater. One interesting conceptual problem concerning the role of organizational factors, uncertainty, and the winner's curse has been suggested by Kahneman: Imagine an organization that funds research and development projects based on proposals that come from the varying units of the organization.[3] To the extent that the organization rewards its units for exaggerating their projects' returns, the noisier the information that the funding group uses to allocate resources will be, and the likelihood of the winner's curse will increase. Interestingly, whereas Kahneman has considered how the structure of such a funding procedure could create a winner's curse, we can easily extend the logic to see that expectation inflation is also likely.

Conclusion

In this chapter we have examined a number of factors associated with decision making that may produce expectation inflation and the winner's curse by influencing the number of alternatives considered and the uncertainty of estimated values of alternatives. We have also considered factors that may inhibit the recognition of expectation inflation and thereby influence the experienced level of decision satisfaction.

Little empirical research has focused on either the number of alternatives or the noise level involved in decision making. Such research is important because these two characteristics of decision-making information directly influence expectation inflation and the winner's curse. This chapter provides guidance for further research by offering hypotheses concerning behavioral and organizational effects on the number of alternatives and uncertainty. Many of these hypotheses can be tested with straightforward experimental designs and can be generalized through the use of field studies.

The emphasis on the number of alternatives and uncertainty is restrictive, because other factors surrounding the decision-making process can influence expectation inflation and the winner's curse. Because of the statistical effects of these two variables, however, it is important to understand their role and the conditions that influence them in order to assess their relative impacts and to provide a baseline for evaluating other effects, such as those caused by biased estimates of decision alternatives. To determine the baseline effect in experimental work, researchers could have disinterested subjects evaluate alternatives, or they could train subjects to avoid cognitive biases and then record the estimated values of the "best" alternatives as the number of alternatives is varied. Or researchers could compute the expected choice values from the equations given in Harrison and March (1984) if the distributions of x and y are known with precision. Differences between these values and the estimated values of chosen alternatives of subjects in various treatment groups could then be attributed to non-statistical biases.

Several options are available for managing expectation inflation and the winner's curse. Managers may choose to misrepresent or conceal expectation inflation and the winner's curse. They may simply monitor the degree to which expectations are met in order to assess the magnitude of the effect, and then decide whether corrective action is necessary. They may correct outcome expectations with statistical adjustments (Harrison & March, 1984), perhaps with the help of data from previous monitoring. They could attempt to influence the level of uncertainty or (when accuracy is the paramount concern) the number of alternatives considered. The best approach may vary with the nature and circumstances of the decision. As noted earlier, influencing the number of alternatives involves a trade-off between outcome values and the accuracy of outcome expectations. Improvements in both outcome values and accuracy through noise reduction must be weighed against the costs involved. Postdecision satisfaction is also a consideration; exposing inflation without reducing it may induce disappointment, whereas concealing inflation may promote satisfaction.

Individuals and organizations often do not consciously compensate for expectation inflation and the winner's curse, partially because they fail to recognize these phenomena. Depending on the situation, this failure of recognition may have either desirable or undesirable consequences. In the hiring of a tenured professor, an academic department, as well as the professor, may have inflated expectations; however, if the department's members, including the new professor, reformulate their expectations and feel satisfied—and this may be likely, at least in the short run, because of the high level of commitment involved— then the stability and atmosphere of the department may be enhanced.

Earlier, we argued that expectation inflation has a cognitive root, whereas the winner's curse has a social root. This has important implications for learning about these effects. The logic in this chapter has emphasized the commonality of these phenomena. However, learning that one needs to consider the number of alternatives examined before making a choice is unlikely to generalize easily to the conclusion that one needs to consider the social context (i.e., number of bidders) of the winner's curse in an auction. The differences in the asocial versus social natures of these two phenomena account for why most people aware of both might still fail to see the underlying parallels.

The consequences of failing to notice expectation inflation and the winner's curse are generally undesirable. This is the case for the manager who is fired for repeatedly making poor investment decisions, and for the manager's firm. Still more troublesome may be poor organizational decisions that are never recognized as falling short of expectations. It is our hope that this chapter, by calling attention to the phenomena of expectation inflation and the winner's curse, and to some of their previously unrecognized behavioral and organizational determinants, will encourage research leading to a better understanding of the causes of expectation inflation and the winner's curse and eventually to effective procedures for their management by organizational decision makers.

Notes

1. Readers who are offended by the example in this paragraph should note that we can ask the same question in relation to virtually any industry.

2. This assumption of common value is not necessary for the winner's curse to exist. However, the assumption provides analytic simplicity. The complexities of noncommon values are not of direct interest in this chapter. See Kagel (1991) for a discussion of the differences between common value and noncommon value auctions.

3. Kahneman suggested this idea in a presentation at Northwestern University in the fall of 1991.

References

Anderson, C. A., Lepper, M. R., & Ross, L. (1980). Perseverance of social theories: The role of explanation in the persistence of discredited information. *Journal of Personality and Social Psychology, 39,* 1037-1049.

Bazerman, M. H. (1990). *Judgment in managerial decision making.* New York: John Wiley.

Bazerman, M. H., & Neale, M. H. (1992). *Negotiating rationally.* New York: Free Press.

Bazerman, M. H., & Samuelson, W. F. (1983). I won the auction but don't want the prize. *Journal of Conflict Resolution, 27,* 618-634.

Brockner, J., & Rubin, J. Z. (1985). *Entrapment in escalating conflicts: A social psychological analysis.* New York: Springer-Verlag.

Capen, E. C., Clapp, R. V., & Campbell, W. M. (1971). Competitive bidding in high risk situations. *Journal of Petroleum Technology, 23,* 641-653.

Connolly, T. (1977). Information processing and decision making in organizations. In B. M. Staw & G. R. Salancik (Eds.), *New directions in organizational behavior* (pp. 205-234). Chicago: St. Clair.

Cox, A. D., & Summers, J. O. (1987). Heuristics and biases in the intuitive projection of retail sales. *Journal of Marketing Research, 24,* 290-297.

Cyert, R. M., & March, J. G. (1963). *A behavioral theory of the firm.* Englewood Cliffs, NJ: Prentice Hall.

Dawes, R. M. (1988). *Rational choice in an uncertain world.* New York: Harcourt Brace Jovanovich.

Downs, A. (1967). *Inside bureaucracy.* Boston: Little, Brown.

Driscoll, J. M., & Lanzetta, J. T. (1965). Effects of two sources of uncertainty in decision making. *Psychological Reports, 17,* 635-648.

Driscoll, J. M., Tognoli, J. J., & Lanzetta, J. T. (1966). Choice, conflict and subjective uncertainty in decision making. *Psychological Reports, 18,* 427-432.

Einhorn, H. J., & Hogarth, R. M. (1978). Confidence in judgment: Persistence of the illusion of validity. *Psychological Review, 85,* 395-416.

Einstein, A. (1905). Über die von der molekularkinetischen Theorie der Wärme geforderte Bewegung von in ruhenden Flüssigkeiten suspendierten Teilchen. *Annalen der Physik, 17,* 549-560.

Feldman, M. S., & March, J. G. (1981). Information in organizations as signal and symbol. *Administrative Science Quarterly, 26,* 171-186.

Festinger, L. (1957). *A theory of cognitive dissonance.* Stanford, CA: Stanford University Press.

Festinger, L., Riecken, H. W., & Schachter, S. (1956). *When prophecy fails.* Minneapolis: University of Minnesota Press.

Fischhoff, B. (1975). Hindsight foresight: The effect of outcome knowledge on judgment under uncertainty. *Journal of Experimental Psychology: Human Perception and Performance, 1,* 288-299.

Fischhoff, B. (1977). Perceived informativeness of facts. *Journal of Experimental Psychology: Human Perception and Performance, 3,* 349-358.

Fischhoff, B., & Beyth, R. (1975). "I knew it would happen": Remembered probabilities of once-future things. *Organizational Behavior and Human Performance, 13,* 1-16.

Fischhoff, B., Slovic, P., & Lichtenstein, S. (1977). Knowing with certainty: The appropriateness of extreme confidence. *Journal of Experimental Psychology: Human Perception and Performance, 3,* 552-564.

George, A. L. (1980). *Presidential decisionmaking in foreign policy: The effective use of information and advice.* Boulder, CO: Westview.

Gilovich, T. (1991). *How we know what isn't so.* New York: Free Press.

Goitein, B. (1984). The danger of disappearing postdecision surprise: Comment on Harrison and March, "Decision making and postdecision surprises." *Administrative Science Quarterly, 29,* 410-413.

Harrison, J. R. (1990). A model of sealed-bid auctions with independent private value and common value components. *Managerial and Decision Economics, 11,* 123-125.

Harrison, J. R., & March, J. G. (1984). Decision making and postdecision surprises. *Administrative Science Quarterly, 29,* 26-42.

Hogarth, R. M. (1980). *Judgment and choice: The psychology of decision.* New York: John Wiley.

Janis, I. L. (1972). *Victims of groupthink.* Boston: Houghton Mifflin.

Janis, I. L., & Mann, L. (1977). *Decision making.* New York: Free Press.

Kagel, J. H. (1991). Auctions: A survey of experimental research. In J. H. Kagel & A. E. Roth (Eds.), *Handbook of experimental economics.* Princeton, NJ: Princeton University Press.

Kagel, J. H., & Levin, D. (1986). The winner's curse and public information in common value auctions. *American Economic Review, 76,* 894-920.

Kahneman, D., Slovic, P., & Tversky, A. (Eds.). (1982). *Judgment under uncertainty: Heuristics and biases.* New York: Cambridge University Press.

Kahneman, D., & Tversky, A. (1973). On the psychology of prediction. *Psychological Review, 80,* 251-273.

Kahneman, D., & Tversky, A. (1979a). Intuitive prediction: Biases and corrective procedures. *TIMS Studies in Management Science, 12,* 313-327.

Kahneman, D., & Tversky, A. (1979b). Prospect theory: An analysis of decision under risk. *Econometrica, 47,* 263-291.

Kahneman, D., & Tversky, A. (1982, February). Psychology of preferences. *Scientific American,* pp. 161-173.

Kiesler, C. A. (Ed.). (1971). *The psychology of commitment.* New York: Academic Press.

Kuhn, T. S. (1962). *The structure of scientific revolutions.* Chicago: University of Chicago Press.

Lepper, M. R., Ross, L., & Lau, R. (1979). *Persistence of inaccurate and discredited personal impressions: A field demonstration of attributional perseverance.* Unpublished manuscript, Stanford University, Department of Psychology.

Lichtenstein, S., Fischhoff, B., & Phillips, L. D. (1977). Calibration of probabilities: The state of the art. In H. Jungermann & G. de Zeeuw (Eds.), *Decision making and change in human affairs* (pp. 275-324). Amsterdam: Reidel.

Lind, B., & Plott, C. R. (1991). The winner's curse: Experiments with buyers and with sellers. *American Economic Review, 81,* 335-346.

March, J. G., & Shapiro, Z. (1982). Behavioral decision theory and organizational decision theory. In G. Ungson & D. Braunstein (Eds.), *Decision making: An interdisciplinary inquiry* (pp. 92-115). Boston: Kent.

March, J. G., & Simon, H. A. (1958). *Organizations.* New York: John Wiley.

McGrath, J. E., & Kravitz, D. A. (1982). Group research. In M. R. Rosenzweig & L. W. Porter (Eds.), *Annual review of psychology* (Vol. 33, pp. 195-230). Palo Alto, CA: Annual Reviews.

Meyer, J. W., & Rowan, B. (1977). Institutionalized organizations: Formal structure as myth and ceremony. *American Journal of Sociology, 83,* 340-363.

Nisbett, R., & Ross, L. (1980). *Human inference: Strategies and shortcomings of social judgment.* Englewood Cliffs, NJ: Prentice Hall.

O'Reilly, C. A., III. (1982). Variations in decision makers' use of information sources: The impact of quality and accessibility of information. *Academy of Management Journal, 25,* 756-771.

O'Reilly, C. A., III. (1983). The use of information in organizational decision making: A model and some propositions. In L. L. Cummings & B. M. Staw (Eds.), *Research in organizational behavior* (Vol. 5, pp. 103-139). Greenwich, CT: JAI.

O'Reilly, C. A., III, & Caldwell, D. F. (1981). The commitment and job tenure of new employees: Some implications of postdecision justification. *Administrative Science Quarterly, 26*, 597-616.

Payne, J. W. (1976). Task complexity and contingent processing in decision making: An information search and protocol analysis. *Organizational Behavior and Human Performance, 16*, 366-387.

Pfeffer, J. (1977). Power and resource allocation in organizations. In B. M. Staw & G. R. Salancik (Eds.), *New directions in organizational behavior* (pp. 235-265). Chicago: St. Clair.

Pfeffer, J. (1981). *Power in organizations.* Marshfield, MA: Pitman.

Ross, J., & Staw, B. M. (1986). Expo 86: An escalation prototype. *Administrative Science Quarterly, 31*, 274-297.

Ross, L., Lepper, M. R., & Hubbard, M. (1975). Perseverance in self-perception and social perception: Biased attributional processes in the debriefing paradigm. *Journal of Personality and Social Psychology, 32*, 880-892.

Salancik, G. R. (1977). Commitment and the control of organizational behavior and belief. In B. M. Staw & G. R. Salancik (Eds.), *New directions in organizational behavior* (pp. 1-54). Chicago: St. Clair.

Simon, H. A. (1957). *Models of man.* New York: John Wiley.

Simon, H. A. (1976). *Administrative behavior* (3rd ed.). New York: Free Press.

Simon, H. A. (1978). Rationality as a process and as product of thought. *American Economic Review, 68*, 1-16.

Slovic, P., & Fischhoff, B. (1977). On the psychology of experimental surprises. *Journal of Experimental Psychology: Human Perception and Performance, 3*, 544-551.

Staelin, R., & Payne, J. W. (1976). Studies of the information-seeking behavior of consumers. In J. S. Carroll & J. W. Payne (Eds.), *Cognitive and social behavior* (pp. 185-202). Hillsdale, NJ: Lawrence Erlbaum.

Staw, B. M. (1974). Attitudinal and behavioral consequences of changing a major organizational reward: A natural field experiment. *Journal of Personality and Social Psychology, 6*, 742-751.

Staw, B. M. (1976). Knee-deep in the big muddy: A study of escalating commitment to a chosen course of action. *Organizational Behavior and Human Performance, 16*, 27-44.

Staw, B. M. (1980). Rationality and justification in organizational life. In B. M. Staw & L. L. Cummings (Eds.), *Research in organizational behavior* (Vol. 2, pp. 45-80). Greenwich, CT: JAI.

Staw, B. M., Sandelands, L. E., & Dutton, J. E. (1981). Threat-rigidity effects in organizational behavior: A multilevel analysis. *Administrative Science Quarterly, 26*, 501-524.

Tetlock, P. E. (1985). Accountability: The neglected social context of judgment and choice. In L. L. Cummings & B. M. Staw (Eds.), *Research in organizational behavior* (Vol. 7, pp. 297-332). Greenwich, CT: JAI.

Tullock, G. (1965). *The politics of bureaucracy.* Washington, DC: Public Affairs.

Tversky, A., & Kahneman, D. (1974). Judgment under uncertainty: Heuristics and biases. *Science, 185*, 1124-1131.

Tversky, A., & Kahneman, D. (1980). Causal schemas in judgments under uncertainty. In M. Fishbein (Ed.), *Progress in social psychology* (Vol. 1, pp. 49-72). Hillsdale, NJ: Lawrence Erlbaum.

Tversky, A., & Kahneman, D. (1981). The framing of decisions and the rationality of choice. *Science, 211*, 453-458.

Vroom, V. H., & Deci, E. L. (1971). The stability of postdecision dissonance: A follow-up study of the job attitudes of business school graduates. *Organizational Behavior and Human Performance, 6*, 36-49.

5

In Dubious Battle

Heightened Accountability, Dysphoric
Cognition, and Self-Defeating Bargaining Behavior

RODERICK M. KRAMER

> I felt that I was being chased on all sides by a giant stampede coming at me
> from all directions. . . . I was forced over the edge by rioting blacks, demon-
> strating students, marching welfare mothers, squawking professors, and
> hysterical reporters. And then the final straw. The thing I feared from the
> first day of my Presidency was actually coming true. Robert Kennedy had
> openly announced his decision to reclaim the throne in the memory of his
> brother. And the American people, swayed by the magic of the name, were
> dancing in the streets. The whole situation was unbearable.
>
> *Lyndon Baines Johnson,*
> *recalling his presidency*
> *(in Kearns-Goodwin, 1976, p. 329)*

The conceptualization of organizational actors as strategic bargainers
who achieve their goals by manipulating and influencing others has occu-
pied a prominent place in organizational theory (e.g., Allison, 1971; Bacharach
& Lawler, 1981; Boulding, 1972; March, 1962; Pfeffer, 1992; Strauss, 1978). It
is central as well to most normative and prescriptive accounts of bargaining

AUTHOR'S NOTE: I am grateful to Jim Baron, Bill Barnett, Jon Bendor, Bob Bies, Joel Brockner,
Peter Carnevale, Robert Cialdini, the late Irving Janis, Jim March, Joanne Martin, Michael Morris,
Jeff Pfeffer, Dean Pruitt, Blair Sheppard, Sim Sitkin, Phil Tetlock, Tom Tyler, Bernie Weiner, Gene
Webb, and Mayer Zald for their thoughtful input at various stages in the development of the ideas
presented in this chapter.

(see Dixit & Nalebuff, 1991; McMillan, 1992; Raiffa, 1982). Indeed, Schelling (1960) characterizes the study of strategic conflict as the examination of "conscious, intelligent, sophisticated conflict behavior—of successful behavior," which he construes as "like a search for rules of 'correct' behavior in a contest winning sense" (p. 3).

The portrait of the organizational actor that emerges from theory and research in this tradition is that of a perceptive and pragmatic bargainer: vigilant, discerning, and cognitively flexible when dealing with opponents. Relative to such characterizations, self-defeating bargaining behavior—behavior that undermines or impedes realization of the very goals it is meant to serve—is both perplexing and paradoxical. If "self-preservation and the pursuit of self-interest are essential features of rational behavior," as Baumeister and Scher (1988, p. 3) suggest, then self-defeating bargaining behavior can be regarded as the quintessential example of negotiator irrationality.

Few instances of self-defeating bargaining behavior have attracted as much scholarly attention as Lyndon Baines Johnson's misperceptions and miscalculations in trying to manage domestic political opposition to the Vietnam War in the late 1960s (see, e.g., Berman, 1982, 1989; Burke & Greenstein, 1989; Califano, 1991; Goodwin, 1988; Halberstam, 1972; Heath, 1975; Herring, 1993; Johnson, 1971; Kearns-Goodwin, 1976; Miller, 1980; Van DeMark, 1991; Wicker, 1981). Throughout his long and tumultuous career, Johnson displayed a remarkable ability to assess his adversaries accurately and, ultimately, to win his way when bargaining with them. He had, as one observer has noted, a "jeweler's eye for the other man's ego" (Matthews, 1988, p. 30). "If Lyndon Johnson was not a reader of books," comments Caro (1982) more wryly, "he was a reader of men—a reader with a rare ability to see into their souls" (p. 287). Johnson was, by all of these accounts, a masterful manipulator and consummate bargainer.

When dealing with opposition to the Vietnam War, however, Johnson displayed a striking level of strategic misperception and miscalculation. As Kearns-Goodwin (1976) observes, whereas "in the past Johnson had displayed a fine sense of discrimination about his political opponents, recognizing that his enemies today might be his allies tomorrow . . . now he became unrestrained and reckless, creating a fantasy world of heroes and villains" (p. 315). Even close associates and aides who appreciated the enormous obstacles Johnson faced in trying to overcome opposition to the war were struck by the extent to which his perceptions and judgments were at first curiously—and later shockingly—out of touch with reality. As Skowronek (1993) concludes in a recent assessment, "The 'tragedy of Lyndon Johnson' is a drama without parallel in modern American politics. It is the story of a master politician who self-destructed at the commanding heights. . . . The Johnson presidency remains one of the great riddles of our time" (p. 325).

How is it possible that such a sophisticated and perceptive bargainer, seasoned by years of experience in the organizational trenches and presumably at "the height of his game," could have so dramatically misperceived his opposition? Why did Lyndon Johnson, who was widely recognized for his political acuity and strategic acumen, embark on a counterproductive and escalatory course of behavior, especially over a war for which he felt little affection?

In trying to account for Johnson's behavior during this period, several explanations have been advanced. First, a number of scholars have focused on psychological and organizational processes that contributed to Johnson's escalating commitment to Vietnam (e.g., Brockner & Rubin, 1985; Staw, 1976). Others have emphasized the impact of dysfunctional group dynamics and other malfunctions in the advisory process that adversely influenced Johnson's decisions (e.g., Janis, 1983). Finally, a third perspective, promulgated primarily by political psychologists, explains Johnson's behavior in terms of the interaction of personality factors and institutional dynamics (e.g., Barber, 1992; Greenstein, 1975).

Although benefiting from these contributions, the present chapter articulates a quite different perspective on the origins and dynamics of Johnson's self-destructive bargaining behavior. Drawing on recent social cognitive theory and research, I argue that Lyndon Johnson experienced a variety of dysphoric cognitive states during the late 1960s that contributed to his adopting a variety of self-defeating bargaining behaviors. To explain the emergence of these dysfunctional cognitions, and the self-destructive behaviors they engendered, I weave together theory and evidence from three distinct streams of research: (a) research on the effects of accountability on judgment and choice (for recent reviews, see Tetlock, 1991, 1992), (b) research on the antecedents and consequences of paranoid cognition in organizations (Kramer, 1993, in press), and (c) research on self-defeating behavior (Baumeister & Scher, 1988; Berglas & Baumeister, 1993).

Method and Approach

In order to derive inductively a model that articulates the links among self-defeating bargaining behavior, heightened accountability, and dysphoric cognition, I adopt a psychohistorical approach. The aim of a psychohistorical account is to articulate how the interplay of psychological and organizational dynamics shape judgment and decision behavior. This method has been employed primarily by historians and political psychologists (see, e.g., Barber, 1992; George & George, 1956; Greenstein, 1975). Although less frequently used by organizational theorists, the method closely resembles, in both form and rationale, the qualitative, idiographic research methods widely used in organizational research (see, e.g., Eisenhardt, 1989; Janis, 1983; Tsoukas, 1989; Weick, 1993).

The conceptual framework that emerges from this psychohistorical analysis is based upon a large volume of archival data on the Johnson administration, including oral histories, recently released transcripts of meetings and telephone conversations, memoirs, and journalistic accounts (particularly the following sources: Anderson, 1993; Barrett, 1993; Berman, 1982, 1988, 1989; Burke & Greenstein, 1989; Califano, 1991; Dallek, 1991; Goodwin, 1988; Gruber, 1991; Halberstam, 1972; Heath, 1975; Herring, 1993; Johnson, 1971; Kearns-Goodwin, 1976; Miller, 1980; Skowronek, 1993; Turner, 1985; Van DeMark, 1991; Wicker, 1991). Although space precludes a review of all of the pertinent evidence, the framework is also consistent with an accumulating body of experimental research (Fenigstein & Vanable, 1992; Kramer, 1993; Lyubomirsky & Nolen-Hoeksema, 1993).

Self-Defeating Behavior: A Social Cognitive Perspective

The study of self-defeating behavior stands at the intersection of clinical psychology and social psychology (for overviews, see Baumeister & Scher, 1988; Berglas & Baumeister, 1993). A variety of different forms of self-defeating behavior have been identified, but the present analysis focuses on situations in which organizational actors do not desire, intend, or foresee the harmful consequences of their strategic acts. In this sense, self-defeating behaviors are counterproductive because the actor "seeks some positive goal but uses a technique or strategy that impairs the chances of success. The focus is neither on normal behaviors that occasionally turn out badly, nor on isolated accidents or mishaps. *Rather, it is on systematic behavior patterns that . . . lead reliably to self-harmful outcomes*" (Baumeister & Scher, 1988, p. 12; emphasis added).

The aim of a social cognitive analysis of self-defeating behavior is to explicate the role that basic cognitive processes play in the development and maintenance of such behavior. In particular, it attempts to articulate how such processes contribute to the misperception and misconstrual of social situations, engendering ineffectual or counterproductive behaviors in those situations. Importantly, it also affords serious attention to the social bases of such misperceptions and misconstruals. In the present case, the emphasis is on how the social context within which organizational bargaining occurs—operationalized in terms of the heightened and diffuse accountability that organizational actors frequently encounter—shapes negotiator cognitions and behaviors.

To make these linkages clearer, it may be helpful first to describe in more detail what dysphoric cognitions are, and how accountability might influence them.

Dysphoric Cognitions

In recent years, a great deal of attention has been directed toward understanding how positive illusions (Taylor & Brown, 1988) and positive affect (Isen & Baron, 1991) influence social judgment and behavior. This research has shown, for example, that cognitive illusions and positive mood states can lead individuals to overestimate their perceived control over events, foster patterns of unrealistic optimism about future events, and contribute to overly positive views about the self. Much of this research has focused on the constructive and beneficial effects of these illusions and mood states. For example, it has been noted that they play a major role in self-regulation, helping individuals maintain a sense of self-efficacy, potency, and competence across the life span (see, e.g., Taylor, Wayment, & Collins, 1993).

In contrast with these positive illusions and mood states, dysphoric cognitions represent a variety of what might be thought of as "negative illusions" about the self and others. These include heightened perceptions of vulnerability, perceived loss of control, feelings of helplessness and hopelessness, worst-case thinking, and fatalistic rumination. The concept of dysphoric cognition represents an amalgam of several clinical and social psychological perspectives on the self in social context (see, e.g., Janis, 1967; Kramer, 1993, in press; Lyubomirsky & Nolen-Hoeksema, 1993; Seligman, 1975). It reflects an accumulating body of psychological theory and research concerning how individuals respond to, or cope with, anxiety-inducing and/or depressive situations, especially those that are construed as presenting identity-threatening predicaments, or threats to the integrity of the self (see e.g., Ginzel, Kramer, & Sutton, 1993; Janoff-Bulman, 1992; Lazarus & Folkman, 1984; Steele, Spencer, & Lynch, 1993).

Heightened Accountability

In exploring how dysphoric cognitions, and the affective states that accompany them, contribute to self-defeating bargaining behavior in organizations, this chapter focuses primarily on the effects of accountability. In particular, I argue that dysphoric cognitions arise when organizational decision makers experience a form of heightened but also diffuse accountability. Because accountability is intense but diffuse, the decision makers are unable to identify a dominant or satisfactory strategy for coping with that accountability.

Over the past several decades, an impressive body of theory and empirical evidence has accumulated documenting the significant effects of accountability on individual judgment and decision making (for recent reviews, see Tetlock, 1991, 1992). This research has shown that accountability affects not only the goals individuals adopt during decision making, but the strategies they use when trying to cope with perceived accountability. Several broad conclusions emerge from this research. First, when individuals feel accountable to others, they are likely to be concerned not only about the objective outcomes associated with a given decision, but with how those outcomes will be perceived and evaluated by those to whom they feel accountable. Accountability, it is argued, activates self-presentational concerns because people seek approval and status from the audiences that observe their behavior (Baumeister & Scher, 1988; Tetlock, 1985). Second, the effects of accountability in a given context are often quite complex, and depend on the specific form of accountability linking decision makers and a given audience. Thus, in some settings, decision makers may be concerned primarily about appearing competent; in other settings, concerns about being perceived as likable or popular may be paramount; and in still other settings, concerns about appearing tough or resolute may dominate their decision calculus. Studies that have examined how accountability affects negotiator judgment and decision making have produced similar conclusions (see, e.g., Ben-Yoav & Pruitt, 1984; Carnevale, Pruitt, & Britton, 1979; Kramer, Pommerenke, & Newton, 1993). These studies show that the effects of accountability on a negotiator's judgment and behavior depend on *whom* they feel accountable to and on how they *construe* that accountability.

In many of these studies, most of which have been conducted in laboratory settings, accountability has been operationalized in terms of accountability to a single constituency. For example, in experimental studies designed to simulate management-labor negotiations, each participant has represented a particular well-defined constituency. When only one constituency is involved, strategic complexity is reduced insofar as a compelling or dominant strategy for coping with perceived accountability exists. For example, most experimental studies have found that accountability to a single constituency leads to increased use of competitive or contentious bargaining tactics (Ben-Yoav & Pruitt, 1984; Carnevale et al., 1979). In explaining such results, Tetlock (1985) suggests that "accountability to constituents (who presumably favor tough negotiation standards) induces concern for appearing strong by refusing to make concessions. People respond by employing competitive bargaining tactics that, although obstacles to resolving conflicts of interest, are quite effective in protecting their images in the eyes of constituents" (p. 311).

However, when negotiating organizational outcomes, decision makers typically confront much more complex and diffuse forms of accountability, for which no single dominant strategy is usually apparent. For example, organizational leaders routinely must accommodate and appease a variety of different constituencies whose demands and preferences differ and, in fact, may be quite incompatible. This "multiple audience problem" introduces a variety of cognitive and strategic complexities into a bargaining process (see, e.g., Ginzel et al., 1993; Kramer, 1991).

The problems that attend diffuse accountability, moreover, can be exacerbated considerably when the conflict happens to be severe or acute, as in an escalating organizational conflict or crisis. Stress and arousal under such circumstances are likely to be high. Relatedly, the time and the opportunity necessary to appraise alternatives adequately are constrained (Janis, 1989). Under these conditions, it may be hard to find a single strategy or stance that can solve all of the problems posed by the diffuse accountability that decision makers are feeling. These conditions, in a classic sense, pose intense avoidance-avoidance conflicts (every strategy has obvious drawbacks and political costs). As a consequence, negotiators may experience a kind of dysphoric cognition.

Lyndon Johnson and
the Lugubrious Limelight of Vietnam

Few examples of an organizational actor caught in the painful and protracted limelight created by such heightened and diffuse accountability can rival Lyndon Johnson's experience as president of the United States during the late 1960s, when domestic political conflict over the Vietnam War was approaching its height. During this period, Johnson felt as if he were under continual scrutiny by a variety of hostile audiences. He viewed himself as surrounded by unrelenting adversaries, including not only his all-too-familiar political enemies in Washington, but a national press whose approval he had assiduously courted since becoming president and a vast citizenry whose love and affection he had long sought (Henggeler, 1991; Wicker, 1981).

As the attacks on his policies and character continued, Johnson renewed his efforts to persuade the public and win over his congressional critics. He became obsessed with trying to find some course of action that would resolve his problems. Insiders within the Johnson administration have described in vivid detail how Johnson would prowl the corridors of the White House, often waking in the middle of the night to ponder the next day's bombing targets and to check casualty figures as they arrived. As Secretary of State Dean Rusk recalled, "We could never break him of the habit, even for health reasons, of getting up at 4:30 or 5:00 every morning to go down to the operations room and check on the casualties from Vietnam, each one of which took a little piece out of him" (quoted in Berman, 1988, p. 144).

Despite every effort, Johnson was unable to find a course of action that would appease or mollify his numerous and diverse critics. In response, he began to withdraw socially, drawing the political wagons in an ever tighter circle around the White House. He became increasingly suspicious of even his closest aides and advisers, convinced they were lined up against him, mocking his failures and, in some cases, waiting in the wings to take his place. "I can't trust anybody anymore," he complained bitterly to Goodwin (1988, p. 392).

In describing Johnson's behavior during this period, Johnson's aide, confidante, and eventual biographer Doris Kearns-Goodwin (1976) notes:

> Members of the White House staff who had listened to the President's violent name-calling were frightened by what seemed to them signs of paranoia. Suddenly, in the middle of a conversation, his voice would become intense and low-keyed. He would laugh inappropriately and his thoughts would assume a random, almost incoherent quality, as he began to spin a vast web of accusations. (p. 316)

No less dramatic incidents are recounted by Johnson's former speechwriter and adviser Richard Goodwin (1988). In assessing Johnson's deliberations during this period, Goodwin notes that it was not so much what he said or did, but rather the

> disjointed, erratic flow of thought, unrelated events strung together, yet seemingly linked by some incomprehensible web of connections within Johnson's mind. . . . It was a giant, if always partial, leap into unreason, an outward sign that the barriers separating rational thought and knowledge from delusive belief were becoming weaker, and more easily crossed. (pp. 401-402)

Commenting on the evolution of Johnson's dysphoric thinking about Vietnam, Kearns-Goodwin (1976) notes further that, although "sometimes it seemed as if Johnson himself did not believe what he was saying . . . at other times [his] voice carried so much conviction that his words produced an almost hypnotic effect. . . . The worse the situation in Vietnam became, the more Johnson intruded his suspicions and his fears into every aspect of his daily work" (p. 317).

By the end of his administration, Johnson had become convinced that he was engaged in a life-or-death struggle in which not only his foreign policy but his presidency and, ultimately, even his legacy in history were at stake. Finally, and tragically, the man who had often expressed the aspiration of becoming the greatest and most beloved president in U.S. history died one of its most embittered and rejected, convinced in the end that he had been betrayed by sinister forces—forces that were not only larger and better organized than any he had encountered before, but greater than others around him realized. As Johnson himself poignantly observed, "The only difference between the Kennedy assassination and mine is that I am alive and [mine] has been more tortuous" (quoted in Matusow, 1984, pp. 150-151).

Viewed in aggregate, these accounts portray an organizational leader who felt as if he were under relentless scrutiny by a variety of hostile audiences to whom he felt accountable, and yet for whom no response seemed adequate. He regarded himself as the hapless and helpless victim of malevolent political forces determined to forge the undoing of his presidency.

Understanding Johnson's Dysphoria: The Suffocating Web of Accountability

Organizational leaders live under the continual scrutiny of multiple audiences and constituencies to whom they feel accountable (see Ginzel et al., 1993; Tetlock, 1992). As Pfeffer (1992) has observed in this regard, "To be in power is to be watched more closely, and this surveillance affords one the luxury of few mistakes" (p. 302). In this respect, being in the limelight was hardly a new or unique experience for Johnson. What *was* different, however, was how he construed that accountability. Johnson seemed to personalize both the real and imagined scrutiny of his every action. Expressions of doubt or criticisms of his policy by others, even when intended as constructive, were transformed in Johnson's mind into personal assaults on his character and his claim on the nation's leadership. As close friend and adviser Clark Clifford (1991) comments, "I often saw Johnson personalize the actions of even the Vietcong, interpreting them as somehow personally aimed at him. He reacted by thinking, '*They can't do this to Lyndon Johnson! They can't push me around this way!*'" (p. 380).

In tracing the development of Johnson's dysphoric thinking about Vietnam, it is important to note that these cognitions did not emerge suddenly or full-blown. Rather, the data suggest they developed gradually in response to the way in which Johnson construed the threat posed by that opposition. In the early phases of his policy, Johnson believed that Vietnam was a manageable political issue and that it would not divert either his attention or the attention of the American people from his ambitious plans for a "Great Society" (see Caro, 1982; Dallek, 1991; Goodwin, 1988; Kearns-Goodwin, 1976). Even as late as 1967, he was convinced that "with a bit of financial tinkering and a dash of vigorous campaigning, both [his] foreign and domestic needs could be met" (Turner, 1985, p. 171).

Equally important, Johnson was confident that he possessed the personal skills and political power needed to overcome whatever opposition he might encounter, just as he had so many times before in his career (Johnson, 1971). When the first rumblings reached him that the road to political consensus might be rocky, Johnson derisively dismissed his critics as "nervous nellies," "knee-jerk liberals," and "half-brights" (a pun he used to refer to Senator Fulbright and other individuals who opposed him) (Berman, 1989; Goodwin, 1988; Kearns-Goodwin, 1976).

However, as his attempts to win over his critics failed, Johnson began to believe that the adversaries lined up against him were more powerful and sinister than any he had encountered before. It was almost as if, in order to explain to himself why his enormous personal skills and institutional advantages as president were not enough, he had to conjure up enemies of comparable stature, cunning, and power. Moreover, the scope of the conspiracy that he imagined marshaled against him grew, seemingly in perverse proportion to the extent to which he felt besieged.

Vietnam as Identity-Threatening Predicament

Equally striking is the extent to which Johnson construed opposition to the war as a threat to his identity as a national leader. Criticism of his policy brought to the surface a variety of long-standing doubts Johnson had, not only about his ability to lead the nation, but about the extent to which he was admired and liked as a leader. As Berman (1989) notes: "As his political maneuverings failed to achieve their anticipated goals, Johnson's great personal insecurities manifested themselves. All presidents feel ill-treated by the press, but with Johnson it became an obsession" (p. 183).

These perceptions were no doubt exacerbated by the way in which Johnson had acquired his presidency. Upon the death of President Kennedy, Johnson had at long last achieved his ultimate political goal (indeed, when asked by a colleague in 1960 why he had accepted Kennedy's offer of the vice presidency, against the advice of so many supporters, Johnson confided, "I'll be a heartbeat away from the presidency"). The dubious circumstances surrounding his ascendancy, however, made the victory Pyhrric: Johnson regarded himself as, at best, an accidental president, the undeserving beneficiary of a tragic turn of fate. More important, he feared that others regarded him as a mere pretender to the throne, an illegitimate heir to Camelot (Gruber, 1991).

Perceived Loss of Control

Another important psychological consequence of the way Johnson construed his accountability is that it appeared to threaten his perceived control over events. Throughout his career, Johnson had labored to control every facet of his political career, trying to leave as little as possible to chance. In his rise to power, he took great pains to orchestrate the social and political forces around him as he saw fit to achieve his ends (Caro, 1982; Dallek, 1991; Gruber, 1991). With Vietnam, however, Johnson found himself, "for almost the first time, encompassed by men and events that he could not control: Vietnam and the Kennedys, and, later, the press, Congress, and even the public whose approval was essential to his own esteem" (Goodwin, 1988, p. 399).

Linked to this perceived loss of control and vulnerability was Johnson's failure to perceive any course of action that would alleviate his anxieties. Johnson felt trapped in an avoidance-avoidance conflict. Movement down any path of the decision tree seemed fraught with peril. Any contemplated decision seemed to have catastrophic political drawbacks. "I feel like a hound bitch in heat in the country," he poignantly complained. "If you run, they chew your tail off. If you stand still, they slip it to you" (Berman, 1989, p. 183).

Dysphoric Self-Consciousness

As a result of perceiving himself under such intense scrutiny, Johnson became increasingly self-conscious, not only about his role in the war's escalation, but about his responsibility for the economic and social costs it was inflicting on the country. The Great Society, which he had once graphically described as being like a beautiful and desirable lady, now seemed to him like an old and withered woman: "She's getting thinner and thinner and uglier and uglier all the time. . . . Soon she'll be so ugly the American people will refuse to look at her; they'll stick her in a closet to hide her away and there she'll die. And when she dies, I, too, will die" (quoted in Kearns-Goodwin, 1976, pp. 286-287)

Even within the cloistered recesses of the White House, Johnson found little respite from these painful feelings of self-consciousness. As Barber (1992) notes: "Johnson felt a stranger among his inherited advisors, extraordinarily sensitive to the slurs by all the 'overbred smart alecks who live in Georgetown and think in Harvard.' And he wondered continually about his adequacy to be what he so desperately wanted to be, a Great President" (p. 79). He imagined that those around him, especially the carryovers from the Kennedy administration, were continually making invidious comparisons between him and his predecessor (Henggeler, 1991). As a result, he felt trapped: unable to relax with them, yet reluctant to remove them, fearing the public would view any change in his cabinet as an act of disrespect toward its recently slain leader (Gruber, 1991).

Johnson also feared that the unfulfilled promise of the Kennedy administration would continue to cast a shadow over his own efforts to sculpt a Great Society. As Goodwin (1988) comments, "The enduring shadow of Camelot—glamorous, popular, intellectual, enshrined in steadily growing myth—seemed to him to obscure the achievements of his own presidency, preventing others from seeing how much more he was accomplishing than had his predecessor" (p. 396).

Hypervigilance

As a result of his heightened self-consciousness, Johnson became extremely vigilant about the conflict over Vietnam. It was, however, a vigilance that differed in form and intensity from the kind of adaptive vigilance that Johnson had displayed so often in the past. As observers of his rise to power have frequently commented, Johnson's intense political preoccupations often played important roles in his early triumphs. As Heath (1975) notes:

> [Johnson] studied, analyzed, catalogued, and remembered the strengths and weaknesses, the likes and the dislikes, of fellow politicians as some men do stock prices, batting averages, and musical compositions. He knew who drank Scotch and who bourbon, whose wife was sick, who needed new post offices . . . who was in trouble with organized labor . . . and who owed him for a past favor. (p. 179)

Such vigilance increased Johnson's effectiveness as a bargainer by helping him recognize subtle opportunities that were strewn across the political landscape, opportunities that others missed (Caro, 1982; Dallek, 1991; Pfeffer, 1992). It also helped inform him how best to tailor his influence approach to the specific person with whom he was dealing. "To gain a senator's vote on a bill, Johnson would spend hours studying every conceivable motivation. . . . The fellow never knew what hit him" (Matthews, 1988, p. 30). In discussing the functional role such vigilance played in Johnson's effectiveness, Matthews (1988) observes:

> It may seem all the more surprising that a man with [Johnson's] towering ego should have climbed to such heights by studying the inner as well as the outer needs of others. Yet it was his willingness to focus on other people and their concerns, no matter how small, that contributed to the near-total communication or at least access that Johnson achieved with those he sought to influence. (p. 27)

As Johnson himself noted, in order to influence someone successfully, "You've got to understand the beliefs and values common to them all as politicians, the desire for fame and the thirst for honor, [but] then you've got to understand the emotion most controlling that particular senator when he thinks about this particular issue" (quoted in Goodwin, 1988, p. 261). Along these lines, Pfeffer (1992) has argued that the ability to take the perspective of the other party is crucial to success in acquiring power: "One has to be able, at least for the moment, to stop thinking about oneself and one's own needs and beliefs. Somewhat ironically, *it is this capacity to identify with others that is actually critical in obtaining things for oneself*" (p. 173; emphasis added).

In sharp contrast to such adaptive vigilance, the data suggest that Johnson began to experience a much less functional form of hypervigilance during the late 1960s. As Herring (1993) comments:

> If Ronald Reagan was the Teflon president, to whom nothing stuck, Johnson was the flypaper president, to whom everything clung. A compulsive reader, viewer, and listener who took every criticism personally and to heart, he was at first intent on, and then obsessed with, answering every accusation, responding to every charge. (p. 95)

Johnson began to scrutinize his interactions—not only those involving his obvious enemies, but even those with his once-trusted aides and advisers—seeking out evidence of their defection or disloyalty.

From Johnson's perspective, of course, such extreme vigilance was justified. As Kearns-Goodwin (1976) notes:

> When every situation is translated into one of power lost or gained, all relationships, including friendships, are reduced to a series of shifting and undependable alliances. In such a world it is easy to succumb to the belief that even one's closest friends must be watched for signs of treason. (p. 388)

Rumination

Another psychological dimension of Johnson's behavior during this period was his intense and seemingly uninterrupted rumination, not only about his role in the escalating political crisis over Vietnam, but about the role that he thought his opponents were playing in his difficulties. According to Kearns-Goodwin (1976), Johnson often

> consciously and deliberately decided not to think another thought about Vietnam. Nonetheless, discussions that started on poverty or education invariably ended up on Vietnam. If Johnson was unhappy thinking about Vietnam, he was even less happy not thinking about it. . . . He found himself unwilling, and soon unable, to break loose from what had become an obsession. (p. 299)

Johnson also ruminated at length about his deteriorating image as a leader. He could not understand how someone whose intentions were obviously so noble, and whose previous legislative accomplishments so great, could suddenly be so universally disdained (Goodwin, 1988; Gruber, 1991; Kearns-Goodwin, 1976). Berman (1989) notes, "It pained him that those he believed had been helped the most by his presidency [e.g., educators, students, blacks, and liberals] were leading the opposition to the war" (p. 183). He was baffled by the sudden erosion of public affection from the same people who, in his eyes, only months before had granted him an enormously strong mandate in the 1964 election. "Why don't people like me?" he once asked Dean Acheson—to which Acheson reportedly replied, "Because, Mr. President, you are not a very likable man" (Barber, 1992, p. 77).

In searching for answers to such questions, Johnson directed his attention outward, toward others, scrutinizing his relationships and pondering the concealed motives and intentions of those he felt had betrayed him. "Discussions on legislation would be interrupted by diatribes against the 'critics.' Private luncheons and dinners would be dominated by complaints about 'the traitors'" (Kearns-Goodwin, 1976, p. 317). Even close aides and long-trusted advisers were not immune to such scrutiny.

Effects of Dysphoric Cognitions on Negotiator Judgment and Behavior

Up to this point, I have described in some detail how Johnson's perceptions of heightened and diffuse accountability contributed to the development of his dysphoric thinking about Vietnam. I have not indicated, however, how such thinking impaired his ability to bargain. The self-defeating consequences of Johnson's dysphoric cognitions become apparent when attention is given to how they affected the accuracy of his political perceptions and the efficacy of the bargaining behaviors he adopted based on those perceptions.

Misperception and Miscalculation

The data suggest several forms of misperception and miscalculation that were closely associated with the dysphoric cognitions that Johnson experienced, including the sinister attribution error, the exaggerated perception of conspiracy, and the biased perception of conflict.

Sinister Attribution Error

The sinister attribution error reflects a tendency for individuals to overattribute hostile intentions and malevolent motives to the actions of others (Kramer, 1993). Several writers have noted that, throughout his career, Johnson frequently expressed suspicions regarding others' motives and intentions, convinced that he was detecting slights and snubs that less discerning observers simply failed to see. For example, Clark Clifford (1991) states that Johnson

saw real or imagined slights everywhere. He told me that on one occasion, while he was sitting in the small room outside the Oval Office waiting to see President

Kennedy, Bobby Kennedy walked rapidly through the room and entered the Oval Office without even acknowledging or greeting him. Whatever the facts of this story, it rankled the proud Lyndon Johnson enormously. (p. 390)

Along similar lines, Henggeler (1991) notes:

[Then Vice President] Johnson's concern about Robert [Kennedy] was so prevalent, and his behavior so peculiar, that those closest to him thought he was 'paranoid.' He was convinced that Robert not only poisoned [President Kennedy's] opinions against him but also the judgments of reporters; together they were engineering his removal from the 1964 ticket. According to Reedy, this possibility became "an obsession" with Johnson—a conviction that peopled the world with agents of the President's brother all seeking to do him in. (p. 62)

Even the seemingly most benign events could take on sinister import in Johnson's mind. For example, when relatives of the Kennedy family accompanied him on one world tour, he was convinced they were acting as spies for Robert Kennedy (Henggeler, 1991, p. 62).

With respect to Vietnam, these suspicions intensified dramatically. Johnson believed that many of the actions of his political enemies, especially those of Robert Kennedy, were intended not only to challenge to his foreign policy, but to mock and humiliate him. (Later, a bemused Bobby Kennedy, perhaps underestimating the threat he posed to Johnson, asked Goodwin, "Why does he keep worrying about me? I don't like him, but there's nothing I can do to him. Hell, he's the President and I'm only a junior senator"; Goodwin, 1988, p. 396).

Exaggerated Perceptions of Conspiracy

Exaggerated perceptions of conspiracy reflect a tendency for individuals to overestimate the extent to which their perceived enemies are engaged in concerted or coordinated actions against them (see Kramer, in press; Pruitt, 1987; Stein, 1988). With respect to undermining U.S. efforts in Vietnam, Johnson believed that a conspiracy of enormous proportions existed.

No longer satisfied with impugning the motives of his critics . . . or attributing his difficulties to 'those Kennedys' or 'those Harvards' or to the traitorous citizens who lived in seeming innocence along the banks of Boston's Charles River, Johnson began to hint privately . . . that he was the target of a gigantic communist conspiracy in which his domestic adversaries were only players—not conscious participants perhaps, but unwitting dupes. (Goodwin, 1988, p. 402)

As he later confided to Kearns-Goodwin (1976):

> Two or three intellectuals started it all, you know. They produced all the doubt, they and the columnists in the *Washington Post*, the *New York Times, Newsweek,* and *Life*. And it spread and spread. . . . Bobby began taking it up as his cause and, with Martin Luther King on his payroll, he went around stirring up the Negroes. . . . Then the communists stepped in. They control the three networks, you know, and the forty major outlets of communication. It's all in the FBI reports. They prove everything. Not just about the reporters, but about the professors too. (p. 316)

Johnson was so convinced his perceptions regarding this conspiracy were correct that he berated CIA director Richard Helms for his inability to find evidence of the "money trail" linking American opposition to the war to its communist origins. "I simply don't understand why it is that you can't find out about that foreign money," he complained (quoted in Miller, 1980, p. 626).

Johnson's belief in this conspiracy persisted long after he left the White House. Even years later, when trying to write his memoirs, he remained fatalistic about his ability to overcome those who were against him: "They'll get me anyhow, no matter how hard I try. . . . No matter what I say in this book, the critics will tear it apart. . . . The reviews are in the hands of my enemies— the *New York Times* and the Eastern magazines—so I don't have a chance" (quoted in Kearns-Goodwin, 1976, p. 357).

Biased Punctuation of Conflict

Biased punctuation of conflict reflects a tendency for individuals involved in a conflict to construe interactions with their adversaries in self-serving and other-derogating terms (Kahn & Kramer, 1990). Thus an actor, A, perceives the history of conflict with another actor, B, as a sequence B-A, B-A, B-A, in which the initial hostile or aggressive move was made by B, causing A to engage in defensive and legitimate retaliatory actions. However, actor B punctuates the same history of interaction as A-B, A-B, A-B, reversing the roles of aggressor and defender.

Just as the exaggerated perception of conspiracy entails an overperception of *social* linkages among actors, so the biased punctuation of conflict entails an overperception of *causal* linkages among events. For example, Johnson once observed:

> Look what happened whenever I went to make a speech about the war. The week before my speech, the *St. Louis Post-Dispatch* or the *Boston Globe* or CBS News would get on me over and over, talking about what a terrible speaker I was. . . . Pretty soon the people began to wonder, they began to think that I really must

be uninspiring if the papers and the TV said so. (quoted in Kearns-Goodwin, 1976, pp. 315-317)

On another occasion, he suggested:

Isn't it funny that I *always* received a piece of advice from my top advisers *right after* each of them had been in contact with someone in the communist world? And isn't it funny that you could *always* find [Soviet official] Dobrynin's car in front of [American journalist] Reston's house the *night before* Reston delivered a blast on Vietnam? (quoted in Kearns-Goodwin, 1976, pp. 315-317; emphases added)

Ironically, the more Johnson ruminated about such links, the more convinced he became of the veridicality of his suspicions. It might seem surprising that rumination would have increased Johnson's confidence in his misperceptions. On prima facie grounds, one might argue just the opposite: that the more people ruminate about the causes of their difficulties, the more likely they should be to generate alternative—and perhaps more realistic—interpretations of their causes. However, research suggests that rumination often works in exactly the opposite direction, fostering unrealistic confidence in people's construals of events. As Wilson and Kraft (1993) note: "Because it is often difficult to get at the exact roots of [many] feelings, repeated introspections may not result in better access to the actual causes. Instead, people may repeatedly focus on reasons that are plausible and easy to verbalize" (p. 410).

Counterproductive Bargaining Behavior

One reason that researchers have emphasized the importance of accurate perception in bargaining is that such perceptions are presumably linked to the efficacy of negotiators' influence attempts. In this respect, dysphoric cognitions contribute to self-defeating behavior because they promote adoption of ineffectual or counterproductive strategies. Consideration of the links between Johnson's thoughts and actions is instructive in this regard.

As noted earlier, Johnson enjoyed a reputation throughout his life as a skilled bargainer and consummate practitioner of the influence process. Accounts of the famous "Johnson treatment" are legendary in Washington. At the top of his form, Johnson's bargaining behavior represented a bewildering, beguiling, and ultimately overwhelming mixture of positive and negative influence strategies. As longtime Johnson associate George Reedy recalls, the Johnson treatment was an "incredible blend of badgering, cajolery, reminders of past favors, promises of future favors, predictions of gloom if something didn't happen. . . . When that man started to work on you, all of a sudden you just felt as if you were standing under a waterfall and the stuff was just pouring on you" (Gruber, 1991). Johnson was, in short, a kind of one-man "good cop/bad cop." Moreover, and significantly, each administration of the treatment was uniquely tailored to fit its intended target.

When dealing with critics of his Vietnam policy, however, Johnson displayed none of his usual flexibility; gone was his willingness to engage in ingratiation, conciliation, or creative bargaining. Instead, as opposition to that policy grew, Johnson turned increasingly to the use of threats and ultimatums to silence his critics. For example, he told Goodwin (1988), "I'm going to get rid of every-body who doesn't agree with my policies. . . . I'll take a tough line" (p. 392). And when one democratic senator (Frank Church) tried to defend himself by telling Johnson that he had, after all, not gone any further in his criticism of Johnson than had Walter Lippman, Johnson put his arm around the senator's shoulders, looked him in the eye, and said, "Well, Frank . . . the next time you need money to build a dam in your state, you'd better go see Mr. Lippman" (Turner, 1985, pp. 184-185).

Moreover, Johnson uncharacteristically abandoned many of his own intui-tions about how to exert influence effectively—finely honed intuitions that had served him well in the past. For example, Kearns-Goodwin (1976) notes that "the more defensive Johnson became about the war, the more he demanded sole credit for the laws Congress passed. [In so doing] he violated his own principle of sharing publicity and credit in order to create a base of good will for the future" (p. 300). Other close associates were similarly struck by the extent to which Johnson increasingly pursued ineffectual and self-defeating strategies when trying to influence others (Goodwin, 1988; Kearns-Goodwin, 1976; Skowronek, 1993).

To be sure, the use of such "hardball" strategies was certainly not new or unique to this situation: Johnson was always tough, especially when the going got rough, as Wicker (1981) once observed. He had been known to reduce grown men, including Vice President Humphrey, literally to tears (Goodwin, 1988). What was distinctive in the late 1960s was the extent to which Johnson relied on such tactics to the exclusion of other approaches that had also character-istically been a part of the "Johnson treatment." Thus, rather than eliciting the concessions he desired or sought from the other party, Johnson's rigid bullying behavior merely escalated his difficulties.

Perseveration

A second form of self-destructive behavior described by Baumeister and Scher (1988) is perseveration. Johnson became unusually rigid with respect to the persistence of his efforts to convert or defeat his adversaries. Rather than changing one approach to another when it was failing, as he had often done in the past, "Johnson dug in further. . . . As the war encroached ever more on his pursuit of the Great Society, [he] accelerated his efforts to convince the doubters and silence the critics" (Turner, 1985, p. 184).

Social Consequences

In assessing the full extent to which Johnson's behavior was self-defeating, it is important to note that his influence attempts were ineffective with respect to changing the attitudes or behaviors not only of those specific individuals at whom they were targeted, but of those who were the observers of his bizarre behavior, especially his supporters and advisers. Without intending to, Johnson disrupted and eroded a number of important social and political relationships on which he depended. For example, his increasingly irrational and harsh actions drove away many of the "best and brightest" in his administration, including such talented policy makers and loyal advisers as Clark Clifford, John Gardner, and Robert McNamara. His behavior also alarmed potential allies whose causes he had often championed and whose respect he had earned through his efforts with respect to civil rights, the War on Poverty, education, and other important domestic issues. Thus Johnson unintentionally estranged himself from those whose counsel and reassurance might otherwise have been enormously helpful to him in trying to manage the predicament of Vietnam.

Putting the Pieces Together: A Framework Linking Accountability, Dysphoric Cognition, and Self-Defeating Bargaining Behavior

In developing the argument that the intense scrutiny Johnson experienced over his Vietnam policy contributed to his dysphoric thinking about the war and, in turn, that such thinking prompted the adoption of self-destructive bargaining behaviors, it has been necessary to cover a fair amount of conceptual ground. Accordingly, it may be helpful to try to pull the various strands of argument together into a more coherent framework. Figure 5.1 represents an attempt to do so. The conceptual framework depicted in the figure illustrates how accountability affects cognition and the links between cognition and behavior.

There are, of course, some obvious omissions in the framework. For example, the roles of political and institutional constraints on behavior are inadequately represented. However, many of these processes have been documented in detail elsewhere (see, e.g., Brockner & Rubin, 1985; Ibarra & Andrews, 1993;

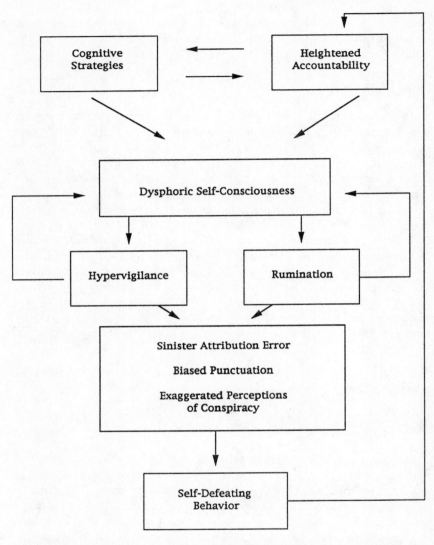

Figure 5.1. Effects of Accountability and Dysphoric Cognitions on Self-Defeating Behavior

Staw, 1976; Staw, Sandelands, & Dutton, 1981). Also, the impact of dispositional and historical influences remains only implicit. However, and again, these influences have been more than amply demonstrated elsewhere (see, e.g., House, 1980; Janis, 1967; Jervis, 1976; Kahn & Kramer, 1990).

Discussion

The primary aim of this chapter is to explore the puzzle of a master bargainer who engaged in inept and self-destructive behavior just at a point in his career when he appeared to have it all. Although focused on explaining the behavior of one extraordinary individual during one extraordinary period in U.S. history, this chapter is also an attempt, more generally, to move us in the direction of a better understanding of the origins and dynamics of self-defeating bargaining behavior in organizations.

At the same time, the present analysis raises as many questions as it answers. It is clear, for example, that many organizational decision makers, when confronted with accountability demands, do not experience the sort of dysfunctional cognitions described here. Accounts of the presidencies of John F. Kennedy and Ronald Reagan reveal little evidence of dysphoric cognition in these presidents, even when their administrations were embroiled in major political crises and identity-threatening predicaments.

Such seeming exceptions prompt consideration of the boundary conditions of the present analysis. First, in trying to explain why seemingly insignificant slights and benign encounters could assume such psychological significance in Johnson's mind, it is interesting to note that Johnson's political identity appeared to be central to his sense of self. As John Connally once observed, "Johnson didn't care about anything but politics. I never saw him read up a book. He slept and ate politics. There wasn't anything else he cared about or was interested in" (Gruber, 1991). This may provide a clue to the dynamics underlying Johnson's extreme reactions. Self-affirmation theorists have recently argued that when threats to one aspect of a person's sense of self occur, most people can attenuate the impact of that threat by affirming other positive personal or social identities (e.g., Steele et al., 1993). In Johnson's case, there seemed to be no other identity to invoke: his whole life was politics. Thus, because his personal and political identities were so heavily intertwined, this coping strategy was unavailable to him. Viewed from this perspective, it is perhaps not altogether surprising that Johnson construed the attacks on his political leadership and policy in such personalistic terms.

A second factor that may influence the likelihood that leaders experience dysphoric cognitions of the sort described above are the coping strategies they use when responding to political threats. Both Kennedy and Reagan, for example, employed a variety of coping strategies that may have helped reduce their susceptibility to irrational suspicion and adoption of self-destructive behavior. Kennedy and Reagan often used humor and self-deprecating remarks when dealing with identity-threatening events. These were used to discount the perceived severity of threats and to frame others' motives and actions in relatively positive and light terms. Along similar lines, Reagan seemed to distance himself psychologically from the Machiavellian machinations around him, viewing the political landscape in benign, almost Pollyannaish, terms. Kennedy, on the other hand, often adopted an unemotional, realist perspective on others' political actions. He resisted construing their behavior in personalistic terms, instead always seeking the rational motives they concealed or revealed.

There are also a number of social and institutional processes that leaders may use to help them engage in more effective reality testing than Johnson displayed (Burke & Greenstein, 1989; George, 1980; Neustadt & May, 1986). Again, Kennedy and Reagan are instructive. Both created very different advisory systems and enjoyed richer social support networks than Johnson. For example, Kennedy was an energetic if erratic reality tester, often probing the veridicality of his political perceptions and assumptions by reaching out to a diverse group of formal and informal advisers. Especially after the Bay of Pigs incident, he made a concerted effort to gather information from diverse sources, including going around close advisers who he feared might be less than motivated to give him critical feedback. The diverse and seemingly erratic search for information may have helped him avoid insular or self-confirming feedback. Similarly, Reagan surrounded himself with those he trusted and tried to minimize political infighting in his advisory groups. Such advisory systems and social support networks operated to reduce the likelihood that irrational and self-defeating cognitions could gain a firm hold.

Caveat

Before closing, I would like to emphasize a few points. The conceptual analysis I have presented thus far has concentrated almost exclusively on the deleterious effects of dysphoric cognition on negotiator judgment and behavior in organizations. To the extent that dysphoric cognitions contribute to dysfunctional cognitions, such as exaggerated perceptions of threat and loss of control, they obviously constitute maladaptive processes. However, it is important to consider the possibility that such cognitions can serve adaptive purposes as well.

There are several ways in which dysphoric cognitions may be useful. First, the results of several recent studies suggest that positive cognitive illusions and positive mood states often contribute to costly misperception and miscalculation in negotiation situations (Carnevale & Isen, 1986; Kramer, Newton, & Pommerenke, 1993; Tyler & Hastie, 1991). To the extent that dysphoric cognitions prompt more vigilant perception and mindful interaction, they may attenuate the impact of such illusions and mood states. Second, dysphoric information processing may be useful in situations where the costs of overconfidence or misplaced trust are high. As already noted, individuals who occupy positions of power in large, complex organizations routinely confront an enormous amount of information that has bearing on the assessment of political risks and opportunities. Somehow, they must sift through and evaluate this information. As Lewis and Weigert (1985) have suggested, distrust and suspicion help reduce such complexity by "dictating a course of action based on suspicion, monitoring, and activation of institutional safeguards" (p. 969). Ultimately, the utility of such a heuristic depends upon how well it maps the actual political terrain of the organization. Whereas its overuse leaves one vulnerable to a Type II error with respect to misplaced distrust, its underutilization exposes one to a potentially more serious Type I error with regard to misplaced trust.

In the final analysis, of course, the trade-offs that attend these two errors depend on context and circumstance. Just as there exists a fine line between adaptive vigilance and dysfunctional hypervigilance, so a distinction needs to be drawn between prudent caution and the self-destructive forms of suspicion displayed by Lyndon Johnson. As with other forms of cognitive illusion and error, the critical question may be, How much is enough?

References

Allison, G. T. (1971). *Essence of decision.* Boston: Little, Brown.
Anderson, D. L. (Ed.). (1993). *Shadow on the White House: Presidents and the Vietnam War, 1945-1975.* Lawrence: University Press of Kansas.
Bacharach, S., & Lawler, E. (1981). *Power and politics in organizations.* San Francisco: Jossey-Bass.
Barber, J. D. (1992). *The presidential character: Predicting performance in the White House* (4th ed.). Englewood Cliffs, NJ: Prentice Hall.
Barrett, D. M. (1993). *Uncertain warriors: Lyndon Johnson and his Vietnam advisers.* Lawrence: University Press of Kansas.
Baumeister, R. F., & Scher, S. J. (1988). Self-defeating behavior patterns among normal individuals: Review and analysis of common self-destructive tendencies. *Psychological Bulletin, 104,* 3-22.
Ben-Yoav, O., & Pruitt, D. G. (1984). Accountability to constituents: A two-edged sword. *Organizational Behavior and Human Performance, 34,* 282-295.
Berglas, S., & Baumeister, R. F. (1993). *Your own worst enemy: Understanding the paradox of self-defeating behavior.* New York: Basic Books.
Berman, L. (1982). *Planning a tragedy: The Americanization of the war in Vietnam.* New York: W. W. Norton.
Berman, L. (1988). Lyndon B. Johnson: Paths chosen and opportunities lost. In F. I. Greenstein (Ed.), *Leadership in the modern presidency.* Cambridge, MA: Harvard University Press.
Berman, L. (1989). *Lyndon Johnson's war.* New York: W. W. Norton.
Brockner, J., & Rubin, J. (1985). *Entrapment in escalating conflicts.* New York: Springer-Verlag.
Boulding, K. E. (1972). The organization as a party to conflict. In J. M. Thomas & W. G. Bennis (Eds.), *Management of change and conflict.* New York: Penguin.

Burke, J. P., & Greenstein, F. I. (1989). *How presidents test reality: Decisions on Vietnam, 1954 and 1965.* New York: Russell Sage Foundation.

Califano, J. A. (1991). *The triumph and tragedy of Lyndon Johnson.* New York: Simon & Schuster.

Carnevale, P. J., & Isen, A. M. (1986). The influence of positive affect and visual access on the discovery of integrative solutions in bilateral negotiation. *Organizational Behavior and Human Decision Processes, 37,* 1-13.

Carnevale, P. J., Pruitt, D. G., & Britton, S. (1979). Looking tough: The negotiator under constituent surveillance. *Personality and Social Psychology Bulletin, 5,* 118-121.

Caro, R. A. (1982). *The path to power: The years of Lyndon Johnson.* New York: Vintage.

Clifford, C. (1991). *Counsel to the president.* New York: Random House.

Dallek, R. (1991). *Lone star rising: Lyndon Baines Johnson.* New York: Oxford University Press.

Dixit, A., & Nalebuff, B. (1991). *Thinking strategically.* New York: W. W. Norton.

Eisenhardt, K. M. (1989). Building theory from case study research. *Academy of Management Review, 14,* 532-550.

Fenigstein, A., & Vanable, P. A. (1992). Paranoia and self-consciousness. *Journal of Personality and Social Psychology, 62,* 129-138.

George, A. (1980). *Presidential decisionmaking in foreign policy: The effective use of information and advice.* Boulder, CO: Westview.

George, A., & George, J. L. (1956). *Woodrow Wilson and Colonel House: A personality study.* New York: John Day.

Ginzel, L., Kramer, R. M., & Sutton, R. (1993). Organizational impression management as a reciprocal influence process: The neglected role of the organizational audience. In L. L. Cummings & B. M. Staw (Eds.), *Research in organizational behavior* (Vol. 15, pp. 227-266). Greenwich, CT: JAI.

Goodwin, R. N. (1988). *Remembering America: A voice from the sixties.* New York: Harper & Row.

Greenstein, F. I. (1975). Personality and politics. In F. I. Greenstein & N. W. Polsby (Eds.), *Handbook of political science: Vol. 2. Micropolitical theory* (pp. 1-92). Reading, MA: Addison-Wesley.

Gruber, D. (Producer). (1991). *LBJ: A biography* [Video]. Dallas: North Texas Public Broadcasting.

Halberstam, D. (1972). *The best and the brightest.* New York: Random House.

Heath, J. (1975). *Decade of disillusionment: The Kennedy-Johnson years.* Bloomington: Indiana University Press.

Henggeler, P. R. (1991). *In his steps: Lyndon Johnson and the Kennedy mystique.* Chicago: Dee.

Herring, G. C. (1993). The reluctant warrior: Lyndon Johnson as commander in chief. In D. L. Anderson (Ed.), *Shadow on the White House: Presidents and the Vietnam War, 1945-1975* (pp. 87-112). Kansas: University Press of Kansas.

House, R. J. (1990). Power and personality in complex organizations. In B. M. Staw & L. L. Cummings (Eds.), *Personality and organizational influence.* Greenwich, CT: JAI.

Ibarra, H., & Andrews, S. (1993). Power, social influence, and sensemaking: Effects of network centrality and proximity on employee perceptions. *Administrative Science Quarterly, 38,* 277-303.

Isen, A. M., & Baron, R. A. (1991). Positive affect as a factor in organizational behavior. In L. L. Cummings & B. M. Staw (Eds.), *Research in organizational behavior* (Vol. 13). Greenwich, CT: JAI.

Janis, I. L. (1967). Effects of fear arousal on attitude change: Recent developments in theory and experimental research. In L. Berkowitz (Ed.), *Advances in experimental social psychology* (Vol. 3, pp. 166-244). New York: Academic Press.

Janis, I. L. (1983). *Groupthink* (2nd ed.). Boston: Houghton Mifflin.

Janis, I. L. (1989). *Crucial decisions.* New York: Free Press.

Janoff-Bulman, R. (1992). *Shattered assumptions: Toward a new psychology of trauma.* New York: Free Press.

Jervis, R. (1976). *Perception and misperception in international politics.* Princeton, NJ: Princeton University Press.

Johnson, L. B. (1971). *The vantage point: Perspectives on the presidency, 1963-1969.* New York: Holt, Rinehart & Winston.

Kahn, R. L., & Kramer, R. M. (1990). Untying the knot: De-escalatory processes in international conflict. In R. L. Kahn & M. N. Zald (Eds.), *Organizations and nation-states: New perspectives on conflict and cooperation.* San Francisco: Jossey-Bass.

Kearns-Goodwin, D. (1976). *Lyndon Johnson and the American dream.* New York: New American Library.

Kramer, R. M. (1991). The more the merrier? Social psychological aspects of multiparty negotiations. In M. H. Bazerman, R. J. Lewicki, & B. H. Sheppard (Eds.), *Research on negotiation in organizations: Vol. 3. Handbook of negotiation research* (pp. 307-332). Greenwich, CT: JAI.

Kramer, R. M. (1993). *The sinister attribution error: Antecedents and consequences of collective paranoia.* Paper presented at the annual meeting of the Academy of Management.

Kramer, R. M. (in press). Perceptions of conspiracy in hierarchical relationships: A social information processing perspective. In R. M. Kramer & T. R. Tyler (Eds.), *Trust in organizations.* Thousand Oaks, CA: Sage.

Kramer, R. M., Newton, E., & Pommerenke, P. L. (1993). Self-enhancement biases and negotiator judgment: Effects of self-esteem and mood. *Organizational Behavior and Human Decision Processes, 56,* 110-133.

Kramer, R. M., Pommerenke, P. L., & Newton, E. (1993). The social context of negotiation: Effects of social identity and accountability on negotiator judgment and decision making. *Journal of Conflict Resolution, 37,* 633-654.

Lazarus, R. S., & Folkman, S. (1984). *Stress, appraisal, and coping.* New York: Springer.

Lyubomirsky, S., & Nolen-Hoeksema, S. (1993). Self-perpetuating properties of dysphoric rumination. *Journal of Personality and Social Psychology, 65,* 339-349.

March, J. G. (1962). The business firm as a political coalition. *Journal of Politics, 24,* 662-678.

Matthews, C. (1988). *Hardball.* New York: Summit.

Matusow, A. J. (1984). *The unraveling of America: A history of liberalism in the 1960s.* New York: Harper & Row.

McMillan, J. (1992). *Games, strategies, and managers.* New York: Oxford University Press.

Miller, M. (1980). *Lyndon: An oral biography.* New York: Ballantine.

Neustadt, R. E., & May, E. R. (1986). *Thinking in time: The uses of history for decision makers.* New York: Free Press.

Pfeffer, J. (1992). *Managing with power.* Cambridge, MA: Harvard Business School Press.

Pruitt, D. (1987). Conspiracy theory in conflict escalation. In S. Moscovici & C. F. Graumann (Eds.), *Changing conceptions of conspiracy.* New York: Springer-Verlag.

Raiffa, H. (1982). *The art and science of negotiation.* Cambridge, MA: Harvard University Press.

Schelling, T. (1960). *The strategy of conflict.* Cambridge, MA: Harvard University Press.

Seligman, M. E. P. (1975). *Helplessness: On depression, development and death.* San Francisco: W. H. Freeman.

Skowronek, S. (1993). *The politics presidents make.* Cambridge, MA: Belknap.

Staw, B. M. (1976). Knee-deep in the big muddy: A study of escalating commitment to a chosen course of action. *Organizational Behavior and Human Performance, 16,* 27-44.

Staw, B. M., Sandelands, L. E., & Dutton, J. E. (1981). Threat-rigidity effects in organizational behavior: A multilevel analysis. *Administrative Science Quarterly, 26,* 501-524.

Strauss, A. (1978). *Negotiations: Varieties, contexts, processes and social order.* San Francisco: Jossey-Bass.

Steele, C. M., Spencer, S. J., & Lynch, M. (1993). Self-image resilience and dissonance: The role of affirmational resources. *Journal of Personality and Social Psychology, 64,* 885-896.

Stein, J. G. (1988). Building politics into psychology: The misperception of threat. *Political Psychology, 9,* 245-271.

Taylor, S. E., & Brown, J. D. (1988). Illusion and well-being: A social psychological perspective on mental health. *Psychological Bulletin, 103,* 193-210.

Taylor, S. E., Wayment, H. A., & Collins, M. A. (1993). Positive illusions and affect regulation. In D. M. Wegner & J. W. Pennebaker (Eds.), *Handbook of mental control.* Englewood Cliffs, NJ: Prentice Hall.

Tetlock, P. E. (1985). Accountability: The neglected social context of judgment and choice. In L. L. Cummings & B. M. Staw (Eds.), *Research in organizational behavior* (Vol. 7, pp. 297-332). Greenwich, CT: JAI.

Tetlock, P. E. (1991). An alternative metaphor in the study of judgment and choice: People as politicians. *Theory and Psychology, 1,* 451-475.

Tetlock, P. E. (1992). The impact of accountability on judgment and choice: Toward a social contingency model. In L. Berkowitz (Ed.), *Advances in experimental social psychology* (Vol. 25, pp. 331-376). New York: Academic Press.

Tsoukas, H. (1989). The validity of idiographic research explanations. *Academy of Management Review, 14,* 551-561.

Turner, K. J. (1985). *Lyndon Johnson's dual war: Vietnam and the press.* Chicago: University of Chicago Press.

Tyler, T. R., & Hastie, R. (1991). The social consequences of cognitive illusions. In M. H. Bazerman, R. J. Lewicki, & B. H. Sheppard (Eds.), *Research on negotiation in organizations: Vol. 3. Handbook of negotiation research.* Greenwich, CT: JAI.

Van DeMark, B. (1991). *Into the quagmire: Lyndon Johnson and the escalation of the Vietnam War.* New York: Oxford University Press.

Weick, K. E. (1993). The collapse of sensemaking in organizations: The Mann Gulch disaster. *Administrative Science Quarterly, 38,* 628-652.

Wicker, T. (1981). *JFK and LBJ: The influence of personality upon politics.* Chicago: Dee.

Wicker, T. (1991). *One of us: Richard Nixon and the American dream.* New York: Random House.

Wilson, T. D., & Kraft, D. (1993). Why do I love thee? Effects of repeated introspections about a dating relationship on attitudes toward the relationship. *Personality and Social Psychology Bulletin, 19,* 409-418.

PART II

The Relational Contexts of Negotiation

As we noted in the preface to this volume, contemporary bargaining theory and research have often characterized negotiators as relatively individualistic and asocial actors. The authors of the chapters in Part II take exception to such views by drawing attention to the importance of relationships in negotiation. They also illustrate the different bases of relationships and their impacts on the negotiation process.

In Chapter 6, Polzer, Mannix, and Neale explore the process of multiparty negotiation, a topic that has received relatively little systematic attention. Polzer et al. argue that coalitional dynamics are a fundamental feature of multiparty negotiation dynamics, and one that differentiates them from dyadic negotiations. They show how coalition processes shape bargaining processes and outcomes, including affecting the distribution of bargaining power and bargainers' incentives for reaching different agreements. Drawing on insights from social identity theory, the authors argue that the social ties that link negotiators can influence the coalitions that form and, by implication, inter-coalitional dynamics. Their chapter is important in that it takes exception to much of the game-theoretic literature on coalitions, which has tended to view coalition formation and maintenance as largely an issue-based and calculative process. As a consequence, coalitions have been construed as shifting, unstable alliances of strategic, self-interested actors. Polzer et al. document the poverty of such a view, suggesting how identity-based ties bind negotiators together in more enduring and stable relations.

Lawler and Yoon, in Chapter 7, address a fundamentally important but much-neglected side of negotiations: the role of emotions. Using the context of a minimal exchange network, the authors examine the importance of relationship-based affective processes. Arguing that such simple networks are characteristic of a wide range of social and organizational situations, they show how the "mere" repeated doing of things jointly creates an emotional attachment that transforms the process and outcome of the exchange relation.

In Chapter 8, Greenhalgh and Chapman attempt to articulate in finer detail than have previous researchers the multidimensionality of negotiation relationships. They note that, because much of the laboratory-based work on negotiations has focused on negotiators' cognitions and utilities, it has tended to highlight calculative and strategic aspects of information processing and behavior. In so doing, such work has attenuated or muted the impact of relationships. In effect, negotiations have been reduced, in a rather ironic fashion, to close encounters between strangers. As a remedy, the authors propose, relationships should be treated as a variable, and as a part of the omnipresent context in which real-world conflicts are played out.

Fittingly, this section concludes with an ambitious contribution that construes relational contexts in their broadest possible terms. In Chapter 9, Robinson asks us to consider the impact of the rapidly evolving institutional and global environments in which tomorrow's organizational conflicts will occur. He points out that the social and economic world in which complex organizations are embedded is changing in ways that negotiation practice—and theory—must acknowledge and accommodate. The old ways won't do. To stimulate broader thinking along these lines, Robinson asks us to consider what attributes the "conflict-competent organization" of the future will need to weather such changes. He notes that it is clear that certain competencies must be in place if organizations are to survive in a competitive, diverse world. At the same time, and appropriately so, he leaves open the question of the precise contours of these emerging organizational competencies. He gives us a call for action, raises the right questions, and, in so doing, offers the research community a daunting but tempting challenge.

6

Multiparty Negotiation
in Its Social Context

JEFFREY T. POLZER
ELIZABETH A. MANNIX
MARGARET A. NEALE

A substantial body of research describes dyadic negotiation behavior and offers prescriptions to actors preparing to enter one-on-one negotiations (Fisher & Ury, 1981; Lewicki & Litterer, 1985; Neale & Bazerman, 1991; Pruitt, 1981; Walton & McKersie, 1965). By comparison, multiparty negotiation remains a neglected topic. This neglect may be a result of the general lack of interest in recent years in small group research. Although small group research boomed in the 1950s and 1960s, interest in the area waned in the following decades. The predominant explanations offered for this shift are the absence of theoretical integration and lack of practical orientation in the small group field (Levine & Moreland, 1990; McGrath & Kravitz, 1982; Zander, 1979). However, Levine and Moreland (1990) propose that although most social psychologists have abandoned the area of small group research, it is now being reexamined by other researchers, notably those interested in organizational settings. One area that can offer a fresh perspective on multiparty interaction and provide a practical and applied context is negotiation research.

In the study of dyadic negotiation, issues that have been addressed frequently include integrative potential, decision biases, power balance, negotiator relationships, communication processes, and the impact of third parties.

Although this research may be informative in a multiparty setting, the direct translation of findings from dyadic to multiparty negotiation contexts can be problematic (Bazerman, Mannix, & Thompson, 1988). A primary reason for this is the higher degree of complexity in multiparty interactions. One of the most obvious and important differences in multiparty compared with dyadic negotiation is the potential to exclude group members from the final agreement (Chertkoff, 1967; Gamson, 1961; Luce & Raiffa, 1957; Murnighan, 1986). This potential results simply from adding a third player to a dyadic interaction; with three (or more) people, subsets of parties can, and indeed are likely to, coalesce to influence the outcome of the group (Caplow, 1956). Issues unique to multiparty negotiation (e.g., the potential for coalitions), which limit the generalizability of findings from dyadic contexts, have led negotiation scholars to call for research on various aspects of multiparty bargaining (Ancona, 1990; Ancona, Friedman, & Kolb, 1991; Bazerman et al., 1988; Brett & Rognes, 1986; Gersick, 1988; Hackman, 1990).

Although research in the negotiation and coalition fields is largely unconnected, both phenomena are typically studied as short-term, self-interested, and politically motivated processes. Our purpose in this chapter is to provide a different lens through which to view coalitions and multiparty negotiation. We propose that by incorporating the social context into an analysis of coalitions, we will add substantially to our understanding of negotiation behavior in the multiparty domain. To do this, we address three broad categories of variables that are most relevant to the social context of small groups: sources of power and power balance, the relationships among the negotiators, and the level of group identification.

Sources of Power in Multiparty Negotiation

Power or negotiating strength has been called the "essence of bargaining" (Bacharach & Lawler, 1980). Certainly the outcomes of a negotiation will be highly related to the amount of power each party has in the negotiation. However, power is not a unitary concept; it can be conceptualized in a number of ways (see Emerson, 1964; French, 1956; Lewin, 1951; Raven & Kruglanski, 1970; Thibaut & Kelley, 1959). We propose that the power sources in multiparty negotiation may be conceptualized as strategic, normative, or relationship based.

Strategic power depends upon the availability of alternative coalition partners. This variable has received the most theoretical and empirical attention, resulting in considerable evidence that bargaining power is a direct function of the alternatives of the negotiators. Normative power, by contrast, has no strategic function. In essence, normative power stems from beliefs about what constitutes a just or fair distribution. These norms can become powerful cues to how resources should be allocated. In a group setting, however, an increased number of norms are available and operating, creating added conflict for negotiators in multiparty contexts.

A third power source is the preference structures of the parties, or relationship-based power. Consider that with the potential for coalition formation, if certain members of the group have compatible preferences on several issues, they are more likely to coalesce, emphasizing their shared interests and excluding or minimizing the input of the remaining group members in fashioning a final agreement. Thus it is in group negotiation that negotiator compatibility and the relationships among negotiators become factors adding to negotiators' bargaining strength.

Strategic and Normative Power

According to Thibaut and Kelley (1959), bargaining power is based on a person's "comparison level for alternatives," which is defined as the "lowest level of outcomes a member will accept in the light of available alternative opportunities" (p. 21). Drawing from this definition, negotiation researchers have focused on how alternatives to a negotiated agreement can affect the power of the parties and the subsequent outcomes they attain (Fisher & Ury, 1981; Pinkley, Neale, & Bennett, in press; Raiffa, 1982; Thibaut, 1968; Walton & McKersie, 1965; White & Neale, in press). Coalition researchers have emphasized the effects of both the number and the value of alternative coalition partners (Chertkoff, 1971; Kelley & Arrowood, 1960; Komorita, Hamilton, & Kravitz, 1984; Komorita & Kravitz, 1979; Kravitz, 1981; Kravitz & Iwaniszek, 1984). From a coalition perspective, parties may bring different amounts of resources, or inputs, to the coalitions they join. The more inputs a party is able to add to a coalition, the more alternative coalition partners that party is likely to have, and the higher will be that party's strategic power.

Empirical research supports the idea that the relative strategic power of the parties in a multiparty negotiation helps to explain which parties will coalesce. Although some studies have found that the weaker parties in a triadic situation are likely to coalesce against the party with the highest power (Chertkoff & Esser, 1977; Kelley & Arrowood, 1960; Psathas & Stryker, 1965; Vinacke & Arkoff, 1957), other work has demonstrated that this phenomenon is partially a function of the game's requirements for a winning coalition (Komorita & Moore, 1976; Kravitz, 1981; Murnighan, 1978b). In so-called simple games, when any two of the parties can form a winning coalition (i.e., when the amount of resources brought to the coalition does not affect the outcome), the two lower-power parties are likely to coalesce. Researchers have recognized that this "strength is weakness" effect is largely a result of the particular role of resources in these types of games. In simple games, resources serve a purely normative function, providing a frame of reference (or norm) for a fair division of rewards (Greenberg & Cohen, 1982; Komorita & Hamilton, 1984; Komorita & Nagao, 1983; Leventhal, 1976). However, normative power carries no recourse for the players in terms of alternatives—it is without strategic value (Komorita & Hamilton, 1984; Komorita & Tumonis, 1980). Researchers have found that both strategic and normative power affect outcomes in coalition games (Komorita & Nagao, 1983; Murnighan, Komorita, & Szwajkowski, 1977) and negotiation exercises (Mannix & White, 1992).

Compatibility of Preferences: Relationship-Based Power

A third type of power present in social contexts is relationship-based power. Relationships take many forms. One force discussed primarily by negotiation researchers is the level of compatibility between negotiators' preferences. In dyadic negotiations, although the two parties may have compatible preferences on some of the issues (L. Thompson, 1991), the majority of the parties' preferences are likely to be opposed (which is the reason they negotiate). By contrast, in a multiparty negotiation it is likely that two or more parties will share compatible preferences on any particular issue.[1] The process of determining compatibility, however, can be complex, as individuals must simultaneously decide with whom to negotiate as well as how to allocate resources among those included in the agreement (Psathas & Stryker, 1965; Sondak, 1992; Sondak & Bazerman, 1989; Stryker & Psathas, 1960). Parties who discover they have compatible preferences are likely to ally and form coalitions, adding to their bargaining strength (Mannix, Polzer, & Neale, 1994; Murnighan & Brass, 1991).

Compatibility, and the subsequent linkages between negotiators that it generates, implies that ties or relationships between negotiators are a form of power. This is beginning to be recognized in the negotiation literature (Greenhalgh, 1987; Greenhalgh & Kramer, 1990; Polzer, Neale, & Glenn, 1993; Shah & Jehn, 1993; Valley & Neale, 1991; Valley, Neale, & Mannix, in press). Interestingly, most coalition theories do not consider compatibility based on ties through qualitative preferences. Exceptions may be found in coalition theories derived from the field of political science. These theories assume that parties who are ideologically close are most likely to be coalition partners (Axelrod, 1970; Leiserson, 1966; Miller, 1979; Miller & Crandall, 1980). Similarly, we argue that closeness based on relationships allows players to gain bargaining strength through the potential for coalition formation.

Coalitions that are based on compatible preferences may enhance the coalition members' outcomes by either excluding incompatible parties from the negotiated agreement or controlling the outcomes of the incompatible parties through an "internal coalition" (Mannix et al., 1994; Psathas & Stryker, 1965; Stryker & Psathas, 1960). An internal coalition is an alliance between a subset of group members that serves to control the final outcomes of the entire group, without excluding other group members from the final agreement. Even when compatibility between negotiators would suggest coalition formation, it is not always rational to exclude members from the final agreement, depending on the structure of the payoffs. In some cases, the inclusion of all group members in the final agreement is necessary to maximize collective gain. In coalition theory this is known as *group rationality,* which becomes more likely as the potential profit available in the grand coalition increases (Aumann & Maschler, 1964; Kahan & Rapoport, 1984). Thus group members with compatible preferences may include the other group members in the final agreement in order to enhance the size of the resource pool, while retaining the largest share of the pie for themselves (Psathas & Stryker, 1965; Stryker & Psathas, 1960).

An Empirical Test

Recently, Mannix et al. (1994) explored the effects of power from the three sources discussed above in an empirical study that integrated research on coalition formation and negotiations. Negotiators role-played three divisional vice presidents in a research and development firm. Their task was to allocate among themselves funding from two resource pools. In doing so, they had to decide both who should be included in the final agreement and the amount of resources each included party should receive. Any two parties could agree to exclude the third party, or all three parties could be included in the final agreement.

The value of the first resource pool varied based on which players were included in the final agreement, in effect manipulating their strategic power (high, medium, and low). For example, if the high- and low-power parties agreed to exclude the medium-power player, the first resource pool was worth more money than if the medium- and low-power players excluded the high-power player. In the words of coalition researchers, the players had different *quota values.* The varying quota values were justified as being based on the sizes of the vice presidents' divisions. The players' normative power, manipulated based on their future potential contributions to the organization, was also linked to this first resource pool. Information on future potential contributions provided the parties with arguments about who could best use the resources.

The second resource pool was composed of a traditional negotiation payoff schedule with two issues and integrative potential (Bazerman, Magliozzi, & Neale, 1985). The two issues involved levels of staff support and computer support. The parties included in the final agreement had to agree on one option (out of five) for each issue. Each party had his or her own preferences and degree of importance for each issue, reflected in the party's payoff schedule. Two of the three players had compatible preferences on both negotiation issues; the third player had incompatible preferences. Compatibility on the issues in this resource pool served as the mechanism for manipulating relationship-based power.

The results of the study indicate that relationships derived from compatibility of interests were an overriding source of power, affecting players' outcomes from both resource pools. Players who had compatible interests were able to achieve higher individual outcomes from both portions of the task. This was true even when compatible players did not form exclusive two-way coalitions. These findings indicate that compatible players formed internal coalitions, acting as allies against the incompatible third party—not necessarily to lock the third party out of the final agreement, but to force him or her to accept a reduced share of both resource pools.

The other types of power (strategic and normative) also affected the allocation of resources. However, they did not have such far-reaching effects as relationship-based power, and were able to improve or decrease a player's outcomes only on the first resource pool to which they were directly linked. In addition, normative power served as an "adjustment" on the outcomes influenced by strategic-power. Thus individuals with high-strategic-power were more likely to be allocated greater portions of the resource pool when they also had high-normative-power. However, when high-strategic-power was combined with low normative power, the ability to obtain resources was reduced.

It is likely that the effects of normative power were strengthened by the multiparty structure of this exercise. Consider the condition where normative power was inconsistent with strategic power—that is, where a high-strategic-power player had low normative power and a low-strategic-power player had high-normative-power. In this condition the low-strategic-power party was likely to invoke his or her entitlement based on normative considerations, and the high-strategic-power party was likely to reject such a justification, instead pressing his or her claim to resources based on strategic considerations. Yet low-strategic-power parties were, in fact, able to increase their outcomes in this situation. It seems likely that normative-based arguments were effective, at least partially, because of their influence on the medium-strategic-power party. In effect, the medium-strategic-power player could act as the swing vote, and thus would actually have more overall power than it might at first appear (Mannix, 1993). This represents yet another way in which the processes and outcomes of multiparty negotiation differ from dyadic contexts.

The empirical study reported above used a structural manipulation of preferences as a proxy for different types of relationships. This is a good starting point, but the conceptual richness of relationships goes well beyond compatible preferences. The next section extends our analysis of the effects of relationships on multiparty negotiations.

Relationships in Multiparty Negotiations

In a recent review article, Valley et al. (in press) suggest that relationships influence negotiations in two critical ways. First, relationships can significantly alter the process of negotiation. That is, when a relationship exists between the parties to a negotiation, there will be a richer set of options and issues from which to choose—the number of potential moves in the bargaining game will be greater. Second, relationships influence the preferences parties have and the associated utilities for outcomes. Kelley (1979), for example, posits that personal relationships influence not only the concrete or direct value of an outcome but also the symbolic value of the relationship independent of the outcome. Relationships give the associated parties a wider range of alternatives, values, and mechanisms by which to evaluate an interaction.

In multiparty negotiations, these same facets of relationships can significantly influence the formation and stability of coalitions. The power that can be derived from relationships—especially as it relates to coalitions—is likely to flow from the opportunity of repeated interactions, the utility that the other's outcomes have for self, the real and perceived compatibility of interests, and trust (Greenhalgh, 1987; Greenhalgh & Kramer, 1990; Heider, 1958; Polzer et al., 1993; Sondak & Moore, 1993; Valley & Neale, 1991).

To the extent that parties share a relationship, they are more likely to experience temporally interdependent outcomes than are those who have no relationship. Because expected future interaction is one of the defining features of relationships (and the most common way in which relationships are operationalized in laboratory settings), parties may explicitly incorporate a temporal dimension into their interaction. Because there is the expectation of repeated plays in the "game," the parties can attempt not only to get their interests met in one particular interaction but also to include future negotiations and allocations in the equation. The "shadow of the future" may lead parties to be less concerned about getting everything they want from the current negotiation. As a result, one side may be willing to support a member of the coalition's agenda today in exchange for support on another issue tomorrow.

The viability of trading off support over time exists only to the extent that the parties expect opportunities for redress. In stranger interactions, maintaining continuous equivalence on the balance sheet is important, as the interactions may not be repeated. O'Connell (1984) finds considerably more tolerance for imbalance in exchanges among friends and kin than among strangers. Using Ekeh's (1974) concept of restricted exchange and Lévi-Strauss's (1969) concept of generalized exchange, O'Connell argues that the imbalance is explained as the parties' willingness to both discount the instrumental value of the exchange and enhance the benefits of socialization and interaction. Parties may also invoke a need norm to explain the imbalance—a norm that emphasizes the inability, rather than the unwillingness, to respond. Thus relationships enhance the stability of coalitions by increasing each member's flexibility regarding acceptable outcomes.

As O'Connell (1984) suggests, relationships are much more than simply the opportunity to interact in the future. In addition, there is real concern for the other's outcomes (Clark, Mills, & Corcoran, 1989). For example, past research has found that (other's) need is more likely to be taken into account when allocations are made to friends than to strangers (Lamm & Schwinger, 1980).

In addition to caring more about the other's outcomes, the existence of a relationship increases the probability that parties will have similar preferences (Heider, 1958).[2] This similarity in objective preferences is likely to affect choices regarding coalition membership and subsequent resource allocation. Furthermore, we propose that compatibility on many issues may lead friends to assume that they share compatibility on other issues, even though they may not have information about the other's preferences. People in relationships, however, often have opposing preferences. What happens when relationships and preferences are inconsistent? Parties often form alliances based on their relationship even when they have differing preferences. Tenbrunsel, Wade-Benzoni, Moag, and Bazerman (1994) provide evidence that friendship ties may dominate objective preferences in a market negotiation, especially for those with high market power. They found that high-power parties were more profitable in markets that did not permit alliances between friends and were less profitable in markets that did. In contrast, low-power parties were more profitable in markets that allowed alliances between friends and were less profitable in markets that did not. This may have resulted because parties made assumptions about their friends' interests or because friends placed more importance on their relationship than on the issue, in this case profitability.

The final way in which relationships influence a party's power in a coalition is through trust. Based on belief about the good intentions of the other's choices, trust is a central component in the psychological assessment of relationships (Davis & Todd, 1985). Trust arises through a sense of certainty about the predictability and intentions of another's actions (Valley et al., in press). Thus the attractiveness of friends as potential coalition partners is greater because of the presence of trust.

Trust, frequency of interaction, compatibility of preferences, and concern for others are central components of relationships. Many of these same components that make relationships relevant in explaining behavior in multiparty negotiations also characterize group membership. In the next section, we discuss how belonging to and identifying with a group can have many of the same effects on behavior as relationships. Our analysis of group membership goes a step further than the discussion of relationships in that we address not only how group memberships can bind people together, but how they can push people apart.

Group Identification

In multiparty negotiations, group membership may affect who forms coalitions, how stable they are, and the nature of interactions within and between coalitions. Each party belongs to several relevant groups, including the total set of negotiating parties along with numerous subgroups composed of various combinations of the parties. Because of these multiple group memberships, the group with which each party *identifies* will go further toward explaining that party's behavior than simply knowing to which groups the party belongs. Group identification is "that part of an individual's self-concept which derives from his knowledge of his membership in a social group (or groups) together with the value and emotional significance attached to that membership" (Tajfel, 1978). A general hypothesis in the group identification literature is that when people identify strongly with a group to which they belong, they are more likely to act in the group's interest (i.e., to cooperate with the other members of the group) (Brewer & Kramer, 1986; Kramer, 1993; Kramer & Brewer, 1984).

Several underlying mechanisms may link group identification to cooperation with the group (Kramer, 1991, 1993). First, people exhibit a positive bias toward members of their own group regarding trustworthiness, honesty, and cooperativeness, resulting in a depersonalized or group-based trust (Brewer, 1979, 1981; Brewer & Silver, 1978). This is tied closely to the idea that identification with a group leads to expectations of reciprocity (Brewer, 1981). When a person identifies with a group, cooperating with that group is perceived as less risky, because the fear that others will be exploitative by not reciprocating cooperation is low. Second, people may be more attracted to members of their own group than to members of other groups, making cooperation more likely within groups (Hogg & Abrams, 1988). Third, when group identity is strong, people may replace self-interest with group interest and place more emphasis on the outcomes of the other group members (Turner, 1987). Finally, people may be concerned about appearing fair and cooperative to other members of their group because of a desire to make favorable impressions (Greenberg, 1990; Kramer, Newton, & Pommerenke, 1993; Tedeschi, 1981).

Along with cooperation within the group, group identification may also be linked to increased competition between groups (Sherif, 1951; Tajfel & Turner,

1986; Turner, 1975). People may engage in intergroup comparisons to enhance their own self-esteem by virtue of belonging to a superior group (Turner, 1975). This motivation leads to competition with other groups, with a focus on relative rather than absolute gain. Intergroup anxiety, whereby group members experience tension or discomfort when interacting with members of other groups, may cause both negative expectations and avoidance of outgroup members. Furthermore, just as expectations of reciprocity for cooperative behavior are high within groups, these expectations tend to be low between groups (Brewer, 1981; Brewer & Campbell, 1976; Insko et al., 1987; Insko, Schopler, Hoyle, Dardis, & Graetz, 1990). Identification with a group, then, may lead to enhanced competition between groups as well as enhanced cooperation within groups (for a thorough discussion of these phenomena, see Kramer, 1991, 1993).

Patterns of behavior among the parties in a multiparty negotiation may vary drastically, depending on the group with which each party identifies. Several sources of identification exist in this context, including (a) a party's constituency, which does not include any other parties in the negotiation; (b) a coalition, including a subset of the other negotiation parties; and (c) the negotiating group as a whole, including the entire set of parties in the negotiation. In the first and third scenarios, the focal negotiator is not involved in a coalition.[3]

Consistent with the earlier discussion, identification with a particular source may occur because of the pattern of preferences in the negotiation. For example, if no other group members share a negotiator's preferences, the incompatible negotiator may identify only with his or her constituency. Alternatively, if the negotiator shares preferences on several issues with a subset of the other group members, that negotiator may identify with a coalition consisting of the compatible parties. When these structural factors are the basis of coalition formation, the process of group identification may have an effect beyond the objective preferences of the parties. For instance, once coalitions based on structural factors are in place, identification with these coalitions may exacerbate competition between coalitions while enhancing cooperation within them. Coalitions may take on a life that goes beyond the initial reason for their existence. When the gears of the group identification machinery start to whirl, all further interactions and information may be filtered through this intergroup screen, and may be biased as a result.

Group memberships may influence which parties coalesce independent of the preference structures in a particular negotiation. Each party brings to the table membership in multiple groups that are not directly connected to the issues being negotiated. For example, people in a multiparty negotiation may vary in terms of their demographic categories (e.g., gender, race, age), societal categories (e.g., Democrat versus Republican), and organizational categories (e.g., marketing versus production, Project Team A versus Project Team B). If a party shares membership in these external groups with a subset of the parties in the negotiation, coalitions may be more likely to form between these parties than between parties who do not share external group memberships. By the same logic, if all the parties share membership in the same external groups, then it may be more likely that no coalitions will form, with the parties instead identifying with the entire set of negotiation parties.

From this, it is not clear that we could predict which of the many potential group identities will form the basis of coalition membership. Despite this uncertainty, it may be that group identification, rather than structural factors such as issues and alternatives, is a primary reason parties coalesce. To test this perspective, Eisenhardt and Bourgeois (1988) investigated the strategic decision processes of executives in an extremely turbulent environment, the micro-computer industry. Several of their findings are directly relevant to and consistent with our analysis of coalitions in multiparty negotiations. Concerning the role of identification with groups external to the particular negotiation, coalitions were based on "demographic factors such as age, office location, similarity of titles, and prior experience together" rather than on compatible preferences on specific issues (Eisenhardt & Bourgeois, 1988). Their empirical findings in a field setting give credence to the existence of a social basis for coalition formation.

A second major finding was that coalition patterns were stable, such that executives predictably sought coalitions with the same one or two people (Eisenhardt & Bourgeois, 1988). This was especially true in the most politically active firms. When the people in these stable coalitions disagreed on an issue, they were more likely to drop the issue or work alone rather than ally with other executives who had compatible preferences on that issue. This finding clearly contradicts the general argument of many coalition researchers that coalitions exist for short periods of time and are inherently unstable (Bacharach & Lawler, 1980; Gamson, 1961; March, 1962; Murnighan & Brass, 1991; Stevenson, Pearce, & Porter, 1985). Eisenhardt and Bourgeois (1988) speculate that their findings may indicate either a reliance on habitual responses to a threatening environment (Staw, Sandelands, & Dutton, 1981) or a lack of cognitive processing and information gathering about the preferences of others (Cyert & March, 1963).

Parties' identification with their constituencies, coalitions, or entire set of negotiation partners may determine whether intergroup or intragroup processes characterize the negotiation. If the parties identify only with their constituencies and not with any of the other parties in the negotiation, intergroup processes among all the parties are likely to dominate the negotiation process.

If parties identify with coalitions, intergroup processes may occur between the coalitions while intragroup processes occur within each coalition. If each party identifies with the entire set of parties, intragroup processes are more likely to occur among all parties in the negotiation. As discussed previously, research on group processes demonstrates that intergroup interactions are characterized by higher levels of competition and lower levels of cooperation and trust than intragroup interactions (Brewer, 1981). Thus negotiators are more likely to share information with others whom they view as in-group members than with those they view as out-group members (Kramer, 1991; Polzer, 1993).

Information exchange, especially regarding the parties' true preferences and objectives on the issues, is a critical factor that facilitates integrative bargaining (Lewicki & Litterer, 1985; Neale & Bazerman, 1991). Based on systematic patterns of information sharing within and between groups, we would expect that more Pareto-efficient agreements will occur in multiparty negotiations when the barriers erected by various coalitions do not exist (Mannix, 1991, 1993). Consistent with this proposition, Eisenhardt and Bourgeois (1988) found that the use of politics (i.e., coalitions) was negatively correlated to the performance of the firm in their study. One reason for this effect on firm performance, they argue, was that coalitions hampered the flow of information. People withheld important information from other parties to influence the group's decision, thereby increasing their own, rather than the group's, outcomes. In the absence of accurate and complete information, people made incorrect assumptions that those in competing coalitions held preferences that were incompatible with their own.

This finding shows an interesting similarity to the "incompatibility bias" described by Leigh Thompson (1991). She has demonstrated that negotiators assume that other parties' preferences are diametrically opposed to their own. Extending Thompson's work to a multiparty context, there may exist an incompatibility bias between coalitions, rather than between individual parties. Furthermore, we propose that a "compatibility bias" might exist within stable coalitions. Coalition members may focus on their similarities to the point that they generalize compatibility on some issues to most or all issues. This is the same phenomenon we earlier suggested may occur within relationships. As Kramer (1991) notes, this idea at the group level is consistent with the research on categorization conducted by Tajfel and his colleagues (Tajfel, 1969; Tajfel, Flament, Billig, & Bundy, 1971). An extension of Tajfel's research suggests that coalition members may overestimate the incompatibility between their coalition's interests and those of the other coalition, and overestimate the compatibility between their own individual preferences and those of their coalition members.

Integration and Discussion

The purpose of this chapter is to suggest that the study of multiparty negotiations—and coalitions as a unique aspect of multiparty negotiations—will be enhanced through the explicit consideration of the social context. Specifically, we argue that the social context significantly influences the relative power (and subsequent behavior) of parties. The primary social bases of power are the relationships between parties and the various group memberships that parties share. Along with patterns of coalition formation, the stability of a coalition seems particularly sensitive to the social context.

Coalitions are typically described as issue based and unstable (Bacharach & Lawler, 1980; Gamson, 1961; Murnighan & Brass, 1991; Stevenson et al., 1985). Coalitions that form around parties' preferences on particular issues are characterized as having a founder, forming behind the scenes, forming one member at a time, and never meeting as a group (Murnighan, 1978a). Such coalitions may be described as a series of dyadic connections, and one might not expect such coalitions to remain intact after their specific purposes have been served (e.g., once the vote has been taken or the allocation made). However, coalitions that function across multiple situations and different issues (i.e., stable coalitions) are common in organizational settings (J. Thompson, 1967). People frequently subjugate their preferences on particular issues if those preferences are inconsistent with preferences of friends or members of their group, especially when the other option is to form a new coalition with people to whom they are not socially connected. From an issue-based perspective, these parties would be expected to form separate coalitions that include only people who share the same preferences on the focal issue. How can these discrepant perspectives be reconciled?

Murnighan and Brass (1991) differentiate coalitions from other types of subgroups (e.g., interest groups or dominant coalitions) based on their instability. In effect, they define coalitions as those subgroups that are unstable. If a coalition is instead defined as a subgroup whose purpose is to influence the decision of a larger group, then stability becomes a variable rather than an assumption. An interesting question then is, What factors explain variance in coalition stability? From an issue-based perspective, some issues may be temporary (e.g., where to build a new building), and others may be more permanent (e.g., how to budget resources). Coalitions that try to influence recurring decisions may be more stable than those assembled to influence a one-time issue. Another possibility is that coalitions that form around issues are unstable, whereas those that form around social connections tend toward stability.

Coalitions that form because of relationships or group memberships are likely to be stable because their existence is based on the structure of the relationship and not limited to the specifics of any particular issue (Valley & Neale, 1991). The stability arises not from a requirement of consensus on every issue, but because the parties recognize the benefits of using temporal trade-offs to integrate long-term interests. Relationships provide an inherent stability or inertia that is rare or even unavailable to potential coalition partners who are strangers. If coalitions are based on issues, then it makes sense that when the issues have been resolved, the coalition would disband. If coalitions are based on relationships and group memberships that remain meaningful after any particular decision is made, then coalitions should remain intact because the relational factors around which they form are still in place.

Another interesting issue concerns ascertaining when coalitions form. Murnighan and Brass (1991), among others, propose that coalitions typically form behind the scenes before a group interaction takes place, and then come to the surface only during the group interaction. From a negotiation perspective, we would also expect coalitions to form during the multiparty interaction as information is shared about preferences and interests. One assumption of most negotiation research is that parties do not have complete information about the preferences of the other parties prior to the actual interaction. Thus one fundamental prescription to negotiators is to gather information from the other parties about their preferences (Neale & Bazerman, 1991). It seems that coalitions that form around preferences would form during the negotiation, when information on preferences is exchanged. When information about preferences is exchanged before the negotiation, we would expect such behavior to occur among parties who share relationships and group memberships (i.e., those who are connected socially). Thus the coalitions that do gather strength before a negotiation are likely to be those that are already in place (i.e., the stable coalitions), so that the members primarily need to confirm their support for each other. Of course, many negotiations occur over extended periods, such that the parties meet, then break, then reconvene. This intermittent information sharing allows coalitions to originate and stabilize both at and away from the table.

The results of the study discussed above that specifically examined the impact of the three types of power—strategic, normative, and relational—suggest some interesting implications for the effects of relationship-based power (Mannix et al., 1994). If relationship-based power has effects across multiple resource pools, its use could lead to inefficient and possibly irrational outcomes in some contexts. As alliances form, in-group members may be able to obtain resources at the expense of out-group members, even when the out-group members are not totally excluded from the final agreement. Furthermore, stable alliances may be able to obtain preferred outcomes on several issues, even though individual members of the alliance have relatively low strategic power. As a result, resources could be allocated to group members who are less able to use them effectively. This type of resource allocation could have detrimental effects, not only for members of the "out-group," but for the group or organization as a whole (Mannix, 1993). Additional evidence of the disadvantages of relationships in marketplace transactions is provided by Tenbrunsel et al. (1994), in that relationships may provide a safety net for low-power players, but the net is built at the direct cost of the high-power players in the market. If this move toward egalitarianism is not highly valued, then such constraints may make the market or the organization worse off.

Our concluding proposition is that in multiparty negotiations, especially in organizations, coalitions tend to be stable because they are based on relationships and group memberships rather than solely on the issues in a specific negotiation. The continuity of relational variables suggests more stability in coalitions than when only structural variables, which change with every negotiation, are considered. Relationships and common group memberships bind people together in a variety of social settings, including multiparty negotiations.

Notes

1. For issues with dichotomous outcomes (e.g., deciding to hire versus not to hire a particular candidate), at least two parties in a multiparty negotiation must logically have compatible interests (assuming that all parties have preferences regarding the issue). For issues with continuous outcomes, if each party prefers one of the two extreme positions on an issue (e.g., provide as much funding as possible versus provide no funding for a particular project), then at least two of the multiple parties will have compatible interests. Of course, there are many issues for which it is possible that multiple parties will all have incompatible preferences (e.g., each party may want to provide a different amount of funding for a project). The point here is simply that, holding the distribution of preferences constant across possible negotiation opponents, it is more likely that parties will share compatible preference in multiparty than in dyadic negotiations.

2. We acknowledge the dual causality that may underlie this correlation. People may become friends because they share compatible preferences, or compatible preferences may develop because of a relationship. This reason for the correlation between relationships and preferences is not as important to our analysis as is the existence of the correlation.

3. An interesting note is that in the first scenario, some parties might coalesce and others may not. This could affect how the parties external to the coalition behave. These external parties may feel some bond because of their common fate (i.e., they share the characteristic that they do not belong to a coalition) (Campbell, 1958), and thus may tend toward cooperation with each other as a direct response to the coalition. In this way, a party may move from the first scenario to the second scenario as a reactive or evolved strategy rather than as a proactive strategy.

References

Ancona, D. (1990). Outward bound: Strategies for team survival in an organization. *Academy of Management Journal, 33,* 334-365.

Ancona, D., Friedman, R., & Kolb, D. (1991). The group and what happens on the way to "yes." *Negotiation Journal, 7,* 155-174.

Aumann, R. J., & Maschler, M. (1964). The bargaining set for cooperative games. In M. Dresher, L. S. Shapley, & A. W. Tucker (Eds.), *Advances in game theory.* Princeton, NJ: Princeton University Press.

Axelrod, R. (1970). *Conflict of interest.* Chicago: Markham.

Bacharach, S. B., & Lawler, E. J. (1980). *Power and politics in organizations.* San Francisco: Jossey-Bass.

Bazerman, M. H., Magliozzi, T., & Neale, M. A. (1985). Integrative bargaining in a competitive market. *Organizational Behavior and Human Performance, 34,* 294-313.

Bazerman, M. H., Mannix, E., & Thompson, L. (1988). Groups as mixed-motive negotiations. In E. J. Lawler & B. Markovsky (Eds.), *Advances in group processes: Theory and research* (Vol. 5). Greenwich CT: JAI.

Brett, J., & Rognes, J. (1986). Intergroup relations in organizations: A negotiation perspective. In P. S. Goodman (Ed.), *Designing effective work groups.* San Francisco: Jossey-Bass.

Brewer, M. B. (1979). In-group bias in the minimal intergroup situation: A cognitive-motivational analysis. *Psychological Bulletin, 86,* 307-324.

Brewer, M. B. (1981). Ethnocentrism and its role in interpersonal trust. In M. B. Brewer & B. E. Collins (Eds.), *Scientific inquiry and the social sciences.* San Francisco: Jossey-Bass.

Brewer, M. B., & Campbell, D. T. (1976). *Ethnocentrism and intergroup attitudes: East African evidence.* New York: Halsted.

Brewer, M. B., & Kramer, R. M. (1985). The psychology of intergroup attitudes and behaviors. In M. R. Rosenzweig & L. W. Porter (Eds.), *Annual review of psychology* (Vol. 36, pp. 219-243). Palo Alto, CA: Annual Reviews.

Brewer, M. B., & Silver, M. (1978). Ingroup bias as a function of task characteristics. *European Journal of Social Psychology, 8,* 393-400.

Campbell, D. T. (1958). Common fate, similarity, and other indices of the status of aggregates of persons as social entities. *Behavioral Science, 3,* 14-25.

Caplow, T. A. (1956). A theory of coalitions in the triad. *American Sociological Review, 21,* 489-493.

Chertkoff, J. M. (1967). A revision of Caplow's coalition theory. *Journal of Experimental Social Psychology, 3,* 172-177.

Chertkoff, J. M. (1971). Coalition formation as a function of differences in resources. *Journal of Conflict Resolution, 15,* 371-383.

Chertkoff, J. M., & Esser, J. K. (1977). A test of three theories of coalition formation when agreements can be short-term or long-term. *Journal of Personality and Social Psychology, 35,* 237-249.

Clark, M. S., Mills, J. R., & Corcoran, D. M. (1989). Keeping track of needs and inputs of friends and strangers. *Personality and Social Psychology Bulletin, 15,* 533-542.

Cyert, R., & March, J. (1963). *A behavioral theory of the firm.* Englewood Cliffs, NJ: Prentice Hall.

Davis, K. E., & Todd, M. J. (1985). Assessing friendship: Prototypes, paradigm cases and relationship description. In S. Duck & D. Perlman (Eds.), *Understanding personal relationships: An interdisciplinary approach.* London: Sage.

Eisenhardt, K., & Bourgeois, L. (1988). Politics of strategic decision making in high-velocity environments: Toward a midrange theory. *Academy of Management Journal, 31,* 737-770.

Ekeh, P. (1974). *Social exchange theory: The two traditions.* Cambridge, MA: Harvard University Press.

Emerson, R. M. (1964). Power-dependence relations: Two experiments. *Sociometry, 27,* 282-298.

Fisher, R., & Ury, W. (1981). *Getting to yes: Negotiating agreement without giving in.* Boston: Houghton Mifflin.

French, J. R. P. (1956). A formal theory of social power. *Psychological Review, 63,* 181-194.

Gamson, W. A. (1961). A theory of coalition formation. *American Sociological Review, 26,* 373-382.

Gersick, C. (1988). Time and transition in work teams: Toward a new model of group development. *Academy of Management Journal, 31,* 9-41.

Greenberg, J. (1990). Looking fair versus being fair: Managing impressions of organizational justice. In B. M. Staw & L. L. Cummings (Eds.), *Research in organizational behavior* (Vol. 12, pp. 111-158). Greenwich, CT: JAI.

Greenberg, J., & Cohen, R. L. (1982). *Equity and justice in social behavior.* New York: Academic Press.

Greenhalgh, L. (1987). Relationships in negotiations. *Negotiation Journal, 3,* 235-243.

Greenhalgh, L., & Kramer, R. (1990). Strategic choice in conflicts: The importance of relationships. In R. L. Kahn & M. N. Zald (Eds.), *Organizations and nation-states: New perspectives on conflict and negotiation.* San Francisco: Jossey-Bass.

Hackman, J. R. (Ed.). (1990). *Groups that work (and those that don't).* San Francisco: Jossey-Bass.

Heider, R. (1958). *The psychology of interpersonal relations.* New York: John Wiley.

Hogg, M., & Abrams, D. (1988). *Social identifications: A social psychology of intergroup relations and group processes.* London: Routledge.

Insko, C., Pinkley, R., Harring, K., Holton, B., Hong, G., Krams, D., Hoyle, R., & Thibaut, J. (1987). Beyond categorization to competition: Expectations of appropriate behavior. *Representative Research in Social Psychology, 17,* 5-36.

Insko, C., Schopler, J., Hoyle, R., Dardis, G., & Graetz, K. (1990). Individual-group discontinuity as a function of fear and greed. *Journal of Personality and Social Psychology, 58,* 68-79.

Kahan, J. P., & Rapoport, A. (1984). *Theories of coalition formation.* Hillsdale, NJ: Lawrence Erlbaum.

Kelley, H. H. (1979). *Personal relationships.* Hillsdale, NJ: Lawrence Erlbaum.

Kelley, H. H., & Arrowood, A. J. (1960). Coalitions in the triad: Critique and experiment. *Sociometry, 23,* 231-244.

Komorita, S. S., & Hamilton, T. P. (1984). Power and equity in coalition bargaining. In *Research in the sociology of organizations* (Vol. 3). Greenwich, CT: JAI.

Komorita, S. S., Hamilton, T. P., & Kravitz, D. (1984). The effects of alternatives in bargaining. *Journal of Experimental Social Psychology, 20,* 116-136.

Komorita, S. S., & Kravitz, D. (1979). The effects of alternatives in bargaining. *Journal of Experimental Social Psychology, 15,* 147-157.

Komorita, S. S., & Moore, D. (1976). Theories and processes of coalition formation. *Journal of Personality and Social Psychology, 33,* 371-381.

Komorita, S. S., & Nagao, D. (1983). The functions of resources in coalition bargaining. *Journal of Personality and Social Psychology, 44,* 95-106.

Komorita, S. S., & Tumonis, T. M. (1980). Extensions and tests of some descriptive theories of coalition formation. *Journal of Personality and Social Psychology, 39,* 256-268.

Kramer, R. M. (1991). Intergroup relations and organizational dilemmas: The role of categorization processes. In L. L. Cummings & B. M. Staw (Eds.), *Research in organizational behavior* (Vol. 13, pp. 191-227). Greenwich, CT: JAI.

Kramer, R. M. (1993). Cooperation and organizational identification. In J. K. Murnighan (Ed.), *Social psychology in organizations: Advances in theory and practice* (pp. 244-268). Englewood Cliffs, NJ: Prentice Hall.

Kramer, R. M., & Brewer, M. B. (1984). Effects of group identity on resource use in a simulated commons dilemma. *Journal of Personality and Social Psychology, 46,* 1044-1057.

Kramer, R. M., Newton, E., & Pommerenke, P. L. (1993). Self-enhancement biases and negotiator judgment: Effects of self-esteem and mood. *Organizational Behavior and Human Decision Processes, 56,* 110-133.

Kravitz, D. (1981). Effects of resources and alternatives on coalition formation. *Journal of Personality and Social Psychology, 41,* 87-98.

Kravitz, D., & Iwaniszek, J. (1984). Number of coalitions and resources as sources of power in coalition bargaining. *Journal of Personality and Social Psychology, 47,* 534-548.

Lamm, H., & Schwinger, T. (1980). Norms concerning distributive justice: Are needs taken into consideration in allocation decisions? *Social Psychology Quarterly, 43,* 425-429.

Leiserson, M. (1966). *Coalitions in politics.* Unpublished doctoral dissertation, Yale University.

Leventhal, G. S. (1976). The distribution of rewards and resources in groups and organizations. In L. Berkowitz & E. Walster (Eds.), *Advances in experimental social psychology.* New York: Academic Press.

Levine, J., & Moreland, R. (1990). Progress in small group research. *Annual Review of Psychology, 41,* 585-634.

Lévi-Strauss, C. (1969). *The elementary structure of kinship.* Boston: Beacon.

Lewicki, R. J., & Litterer, J. A. (1985). *Negotiation.* Homewood, IL: Irwin.

Lewin, K. (1951). *Field theory in social science.* New York: Harper & Row.

Luce, R. D., & Raiffa, H. (1957). *Games and decision: Introduction and critical survey.* New York: John Wiley.

Mannix, E. A. (1991). Resource dilemmas and discount rates in organizational decision making groups. *Journal of Experimental Social Psychology, 27,* 379-391.

Mannix, E. A. (1993). Organizations as resource dilemmas: The effects of power balance on group decision making. *Organizational Behavior and Human Decision Processes, 55,* 1-22.

Mannix, E. A., Polzer, J. T., & Neale, M. A. (1994). *Multi-party negotiation: The effects of power, entitlement, and preference structure* (Working paper). Chicago: University of Chicago, Graduate School of Business.

Mannix, E. A., & White, S. (1992). The effect of distributive uncertainty on coalition formation in organizations. *Organizational Behavior and Human Decision Processes, 51,* 198-219.

March, J. G. (1962). The business firm as a political coalition. *Journal of Politics, 24,* 662-678.

McGrath, J., & Kravitz, D. (1982). Group research. *Annual Review of Psychology, 33,* 195-230.

Miller, C. (1979). Coalition formation in triads with single-peaked payoff curves. *Behavioral Science, 24,* 75-84.

Miller, C., & Crandall, R. (1980). Experimental research on the social psychology of bargaining and coalition formation. In P. Paulus (Ed.), *Psychology of group influence.* Hillsdale, NJ: Lawrence Erlbaum.

Murnighan, J. K. (1978a). Models of coalition behavior: Game theoretic, social psychological, and political perspectives. *Psychological Bulletin, 85,* 1130-1153.

Murnighan, J. K. (1978b). Strength and weakness in four coalition situations. *Behavioral Science, 23,* 195-208.

Murnighan, J. K., & Brass, D. (1991). Intraorganizational coalitions. In M. H. Bazerman, R. J. Lewicki, & B. H. Sheppard (Eds.), *Research on negotiation in organizations: Vol. 3. Handbook of negotiation research.* Greenwich, CT: JAI.

Murnighan, J. K., Komorita, S. S., & Szwajkowski, E. (1977). Theories of coalition formation and the effects of reference groups. *Journal of Experimental Social Psychology, 13,* 166-181.

Neale, M. A., & Bazerman, M. H. (1991). *Cognition and rationality in negotiation.* New York: Free Press.

O'Connell, L. (1984). An exploration of exchange in three social relationships: Kinship, friendship, and the marketplace. *Journal of Social and Personal Relationships, 1,* 333-345.

Pinkley, R. L., Neale, M. A., & Bennett, R. J. (in press). Alternatives, reservation prices and outcomes: The impact of alternatives to settlement in dyadic negotiation. *Organizational Behavior and Human Decision Processes.*

Polzer, J. T. (1993). *Intergroup negotiations: The effects of negotiating teams* (Working paper). Evanston, IL: Northwestern University.

Polzer, J. T., Neale, M. A., & Glenn, P. (1993). The effects of relationships and justification in an interdependent allocation task. *Group Decision and Negotiation, 2,* 135-148.

Pruitt, D. G. (1981). *Negotiation behavior.* New York: Academic Press.

Psathas, G., & Stryker, S. (1965). Bargaining behavior and orientations in coalition formation. *Sociometry, 28,* 124-144.

Raiffa, H. (1982). *The art and science of negotiation.* Cambridge, MA: Belknap.

Raven, B. H., & Kruglanski, A. W. (1970). Conflict and power. In P. Swingle (Ed.), *The structure of conflict.* New York: Academic Press.

Shah, P., & Jehn, K. (1993). Do friends perform better than acquaintances? The interaction of friendship, conflict and task. *Group Decision and Negotiation, 2,* 149-166.

Sherif, M. (1951). Experimental study of intergroup relations. In J. Rohrer & M. Sherif (Eds.), *Social psychology at the crossroads* (pp. 388-426). New York: Harper.

Sondak, H. (1992). *Negotiating in a matching market* (Working paper). Durham, NC: Duke University, Fuqua School of Business.

Sondak, H., & Bazerman, M. H. (1989). Matching and negotiation processes in quasi-markets. *Organizational Behavior and Human Decision Processes, 44,* 261-280.

Sondak, H., & Moore, M. (1993). Relationship frames and cooperation. *Group Decision and Negotiation, 2,* 103-118.

Staw, B. M., Sandelands, L. E., & Dutton, J. E. (1981). Threat-rigidity effects in organizational behavior: A multilevel analysis. *Administrative Science Quarterly, 26,* 501-524.

Stevenson, W., Pearce, J., & Porter, L. (1985). The concept of "coalition" in organization theory and research. *Academy of Management Review, 10,* 256-268.

Stryker, S., & Psathas, G. (1960). Research on coalitions in the triad: Findings, problems and strategy. *Sociometry, 23,* 217-230.

Tajfel, H. (1969). Cognitive aspects of prejudice. *Journal of Social Issues, 25,* 79-97.

Tajfel, H. (1978). *Differentiation between social groups: Studies in the social psychology of intergroup relations.* London: Academic Press.

Tajfel, H., Flament, C., Billig, M., & Bundy, R. (1971). Social categorization and intergroup behavior. *European Journal of Social Psychology, 1,* 147-175.

Tajfel, H., & Turner, J. (1986). The social identity theory of intergroup behavior. In S. Worchel & W. G. Austin (Eds.), *Psychology of intergroup relations* (pp. 7-24). Chicago: Nelson-Hall.

Tedeschi, J. T. (1981). *Impression management theory and social psychological research.* New York: Academic Press.

Tenbrunsel, A., Wade-Benzoni, K., Moag, J., & Bazerman, M. (1994). *When is a friend not a friend? The effects of strong ties on matching efficiency, individual effectiveness, and barriers to learning* (Working Paper No. 108). Evanston, IL: Northwestern University, Dispute Resolution Research Center.

Thibaut, J. W. (1968). The development of contractual norms in bargaining. *Journal of Conflict Resolution, 12,* 102-112.

Thibaut, J. W., & Kelley, H. H. (1959). *The social psychology of groups.* New York: John Wiley.

Thompson, J. (1967). *Organizations in action.* New York: McGraw-Hill.

Thompson, L. (1991). Information exchange in negotiation. *Journal of Experimental Social Psychology, 27,* 161-179.

Turner, J. (1975). Social comparison and social identity: Some prospects for intergroup behavior. *European Journal of Social Psychology, 5,* 5-34.

Turner, J. (1987). *Rediscovering the social group: A self-categorization theory.* New York: Basil Blackwell.

Valley, K., & Neale, M. (1991). *The role of relationships in negotiations at work* (Working paper). Evanston, IL: Northwestern University, Dispute Resolution Research Center.

Valley, K., Neale, M., & Mannix, E. A. (in press). Friends, lovers, colleagues, strangers: The effects of relationship on the process and outcome of negotiation. In R. J. Lewicki, B. H. Sheppard, & R. Bies (Eds.), *Research on negotiation in organizations* (Vol. 5). Hillsdale, NJ: Lawrence Erlbaum.

Vinacke, W., & Arkoff, A. (1957). An experimental study of coalitions in the triad. *American Sociological Review, 22,* 406-414.

Walton, R. E., & McKersie, R. B. (1965). *A behavioral theory of labor negotiations: An analysis of a social interaction system.* New York: McGraw-Hill.

White, S. B., & Neale, M. A. (in press). The role of negotiator aspiration and settlement expectancies on bargaining outcomes. *Organizational Behavior and Human Decision Processes.*

Zander, A. (1979). The psychology of group process. *Annual Review of Psychology, 30,* 417-451.

7

Structural Power and Emotional
Processes in Negotiation
A Social Exchange Approach

EDWARD J. LAWLER
JEONGKOO YOON

When two individual actors negotiate repeatedly over time, some sort of social relationship is likely to develop. Sometimes the relationship is remote, distant, and hostile; sometimes it is open, close, and friendly; most often it falls somewhere between these possibilities. The relationship that develops is likely to be contingent on the social context giving rise to negotiations in the first place, the strategic action people adopt in response to that context, and the results they produce jointly. In this chapter, we suggest how one part of the social context—the structurally based power of individual actors—affects the relationship developed in repeated explicit negotiations.

The social context we assume is a network in which each of two focal actors has at least one alternative negotiation partner. This might be termed a minimal "exchange network" consisting of a four-position line. Each actor can exchange

AUTHORS' NOTE: This research was supported in part by the Duane C. Spriestersbach Professorship while held by the first author at the University of Iowa, and in part by a grant from the National Science Foundation (SES-9222668). We thank Roderick M. Kramer and Jennifer Halpern for comments on an earlier draft. Direct correspondence to Edward J. Lawler, Department of Organizational Behavior, School of Industrial and Labor Relations, Cornell University, Ithaca, NY 14853.

with only one of the others at any point in time, which makes it a negatively connected exchange network, in Cook and Emerson's (1978; Cook, Emerson, Gilmore, & Yamagishi, 1983; Emerson, 1972) terms. Many interorganizational buyer-seller relations, international trading relations, and even close personal relations have the properties of such an exchange network. Social exchange theory treats the nature (i.e., expected value) of prospective agreements from an alternative actor as a structural dimension of each actor's potential power or dependence on another (Emerson, 1972, 1981; Thibaut & Kelley, 1959). Previous research on exchange networks has documented purely structural effects of such power on action in negotiated exchange (Cook et al., 1983; Markovsky, Willer, & Patton, 1988) by revealing that the effects of such power conditions are not contingent on an actor's awareness of the network-based power. The action produced by structural power, however, can alter the context for future negotiations, and this is our point of departure.

Structural power establishes the contextual conditions for negotiations between some pairs of actors in a network by providing incentives for them to negotiate repeatedly and to arrive at satisfactory agreements. The incentives are that the focal relation is likely to provide greater benefit (expected value) to each actor than is the relation with his or her respective alternative negotiation partner. We take such power and incentive conditions as a given and ask what happens to the resulting exchange relation. We argue that if people act on these power conditions and repeatedly negotiate satisfactory agreements with each other, they will develop an emotional/affective commitment to their relationship that, in turn, changes the context for future negotiations. Behaviorally, emotional/affective commitment should be manifest in a propensity (a) to give each other benefits without strings attached (e.g., gifts), (b) to stay in their relationship even if the expected payoff from an alternative actor becomes equal to or better than that of the focal relation, and (c) to invest in a joint venture that takes the form of a social dilemma. We propose a theory that treats mild, everyday emotions as mediators of such commitment behavior, making endogenous emotional processes in the dyad an integral part of the explanation for emergent commitment formation.

Theory and research on a focal dyad embedded in a larger network, though decidedly micro in emphasis, could have important broader implications for the role of "pivotal dyads" in organizations, that is, dyadic relations among persons at key junctures in the organizational structure. Negotiations between pairs of actors who represent different parts of the organization are often critical to "fill in the gaps" between or to bridge institutional and technical levels, organizational policies and everyday practices, or conflicting external pressures that have different impacts on subparts of the organization. These negotiations are especially important where institutionalized rules and procedures do not offer ready-made solutions to the varied problems that confront actors representing different subunits in the organization (e.g., union and management, marketing and finance), and where there are incentives for two particular persons to deal with these matters repeatedly over time. In the course of responding to such problems, one-on-one negotiations between key actors may even change institutional patterns—that is, taken-for-granted ways of doing things.

This chapter focuses in the abstract on when and how repeated negotiations between the same actors foster positive feelings or emotions and, in turn, an affective commitment to their relationship. However, we have in mind applications to pivotal dyads within organizations and also to the emergence of "friction" or "stickiness" in market relations. Implicit in the idea that negotiations in pivotal dyads shape institutional patterns is the notion that repeated negotiations between the same two actors are likely to become more than instrumental ways for the particular actors to get work done. We suggest a simple process by which dyadic negotiations give rise to incipient affective commitments that make the relationship an expressive object of attachment in its own right. When such transformations occur, future negotiations are not just efforts to solve yet another concrete issue or problem that the particular actors face; they come to symbolize or express the existence of a positive, productive relationship. Commitments that have an emotional/affective component tend to make the exchange relation an objective reality with intrinsic value to actors. In Berger and Luckmann's (1967) terms, the relation becomes a "third force."

The Role of Everyday Emotions in Negotiations

Social exchange theorists, like theorists of bargaining and negotiation, have relegated emotions to a subsidiary position. Behaviorism and cognitivism have been the dominant theoretical guides for explaining how aspects of the social context affect negotiation behavior and outcomes (e.g., Emerson, 1981; Neale & Bazerman, 1991). These emphases are understandable given the zeitgeist of the larger disciplines of psychology, sociology, and organizational behavior. Emotions are soft, vague, elusive phenomena to theorize and research. Also, the pathways to making emotional processes more central to analyses of bargaining and negotiation are likely to have several potholes and unexpected twists and turns, because there are several fundamental unanswered questions about emotion as a phenomenon, including the distinctiveness—physiologically and psychologically—of different emotions, their involuntariness, and the interrelationship of cognition and emotion (e.g., Forgas, 1992; Izard, 1977, 1992; Kemper, 1978; Lazarus, 1984; Zajonc, 1984).

However, this is an appropriate time to think more systematically about the role of emotions in negotiations. In the larger social psychological literature, there is a rapidly growing body of research on emotion with applications to phenomena such as social judgment, prosocial behavior, persuasion, identity, self-presentation, and affective group attachment, to mention just a few (see Forgas, 1992; Hochschild, 1983; Isen & Baron, 1991; Kemper, 1978; Lawler, 1992a; Smith-Lovin & Heise, 1988). One important feature of this literature is a rejection of the historic sharp distinction between cognition and emotion in favor of the view that the two are intertwined in a variety of important ways. A second important feature is a focus on mild, everyday emotions, feelings, or moods rather than on "hot" or extreme emotions such as fear and anger. Feeling good or happy, feeling sad or unhappy, feeling excited or energized, feeling tired or unmotivated—all exemplify mild emotions we experience regularly in social contexts (see Isen, 1987). Mild, everyday emotions can be a positive motivating force in or a subtle hindrance to successful negotiations.

Consider a few examples of the impact of emotion on phenomena of relevance to negotiation. In a review of affect in social judgment, Forgas (1992) makes the general point that positive emotion leads to more heuristic information processing. For example, Schwarz and associates have found that targets of a persuasive communication who are in a positive mood process the information received in less systematic ways than do targets who are in a neutral or mildly depressed mood (Schwarz & Bless, 1991; Schwarz, Bless, & Bohner, 1991; Schwarz & Clore, 1988). In a study of how mood affects subjective probability judgments, Wright and Bower (1992) found that positive moods produce higher subjective probabilities for positive consequences of a choice and lower for negative consequences; negative moods produce the opposite effects. Apparently, mood affects the positivity of what is retrieved from memory (mood-consistent retrieval). Finally, Isen and Daubman (1984) have shown that a mild positive mood increases the degree to which persons categorize as similar items (e.g., colors) that are only marginally similar or even dissimilar; and Kraiger, Billings, and Isen (1989) have demonstrated that positive emotion, generated independent of a task, fosters more satisfaction upon completion of the task, suggesting that reports of satisfaction are mood congruent. Overall, research shows that mild positive emotions generate more global and heuristic information processing, a tendency to group together objects or elements of the situation and to make mood-congruent inferences about future events. These sorts of processes should occur on negotiation contexts as well, and should bear on the relationships that evolve in repeated negotiations.

A few studies have examined the effects of emotion in negotiations. For example, Carnevale and Isen (1986) tested the hypothesis that positive emotion or mood would increase the degree to which actors in bargaining would find and arrive at better integrative solutions. The rationale for this hypothesis was that mild positive emotion leads people to view a situation more broadly and to attempt to pull together or interrelate more elements of it; that is, positive mood leads to more heuristic information processing. The researchers found that when subjects in a positive mood bargained face-to-face, they reached higher joint outcomes (more integrative solutions) and used fewer contentious tactics; both findings support their hypothesis. Kramer, Newton, and Pommerenke (1993) replicated these results and also found that people experiencing positive emotion are more optimistic about future negotiations. More generally, Isen's (1987) review of work on mild feelings or moods suggests that positive emotion promotes cooperation and helping of others. One can extrapolate from such effects and argue that mild positive emotions, regardless of their source, lead people in negotiations to see more similarity among themselves and to develop a "dual concern" about their own and others' payoffs or outcomes. An emergent dual concern may be integral to commitment formation.

Clearly, there is a need for more research on how mild, everyday emotions and feelings come about in negotiations and what impact these have on negotiation tactics and on future negotiations in the case of ongoing exchanges. Our theory and research constitute a modest step in that direction. The following sections present a social exchange framework, incorporate some basic forms of everyday emotion, offer a theoretical model explaining the role of emotional/affective processes in negotiation, and summarize recent evidence on that role. Finally, we point to some broader implications for networks, group formation, and commitment in organizations.

A Social Exchange Framework

Dimensions of Structural Power

Social exchange theory portrays all social relationships, not just negotiation ones, as having an instrumental foundation. People ostensibly form and remain in relationships of whatever sort as long as they receive individual rewards better than those available elsewhere (Blau, 1964; Emerson, 1962; Homans, 1961; Thibaut & Kelley, 1959). Richard Emerson (1962, 1972, 1981), in his seminal theoretical work, has developed a comprehensive theory of power from these basic ideas and assumptions of exchange theory. He has formulated an explicitly structural theory of power in which power capabilities are based on the dependencies or interdependencies within a network of more than two actors. The concept of *structural power* communicates not only that power is conceived of as a potential but that it is grounded in a network of dyadic relations. Emerson's concept of power as dependence captures some of the important features of negotiation contexts.

In negotiations, structural power concerns the objective relations of dependence and interdependence of the two actors (Bacharach & Lawler, 1981; Emerson, 1981). The power of A is based on the dependence of B on A, and vice versa. The degree of dependence varies positively with the value actors ascribe to the outcomes, resources, or issues at stake, and negatively with the availability of such outcomes or resources from elsewhere (Bacharach & Lawler, 1981). This is a fairly standard rendition of Emerson's power dependence theory that also dovetails with the larger social exchange tradition (e.g., Blau, 1964; Thibaut & Kelley, 1959). Thus in an exchange situation in which two parties, A and B, can provide rewards x and y to each other, A's power over B is equal to B's dependence on A for x and B's power over A is equal to A's dependence on B for y. Each party's dependence in turn has a positive relation with the value of x and y to B and A, respectively, and a negative relation with the availability of x and y from alternatives. Like others who examine exchange networks (e.g., Cook et al., 1983; Cook & Yamagishi, 1992; Markovsky et al., 1988), we focus on the "alternatives" dimension of dependence and essentially assume that value is constant.

Implicitly, Emerson's theory treats power in "absolute" terms, because each actor's power is based only on the other's dependence and not on his or her own. Bacharach and Lawler (1981) develop this idea further and propose a non-zero-sum theory of power dependence (see also Lawler 1992b; Lawler & Ford, 1993). A non-zero-sum theory allows for variation in the total (or average) amount of power potential in an exchange relation, whereas a zero-sum conception assumes a fixed total. With a non-zero-sum conception, both the total power (or mutual dependence) and relative power (dependence difference) are important structural dimensions of the relation—thus an increase in the power of one does not necessarily imply a decrease in the power of the other. Both actors can experience an increase in power without a change in their relative power (see Bacharach & Lawler, 1981; Lawler, 1992a; Lawler & Bacharach, 1987). We suggest that in combination these dimensions of power grasp in a simple and parsimonious way the fundamental underpinning of an exchange relation such as that found in dyadic negotiations.

The broader import of a non-zero-sum approach to power is illustrated in Kanter's (1977) analysis of "empowerment" in organizations. She shows, for example, that if middle managers are "empowered" by becoming more involved in strategic planning and other activities external to their subunits, their subordinates also are "empowered" by having greater discretion and autonomy over day-to-day activities. The power of both middle and lower managers may change in the same direction. Tannenbaum (1968) makes a similar point, suggesting that if the participation of employees in organizational decision

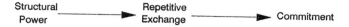

Figure 7.1. Classic Social Exchange Model of Commitment

making increases, their "control" over managers is enhanced, but so is the managers' control over them.

Repetitive Negotiations in Exchange Relations

Mutual (total) and relative dependence should have an important effect on negotiations and the development of an ongoing "exchange relation." Previous research on one-shot negotiations shows that greater mutual or total dependence and more equal dependence increase the likelihood of an agreement (Bacharach & Lawler, 1981; Lawler, 1992b, 1993; Lawler & Bacharach, 1987). Mutual dependence reflects the opportunity costs of failing to reach agreement with a particular other, and relative dependence bears on the prospects of mutually satisfactory agreements (Lawler, 1992b). In repeated negotiations, the objective power dependence context that brings actors together to negotiate in the first place will bring them together time and time again to resolve problems through negotiation (see Cook & Whitmeyer, 1992; Lawler & Yoon, 1993).

To infer or argue that stable structural-power conditions produce commitment in ongoing, repeated encounters is not a new idea. The classic position of Emerson's exchange theory takes the form of a simple causal chain in which structural power is linked to commitment through the frequency of exchange (Cook & Emerson, 1984), as portrayed in Figure 7.1.[1] Frequent exchange among the same actors produces commitment by reducing uncertainty (Cook & Emerson, 1984) or increasing interpersonal attraction (Tallman, Gray, & Leik, 1991). Thus two additional intervening mechanisms ostensibly can explain the link of repetitive exchange and commitment—the actors come to know each other better (uncertainty reduction) or they come to like each other more (interpersonal attraction). In both, the explanation for commitment formation is still that the rewards within the relationship are better than elsewhere—that is, *people stay because it pays.*

Our approach recasts and elaborates the causal chain proposed by the classic social exchange model by incorporating the emotional/affective dimension of commitment suggested in theory and research on organizational commitment (Kanter, 1972; Lincoln & Kalleberg, 1985; Meyer, Allen, & Gellatly, 1990; Mowday, Porter, & Steers, 1982; Mueller, Wallace, & Price, 1992). Whereas Emerson (1972, 1981) assumes that exchange relations are formed from repeated instrumental encounters, we go further by suggesting that, in the process, exchange relations become partly expressive owing to emotional processes endogenous to the dyadic negotiations (Lawler & Yoon, 1993; Lawler, Yoon, Baker, & Large, in press). Our analysis of this phenomenon is inspired by Homans's (1950) classic notion that frequent exchange among the same actors is sufficient to produce sentiment relations among them if two conditions are met: (a) They have alternative relations and (b) these are not likely to provide benefits as good as the focal ones. These conditions are integral to select dyads within most any network and are assumed as given by our theory.[2]

Our theory contends that under the conditions put forth by Homans, the emotional/affective consequences of "doing things jointly with others" warrant particular attention (see Lawler & Yoon, 1993, p. 467). If a network gets the same two people together to do something jointly and they repeatedly accomplish their joint task, they are likely to feel good about this. Adapting Berger and Luckmann's (1967) ideas about "incipient institutionalization," more frequent exchange therefore should lead actors to perceive themselves as linked and as constituting a "unit" somewhat distinct from other dyads or relations in the situation. This is tantamount to the "objectification" of the exchange relation (Berger & Luckmann, 1967), that is, the perception of it as an objective reality apart from the actors composing it. Once objectified, the relation is likely to be perceived as partly responsible for the positive emotion, and therefore it becomes somewhat expressive (Lawler, 1992b; Lawler & Yoon, 1993). Objectification can be construed as "psychological group formation," in Tajfel and Turner's terms (Tajfel, 1982; Tajfel & Turner, 1986; Turner, 1987), and "expressiveness" as an emotional result of perceived interdependence (Gaertner, Mann, Murrell, & Dovidio, 1989; Kramer, 1991, 1993; Rabbie & Horowitz, 1988).

"Expressiveness" of the relation is different from the liking or interpersonal attraction of the actors for each other (Hogg & Turner, 1985; Lawler, 1992b; Markovsky & Lawler, 1994; Parsons, 1951). Both the other actor and the social relation can be distinct social objects for actors, just as the "generalized other" and specific others are distinct social objects in George Herbert Mead's (1934) theorizing and "the organization" is a distinct object of attachment in research on organizational commitment (Lincoln & Kalleberg, 1985; Meyer et al., 1990; Mowday et al., 1982; Price & Mueller, 1986). Thus instrumental exchange relations, created and maintained by structural-power conditions, can become distinct targets of affective attachment regardless of the interpersonal attraction between the particular actors. Hogg and Turner (1985) make a similar distinction and provide some supporting evidence for the idea that interpersonal liking is not sufficient to foster group formation.[3]

Thus, compared with the standard exchange viewpoint, our theory inserts an intervening emotional/affective process between repetitive exchange (agreements) and commitment behavior. In this framework, uncertainty reduction

Figure 7.2. Modification of the Social Exchange Model

and liking for the other stem from the emotional/affective consequences of reaching agreements, consequences that also make the relation a social object for actors and a potential target of attachment; these other interpretations are subsumed by the collective impact of the emotional/affective process. To examine this emotional process further in the context of an exchange relation, we now turn to some recent work on mild, everyday emotions or feelings.

Mild Emotions/Moods/Feelings

We adopt an approach to emotion heavily informed by the circumplex model and some sociological theorizing about everyday emotions (Kemper, 1978, 1987; Larsen & Diener, 1992; Watson & Tellegen, 1985). The emotions produced by negotiations are treated as normal, mild feelings that we all feel in our daily lives and that we can generally report and describe with accuracy. Such emotions include, for example, mild sensations of feeling happy, unhappy, elated, sad, excited, bored, enthusiastic, and unenthusiastic.

An emotion is defined as a transitory positive or negative evaluative state that involves neurophysiological, neuromuscular, and often cognitive components (Izard, 1992). Given relatively little consensus in the psychological and sociological literatures on the meanings of obviously related terms such as *mood, emotion, affect,* and *feeling,* we adopt a simple framework useful for our particular concerns. Following Kemper (1978) and Gordon (1981), we define *emotion* as a transitory feeling and *affect* as an enduring sentiment; emotions are relatively diffuse feelings emerging from negotiations, whereas affect is a sentiment attached to the relation as an object. We focus solely on normal, mild, self-reportable feelings and sentiments. Although this necessarily skirts many fundamental theoretical and empirical issues about emotion, such an approach to emotions and affect has been used with substantial success by Isen and her colleagues (Isen, 1987; Isen & Baron, 1991) and by those who work with the circumplex model (Larsen & Diener, 1992).

The circumplex approach to emotion identifies pleasure and arousal as the main dimensions of emotion (Larsen & Diener, 1992). Pleasure is most basic and the emotion treated by Isen and her colleagues; the arousal dimension has been a theoretical and empirical problem in the literature because of its diffuseness and its potential to take either negative or positive forms. Arousal has varied positive forms, one of the most important of which is what Izard terms "interest/excitement." Interest/excitement is a distinct and separate positive emotion, defined as a motivating state of curiosity and fascination (Izard, 1992; MacDowell & Mandler, 1989). Interest/excitement is "feeling energized," whereas pleasure is "feeling satisfied." We focus on these two forms of positive emotion.

As Izard (1992) indicates, interest/excitement is anticipatory or oriented to future events and involves an "awareness of potential satisfaction" (see also Deci, 1980). Pleasure/satisfaction, narrowly construed, is oriented to the past, a response to outcomes already received rather than those anticipated or hoped for in the future. This implies a distinction between emotions that stem from "looking backward" and those that stem from "looking forward" (see Lawler & Yoon, 1993). Such a distinction could help capture a fundamental aspect of social interaction in general and negotiation in particular. Actors tend to look both backward and forward, to think about what has happened recently and what might come next, to orient themselves to the past and to the future. When negotiations occur in ongoing relations, the salience of and attention to past and future obviously increase (Axelrod, 1984), and actors more vigilantly monitor and interpret the meaning of past events and the prospects of positive future events. Thus treating pleasure/satisfaction and interest/excitement as basic, everyday emotions of particular importance to bargaining and negotiation makes considerable sense and could lead to important insights.

The Theoretical Model

The theory takes the form of a theoretical (causal) model that specifies the series of *indirect* paths through which structural power fosters commitment behavior (Figure 7.3). There are two exogenous variables, representing the zero-sum (differential dependence) and non-zero-sum (mutual dependence) dimensions of power. *Total power* or mutual dependence is the sum of each actor's absolute power over the other; *relative power* is the difference between the two actors' power. The first endogenous variable is the *frequency of agreement* across repetitive and independent instances of negotiation; the next is *positive emotion,* taking the form of mild, everyday feelings of pleasure/satisfaction or interest/excitement. Satisfactory agreements or exchanges ostensibly produce such emotion, with *satisfactory* defined as an agreement better than likely from the alternative partner. Given the structural-power conditions, it is reasonable to assume that conditions producing more agreements are also producing more satisfactory ones.

Objectification refers to actors' perceptions of being linked to one another and constituting a unit distinct from other potential or actual relations in the

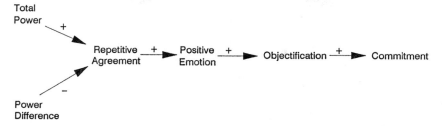

Figure 7.3. The Theory of Relational Commitment

context (Lawler & Yoon, 1993). Based on the work of Berger and Luckmann (1967), when relations become objects unto themselves, they become a "third force" impinging on actors (see also Markovsky & Lawler, 1994; Parsons, 1951). *Commitment* is the tie of an individual to a collective social object, such as a relationship, group, or organization. Affective commitments are individual-to-group ties that are emotional or cathectic (Kanter, 1972), rather than instrumental.

In testing the theoretical model, *indirect* effects of power and repetitive agreements through positive emotion indicate affectively based commitments, whereas direct effects for power or agreements suggest instrumentally based commitments. The following subsections discuss each step or link in the theoretical model, moving from left to right.

Structural Power and Repetitive Agreements

Total power (mutual dependence) is a primary facilitator of exchange because dyads containing greater mutual dependence entail more "relational cohesion," that is, a structural push toward cooperative action (Emerson, 1972; Lawler & Yoon, 1993; Lawler et al., in press). A negotiation relation with greater total power provides each actor more flexibility to adapt to the vicissitudes of the other's behavior and to the larger network because such contexts entail a larger number and range of negotiated agreements that meet a "sufficiency" criterion. Mutual power or dependence in negotiations reflects the extent to which an ongoing relationship is susceptible to disruption by misjudgment, miscalculation, or changes in the larger network.

Research applying power dependence to negotiations has shown that greater total power makes agreement more likely in one-shot negotiations where parties are aware of each other's alternatives (Bacharach & Lawler, 1981; Lawler, 1992b; Lawler & Bacharach, 1987). In recent work on repeated negotiations (Lawler et al., in press), a similar effect was observed where actors know the nature of their own, but not the other's, alternative. This suggests a purely structural effect for total power, attributable to the conjoint effects of each person acting on his or her own power position without being aware of the other's.

Turning to unequal power, the problem actors face shifts to what is a fair and reasonable agreement. The theory predicts that equal power will produce more frequent agreements than unequal power, despite the fact that more benefits accrue to both actors from agreement. It is well known that those with more power tend to argue for agreements that treat power as an appropriate input in an equity equation and that therefore favor themselves, whereas those with lower power argue for agreements that are equal (see, e.g., Bacharach & Lawler, 1981; Hegtvedt & Cook, 1987; Komorita, 1984). Unequal power complicates the bargaining agenda by bringing the meaning and implication of the power difference under dispute.

Various studies of two-party bargaining have suggested that unequal power tends to produce fewer agreements or make conflict resolution more difficult (Lawler, 1992b; Lawler & Bacharach, 1987; Lawler, Ford, & Blegen, 1988). In a recent study of unequal power in a multiparty social dilemma situation, Mannix (1993) also found that larger groups with unequal (compared with equal) power produced more focus on individual gain and generated poorer outcomes overall. It seems clear that unequal, compared with equal, power creates additional obstacles for actors in negotiations.

Repetitive Agreements and Positive Emotion

Our theory predicts that more frequent agreements (exchange) between the same actors produce and crystallize mild positive emotions or feelings. These emotions may involve pleasure/satisfaction with agreements that have already been negotiated and/or interest/excitement about the prospects of future negotiations. The strength of each emotion should depend on the degree to which the context stimulates actors to attend more to the past or to the future of their negotiations with each other. Both the past and the future "cast shadows" over current negotiations, and one question not yet addressed by the theory is what conditions determine the relative size of these shadows.

As we indicated earlier, our argument is that people also feel good as a result of accomplishing joint tasks with other people. This means that doing something jointly with another produces positive feelings (e.g., an "emotional buzz") beyond those generated by the instrumental rewards. The overall strength of the emotions, of course, will likely vary with the task and a number of other aspects of the situation, but, in general, more challenging tasks should produce stronger emotional buzz. Negotiation contexts are particularly challenging, because actors have conflicting interests (or believe they do) and typically face considerable uncertainty and ambiguity. Such situations induce "cognitive work." For these reasons, the emotions actors experience as a result of their joint activity should be somewhat stronger, more salient, and more easily self-reportable than those they experience in many other types of social situations. More important, actors should be prone to give these emotions larger meanings by making inferences about their relationship to the other.

Positive Emotion, Objectification, and Commitment Behavior

The theory stipulates that positive emotions produced by negotiations, if repetitive or frequent, make the people involved perceive a relationship with one another. They become more aware of their interdependence, as manifest in the social structure, and as their perceptions of interdependence grow, so does their sense of having a relationship. This is comparable to the "psychological group formation" process specified by Rabbie and associates, who argue and show empirically that perceptions of interdependence are the key foundation for group formation (Rabbie & Horowitz, 1988; Rabbie, Schot, & Visser, 1989). The mild positive feelings engendered in negotiations should strengthen this group formation process in a dyad within a larger network by enhancing mutual perceptions of interdependence.

The emergence of the relation as a distinct object makes it a likely target for emotions to the degree that the relation is perceived as a cause of these feelings. Lawler (1992a) recently developed a general theory of affective attachments that suggests an explanation for the objectification-to-commitment links in the theory. If a relation or group provides actors a sense of control over their situation—in this case, the uncertainty of the negotiation context—then the relation or group is likely to be a target for the positive feeling produced in the relation or group. The result is stronger affective attachment to that relation or group (Lawler, 1992a) and a propensity to treat it as valuable in its own right or as an end in itself (i.e., as an expressive object). The theory of affective attachments (Lawler, 1993) identifies a general process by which persons form affective ties to collectivities, whether a dyadic relation in a network, a small group in a larger organization, or an organization in a society.

Given the actors' interdependence, reaching agreement in negotiations should enhance each actor's sense of control over the uncertainty of the situation; and the fact that actors jointly accomplish agreements should lead them to credit their relationship, at least in part, for the sense of control and related positive feeling. Thus the relationship should take on intrinsic value, and the actors should be more willing to do things to nurture and maintain the relationship. Continuing to negotiate agreements with the same other maintains the sense of control and enables each actor to reproduce the positive feelings.

To summarize, there are two main parts to the theory that reflect the two sides of the context-action relationship. The first specifies how social contexts initiate commitment processes by generating repetitive agreements among the same actors. Social contexts with high total power and equal power produce the most frequent or repetitive agreements. This is the context-to-action aspect of the theory. The second part of the theory specifies an endogenous process through which repetitive agreements lead to commitment behavior. Repetitive agreement increases positive emotions in the form of mild pleasure/satisfaction and interest/excitement, and positive emotions in turn produce a perceived relationship that leads the actors to engage in behavior that contributes to the relationship. This is the action-to-context aspect of the theory, indicating that commitment formation changes the context for future negotiations.

Evidence for the Theory

We tested several key parts of the theoretical model in two recent studies (Lawler & Yoon, 1993; Lawler et al., in press). The first focused on the impact of equal versus unequal power, and the second on low versus high mutual dependence (total power). In both studies, two actors representing organizations negotiated over the price of a product, and each had one alternative. Negotiation with the alternative was likely to give a lower payoff than negotiation with the focal relation (i.e., it had a lower expected value). The actors engaged in explicit negotiations across 8 to 10 episodes of negotiation (which varied by study), with a maximum of 5 rounds in each year. Each episode set the terms of an exchange for a year, and the negotiations started anew in the next year.

After several episodes (years) of negotiation, actors had the option to give each other unilateral gifts; this was the form of commitment behavior common across the two studies. Actors did not receive information on the number of gifts given by each other until the experiment was over (see Lawler & Yoon, 1993; Lawler et al., in press), so they could not implicitly negotiate reciprocal gifts.[4]

The results of these studies support some key parts of the theoretical model (Figure 7.3). As predicted, the impact of structural power on commitment was mediated by emotional/affective processes in both studies. In the first study, we found that equal, compared with unequal, power produced more commitment behavior, indirectly, through the emotional effects of more frequent agreements under equal power (Lawler & Yoon, 1993). In other words, equal power increased the frequency of agreement, which in turn increased positive emotion, which in turn increased commitment behavior (e.g., gift giving). It is important to note that at each step, the direct effects of antecedent variables were nonexistent or relatively small. The second study revealed that greater mutual dependence produced more frequent agreements, which in turn produced more positive emotion and commitment behavior (Lawler et al., in press). Although neither study could test the role of objectification, the results were consistent with an "objectification-to-expressiveness" interpretation. Moreover, the second study showed that higher mutual dependence produced perceptions of a closer relationship on a postexperimental questionnaire, and that this effect was mediated by the frequency of agreement. In sum, initial evidence supports the theoretical model displayed in Figure 7.3.

The evidence also suggests that the forward-looking emotion, interest/ excitement, may have more to do with the commitment process than the backward-looking emotion, pleasure/satisfaction. We found that the impact of repetitive agreements on commitment behavior was mediated by inter-est/excitement rather than pleasure/satisfaction; the degree of pleasure/satis-faction was determined primarily by the payoffs from actual (past) agree-ments (Lawler & Yoon, 1993). Pleasure/satisfaction may be a function of the nature of agreement, whereas interest/excitement is a function of the frequency of agreement. More frequent agreements may yield hope and an expectation of better things to come, which could account for a greater impact on affec-tively based commitments (for more discussion, see Lawler & Yoon, 1993). This interpretation is made more plausible by the fact that some research on organizational commitment similarly indicates that interesting and challeng-ing work has a stronger impact on organizational commitment than tangible rewards, such as pay, fringe benefits, promotions, and security (see Mottaz, 1988). Clearly, pleasure/satisfaction and interest/excitement are not mutually exclusive emotional responses, and future work should determine whether and when these backward-looking and forward-looking emotions have dif-ferent effects on commitment formation.

Some Broader Implications

We interpret the development of commitment in a relationship within a network as a "group formation" process driven by the positive feelings of pleasure/satisfaction or interest/excitement that result from solving problems (reaching agreements) with the same other over time. Positive emotions are individual-level phenomena that make salient to actors their interdependence and common fate, a key condition for group formation (Brewer & Kramer, 1986; Kramer, 1991, 1993; Kramer & Brewer, 1984; Rabbie & Horowitz, 1988; Rabbie et al., 1989). If group formation is a result of perceptions of interde-pendence (Kramer, 1991, 1993; Kramer & Brewer, 1984; Rabbie & Horwitz, 1988) rather than the mere sharing of a social category (Tajfel & Turner, 1986), it becomes important to integrate power dependence theory with extant notions about group formation. The two dimensions of power dependence, relative and total power, are social-structural conditions that should foster incipient perceptions of interdependence at the outset, but then shape and solidify them by virtue of the interactions these power conditions produce in the actual negotiations. Our theory of commitment offers an emotional/affective explanation for such group formation that reaches beyond the cognitive accounts of previous work. The general processes suggested by our theory also should apply beyond the dyadic relations that are of primary concern in this chapter. We next consider some implications for networks, transaction-costs economics, and organizational commitment.

Applied to networks, the process of group formation in dyadic negotiations poses a dilemma. In networks of exchange, such as those studied by Cook and associates (Cook & Emerson, 1978; Cook et al., 1983) and Markovsky and associates (Markovsky et al., 1988; Willer, Markovsky, & Patton, 1989), dyadic negotiations among the same pairs of actors over time should create pockets of "relational cohesion" that satisfy individual actors but also fragment the network. Over time, ties within a subset of dyads become stronger and more resilient, whereas ties in other potential or actual relations become weaker to nonexistent or virtually impossible. Such processes are readily visible in almost any organization, as people come and go and relations strengthen and weaken accordingly. If our theory is correct, structural theories of exchange cannot account for the ebb and flow of relational strength. Endogenous emotional processes will make some dyads more resilient and less vulnerable to changes of the larger network than structural theories would predict, even with the addition of strategic and cognitive principles.

Applied to transaction-costs economics (Williamson, 1975, 1981), our theory shows how exchange relations can become objects of intrinsic value in their own right, or ends in themselves. The emergence of the relationship as a positive object can be construed as an incipient "governance" structure or a form of "internal organization" that responds to the uncertainty of the negotiation setting (bounded rationality condition), the options both actors have to go elsewhere at any time (potential for opportunism), and the small number of exchanges involved (small-numbers bargaining). The important point of our theory is that the mere frequency of exchange is sufficient to unleash a commitment process, and the resulting "relational cohesion" is based on the emotional/affective consequences of such frequent exchange. Commitment, in our theory, signifies the development of relationship-specific assets that enhance the social costs of exchanging with alternative partners. Asset specificity with such an emotional foundation should have an even more pronounced effect on contracting than predicted by Williamson (1981).

Commitments developed as our theory predicts would involve strong ties between the actors. In organizations, such strong ties can be a double-edged sword. On the one hand, strong ties between key actors are likely to help get the work of the organization done; in fact, as long as actors maintain a focus on organizational tasks, such ties should improve efficiency and performance.

Our theory implicitly highlights the importance of one-on-one relations to getting things done. On the other hand, the fragmenting effects of pockets of "relational cohesion" are a problem if these become vehicles of opposition to organizational goals and procedures. Those with strong personal ties may provide each other mutual affirmation and support for action that reduces organizational performance and efficiency. Network theories offer a possible solution: If weak ties are maintained among dyads with strong ties, the contribution of strong ties to getting the work done may proceed without excessive insulation, and the weak ties (see Granovetter, 1973) may provide informal "oversight" for each of the pivotal or key dyads. This is one way that networks may be a viable alternative to both markets and hierarchies as a method of organizing dyadic transactions (Powell, 1990).

One overall result of dyadic relations with strong expressive links within them and weak instrumental links between them could be more widespread "organizational citizenship" behavior—that is, a tendency to do such things as taking on additional organizational tasks voluntarily, without compensation (Bateman & Organ, 1983; Organ, 1990). Such "citizenship" in an organizational member could be motivated by a strong tie with another with whom the member works repeatedly on organizational tasks rather than loyalty to the organization per se, but it may appear to be "organizational" because of the coordination induced by weak ties to others in the organization. Some organizational citizenship behavior may in fact be "relational citizenship behavior."

If one accepts this network imagery for viewing dyadic negotiations, it also is reasonable to suggest that organizational commitments are mediated in part by the formation of expressive relations among actors, something that organizations often attempt to prevent. If such relations emerge from instrumental ones fostered by the organizational structure and remain focused on the joint activity involved in getting the work of the organization done, they can be quite helpful to organizations. Homans's (1961) classic analysis of 10 cash posters working at a utility company illustrates the organizational benefits of expressive relations in the workplace. The cash posters' duty was to record customers' payments on ledger cards at the time of receipt. The company's standard was 300 postings per hour, and detailed records of the speed of work were kept. Homans observed that the employees significantly exceeded the standard, even though pay was not yoked to production, promotions were rare, and working below the standard resulted in only a "mild rebuke" from the supervisor. Over time, faster workers did not reduce their speed to the standard, and the company did not raise the standard to fit the faster workers' speed. Homans argues that it was not salary, promotion, or other extrinsic benefits that produced the additional production of the workers, but the positive sentiment that developed among the workers and between the workers and the larger organization. One interpretation is that affectively based

commitments to the organization developed in part from the frequent positive interaction of the cash posters with each other and the mutual sharing of
positive experiences with the larger organization. Although there are certainly
other interpretations for Homans's observations (see, e.g., Kelley, 1979), this
example at least serves to suggest how affectively based commitments to relations
and groups in the workplace might be relevant to organizational commitment
(see also Lincoln & Kalleberg, 1985; Mowday et al., 1982; Mueller et al., 1992).

Conclusions

In this chapter we have put forth and modified the classic social exchange
approach to power and commitment behavior. The classic view is that structural power produces commitments by laying the foundation for repetitive
exchange among the same actors. Our theory elaborates this process by arguing
that repetitive exchange arouses positive feelings that are attributed to the
relation. This introduces an emotional/affective component to the commitment process. Whereas exchange theory can explain only instrumental forms
of commitment, our theory explains how and why affective commitments to
an exchange relation can develop and thereby transform an instrumental exchange relation to an expressive relation.

Emotional processes, in our view, forge a link between the existing social
context and subsequent changes in that social context. The initial push toward
change is embedded in the structural power and associated potentials and
tendencies in the social context. People respond to the context with behaviors
that produce emotions at the individual level; these individual emotions
change how people perceive their relationships to one another, strengthening
in particular their sense of interdependence. This makes the relation a salient
"social object" and a target of affective commitment, which is manifest in stay
behavior, a propensity to give things to each other without strings attached,
and an inclination to contribute to a joint venture (i.e., a public good).

In a larger sense, the reciprocal connections of context and behavior involve
macro-to-micro effects (structure to action) and subsequent micro-to-macro
effects (action to structure). Neither set of effects can be subsumed under the
other; both are essential to understanding the role of context in negotiations.
Applying a recently published framework for micro-macro linkages (see Lawler,
Ridgeway, & Markovsky, 1993), negotiations involve *encounters* that are produced by a *macro structure* (the minimal network, in this case). In these
encounters, actors are purposive (have instrumental goals) and are responsive
to each other (take account of each other). Their interaction produces a *micro
structure*, which takes the form of a dyadic relation that is viewed and treated
by the actors and others as an objective reality or unit unto itself. This relation-

ship, once developed, shapes the actors' future encounters with each other but also limits their encounters with others in the larger network. Thus the connections among structurally based power, repetitive exchange, and commitment formation in dyadic negotiation relationships reflect an intertwining of micro-to-macro and macro-to-micro processes.

Notes

1. An assumption of interdependent actors who engage in repetitive exchange helps distinguish exchange theory from neoclassical economic theory (Emerson, 1972, 1981), which assumes a frictionless market and focuses exclusively on discrete and interchangeable transactions. In the classical market, a buyer and a seller will not enter into repeated transactions with each other unless the price is the best each time, and if this occurs, repetitive exchanges will not have any effects per se. Social exchange theory (Blau, 1964; Emerson, 1962, 1972; Homans, 1961; Thibaut & Kelley, 1959) contends that repetitive transactions engender social effects that cannot be explained by economic theory and require a social-structural explanation (Emerson, 1981).

2. We analyze the frequency of agreement in repeated negotiations and take for granted that negotiated exchange will not occur with much frequency in focal relations unless those relations are perceived as providing more benefits than alternative relations. Suboptimal agreements are enough to produce an emotional/affective commitment process as long as the agreements yield payoffs greater than the expected value of the alternative.

3. The transformation of instrumental exchange or negotiation into an expressive relation does not imply that the original instrumental foundation of the relationship has disappeared, only that expressiveness has been superimposed on the instrumental base. In markets, expressive relations are an emotional/affective form of stickiness or friction.

4. Gift giving is defined by actors as a unilateral, noncontingent benefit from a different value domain than that under negotiation (Ekeh, 1974; Heath, 1975; Lawler & Yoon, 1993). Gifts are often small, token gestures such as "showing interest" in new employees, volunteering to help a friend with a difficult task, or putting extra effort into a collective task (Lawler & Yoon, 1993, p. 486). Various "organizational citizenship behaviors" essentially represent gift giving of this sort (see Bateman & Organ, 1983; Organ, 1990). Organ (1990) defines organizational citizenship as "organizationally beneficial behaviors and symbolic gestures that can neither be enforced on the basis of formal role obligations nor elicited by contractual guarantee of recompense" (p. 46). Included are constructive statements about a department, expression of personal interest in the work of others, and suggestions for improvement.

References

Axelrod, R. (1984). *The evolution of cooperation.* New York: Basic Books.
Bacharach, S. B., & Lawler, E. J. (1981). *Bargaining: Power, tactics, and outcomes.* San Francisco: Jossey-Bass.
Bateman, T. S., & Organ, D. W. (1983). Job satisfaction and the good soldier: The relationship between affect and employee citizenship. *Academy of Management Journal, 26,* 587-595.
Berger, P. L., & Luckmann, T. (1967). *The social construction of reality: A treatise in the sociology of knowledge.* Garden City, NY: Doubleday.

Blau, P. (1964). *Exchange and power in social life.* New York: John Wiley.

Brewer, M. B., & Kramer, R. M. (1986). Choice behavior in social dilemmas: Effects of social identity, group size, and decision framing. *Journal of Personality and Social Psychology 50,* 543-549.

Carnevale, P. J., & Isen, A. M. (1986). The influence of positive affect and visual access on the discovery of integrative solutions in bilateral negotiation. *Organizational Behavior and Human Decision Processes, 37,* 1-13.

Cook, K. S., & Emerson, R. M. (1978). Power, equity, and commitment in exchange networks. *American Sociological Review, 27,* 41-40.

Cook, K. S., & Emerson, R. M. (1984). Exchange networks and the analysis of complex organizations. In S. B. Bacharach & E. J. Lawler (Eds.), *Research on the sociology of organizations* (Vol. 3, pp. 1-30). Greenwich, CT: JAI.

Cook, K. S., Emerson, R. M., Gilmore, M. R., & Yamagishi, T. (1983). The distribution of power in exchange networks: Theory and experimental evidence. *American Journal of Sociology, 89,* 275-305.

Cook, K. S., & Whitmeyer, J. M. (1992). Two approaches to social structure: Exchange theory and network analysis. *Annual Review of Sociology, 18,* 109-127.

Cook, K. S., & Yamagishi, T. (1992). Power in exchange networks: A power-dependence formulation. *Social Network, 14,* 245-265.

Deci, E. L. (1980). *The psychology of self determination.* Lexington, MA: Lexington.

Ekeh, P. (1974). *Social exchange theory: The two traditions.* Cambridge, MA: Harvard University Press.

Emerson, R. M. (1962). Power-dependence relations. *American Sociological Review, 27,* 31-40.

Emerson, R. M. (1972). Exchange theory: Part II. Exchange relations and networks. In J. Berger, M. Zelditch, Jr., & B. Anderson (Eds.), *Sociological theories in progress* (Vol. 2, pp. 58-87). Boston: Houghton Mifflin.

Emerson, R. M. (1981). Social exchange theory. In M. Rosenberg & R. H. Turner (Eds.), *Social psychology: Sociological perspectives* (pp. 30-65). New York: Basic Books.

Forgas, J. P. (1992). Affect in social judgements and decisions: A multiprocess model. *Advances in Experimental Social Psychology, 25,* 227-275.

Gaertner, S. L., Mann, J., Murrell, A., & Dovidio, J. F. (1989). Reducing intergroup bias: The benefits of recategorization. *Journal of Personality and Social Psychology, 57,* 239-249.

Gordon, S. L. (1981). The sociology of sentiments and emotion. In M. Rosenberg & R. H. Turner (Eds.), *Social psychology: Sociological perspectives* (pp. 562-592). New York: Basic Books.

Granovetter, M. S. (1973). The strength of weak ties. *American Journal of Sociology, 78,* 1360-1380.

Heath, A. (1975). *Rational choice and social exchange.* Cambridge: Cambridge University Press.

Hegtvedt, K. A., & Cook, K. S. (1987). The role of justice in conflict situations. In E. J. Lawler & B. Markovsky (Eds.), *Advances in group processes* (Vol. 4, pp. 109-136). Greenwich, CT: JAI.

Hochschild, A. R. (1983). *The managed heart: Commercialization of human feeling.* Berkeley: University of California Press.

Hogg, M. A., & Turner, J. C. (1985). Interpersonal attraction, social identification and psychological group formation. *European Journal of Social Psychology, 15,* 51-66.

Homans, G. L. (1950). *The human group.* New York: Harcourt Brace Jovanovich.

Homans, G. L. (1961). *Social behavior: Its elementary form.* New York: Harcourt Brace Jovanovich.

Isen, A. M. (1987). Positive affect, cognitive processes, and social behavior. *Advances in Experimental Social Psychology, 20,* 203-253.

Isen, A. M., & Baron, B. A. (1991). Positive affect as a factor in organizational behavior. In L. L. Cummings & B. M. Staw (Eds.), *Research in organizational behavior* (Vol. 13, pp. 1-53). Greenwich, CT: JAI.

Isen, A. M., & Daubman, K. A. (1984). The influence of affect on categorization. *Journal of Personality and Social Psychology, 47,* 1206-1217.

Izard, C. E. (1977). *Human emotions.* New York: Plenum.

Izard, C. E. (1992). Basic emotions, relations among emotions, and emotion-cognition relations. *Psychological Review, 99,* 561-565.

Kanter, R. M. (1972). *Commitment and community: Communes and utopias in sociological perspective.* Cambridge, MA: Harvard University Press.

Kanter, R. M. (1977). *Men and women of the corporation.* New York: Basic Books.

Kelley, H. H. (1979). *Personal relationships.* Hillsdale, NJ: Lawrence Erlbaum.

Kemper, T. D. (1978). *A social interactional theory of emotions.* New York: John Wiley.

Kemper, T. D. (1987). How many emotions are there? Wedding the social and autonomic structure. *American Journal of Sociology, 93,* 263-289.

Komorita, S. S. (1984). The role of justice and power in reward allocation. *Progress in Applied Sociology, 2,* 185-206.

Kraiger, K. R., Billings, S., & Isen, A. M. (1989). The influence of positive affect states on task perception and satisfaction. *Organizational Behavior and Human Decision Processes, 44,* 12-25.

Kramer, R. M. (1991). Intergroup relations and organizational dilemmas: The role of categorization processes. In L. L. Cummings & B. M. Staw (Eds.), *Research in organizational behavior* (Vol. 13). Greenwich, CT: JAI.

Kramer, R. M. (1993). Cooperation and organizational identification. In J. K. Murnighan (Ed.), *Social psychology in organizations: Advances in theory and research.* Englewood Cliffs, NJ: Prentice Hall.

Kramer, R. M., & Brewer, M. B. (1984). Effects of group identity on resource use in a simulated common dilemma. *Journal of Personality and Social Psychology, 46,* 1044-1057.

Kramer, R. M., Newton, E., & Pommerenke, P. L. (1993). Self-enhancement biases and negotiator judgment: Effects of self-esteem and mood. *Organizational Behavior and Human Decision Processes, 56,* 110-133.

Larsen, R. J., & Diener, E. (1992). Promises and problems with the circumplex model of emotion. In M. S. Clark (Ed.), *Emotion* (pp. 25-59). Newbury Park, CA: Sage.

Lawler, E. J. (1992a). Choice processes and affective attachments to nested groups: A theoretical analysis. *American Sociological Review, 57,* 327-339.

Lawler, E. J. (1992b). Power processes in bargaining. *Sociological Quarterly, 33,* 17-34.

Lawler, E. J. (1993, June). *Affective attachments to nested groups: The role of rational choice processes.* Paper presented at the annual meeting of the International Institute of Sociology, Paris.

Lawler, E. J., & Bacharach, S. B. (1987). Comparison of dependence and punitive forms of power. *Social Forces, 66,* 446-462.

Lawler, E. J., & Ford, R. S. (1993). Metatheory and friendly competition in theory growth: The case of power processes in bargaining. In J. Berger & M. Zelditch, Jr. (Eds.), *Theoretical research programs: Studies in the growth of theory.* Stanford, CA: Stanford University Press.

Lawler, E. J., Ford, R. S., & Blegen, M. A. (1988). Coercive capability in conflict: A test of bilateral deterrence vs. conflict spiral theory. *Social Psychology Quarterly, 51,* 93-107.

Lawler, E. J., Ridgeway, C., & Markovsky, B. (1993). Structural social psychology and the micro-macro problem. *Sociological Theory, 11,* 268-290.

Lawler, E. J., & Yoon, J. (1993). Power and the emergence of commitment behavior in negotiated exchange. *American Sociological Review, 58,* 465-481.

Lawler, E. J., Yoon, J., Baker, M. R., & Large, M. D. (in press). Mutual dependence and gift giving in exchange relations. In B. Markovsky, J. O'Brien, & K. Heimer (Eds.), *Advances in group processes* (Vol. 15). Greenwich, CT: JAI.

Lazarus, R. S. (1984). On the primacy of cognition. *American Psychologist 39,* 124-129.

Lincoln, J., & Kalleberg, A. L. (1985). Work organization and workforce commitment: A study of plants and employees in the U.S. and Japan. *American Sociological Review, 50,* 738-760.

MacDowell, K. A., & Mandler, G. (1989). Constructions of emotion: Discrepancy, arousal, and mood. *Motivation and Emotion, 13,* 105-124.

Mannix, E. A. (1993). Organizations as resource dilemmas: The effects of power balance on coalition formation in small groups. *Organizational Behavior and Human Decision Processes, 55,* 1-22.

Markovsky, B., & Lawler, E. J. (1994). A formal theory of group solidarity: Part 1. Conceptual framework and application to emotions. In B. Markovsky, J. O'Brien, & K. Heimer (Eds.), *Advances in group processes* (Vol. 11). Greenwich, CT: JAI.

Markovsky, B., Willer, D., & Patton, T. (1988). Power relations in exchange networks. *American Sociological Review, 53,* 220-236.

Mead, G. H. (1934). *Mind, self, and society: From the standpoint of a social behaviorist.* Chicago: University of Chicago Press.

Meyer, J. P., Allen, M. J., & Gellatly, I. R. (1990). Affective and continuance commitment to the organization: Evaluation of measures and analysis of concurrent and time-lagged relations. *Journal of Applied Psychology, 75,* 710-720.

Mottaz, C. (1988). Determinants of organizational commitment. *Human Relations, 41,* 467-482.

Mowday, R. T., Porter, L. W., & Steers, L. M. (1982). *Employee-organization linkages.* New York: Academic Press.

Mueller, C. W., Wallace, J. E., & Price, J. L. (1992). Employee commitment: Resolving some issues. *Work and Occupations, 19,* 211-236.

Neale, M. A., & Bazerman, M. H. (1991). *Cognition and rationality in negotiation.* New York: Free Press.

Organ, D. W. (1990). The motivational basis of organizational citizenship behavior. In B. M. Staw & L. L. Cummings (Eds.), *Research in organizational behavior* (Vol. 12, pp. 43-72). Greenwich, CT: JAI.

Parsons, T. (1951). *The social system.* New York: Free Press.

Powell, W. W. (1990). Neither market nor hierarchy: Network forms of organization. In B. M. Staw & L. L. Cummings (Eds.), *Research in organizational behavior* (Vol. 12, pp. 295-336). Greenwich, CT: JAI.

Price, J. L., & Mueller, C. W. (1986). *Absenteeism and turnover of hospital employees.* Greenwich, CT: JAI.

Rabbie, J. M., & Horowitz, M. (1988). Category versus groups as explanatory concepts in intergroup relations. *European Journal of Social Psychology, 19,* 172-202.

Rabbie, J. M., Schot, J. C., & Visser, L. (1989). Social identity theory: A conceptual and empirical critique from the perspective of a behavioral interaction model. *European Journal of Social Psychology, 19,* 171-202.

Schwarz, N., & Bless, H. (1991). Happy and mindless, but sad and smart? The impact of affective states on analytic reasoning. In J. P. Forgas (Ed.), *Emotion and social judgements.* Oxford: Pergamon.

Schwarz, N., Bless, H., & Bohner, G. (1991). Mood and persuasion: Affective states influence the processing of persuasive communications. In M. Zanna (Ed.), *Advances in experimental social psychology* (Vol. 24). San Diego: Academic Press.

Schwarz, N., & Clore, G. L. (1988). How do I feel about it? The informative function of affective states. In W. Stroebe & M. Hewstone (Eds.), *European review of social psychology* (Vol. 2). Chichester, UK: John Wiley.

Smith-Lovin, L., & Heise, D. R. (1988). *Analyzing social interaction: Advances in affect control theory.* New York: Gordon & Breach.

Tajfel, H. (1982). *Social identity and intergroup relations.* Cambridge: Cambridge University Press.

Tajfel, H., & Turner, J. C. (1986). The social identity theory of intergroup behavior. In S. Worchel & W. S. Austin (Eds.), *Psychology of intergroup relations* (pp. 7-24). Chicago: Nelson-Hall.

Tallman, I., Gray, L., & Leik, R. (1991). Decisions, dependency, and commitment: An exchange-based theory of group development. In E. J. Lawler, B. Markovsky, C. Ridgeway, & H. Walker (Eds.), *Advances in group processes* (Vol. 8, pp. 227-257). Greenwich, CT: JAI.

Tannenbaum, A. S. (1968). *Control in organizations.* New York: McGraw-Hill.

Thibaut, J. W., & Kelley, H. H. (1959). *The social psychology of groups.* New York: John Wiley.

Turner, J. C. (1987). *Rediscovering the social group: A self-categorization theory.* Oxford: Basil Blackwell.

Watson, D., & Tellegen, A. (1985). Toward a consensual structure of mood. *Psychological Bulletin, 98,* 219-235.

Willer, D., Markovsky, B., & Patton, T. (1989). Power structures: Derivations and applications of elementary theory. In J. Berger, M. Zelditch, Jr., & B. Anderson (Eds.), *Sociological theories in progress: New formulations* (pp. 313-353). Newbury Park, CA: Sage.

Williamson, O. E. (1975). *Markets and hierarchies: Analysis and antitrust implications—a study in the economics of internal organization.* New York: Free Press.

Williamson, O. E. (1981). The economics of organization: The transaction cost approach. *American Journal of Sociology, 87,* 549-577.

Wright, W. F., & Bower, G. H. (1992). Mood effects on subjective probability assessment. *Organizational Behavior and Human Decision Processes, 52,* 276-291.

Zajonc, R. B. (1984). On the primacy of affect. *American Psychologist, 39,* 117-123.

8

Joint Decision Making
The Inseparability of Relationships and Negotiation

LEONARD GREENHALGH
DEBORAH I. CHAPMAN

Early studies of negotiations were dominated by economic theory, particularly game theory (see, e.g., Nash, 1950). These studies concentrated on how a focal negotiator could optimize the utility gained from a situation by negotiating with another individual who had at least some conflicting goals and who could constrain the focal negotiator's achievement of his or her desired utility gain. Social and personality psychologists embellished the economic paradigm by adding the effects of individual differences, behavioral tactics, and exchange dynamics. The most recent contributions to understanding the basic process posited in this line of research focus on demonstrable limitations to rational choice (see, e.g., Neale & Bazerman, 1991) and show that negotiator cognitions are biased in predictable ways. As a result, we have a body of knowledge about negotiation that construes it as a basically rational process of transactional (or multitransactional) decision making by two or more individuals

AUTHORS' NOTE: A much earlier version of this chapter was presented at the 1993 annual meeting of the Academy of Management in Atlanta, and a more recent version was presented at the Stanford Conference on the Social Context of Negotiation, Stanford Graduate School of Business, March 1994. We are grateful for the critiques and suggestions of colleagues in advancing this chapter to its present form. Direct correspondence to Leonard Greenhalgh, Amos Tuck School of Business Administration, Dartmouth College, Hanover, NH 03755, or via e-mail to Leonard.greenhalgh@dartmouth.edu.

whose goal is to improve their utilities in situations where there is an opportunity to gain or lose utility.

The problem with this body of knowledge, in our view, is its failure to encompass—or even address—the ordinary experience of the phenomenon it purports to explain. As a result, it seems appropriate to step back and reexamine the nature of interpersonal negotiation, review the implicit assumptions underlying traditional research approaches, and assess the success of these approaches in producing a cogent and comprehensive understanding of the phenomenon.

In the interests of clarity, we will discuss interactions between two individuals, although the points made here are largely generalizable to negotiations within and between groups.

Theoretical Framework

Negotiation is a response to conflict. Conflict arises at a decision point when (a) one has interests perceived to be incompatible with the interests of others, and (b) these particular others are capable of affecting achievement of one's interests. Negotiation is one of three alternatives for pursuing one's interests in the conflict. The other two are using power (the ability to impose a solution) and conflict resolution (which involves reconceptualizing the dispute in less divisive terms). Negotiation differs from the use of power in that negotiating parties voluntarily commit themselves to the course of action they agree upon, whereas power users overcome resistance in a way that results in compliance rather than commitment. Negotiation differs from conflict resolution in that the latter, as the term is used here, involves a cognitive restructuring that actually diminishes the perceived incompatibility of interests between the parties (Greenhalgh, 1986). Negotiation, therefore, involves acceptance of an outcome that, except in the case of perfect integrative solutions of the bridging variety (see Pruitt, 1981), only partially serves the negotiator's interests. From this perspective, negotiation can be construed as interactive decision making in that each party decides whether or not to accept a particular settlement as a result of the interaction; power-induced outcomes are unilateral rather than interactive decisions.

The economics-based paradigm attempts to understand negotiation as "interdependent" decision making. The term *interdependence,* in this context, denotes that the focal negotiator has to decide on a course of action that both optimizes his or her utilities and is acceptable to the other party. In other words, optimizing one party's utility is dependent on at least satisfying the other party's minimum needs, and sometimes involves joint utility maximization. Construed in this way, interdependence is clearly different from independence; in the latter situation, decision making involves the unconstrained

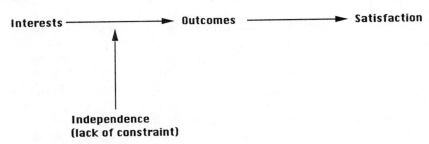

Figure 8.1. The Economic Theory-Based Model of Independent Utility Maximization

selection (or creation) of alternatives that focus solely on maximizing the decision maker's utility (see Figure 8.1). If we deconstruct this conceptualization, we see that independence is being posited as the basic relationship between entities and that interdependence is a special case that occurs when independence is constrained by the need to gain the other party's consent. The conceptual foundation of interdependence in the economics-based model thus lies in independence, which presumes as a base state the separateness of individual decision makers and the primacy of self-interest in their motivational structures (see Bergman, 1991; Greenhalgh, in press).

Figure 8.2 summarizes the principal elements of this paradigm for studying negotiations. An interdependent decision is the outcome of a process that reconciles the preference structures of the two negotiators. The focal negotiator's preference structure (see Greenhalgh, Neslin, & Gilkey, 1985) arises from his or her experienced interests (utilities arising from desires or needs) that are made salient by a perceived opportunity (a situation that can potentially satisfy those needs, a "decision point"). According to this paradigm, the preference structure forms in anticipation of a competitive interaction with the other negotiator (perhaps diluted by the motive to ensure that the other party will get his or her needs met too, in which case we call it a mixed-motive interaction). The preference structure articulates the focal negotiator's interests in terms of the set of feasible outcomes of the interaction, rank ordered by their relative utility (Neslin & Greenhalgh, 1983). Some excellent research has shown that this step is not a purely rational articulation of interests because decision-maker rationality is imperfect: Individuals often fail to maximize their utility because of self-defeating biases in their reasoning processes (for an overview, see Bazerman & Neale, 1992). Note that imperfect rationality is not dismissed as error variance but rather is treated as interesting and worthy of scholars' attention. What makes it interesting is its perverse, aberrant nature when judged in the context of the essentially normative economics-based model; that is, there is an inescapable implication that negotiators ought to be rational in their quest for utility gain.

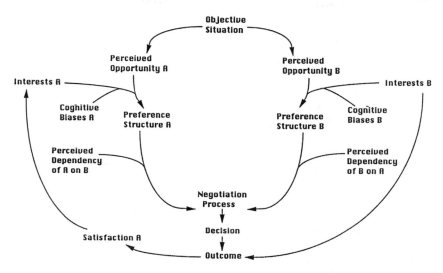

Figure 8.2. Principal Elements of the Traditional Transactional Model of the Pursuit of Self-Interest Through Negotiation

Thus far, we have concentrated entirely on the realm of the cognitions of the focal negotiator (shown as person A in Figure 8.2). A parallel phenomenon is occurring in the other negotiator (person B), who also forms a preference structure on the basis of his or her own unique interests, perceived opportunity, and limited rationality. The key factor that differentiates Figure 8.1 from Figure 8.2 is dependency. In Figure 8.2, the other party has the power (Emerson, 1962) to prevent the focal negotiator from achieving his or her desired utility gain, and vice versa. When the two negotiators interact, the result is a negotiation process, which leads to an outcome that is characterized as an interdependent decision. Let us pause to assess the usefulness of this approach to the study of negotiation.

Judged by its predictive power in laboratory simulations, where researchers can create the conditions and constraints that would induce subjects to engage in utility-oriented cognitive decision making, this approach to studying negotiation is reasonably successful: The variables in the model account for enough variance in outcomes to satisfy other scholars working in this paradigm, and the results can be shown to be significant in the sense that a chance explanation of the laboratory findings is highly unlikely. However, this approach also needs to be judged for its external validity and descriptive value—its ability to mirror real-world negotiations and provide an understanding of common experience. A key question for scholars interested in the phenomenon of negotiation is whether the rather exclusive focus (note our emphasis on what gets excluded) of the dominant theory and methods impedes the broader search for understanding of this phenomenon even while producing valuable understandings of some cognitive processes.

One test of the value of the currently dominant model as an analytic tool would be an assessment of its content validity—whether it includes the variables found most important in participant observer studies of negotiation. Conflict—and negotiation to resolve it—is so ubiquitous that all of us experience it daily, and therefore all of us are participant observers. Our observations indicate that our everyday experiences are quite different from the ones usually studied in laboratory simulations. Specifically, on the basis of their own observations, most scholars would readily agree that (a) actual conflict and negotiation experiences are typically *not* one-shot transactions with strangers, (b) people in real negotiations often sacrifice utility (the nonrefutable, teleological properties of utility theory notwithstanding), (c) people do not conceptualize decision preferences in a social vacuum, and (d) the outcome of greatest importance to negotiators is often the ongoing relationship rather than a utility-enhancing solution to the manifest problem they face.

An alternative model, instead of eliminating the relationship between the parties, includes it as the central explanatory concept for understanding negotiation: It views the relationship as the *context* in which conflict and negotiation occur and through which they are given meaning. Connectedness in this relationship-based model is qualitatively different from interdependence in the economics-based model. In the latter, interdependence is defined as a constraint on utility maximization and as a deviation from the base state of independent or autonomous decision making; in the relationship-based model, connectedness is the base state that, when strained by conflict, must be restored if an optimum outcome is to be reached. Construed this way, interdependence is an experience of communality (Clark & Mills, 1993) in which it is difficult to separate A's interests from B's clearly or cleanly. The individuals' experience of their relationship is better understood as psychic and social connectedness than as economic interdependence.

The process by which the rift in connectedness gets restored, as a conflict is resolved, is interaction. This social encounter gets its meaning and direction from the relationship between the parties; that is, resolution occurs within a context that already joins the two parties in a shared pursuit rather than from interaction that merely coordinates two separate pursuits. The process we are depicting is "joint" rather than "interdependent" decision making, and it characterizes the majority of negotiations. In unusual types of relationships between negotiators (for example, in the rare case of negotiations between strangers), there is little to guide the parties' choices of approach other than their own autonomous interests, the demand characteristics of the situation, and, perhaps, the possibility of a future relationship. As a result, it is not surprising that laboratory studies get the results they do: They have artificially structured the context so as to evoke the paradigm case. In so doing, however, they have distorted the relationship context within which conflict occurs and in which the dispute (and the process used to address it) are given meaning in organizational, family, and social life.

Competitive Posture in a Relationship

Having shown the Hobbesian view of human nature (which would justify the emphasis on economic man) as inconsistent with our everyday experience as participant observers, we are not arguing that interdependent decision making is no more than an artifact of laboratory manipulations. Rather, we are saying that, viewed from a global perspective, joint decision making is the human norm, but interdependent decision making is prominent in situations that evoke it—primarily contexts in which a competitive posture has come to dominate the way the person experiences the relationship (at least momentarily). This type of context can be created by the impulses of particular individuals that get triggered across situations, or by the demand characteristics of the particular situation to which individuals respond.

People are sociobiologically collaborative within an identity group, but their competitive impulses can be triggered by the experience of threat. The most commonly encountered threats do not involve economic deprivation—which the economics-based study of negotiation has taken as the paradigm case—but rather status, approval, validation of an individual's value system, and self-esteem. The competitive impulse first arises in early childhood, when a child perceives a sibling or a parent to be getting some of the attention the child wants from the other parent. The parent whose attention is sought can manage or foster the competitive response. Parents who foster this response create a "need for achievement" in the child (McClelland, 1961) that later predisposes the individual to be competitive in relationships with others. The need-for-achievement syndrome results from a reinforcement history that makes the child feel loved when he or she is excelling over comparison others (i.e., competing successfully). Conversely, however, the child can feel unworthy of parental love in the absence of achievement; the child feels deprived of unconditional positive regard (which is virtually a prerequisite of healthy self-esteem). For individuals high in need for achievement, however, the quest to excel can never be fulfilled, because life presents an endless series of challenges in which self-esteem is at stake.

Throughout the life span, situations that in some way resemble early threats can trigger the competitive impulse. Clinical psychologists refer to this as transference (see Greenhalgh & Gilkey, 1994), although the same process has been described in neuroscience (see Powers, 1973) and behaviorism (in the case of stimulus generalization). As a result of transference, certain others—and particular scenarios—will trigger a competitive impulse. Colloquially, we might say, in explaining aggressive responses in ourselves, "That person is pushing one of my buttons." This often means that we recognize the triggered impulse, and the feelings that accompany it, but are not able to connect it logically to the immediate situation. We sense we are overreacting to the present situation, but (often) are unable to identify the underlying competitive dynamics being aroused. The impulse is usually detectable by others, perhaps because of nonverbal behavior, and creates a threat that spawns a protective counterimpulse. The concomitant rise in adrenaline fuels aggressive behavior in the subsequent interaction, which creates a positive feedback loop that escalates competition. We now see individuals thinking and behaving toward each other like "economic man." This event does not validate the economics-based model's assumption about human nature; rather, it acknowledges that sometimes people think and behave as if they are basically self-interested rather than communal.

Likewise, some *situations* will evoke competitive behavior, irrespective of whether the individual involved is predisposed to be competitive. For example, a "meritocracy," by definition, pits people against each other by putting their prosperity at stake. "Up-or-out" tenure systems in colleges and consulting firms are particularly provocative meritocratic forms. Meritocracies are so commonplace in Western social institutions that we take them for granted; we fail to see them as a manifestation of the ideology of the power elite (see Salem, 1994) and choose instead to view them as evidence of good social science applied to motivating workers. The unexamined assumption is that putting peers in competition with each other will maximize effort, productivity, and excellence. But is this consonant with our experience as participant observers? Don't we have increasing evidence that meritocracy introduces a divisive dimension to the peer relationship that, instead of leading individuals to excel, kills off the collaboration the organization needs to be effective? In fact, those of us who have worked in academic departments where "colleagues" refuse to collaborate with each other know only too well the dysfunctional effects organizationally induced competition can have on cohesive organizational functioning.

Another situation where we *create* competition among people who otherwise might collaborate is in laboratory studies. In many studies of negotiation, we "define the situation" in which we study behavior by handing the participants a zero-sum payoff matrix, or a scenario that is stripped of all detail save the competitive strains in the relationship, or a coalition "game" in which the parties must strive to coalesce or be deprived of resources. We do, indeed, observe competitive behavior in these situations, and we have built a body of knowledge about negotiation on the foundation of the reactions evoked by "staged" scenarios.

When we have studied collaboration as a phenomenon, we have done so by *extending* the competitive paradigm, typically by substituting a mixed-motive payoff matrix for the basic zero-sum scenario. The implicit research question being addressed is, How do basically self-interested, competitive people adapt to situations where there is some benefit to collaborating? A literature has evolved that describes laboratory-evoked processes and outcomes that show many of the shortcomings in external validity we saw in the earlier zero-sum studies. Observational studies outside of the laboratory, to which we will turn next, suggest that it is not difficult to find interpersonal, inter-group, and interorganizational collaboration; it is actually rarer to find the kind of competition we have been devoting so much attention to studying. Yet the economics-based model produces an observational bias that sensitizes us to notice the competing and accept it as the base state of relationships, forming the foundation for the field's research on collaboration.

Field Research

To illustrate the shortcoming in explanatory power of the economics-based model, let us consider the following account of three real-life (as contrasted to laboratory-simulated) negotiations, involving thousands of dollars, as reported by Larry, a landowner who was directly involved in two of them. Following presentation of the cases, we will show how an understanding of the relationships among the parties illuminates the "economically irrational" behavior of the participants.

Larry's Negotiation With Rolf

In 1986, Larry bought a 30-acre plot of land in a bankruptcy proceeding as a long-term investment. He wanted to improve the land gradually, doing much of the work himself in his spare time for its intrinsic recreational value (he was president of a small corporation and craved productive physical exercise as well as an outlet for his creative energies), and hiring others to do work for him as his cash situation allowed. At the outset, he hired a part-time bucket-loader operator, John, to help him remove rock and smooth out the land closest to the house. This operation required buying a lot of "fill"—mostly sand and clay—to fill in gullies and holes. John recommended buying the fill from Rolf Lundquist, one of three large suppliers in the area. John did not seek competitive bids on the fill, even though the volume was large and the cost in the thousands. John said he had always bought from Rolf because John knew Rolf's father, Olaf, well.

Rolf visited the work site several times, and a friendship developed among Rolf, Larry, and Larry's wife, Jane. The next year, John got a full-time job with the town and no longer had the time to do freelance work, so Larry began buying his own earth-moving equipment (at bankruptcy auctions) to continue progress on the property. Larry continued to buy all his materials from Rolf, and Larry and Jane kept up a social relationship with Rolf as well as with Rolf's wife and employees. In addition, Larry and Rolf regularly helped each other out. For example, when Rolf needed a boat for a special family outing, Larry loaned him his boat; when Larry needed surveying equipment, Rolf loaned it to him and showed him how to use it; when Rolf needed some business advice, Larry gave it to him free; when Larry needed material immediately, Rolf found a way to get it to him; when Rolf needed to delay delivery, Larry found a way to accommodate the delay. Over time, as their liking and trust for each other grew, so too did their sensitivity to the difference between convenience and real need.

In 1992, after suffering through two years of recession in the construction industry, Rolf emerged as the low bidder on a very large construction site project. He was desperate for business to cover his large fixed costs, and was bidding on every job that came up, usually losing to other construction companies who were on the verge of bankruptcy and were taking jobs at minimal margins in order to meet cash needs. Rolf was surprised to win this particular job, because he had bid high enough to cover all his costs. His problem was that he did not own enough equipment to actually do the work.

Larry had bought a large excavator the year before, so Rolf asked Larry if his company could lease it. Although Larry was not surprised at the request, he was anxious about it. He said that he would talk it over with Jane and get back to Rolf very soon. Larry and Jane did not want to lease out the excavator for two reasons: First, heavy equipment is very dangerous, and they were afraid of liability exposure if someone got hurt; second, they wanted to minimize the wear and tear put on the excavator because it was old and they were afraid it would break down before they had finished the project for which they had bought it. They did not need the cash that the lease would generate as much as they needed the peace of mind that would come from not leasing it. Larry called Rolf and expressed these concerns, and Rolf said he understood them, but had put himself in a jam. Larry said he would discuss it some more with Jane.

Larry and Jane remained very reluctant to lease the excavator, but felt uncomfortable saying no. First, refusing to lease the excavator seemed out of place in their relationship with Rolf; second, they felt that they ought to help because Rolf was in need and they had the ability to help him out. Larry called

Rolf and gave Rolf permission to take the excavator. They discussed the lease price briefly, but neither had leased such large equipment before. Rolf said he would "ask around" to see what other construction companies were being charged for similar equipment and get back to Larry.

Three months later, Rolf returned the excavator, and he and Larry began discussing the per hour lease price. Based on what Rolf and others had told them in the meantime about leasing prices, Larry and Jane had been expecting to get about $50 per hour, but Rolf was continuing to experience cash flow problems and could only comfortably afford $35 per hour. They settled on that figure, to be paid at some point in the future.

Larry's Negotiation With Vito

Four months later, Larry hired a crew of Rolf's workers to do some high-quality finish work on a section of his land. Larry was preparing it to be planted with grass. The area was so large that it needed to be seeded with special seed-spraying equipment that Rolf's company did not have. Rolf had recommended contacting Vito, his biggest competitor in the area, who had special "hydro-seeding" equipment. The seed-spraying job was scheduled for the Friday before the Memorial Day weekend, so on the preceding Thursday, Vito visited the site to perform final inspection to make sure the topsoil was ready for seeding.

Rolf's crew was running late and had run out of topsoil about the time Vito arrived. They could not get more because their topsoil-screening unit (a large machine that removes rocks and debris from the material) had broken down and could not be fixed before early the next week. Larry needed the hydro-seeding job finished before Memorial Day weekend, so he asked Vito if Vito's company could supply the extra topsoil needed to finish the job. Vito explained that he had plenty of topsoil available, but he didn't want to take the business away from Rolf. Larry offered to call Rolf and explain the problem and see if Rolf objected to his obtaining the last three truckloads of topsoil from Vito. Vito said he'd rather not, and instead called his own staff and told them to send their own screening unit over to Rolf's place so that Rolf could screen the extra topsoil the next morning. Vito completed the seeding job on Saturday, paying his crew time and a half at no extra cost to Larry.

Rolf's Negotiation With Sterling

Sterling, whose ancestors came over on the Mayflower, had used inherited wealth to become a large-scale developer in the area where Larry's land was located. He was bidding on a municipal project and contacted Rolf to get a bid for excavation and fill. Virtually all of Sterling's previous business had been with James Oxley III, another WASP and a competitor to Vito and Rolf.

Rolf did a considerable amount of work to arrive at the estimate, and took a low profit margin to establish himself as a supplier to this large developer. His bid came in 10% lower than that of Oxley. Sterling's bookkeeper (who, unbeknown to Sterling, was a cousin to Rolf's wife) reported that Sterling made a telephone call to Oxley and told him he was 10% high, and that he would have to take less profit if he wanted this business (a large project). Sterling went on to say that if Oxley claimed he had made a mathematical error, he would be allowed to submit a revised bid, and that if this came in at or below Rolf's bid, Oxley could have the business. Oxley complained that Sterling had solicited Rolf's bid as a pressure tactic to provide more of the profit to Sterling and less to Oxley. Sterling laughed and said, "I'm just keeping you honest, James!"

Rolf was furious when he learned of how the subcontractor selection process had been handled. He felt he had done a lot of work to bid for the job, and that he had not been given a chance to compete fairly for the business. He vowed never to do business with Sterling again, and told everyone he knew in the business how unscrupulous Sterling had been.

Let us examine the usefulness of the economics-based model in understanding the three real-life negotiations described above. From an economic perspective, Larry behaved incomprehensibly in his dealings with Rolf, and Vito behaved just as incomprehensibly in his dealings with Larry. Their failure to pursue their own interests adequately (Larry agreed to loan the excavator despite the risks this created for him, and agreed to a price below his own expectations; Vito turned down business and, in so doing, incurred overtime costs he chose to absorb) cannot be explained by the known limits to rationality (Neale & Bazerman, 1991). The economics-based model, which is normative in essence, portrays both of them as duffers because they did not act in response to the opportunities for utility gain available to them; in fact, they acted against their own best interests without being constrained to do so. Yet Larry is a company president with an M.B.A. degree and works as a management consultant, and Vito has an engineering degree and is an experienced executive vice president of a successful multimillion-dollar venture. Furthermore, when viewed in light of situations familiar to most of us, their behavior makes quite a bit of sense. We believe that the relationship-based model can explain how this is possible and, specifically, how both Larry's and Vito's behavior in the negotiations is wholly understandable and predictable.

In the first two case situations, the people involved looked at the conflict itself as well as alternative responses *within the context* of the ongoing relationship; in addition, preservation of the relationship was a primary objective for all of the parties involved. In the first, Rolf's requests as well as any action Larry and Jane would take were looked at in terms of the past pattern of trust, liking, and reciprocal assistance; inasmuch as the relationship *comprised* the dimensions of trust, liking, and reciprocity, refusing to loan the excavator in this case would be a denial of all three and, therefore, the relationship. Such denial was neither desirable nor necessary; in fact, pursuing "their own interests" *as separate and distinct from those of Rolf* was simply not possible. The relationship connects these interests in a way that makes indifference of one party to the satisfaction of the other party's needs no longer a "rational" or even a feasible response. Thus, because of the relationship, Rolf's interests were now included in Larry and Jane's interests, and meeting all of these interests became the only desirable outcome. In addition, in this case, relationship-oriented values influenced Larry and Jane's decision. As Jane articulated this decision factor, if one has the capacity to help a friend in need, one has some responsibility to provide that help, despite reasonable levels of inconvenience and risk.

In the second case also, it is the interpersonal relationship, especially its history and its unwritten rules, together with Vito's desire to preserve the relationship, that provides the context or set of meanings that makes sense of what was done to resolve the conflict. Vito clearly believes that the ongoing base state for the two businesses is communal, rather than exchange-oriented interdependence (see Clark & Mills, 1993). He does not view Rolf *primarily* as a competitor with whom he must vie for scarce business (even though an uninformed or biased observer would see *only* this dimension to their relationship); rather, Rolf is a man Vito likes, trusts, and respects, and with whom he has much in common because they are in the same business. Their business activities present circumstances in which they compete through bidding (in which case the competing dynamic in their relationship becomes temporarily salient), but taking advantage of the zero-sum opportunities they both address is subordinate to their communal relationship.

The third negotiation, between Sterling and Rolf, at first glance seems better suited to explanation by the traditional model, but the explanation this model yields is not as comprehensive or illuminating as the one provided by the relationship-based model. Sterling apparently was pursuing his self-interest in "using" Rolf as a means of gaining a greater share of the contract's profits at subcontractor Oxley's expense. Departures from rationality are not particularly useful in explaining the behavior, but personality theory may be: Perhaps Sterling is high in Machiavellianism, and has no qualms about exploiting others; alternatively, perhaps Sterling has a high need for power, and his behavior toward Oxley was an intrinsically rewarding expression of dominance.

Although it represents a situation that is consistent with the economics-based model, the most interesting aspect of the Sterling-Oxley interaction is what it tells us about differences in relationships. We can surmise that Sterling's relationship with Oxley is qualitatively different from the relationships Rolf has generated with Larry and Vito. Oxley has been Sterling's primary supplier for more than 20 years, and the two share the same "old riche" social circle, but Sterling apparently feels there is nothing in the relationship to inhibit him from exploiting Oxley when this is feasible. In fact, his relationship with Oxley is remarkably similar to his relationship with Rolf: Both are suppliers with whom he has few other bonds. Clark and Mills (1993) might say that Sterling's actions reflect an exchange rather than a communal relationship.

The economics-based model would view the principal outcome of the interaction between Sterling and Rolf as impasse. A relationship-based model would focus instead on the effects of the interaction on the ongoing relationship, which was, in fact, dominated by Rolf's enmity toward Sterling and his strong motive surreptitiously to cost him business in other transactions. By being so transaction focused, the traditional model misses the most important outcome arising from this event—why the *next* negotiation between these parties will *not* take place. Instead, the model would assume that no transaction means no relationship, which is false and has the effect of masking an important organizational phenomenon—rejection in a relationship.

The transactional emphasis of the economics-based model blinds us to just how important relationship rejection is in comparison with loss of utility. A striking way to illuminate the relative importance is to ask people to describe their earliest memories of being involved in a team sport. Participating in a team sport is an opportunity to gain utility by beating the other side, or, if faced with an unbeatable opponent, by feeling good about putting on the best effort possible. But the actual memories reported by most individuals do not reflect the utility gain or loss; rather, almost invariably, people vividly remember the phenomenon of "choosing up sides." That is, what made the event memorable was the anxiety of wondering whether one was going to be picked. Thus outcome utility pales, then as now, in comparison with the risk of relationship rejection.

The three cases above give us insight about the typical context of negotiation. People are likely to seek out interaction differentially with those with whom they feel a positive bond. This leads to repetitive interactions and the deepening of relationship ties. Social and business networks evolve as a result of these processes, and individuals participating in the interactions experience identity as network members. Over time, work and nonwork boundaries become blurred as business associates share leisure activities and individuals preferentially patronize friends' businesses. The result is a social community.

When individuals interact, either acting on their own behalf or as representatives of an organization, imperfect alignment of preferences is inevitable, so all interactions involve some degree of conflict. The nature of the relationship that has formed is likely to be the strongest predictor of how the negotiation ensues: One does not sell one's car to one's college-age son the same way one sells it to a used-car dealer, even though the economic forces experienced by the buyer might be essentially identical. Because of the human tendency to form and interact within identity-based networks, the typical negotiation has more in common with the sale to one's son than with the sale to the used-car dealer, yet the existing body of theory covers only our stereotypes of the latter case.

A Relationship-Based Model of Joint Decision Making

What, then, do we know about relationships, and especially what do we know about them that will make the alternative model useful in understanding the general phenomenon and not just specific instances of negotiation? Fortunately, theory development and research on relationships have mush-roomed in recent years (for examples, in addition to the works in this volume, see Greenhalgh & Chapman, 1993; Greenhalgh & Kramer, 1990; Halpern, 1992; Loewenstein, Thompson, & Bazerman, 1989; Mannix, 1991; Northcraft & Neale, 1991; Sondak & Moore, 1993; Thompson & DeHarpport, 1991; Tuchinsky, Escalas, Moore & Sheppard, 1994; Valley, 1991; Valley & Neale, 1991), and although there is as yet no clear science of relationships in the traditional sense, there is a body of knowledge emerging that has yielded both a conceptual and an operational definition of *relationship*.

The conceptual definition is as follows: A relationship can be defined tenta-tively as the meaning assigned by two or more individuals to their *connected-ness* or coexistence. In the context of negotiation, a relationship involves the set of cognitions that determine the focal negotiator's posture toward the other party. The term *posture* is chosen for its breadth and neutrality: The relationship construct needs to encompass the spectrum of cohesive and divisive forces (Greenhalgh, in press). We offer an operational definition of a relationship elsewhere (Greenhalgh & Chapman, 1993); this instrumentation is based not on potentially biased theory, but rather on empirical field research to investigate how people construe relationships. The dimensions in terms of which individuals construe relationships are shown in Table 8.1 (see Tuchinsky et al., 1994).

The theory of relationships being discussed here has as its central construct identity rather than utility. Identity is not interdependence in the power/ex-change sense (see Greenhalgh, in press), but is a much broader concept. Whereas the economics-based model sees others as sources of (or barriers to) utility gain, the relationship-based model sees others as part of our definition of who we are. In marriages, the centrality of identity was until recently reflected in the wife's becoming "Mrs. John Doe." The title is no longer socially acceptable to many, but the joint identity is still the relationship in healthy marriages. In

──────── TABLE 8.1 ────────────────────────────────────
Empirical Dimensions of Relationships

Dimension	Positive Pole	Negative Pole
Scope	multidimensional	role-limited
Commonality	a lot in common	little in common
Alliance	allies	enemies
Trust	strong trust	distrust
Disclosure	open, vulnerable	reserved
Values	respect	disrespect
Stimulation	interesting	boring
Acceptance	unconditional	rejection
Control	autonomy	dominance
Exchange	rich, balanced	minimal, owing
Fondness	like	dislike
Attraction	find attractive	find repulsive
Dependency	self-sufficient	very needy
Competition	collaborating	competing
Empathy	empathic	nonempathic
Continuity	long-term	transactional

SOURCE: Greenhalgh and Chapman (1993).

other collectivities, individuals' strength of identity is reflected in the extent to which they experience a "sense of community" (see Clark & Mills, 1993).

In the second case presented above, Rolf and Vito experienced a sense of identity that made Vito's apparently self-defeating behavior (he voluntarily reduced his own net utility, without letting Rolf know he had done so) not only understandable but expected. In contrast, the sense of identity between Oxley and Sterling was either weak and superficial or perhaps even negative. The negative range of identity is encompassed by the notion of an out-group in the ethnocentric sense (see, e.g., Levine & Campbell, 1972): It appears that even though Sterling and Oxley saw each other as in-group members from the perspective of social class, they treated each other as out-group members in deciding on the terms of business arrangements, decisions they construed as episodic transactions.

These notions of relationship and the effect on negotiated outcomes are depicted in Figure 8.3. Joint decision making is triggered by some stimulus that focuses attention on the incompatibility of interests; this is the "occasion for decision making" that is perceivable by both parties. Economics-based theories assume that individuals experience the stimulus as an opportunity for utility gain. In using an alternative model to understand the social context of negotiation, we see the stimulus as generating a "definition of the situation." In virtually unidimensional, competing relationships, the focal indi-

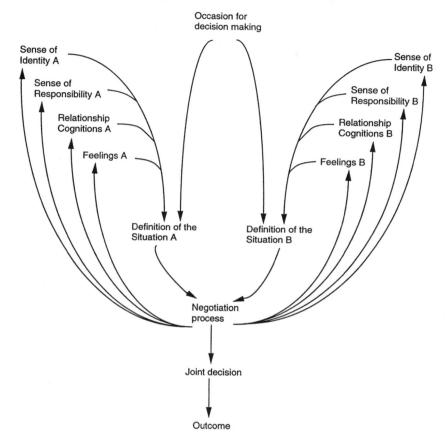

Figure 8.3. A Relationship-Based View of Joint Decision Making

vidual may, indeed, react to the stimulus simply as an opportunity for utility gain. In more typical, multidimensional relationships, however, we have found that the focal individual is likely to see the conflict as a strain in the ongoing relationship.

Each actor evolves a "definition of the situation" (which is equivalent to how the problem is "framed" in the broadest sense). The definition of the situation is shaped by the focal individual's degree of identification with the other party and sense of responsibility in the salient community. Responsibility may actually be a very broad sense of what one ought to do from a moral standpoint (see, e.g., Salem, 1994), or it may be individually focused, such as (in the extreme) a parent's responsibility for a family member (see Clark &

Mills, 1993). The salient community may be a dyad, a group, or a larger collectivity or network, depending on the particular individual's breadth of focus. As a result of this thought process, the focal individual will determine to what extent the current situation is viewed as "our problem" as contrasted with "my" or "your" problem."

Next (or simultaneously), the individual will factor in a set of cognitions concerning the various dimensions of the relationship (as shown in Table 8.1). For example, the individual may wonder, Can I trust this person? Is this person a strong ally who can be expected to be loyal? How will our significant others and friends react to various scenarios that might unfold in the negotiation? What do we have in common that will foster rapport, and perhaps lead to integrative solutions of the bridging variety? Is this person competing with me, perhaps subconsciously? Is this person going to approach the interaction from a power-up/power-down perspective? Do I want this person's acceptance of me? Is the interaction likely to be stimulating or boring? Do I feel indebted to this person? Is there sexual tension between us? Is this person being open about his or her "agenda"? Can (or, more important, does) this person see the situation from my perspective? Is this person focusing on the immediate opportunity or the long-term relationship? Added to these cognitions is the set of feelings the relationship and the situation generate; the result is a "definition of the situation."

To illustrate, in the first case above, Jane defined the situation as reluctantly but voluntarily taking care of a friend in need, and Larry defined it as an opportunity to strengthen an already deep relationship. (Larry is depicted as A in Figure 8.3, Rolf as B; Jane is so close to Larry that her definition of the situation might be depicted as "A prime.") Larry and Jane's definitions of the situation were different, but compatible, and grew into a synthesis as they discussed it further. Larry came to understand and feel the responsibility to take care of a friend in need, and Larry's friendship bonds with Rolf became important to Jane. Larry experienced anxiety, fondness for Rolf, mild resentment at being put in an anxiety-producing predicament, satisfaction that he was able to help Rolf, frustration that he had lost some control of the use of the excavator, gratitude toward Jane for helping him think through the ambivalence-producing situation, and annoyance that Jane was not letting him make the decision unilaterally. Rolf, meanwhile, had been going through a parallel process in defining the situation, except that he did not involve others in the process itself.

When the two parties interacted, there occurred an objective negotiation process, leading to a joint decision and a tangible outcome. Note that Figure 8.3 suggests that the impact on the relationship is a function of the negotiation *process* rather than the outcome. This is consistent with empirical investigation of the determinants of the future relationship (Greenhalgh & Chapman,

1993). That is, the future relationship depends more on how the individual was treated than on the utility gain (as economic theory and exchange theory would predict).

Implications for Future Research

The scenario to which the negotiators actually react is their definition of the situation, which is a product of the objective circumstances and the relationship as it is experienced consciously, subconsciously, and emotionally. The economics-based model imposes a definition of the situation and explores outcomes and, on occasion, process. Imposing the definition of the situation has the advantage of standardizing laboratory research, but carries with it the disadvantage of being unrepresentative of common experience. The paradigm cases we have studied involve strangers who are given minimal detail about their relationship (such as only whether they are potential buyers or sellers) and a payoff matrix that induces them to focus on the economic gain from the transaction. The participants know nothing of their history or future, except perhaps that they may have to interact in a future transaction if the research design calls for subjects to expect a repeated-trials experiment. This paradigm has produced a highly developed science of something that does not happen very often. Expanding the old paradigm to look at different definitions of the situation (e.g., a mixed-motive scenario) produces incremental gains in knowledge, but has little promise of moving the discipline forward very far or very fast (see Greenhalgh, in press).

Instead, we need to understand what produces the idiosyncratic definitions of the situation to which real people react in real situations, something we can call the "relationship context." In the early stages of this endeavor, we will have to rely on descriptive and clinical research rather than on laboratory studies. For our theoretical development we will have to do some heavy borrowing from outside the field of traditional negotiation research. The relevant literature is in the field of interpersonal relationships (see, e.g., Duck, 1988), gender differences (see, e.g., Greenhalgh & Gilkey, 1993), racial differences (see, e.g., Cox, Lobel, & McLeod, 1991), and cross-cultural differences (see, e.g., Hofstede, 1980; Salem, 1994). The reason for borrowing from these particular disciplines is that they take us beyond a study of the economic behavior of Western-socialized white males—the primary focus of the current negotiation paradigm (Gray, 1992; Greenhalgh & Gilkey, 1993)—and into the realm of greater awareness of the relationships between people in conflict.

The expanded paradigm will lead us to ask research questions that are quite different from the ones that have thus far dominated inquiry into negotiations. The future relationship is likely to be the most important outcome variable to research, not because of the risk of retaliation or the hope of utility gain in the next transaction, but because humans are social animals and therefore relationships—not economic gains—are the core of human existence. The process of negotiation is likely to eclipse outcomes as the modal independent variable. Studies of framing will expand in scope beyond the behavioral decision theory paradigm to encompass the negotiator's idiosyncratic definition of the situation. Personality theorists (and perhaps clinical psychologists) will investigate what leads some individuals to focus primarily on economic utility, ignoring other contextual and temporal considerations. Coalition theorists will try to understand the bonds that give subgroup members a sense of shared identity in the real world: Does the sense of cohesion arise from cognitions, emotions, unconscious dynamics, or some combination? What gives rise to the bonds? How is bondedness communicated in a conflict situation? Finally, negotiation researchers will devote less attention to the cognitive side of interactive decision making and more to emotions, impulses, negotiator ethics as a function of moral development, and retrospective sense making to provide economically rational explanations of their responses in relationships strained by conflict.

References

Bazerman, M. H., & Neale, M. H. (1992). *Negotiating rationally*. New York: Free Press.

Bergman, S. J. (1991). *Men's psychological development: A relational perspective* (Work in Progress No. 48). Wellesley, MA: Stone Center.

Clark, M. S., & Mills, J. (1993). The difference between communal and exchange relationships: What it is and is not. *Personality and Social Psychology Bulletin, 19*, 684-691.

Cox, T. H., Lobel, S. A., & McLeod, P. L. (1991). Effects of ethnic group cultural differences on cooperative and competitive behavior on a group task. *Academy of Management Journal, 34*, 827-847.

Duck, S. (Ed.). (1988). *Handbook of personal relationships*. New York: John Wiley.

Emerson, R. M. (1962). Power-dependence relations. *American Sociological Review, 27*, 31-41.

Gray, B. (1992). The gender-based foundations of negotiation theory. In B. H. Sheppard, R. J. Lewicki, & R. Bies (Eds.), *Research on negotiation in organizations* (Vol. 4). Greenwich, CT: JAI.

Greenhalgh, L. (1986). Managing conflict. *Sloan Management Review, 27*(4), 45-52.

Greenhalgh, L. (in press). Competition in a collaborative context: Toward a new paradigm. In R. J. Lewicki, B. H. Sheppard, & R. Bies (Eds.), *Research on negotiation in organizations* (Vol. 5). Hillsdale, NJ: Lawrence Erlbaum.

Greenhalgh, L., & Chapman, D. I. (1993). *The influence of negotiator relationships on the process and outcomes of business transactions* (Working paper). Hanover, NH: Dartmouth College, Amos Tuck School of Business Administration.

Greenhalgh, L., & Gilkey, R. W. (1993). The effects of relationship orientation on negotiators' cognitions and tactics. *Group Decision and Negotiation, 2*, 167-186.

Greenhalgh, L., & Gilkey, R. W. (1994). *Clinical assessment methods for the laboratory: The study of narcissism and negotiator effectiveness* (Working paper). Hanover, NH: Dartmouth College, Amos Tuck School of Business Administration.

Greenhalgh, L., & Kramer, R. M. (1990). Strategic choice in conflicts: The importance of relationships. In R. L. Kahn & M. N. Zald (Eds.), *Organizations and nation-states: New perspectives on conflict and cooperation.* San Francisco: Jossey-Bass.

Greenhalgh, L., Neslin, S. A., & Gilkey, R. W. (1985). The effects of negotiator preferences, situational power, and negotiator personality on outcomes of business negotiations. *Academy of Management Journal, 28,* 9-33.

Halpern, J. J. (1992). *The effect of friendship on bargaining: Experimental studies of personal business decisions.* Paper presented at the annual meeting of the Academy of Management.

Hofstede, G. (1980). *Culture's consequences: International differences in work-related values.* Beverly Hills, CA: Sage.

Levine, R. A., & Campbell, D. T. (1972). *Ethnocentrism: Theories of conflict, ethnic attitudes, and group behavior.* New York: John Wiley.

Loewenstein, G. F., Thompson, L. L., & Bazerman, M. H. (1989). Social utility and decision making in interpersonal contexts. *Journal of Personality and Social Psychology, 57,* 426-441.

Mannix, E. A. (1991). *Negotiation and dispute resolution in small groups: The effects of power, justice norms, and the anticipation of a future relationship* (Working Paper No. 76). Evanston, IL: Northwestern University, Dispute Resolution Research Center.

McClelland, D. C. (1961). *The achieving society.* New York: Van Nostrand Reinhold.

Nash, J. F. (1950). The bargaining problem. *Econometrica, 18,* 155-162.

Neale, M. A., & Bazerman, M. H. (1991). *Cognition and rationality in negotiation.* New York: Free Press.

Neslin, S. A., & Greenhalgh, L. (1983). Nash's theory of cooperative games as a predictor of the outcomes of buyer-seller negotiations. *Journal of Marketing Research, 20,* 368-379.

Northcraft, G. B., & Neale, M. A. (1991). *Negotiating successful research collaboration* (Working Paper No. 78). Evanston, IL: Northwestern University, Dispute Resolution Research Center.

Powers, W. T. (1973). *Behavior: The control of perception.* Chicago: Aldine.

Pruitt, D. H. (1981). *Negotiation behavior.* New York: Academic Press.

Salem, P. E. (1994). A critique of Western conflict resolution from a non-Western perspective. *Negotiation Journal, 4,* 361-370.

Sondak, H., & Moore, M. C. (1993). Relationship frames and cooperation. *Group Decision and Negotiation, 2,* 103-118.

Thompson, L. L., & DeHarpport, T. (1991). *Effects of relationship, task expectancy, and communal orientation on interpersonal conflict* (Working paper). Seattle: University of Washington, Department of Psychology.

Tuchinsky, M., Escalas, J. E., Moore, M. C., & Sheppard, B. H. (1994). *Beyond name, rank and function: Construal of relationships in business* (Working paper). Durham, NC: Duke University, Fuqua School of Business.

Valley, K. L. (1991). *Relationships and resources: A network exploration of allocation decisions* (Working paper). Evanston, IL: Northwestern University, Dispute Resolution Research Center.

Valley, K. L., & Neale, M. A. (1991). *The role of relationships in negotiations at work* (Working paper). Evanston, IL: Northwestern University, Dispute Resolution Research Center.

9

The Conflict-Competent Organization
A Research Agenda for
Emerging Organizational Challenges

ROBERT J. ROBINSON

The Notion of "Conflict Competence"

One of the most important issues scholars in a given field must address concerns the question, "is our knowledge cumulative?" That is, is there progress, or merely the discovery and rediscovery of certain principles, arguments by analogy, and subjectivism? To be sure, these are questions that those in any field should continually ask themselves, but when the subject matter is essentially human—as opposed to the physical—the questions become all the more important, because as our society changes, what was once "truth" (such as the inability of women to be anything but child rearers and housekeepers) becomes yesterday's prejudiced, ignorant, "unscientific" beliefs (Gergen, 1978).

Organizations parallel and reflect our changes as a society. They mirror our culture, our assumptions about the workings of things both material and metaphysical, and our models of economic and social exchange, and they embody the codes of behavior, both civil and criminal, to which a society subscribes. Thus many of the points of stress in organizations are the result of tensions without, in the greater society: the tension between the pursuit of wealth and the role of social conscience; the freedom to act as we wish versus obedience to a political system and agenda; the right to hire and fire versus rules of conduct and antidiscrimination legislation. None of this is strange, nor is any of it really to be avoided. However, if we accept that changes in the larger society create new challenges, and that these are reflected within organizations, then it seems logical that an understanding of the ways in which our society is changing will instruct managers and practitioners alike as to the future challenges and points of friction they can anticipate.

In this chapter I discuss some "traditional" research within the area of social cognition and conflict resolution. This individually oriented perspective can, I suggest, be profitably integrated into a larger consideration of the context within which organizations are operating. To this end, I present an early sketch of the outlines of several major trends that I believe are pertinent to the study of organizations, particularly from the orientation of understanding and anticipating various kinds of organizational conflicts. In a classic dialectical sense, each new trend not only carries within it the solutions to previous problems, but embodies the problems and challenges for the future. New challenges require new competencies; to the extent that some organizations are better able to anticipate future changes and develop the competencies necessary for dealing with them, they will be more successful than organizations that do not react adaptively (Beer, Eisenstadt, & Spector, 1990), or that attempt to apply old models of conflict competence to new problems, particularly those unique challenges that will become part of organizational life in the next century.

It is worth pausing at this point to note that conflict is nothing new to organizations; indeed, it has long been recognized that one of the major challenges facing the organization is how to avoid being torn apart by internal divisions and tensions (e.g., Lawrence & Lorsch, 1967). I am therefore not suggesting that we are necessarily about to see the unfolding of a new process or dynamic; rather, I am pointing out that an opportunity currently exists: If we can predict future challenges to organizations and attempt to visualize the sorts of conflicts that these new challenges will engender, as a field we can position ourselves to observe, describe, learn, and prescribe as organizations encounter the immediate future. The insights gleaned from the unfolding of this process will help us to anticipate the skills that will be required by the conflict-competent organization.

In this piece I also suggest that "negotiation" should be more broadly interpreted. We negotiate challenges and opportunities, not just deals (Lax & Sebenius, 1986). Although it is possible to imagine a narrow version of this chapter, in which each trend is addressed from the perspective of how it affects traditional negotiation between parties, what I want to argue here is that it is the *organization itself* that must negotiate the challenges ahead. We must arrive at a new understanding and vision of the nature of basic relationships among individuals, their organizations, and the larger economy and society, and it is the evolution of the skills, or competencies, needed to deal with this most macro of consensus exercises that is the thrust of this chapter.

To return to an earlier point, therefore, it is arguable that the field of organizational studies has shown signs of maturing as a discipline, not necessarily
solely because of the stability and generalizability of the theory it has produced, but because of its ability to anticipate changes in the environment it is
describing. I shall argue that we are at the point where it is possible to paint,
with broad strokes, the portrait of several major trends that are unfolding, and
that will transform the business environment from what it is to what it must
become. The ability to "see" the future is a major triumph for a field, and what
must follow is a concentrated effort to translate this vision into usable theory
that anticipates what will be and makes prescriptively useful assertions, rather
than merely reacts to what has transpired.

Social Psychological Mechanisms
of Conflict Escalation

In addition to getting a clearer picture of where organizations are heading,
let us briefly consider the contribution of some basic social psychological
research that has accumulated in recent years with respect to various mechanisms that inhibit negotiation and that can lead to escalation. Thus in seeking
an understanding of individual behavior, particularly in conflict-prone situations, we have seen the development of a series of theoretical constructs such
as the "fundamental attribution error," a particular cognitive tendency to
favor dispositional explanations over situational ones (Ross, Greene, & House,
1977; see also Nisbett & Ross, 1980; Ross, Bierbrauer, & Hoffman, 1976; Ross
& Nisbett, 1991). This kind of phenomenon can have profound behavioral
implications. For instance, Kelley and Stahelski (1970) have shown how, in the
Prisoner's Dilemma game, a competitive player can perceive a cooper- ative
opponent to be competitive. In cases where there are clearly defined in- and
out-groups, these tendencies appear even more extreme, in the form of the
so-called ultimate attribution error (Pettigrew, 1979), which predicts that
favorable actions of in-group members will be explained by dispositional
attributions and unfavorable actions will be attributed to external forces,
whereas the reverse will be true regarding the actions of out-group members.

Scholars have long recognized the central role of misperception in social
conflict (Asch, 1951; Schelling, 1960; White, 1977). Beliefs that enemies act as
they do because of dispositional factors, that enemies are extreme and unreasonable, greatly impede the possibility of positive outcomes and conflict
resolution. Stillinger, Epelbaum, Keltner, and Ross (1994) have demonstrated
how any concessions offered by the "other side" may be "reactively devalued,"
and how their motives in offering the concessions are seen as questionable.

In an ongoing line of research, my colleagues and I have examined the views of partisans to the disputes over abortion, capital punishment, racial discrimination, and multicultural education (Keltner & Robinson, 1993; Robinson & Keltner, 1994; Robinson, Keltner, Ward, & Ross, in press). In these studies, partisans offered their own views of issues central to a given dispute and estimated the views of "typical" or "average" members of the opposition. We documented two typical kinds of misperceptions (or "misconstruals"): First, whereas *actual* disagreement was limited to certain issues within the topic under debate, opposing partisans assumed that their differences permeated all aspects of the question; second, partisans imputed ideological extremity and bias to members of the opposition, who in reality (based on data collected from both sides) were typically more moderate than their opponents imagined. This tendency to dismiss the beliefs of others as subjective and biased, and to hold firmly to the conviction that only our own views are founded in reason, principle, and evidence, whereas the other side is extreme, willful, wicked, and immoral, is referred to as "naive realism" (Bar-Tal & Geva, 1986; Brewer, 1979; Levine & Campbell, 1972; Sumner, 1906).

The assumption of diametric differences and extremist opposition creates specific problems in face-to-face negotiation. Negotiators who assume complete disagreement with their counterparts fail to recognize the possible and likely areas of agreement between the parties. Furthermore, negotiators who assume their counterparts are extremist are less likely to understand the other side's actual views or to incorporate those views in integrative solutions—actions critical to reaching substantive agreement (Fisher & Ury, 1981; Kelman & Cohen, 1986; Selman, 1980; Susskind & Cruikshank, 1987). This phenomenon engenders mutual views that emphasize blame and hostility, and thus increase conflict (Deutsch, 1973; Jervis, 1976; Kelley & Stahelski, 1970; Pruitt & Rubin, 1986). Specifically, negotiators who assume their opposition is extremist and biased have a salient attribution to explain their negotiation difficulties: the other side's unwavering extremism and ideological bias.

These findings challenge both the premise and prescription, so central to analyses of conflict resolution, that successful negotiations depend upon opposing partisans' accurate, mutual understanding (e.g., Fisher & Ury, 1981; Kelman & Cohen, 1986; Pruitt & Rubin, 1986; Selman, 1980; Susskind & Cruikshank, 1987). Instead, our research illustrates a persistent pattern of exaggeration and misperception (see Figure 9.1). Thus any attempt to develop competencies to deal with conflicts that are likely to emerge in organizations in the future are also going to have to be cognizant of, and to find ways to deal with, the kinds of psychological phenomena that can lead to the escalation, rather than the resolution, of conflict.

Up until now, there have been relatively few attempts to unite these individual-level theories with larger organizational questions. This chapter is

Actual
construals:

Circles'
perceptions:

Triangles'
perceptions:

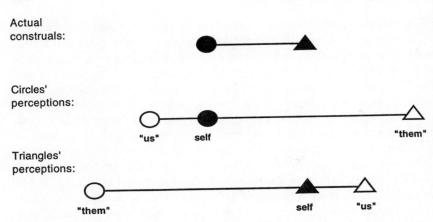

Figure 9.1. Typical Pattern of Exaggerated Construal Between Partisans

conceived of as an early attempt in this regard, with respect to at least asking (if not necessarily answering) what such an approach may offer to an analysis of organizational conflict. With regard to the sorts of phenomena outlined above, I am suggesting that organizations have to learn to deal with human bias and cognitive shortcomings (bounded rationality) in their individual employees; and they will have to discover how to avoid engaging in the collective/organizational analogue of the individual-level phenomena described above.

Five Major Trends

I wish to turn now to a discussion of five specific changes identifiable by our present state of knowledge. These changes are going to require new conflict competencies from organizations in the future; if not addressed, they will gradually paralyze organizational effectiveness. In addition to these five major trends, to be discussed in greater length below, there are several other trends that are still emergent or poorly understood at this time. What is remarkable is how intertwined the five discussed below already are, and how they are interacting with one another to produce powerful effects on the organizational landscape, beyond the simple expectations we might have of any one, or even beyond the predictions of some of the authors who first wrote about them. Indeed, it is not the case that I am necessarily documenting new intellectual discoveries; all of the trends discussed in this chapter are represented in existing (and sometimes extensive) literature, which is what makes them of obvious importance. Rather, I wish to build on the contribution of these other authors in two major ways. First, I want to consider specifically the implications of these trends for increasing conflict in organizations, and therefore what kinds of competencies must be developed (including negotiation skills) to manage these new conflicts. Second, these various trends are frequently discussed in completely separate literatures that fit onto different points on the "macro-micro" continuum that divides up the field of organizational studies. My hope is to demonstrate how these major forces, with complete disregard for the arbitrary academic distinctions, are acting, and interacting, to produce profound new challenges to managers, organizations, and academicians alike. I also intend to reflect briefly on each point from the perspective of some of the lessons available from the kinds of individual-level social cognition phenomena described above, which may in fact lead to the exacerbation rather than the abatement of the sorts of organizational conflicts we can expect to see in the future. I will address the interactions of these various trends briefly after discussing each trend separately. The major trends discussed below are the emergence of new political and social agendas in the workplace, the increasing diversity of the workforce, the growing role of information technology, the move away from traditional hierarchical bureaucracies, and the globalization of the world economy and markets.

Emergence of New Social and
Political Agendas in the Workplace

One of the most interesting and, to this point, underexplored recent trends in organizations has been the intrusion of various social and political questions into the workplace. Not only are employees of various companies frequently pressured by fellow employees to wear AIDS awareness ribbons, or to recycle, or to bring their daughters to work, or to boycott various products, or to sign petitions for various political causes, but organizations themselves are entering into the fray, declaring positions on issues from the environment to the abortion debate. Additionally, organizations are being confronted with demands from their employees regarding issues that would not have been regarded as legitimate workplace questions a decade or so ago. Questions of maternity leave, or day care for employees' children, or a company's environmental policies have become legitimate topics of discussion between organizations and their workers. Other issues, such as company benefits policy toward same-sex or unmarried partners, are on the threshold of becoming discussible by companies. Thus the question of what constitutes acceptable workplace issues, open for negotiation, changes constantly—partially as a function of changing and evolving attitudes and politics in the larger society. Further, as the number of issues, and therefore constituencies, multiplies, so does the complexity of dealing with any given group without somehow offending or alienating others.

This social phenomenon, although fascinating to the social scientist, would not legitimately belong to this list of major trends were it not for the fact that other factors are contributing to making this a particularly volatile time for the role of political issues in organizations. After all, issues of controversy have always leaked into the firm, even when the receptivity to external employee concerns was far lower than it is today. What is different about today is that there is an emerging ethos of intolerance around controversial issues in our society. In my own research, I have documented this tendency of extreme reaction toward individuals with views that differ from our own (see, e.g., Keltner & Robinson, 1993; Robinson et al., in press). Additionally, individuals are arriving in organizations "preoffended," or primed to take offense at perceived instances of discrimination, sexism, or other inequities.

The source of this hypersensitivity, or preoffense, and antagonism toward dissenting perspectives is a complicated story, interwoven with the issues considered further in the following subsection: Gains by women and minorities in various arenas have led to a "backlash" from the groups most threatened by such gains; "political correctness" has become a club with which to punish perceived offenders; there is once again a questioning of formal authority structures, but this time it is not based, as was the case in the 1960s, on pseudo-Marxist notions of property, the military-industrial complex, and control of production and information, but on the premise that institutions formed and maintained by "Eurocentric" white males are inherently suspect and manifestly discriminatory toward nonmembers of the power elite, specifically, women and minorities; and, most recently, a difficult economic climate has intensified the competition for resources as well as the attendant debate over the equity with which such resources are allocated (Hughes, 1993). These factors have led, for reasons that are probably still not well understood by social theorists, to debate's becoming a threatened activity. The First Amendment no longer seems to be a compelling standard in deciding whether or not someone "should" say or think certain things. Instead, there are any number of hot-button issues around which civilized debate is frequently impossible. Rather, a certain inarticulate rage surrounds these issues, so that merely raising a question can be tantamount to opening oneself up to virulent and personal attack. Such issues include abortion, capital punishment, affirmative action, rape, child molestation, pornography, legalization of drugs, homosexuality, and broad categories of religious preference.

What we can understand, with our knowledge of human reactions to divisive ideological issues, is that with ideologies and deeply held beliefs come very strong emotions and unwillingness to compromise. As such issues work their way into organizations, compromise becomes unacceptable to all sides. To partisans on both sides, deciding whether or not an organization should extend benefits usually reserved for employees' legal spouses to homosexual employees' same-sex partners is *not* like a budget negotiation, where each side can give a little and get a little. Ideological debates go beyond whatever the current debate might be to abstract questions of identity, religion, and morality. These are conflicts over *belief*, not profit. As such, they represent profound challenges to the organization's ability to deal with, let alone resolve, such issues.

Companies need to rebuild trust in their authority and reestablish a covenant with their workers. If they do not develop the competencies to do these things, they will suffer the death of a thousand cuts, as each minor disagreement and dispute, instead of being negotiated satisfactorily, will become inflamed within a framework of larger social and political grievances. In this sense, a key requirement for organizations in the future is going to be the competence to figure out how to deal with the diversity of opinion that exists among members of the workforce and that mirrors various contentious social issues. Tolerance for differences of outlook, rather than traditional consensus building, may well be the approach for the future, with managers seeking ways to get employees to agree to disagree peaceably on certain issues. Providing rules and principles to guide this process is likely to be a growth industry (for discussion of dealing with and explaining negative events when various group interests are involved, see Friedman & Robinson, 1993; Robinson & Friedman, 1994).

Increasing Diversity of the Workforce

In some ways, the issue of diversity of the workforce is the most salient, and complete, example of the sort of social-political issue being played out in the workplace. Increasing workplace diversity brings with it a host of new conflicts and management problems. Much of traditional management theory is based on a post-World War II model of fairly rigid, formal authority. Today, this model is no longer appropriate. Thus the development of a vast literature on the integration of women and various minority groups into the workforce, and the accompanying challenges for organizations, has led to the concept of "managing diversity," a major new area of research, writing, and debate (e.g., Alderfer, 1982; Cox, Lobel, & McLeod, 1991; Ibarra, 1992; Jackson & Alvarez, 1992; Nkomo, 1992; Thomas, 1993). Various laws have been enacted that are intended to ensure fairness to all in the workplace, and huge federal and state bureaucracies devote many resources to this end. There have been a number of contentious issues in recent years: affirmative action, maternity leave, reverse discrimination, various religious and ethnic rights. Yet for all the publicity, effort, and money devoted to workplace fairness and nondiscrimination, companies' successes in achieving their stated goals have been mixed at best. Much of this problem arises from the fact that as a society, we are still struggling with the notion of diversity, especially in organizations. Most models of management assume reasonably homogeneous work groups to be managed, with normally distributed attributes such as skills, motivation, and education. The basic managerial schema for an employee involves a traditionally educated white male wearing a tie, who is going to follow one of the well-trodden organizational career paths. There is no existing schema for the woman employee who has children, leaves the workforce for some period to be a full-time mother, and returns in her late 30s to resume a career. We don't really know how to treat minorities who have not had traditional educational experiences, or physically challenged individuals who cannot run to get a cab, or homosexual employees who would like to be able to bring their partners to the company picnic.

It is not my intention to enter into the debate over affirmative action, quotas, or statistical representation versus free market forces—or, for that matter, any of the other contentious debates that continue. Instead, I wish to make the rather general observation that most companies, regardless of their diversity objectives, are rather bad at managing the process whereby they go about achieving these goals. Should this statement appear to be merely a vaguely negative finger-waggle, let me be more forceful: We are currently observing a huge transfer of wealth in the United States, away from organizations and their stockholders and into the hands of lawyers whose task it is either to prosecute or to defend organizations in what are literally hundreds of thousands of discrimination lawsuits in progress across the country every year. Some of these cases, such as the recent one involving the Denny's restaurant chain, result in settlements or judgments in the tens of millions of dollars.

An example here may be useful; the following is based loosely on several recent reports in national newspapers. A large manufacturing company decides to implement an affirmative action program to increase the percentages of women and minorities in the organization's upper echelons. The company needs a basis on which to make the necessary accelerated promotions, but, unfortunately, the existing performance appraisal system is, if anything, an impediment to this goal. In fact, the existing system is already the basis for several lawsuits by minorities, who claim it is "culturally biased," and is also under attack by women in the company. The firm scraps the performance appraisal system and introduces a more subjective set of criteria, which allows for the possibility of a "cultural diversity audit." The first thing that happens is that several young women and minority members are promoted over more senior white men. The second thing that happens is that the company is sued for reverse discrimination by these same senior white males. Now the company faces two sets of lawsuits, both of which assert that its promotional practices are unfair. In the meantime, the company atmosphere has been poisoned, the employees are at each others' throats (mostly along ethnic and gender group lines), and talented individuals are leaving for positions where they will be "evaluated on their own merits."

The above illustrates what can happen when an organization fails to negotiate the question of diversity or approaches it in a naive way. Even in organizations where there are no pending lawsuits to worry about, most management tactics involve defensive, cover-the-rear tactics, rather than capitalize on the immense potential inherent in a multitalented and diverse workforce. In the immediate future (just as in the immediate past), vast sums of money and energy will continue to be expended by organizations, both inside of and outside the courtroom, as payment for their inability to develop the necessary competencies to deal with, and address profitably, issues of diversity. Subjects such as sexual harassment, racial discrimination, and affirmative action, and the ever-increasing litigation around them, create a powder keg that needs to be watched and constantly defused.

One area of established knowledge that has potential contributions to make to the dynamics of managing diversity is the intergroup literature, particularly with regard to in-group/out-group phenomena. We know quite a lot, for example, about how stereotypes are formed and about how to promote cooperation among groups (e.g., Allport, 1954; Hackman, 1990). Allport's "contact hypothesis" suggests that we need circumstances in which there is great situational support for cooperation, where the members of various groups are of roughly equal status, and where highly desirable superordinate goals cannot be achieved without the close cooperation of all parties. We should be looking with great interest for organizational models of companies that have succeeded in this most difficult of arenas, and should seek to catalog and understand the skills and techniques they are evolving to negotiate these questions.

The Growing Role of Information Technology

Consider the following scenario, circa 1950. A letter, mailed two weeks previously, arrives on a manager's desk from a client in Europe. It contains various questions and proposed modifications to an agreement reached, at great expense, during the manager's visit to the Continent some two months previously. Upon reading it, the manager (in the 1950s, definitely a man) flies into a rage, stomps up and down the office, throws an in-tray, and generally has a tantrum. Then, upon calming down, the manager dictates a letter and edits it several times as his secretary brings successive drafts to him for approval. About two weeks later, the manager's letter arrives on the desk of the European counterpart. "Dear M," it begins, "Thank you for your thoughtful comments. I have given them a great deal of consideration, and believe I may have found a way to accommodate your wishes while staying within the framework of the original deal."

Now consider the following scenario, set in the immediate future. A fax arrives on a manager's desk. "The proposed contract modifications are most urgent," reads the message. "Please respond by the end of the day, or a another supplier will be engaged." With no time to fax back, the manager punches up a video link. "What the #@!$* is this all about?" the manager shouts. Annoyed and embarrassed, the client shouts back. The manager heatedly replies—and so on.

This little vignette illustrates just one of the effects of information technology on the way business is conducted. Now, it is true that this interaction could have gone just the other way. Our resolute manager could have saved a deal, thanks to real-time access, that would have failed in the 1950s because of time constraints. The point is simply that information technology continues to transform many aspects of business interactions, and, for the most part, organizations traditionally spend little time considering the potential problems these almost miraculous new technologies might bring, along with all their undoubted benefits.

More generally, there is currently much hullabaloo over the so-called information superhighway, which is supposed to transform how communication, business, and even social interactions will occur, thanks to the role of information technology and the relatively "thicker" information flow and interaction age of which we will all increasingly become a part (Gerstein, 1987; Zuboff, 1988). Whether the superhighway turns out to be just that or an overheated political metaphor, one thing is clear: As a society we have finally reached the point where advanced information technology is a normal medium for doing business, rather than a curiosity. Fax technology, e-mail, computer networking, mobile/cellular phones, teleconferencing, and so on have become business staples, and soon-to-be available technologies such as virtual reality will surely join the fray in short order.

To be sure, information technology brings with it many day-to-day operational dilemmas and conflicts for the organization. What technology to invest in? What software to train workers with? Who gets to take part in the high-tech training courses, which are now part of the perceived fast track for employees? What about workers who want computers on their desks? At the organization where I work, the Harvard Business School, it has been enormously difficult to define a policy that addresses the needs of younger, computer-literate faculty members yet still keeps an eye on financial constraints and also makes sure that older professors don't feel "left out." As a senior colleague once told me, the computer issue is "the single most divisive issue" that has to be dealt with on a daily basis. This same dynamic continues to unfold in various forms in organizations across the United States.

The extent to which we are going to be able to capitalize on the opportunities offered by technological advances will depend, in large degree, on our ability to manage the conflicts inherent in their introduction. In addition to familiar basic questions of human capacity (for example, as a teacher, do I *really* want my students to be able to e-mail me at any time?), there are other issues to be dealt with. Does the notion of a "corporate headquarters" have a role anymore if people will soon (in some cases, already can) do all their work from remote locations? How are these telecommuters to be treated by the organization? What career paths exist for them? This question is particularly relevant when we consider the diversity of the workforce and the needs of various individuals, such as parents with small children and people with physical disabilities. Why should R&D labs be built in specific locations if "virtual" labs can be built and experts from around the world can assemble in "cyberspace" for the workday? Does the concept of an eight-hour workday have any meaning anymore?

These questions, as well as thousands more not asked here, represent profound challenges to organizational unity and identity, although some still believe they smack of science fiction. However, as the January 1994 earthquake in Southern California showed, companies set up for telecommuting options are able to get back on their feet, and to protect core activities, much faster after such a setback than are old-style brick-and-plaster corporations. Understanding what information technology is doing to the way we do business is a critical competency for organizations to acquire. To return to the metaphor of the day, if these companies fail, they will find themselves in a technological cul-de-sac while their competition thunders past on the information superhighway.

The Move Away From Traditional Hierarchy

Much has been made in recent years of the postindustrial, or late-capitalist, organizational form (Handy, 1990; Kanter, 1989). There is also much debate over whether or not such a creature exists outside of the imagination of theorists. What is clear is that the old-style, large, stable bureaucracy is being replaced by organizations that, although not necessarily any smaller than the old behemoths, are more flexible and adaptive. This is partially the result of a more volatile environment. As Kotter (1994), among others, has shown, the business environment changed radically in the late 1970s, when the great oil price shock was the first signal of a series of rapid changes that old-style hierarchical organizations—the Xeroxes, the General Motorses, the U.S. Steels—were ill equipped to roll with. Traditional bureaucracy functions by having rules to guide operations; the usual environment is well described by these rules. Sudden changes are not easily dealt with, and they require new rules that may well be superseded by yet more changes. To be sure, factors such as globalization and changes in the nature and pace of technological development have contributed to this shift, the effect being a series of changes that have resulted in new sources of conflict and new challenges to be negotiated.

Weber himself noted that one of the important functions of bureaucracies is to reduce conflict by having clear, impartial rules for all members of the organization. But increasingly, systems of formally designated responsibility and authority are being replaced by project teams, temporary work groups, and one-off activities. As organizations become flatter, more permeable, more "virtual," resources must increasingly be negotiated for, project teams become more ephemeral, everything becomes less routine, and the potential for conflict, and therefore the necessity for negotiated outcomes, becomes more pronounced.

As the amount of negotiation required in a traditional rule-based bureau-cratic organization increases, it becomes increasingly important that the organization become competent at managing, and institutionalizing, the negotiation process and other necessary conflict resolution techniques. Questions that would never have arisen under an old-style bureaucracy become critical: How is credit to be assigned? Who has what responsibilities? What is the remunera-tion profile of the group to be? What responsibility do other departments have to a project team? As important as these questions are, even more profound ones are becoming apparent as this process continues to unfold. These ques-tion would scarcely have been conceivable 25 years ago. Where does the organi-zation begin and end? When does someone cease to be an employee and become a private contractor? If no division owes allegiance to the rest of the organization, if supplies can be obtained from outside at a lower price, what is the purpose of a corporate identity?

From the perspective of organizational identity as it is currently under-stood, these questions represent perhaps the most fundamental kind of threat. Even the "newer" big corporations, such as Microsoft, Nike, or United Parcel Service, must involve themselves with negotiating these questions as actively as must the older, less-flexible giants. If organizations do not acquire the competencies necessary to evolve into new forms that can scarcely be imag-ined at this point, they, like the dinosaurs, will vanish from the earth. Certainly, at a minimum, a key competency is going to be the organization's ability to reconceptualize itself in terms other than a classic geographically centered, pyramidal corporation. The way this new vision is created, shared, and imple-mented will require renegotiating the values and assumptions that make up the corporate identity and the culture within which it is embedded.

Globalization of the World Economy

One can barely pick up a business publication today, or turn to a television segment on the economy, without seeing a report on some aspect of the increasingly global market. GATT, NAFTA, the European Economic Union, the emerging Eastern European and ex-Soviet economies, the "little dragons" of the Pacific Rim, the burgeoning economies of South America, and the anticipation over China are all stories that represent the incredible interconnectedness of markets and, therefore, the environment in which organizations must operate (Kanter, 1991). In a sense, everyone is becoming a global player, since even a little local firm must compete against foreign imports. It does not matter whether you make computer chips for the world or kitchen cabinets for the local market in Dayton, Ohio—you are a global player. For the cabinetmaker, cheap developing-nation labor may be as much a threat to economic survival as high-tech labs in Paris or Tokyo may be to Motorola.

Within this new global economy, old, long-standing relationships with a small number of stable clients or suppliers are soon likely to belong to the realm of nostalgia. Products and parts are bought from wherever they are cheapest, and output goes to wherever the money is. If the move toward larger and larger markets and lower barriers and tariffs continues, this trend can only become more pronounced. From a negotiation context, the implication is one of new partnerships and alliances being formed, new distribution networks that must be negotiated. Foreign cultures, foreign customs, tariffs, and so on must be addressed. This multiplication of new interfaces provide surfaces for friction and conflict that will require careful management.

The kinds of skills that globalization is going to require of organizations in the immediate future are myriad. In addition to understanding basic logistical questions of how to negotiate different legal, economic, and bureaucratic systems in various countries, U.S. organizations must realize that the basic assumptions of business in the United States are in fact simply specific cultural manifestations (Hofstede, 1980). At a recent conference on venture capital, for instance, one participant explained how in Poland, great confusion still exists over the role of capital and its rights. Once investors get their contributions back, there is no assumption that they should be entitled to continue to receive dividends; indeed, taking such profits is often seen as "theft." Organizations that make a profit are often subject to harassment by the police, and executives may be jailed on suspicion of some sort of illegal activity if they make too much money. Clearly, there is a need for a set of macro competencies in understanding other countries' histories and their social, political, economic, and legal systems.

There are also many necessary micro competencies, often traditionally thought of as "cultural" smarts, such as knowing not to enter a home in certain Asian countries with one's shoes on, or not to talk business over dinner, or to drink a lot of vodka in Eastern Europe in order to cement a deal. Although these examples are interesting and salient manifestations of cultural differences, by far the most important issues in global negotiations involve questions that simply do not exist in internal U.S. transactions: What currency is the deal in? What if the exchange rates change? What if next month's elections bring a group with a different political philosophy to power? All of these questions stem from a situation where business is unlikely to be routine, and special contingencies and clauses will influence how things are done: The custom-made contract will increasingly be the norm, and thus not only will contracts become much more a question of negotiation than of bureaucracy, but the conflict-competent organization will build in specific conflict resolution possibilities for when the inevitable problems and disagreements arise. What if A happens? What if B? What if this "class" of problem arises? Who decides? What process will be followed that, before the situation actually arises, is seen by each party as "fair," given the particular circumstances?

The Japanese have a saying that "problems are opportunities in working clothes." Perhaps globalization, so often heralded as a great opportunity for business, is an area where shabbily clad problems have not been given their due. There are new challenges to be faced, and new competencies to be acquired, before organizations hoping to exploit global opportunities will find their dreams being realized rather than frustrated.

Interactions Among the Major Trends

In choosing certain issues to discuss in this chapter, I have clearly had to neglect many others that may emerge in organizations in the future and that may be equally as relevant to an understanding of conflict management and negotiation skills. One such area might be macropolitical changes. Taking a snapshot of the world in early 1995, we see terrible conflicts in the former Yugoslavia and in Rwanda, instability and danger in the former Soviet Union and North Korea, and great signs of hope in the Middle East and South Africa. Organizations are going to have to learn to deal with conflicts that may be far bigger than they are and beyond their ability to address directly; they will face challenges and danger as they traverse the bumpy road of the "new world order."

However, even if we restrict ourselves to the five major trends discussed in this chapter—the emergence of various social and political questions in the workplace, the increasing diversity of the workforce, the growing role of information technology, the move away from traditional hierarchical bureaucracies, and the globalization of the economy—we can see the enormous potential for interaction in both predictable and unpredictable directions. We can thus anticipate, for example, that it is members of "nontraditional" employee groups (women, minorities) who will be more concerned with issues of justice and equity principles in organizations in the future. In the same way, we can imagine that information technology will offer both opportunities and challenges for the parent who wants to stay home to look after children and still have telecommuting options. Similarly, global project teams will be made possible both by the more permeable organization and by the technology that allows them to meet "virtually" without degradation of interactional quality.

We must also return to a point made earlier: As people of diverse beliefs and backgrounds enter organizations, how are the basic psychological traps of attribution error, stereotyping, and polarization to be avoided? Will cultural and global heterogeneity lead to an upsurge of destructive in-group/out-group attitudes and behaviors? What additional insights does basic psychological research have to offer with regard to the sorts of challenges and problems organizations are going to face in the future?

Less obvious than the examples given above are the impacts of trends that are still difficult for us to imagine here in the twilight of the twentieth century. What new social debates will emerge to transform the nature of workplace interaction? How will global markets change the approach of organizations to the question of diversity? (One suspects that diversity programs may, unless managed very competently, become an increasingly expensive luxury for U.S. firms.) Will information technology accelerate the pace of corporate fragmentation or provide a new model of structure that we are still groping for? We do not know the answers to these questions yet. What is clear is that organizations must attempt not only to consider specific problems, but to develop means to update their competencies continually in the face of unrelenting change and challenge.

Moving Forward: A Research Agenda for the Future

The reader will have noted that I have raised various warnings and have asked a lot more questions than I have offered specific solutions with regard to organizations' need to develop various competencies if they are to survive the challenges defined here. Indeed, this chapter is largely conceived as a call for a new research agenda that addresses the identification and understanding of exactly what skills are currently being developed by organizations to deal with these questions. The prescriptive lessons obtained by studying these organizations in the future will be at least as important as any abstract theorizing done here.

However, even if it is not possible at this time to describe definitively the kinds of solutions that organizations are going to produce or the specific competencies they will be developing, it is possible to imagine the kinds of processes in which organizations will need to engage in their search for new competencies. One can imagine that all the challenges described in this chapter will require, as a beginning point, an efficient means of achieving a shared vision of the future and of building agreement about the best solutions, and the means by which these will be pursued. Although this is a literature well described by leadership theorists (e.g., Kotter, 1982), the field of negotiation has much to offer in describing the ways in which the agendas of various parties in the organization can be accounted for, and how an integrative agreement that is good for the organization can be arrived at without undue defensiveness or protection of turf or local interests. In the same way, the social psychological literature offers suggestions and warnings as to the potentials and pitfalls of dealing with human decision making under uncertainty and the effects of interindividual and intergroup perceptions.

In terms of future research, I am proposing that researchers identify and examine organizations that are doing particularly good jobs of managing one or more of the trends discussed in this chapter. These organizations should be compared with others that are perhaps not doing as well within specific domains. I would also suggest a careful consideration of the tangible bottom-line implications of having (or not having) these competencies in terms of traditional performance indices such as profitability, growth, market share, and stock price. My hope is that a prescriptive analysis of what organizations need to do to become conflict competent in the future will emerge from such analyses, as well an understanding of the consequences of not possessing such competencies.

Another challenge facing the researcher is to go from fairly well described, experimentally driven phenomena such as the ultimate attribution error and naive realism, and apply them to the sorts of collective organizational challenges described here. An understanding of "micro" psychological processes and "macro" organizational issues (such as organizational defensiveness [Argyris, 1990] and organizational learning [e.g., Argyris, 1990; Senge, 1990]) and social trends such as the ones discussed in this chapter will be necessary for this effort to be successful. Such an exercise may well also serve to unite various schools of analysis that deal with the same kinds of phenomena (conflict, misperception, miscommunication, dispute resolution, negotiation, and the like), but that, up until to now, have had little success at communicating with one another.

To conclude, there are many diverse challenges facing the organizations of tomorrow, but these challenges have one thing in common: They will increase the potential for conflict in organizations (Greenhalgh, 1986; Kolb & Putnam, 1992; Tjosvold, 1991). Perhaps it is time for the area of negotiation and conflict resolution to mature further, using the opportunity afforded by these new challenges to observe, describe, and address these emergent trends, to work toward an understanding of the new skills or competencies being acquired by organizations. Perhaps even more important than *what* solutions are arrived at is the process of *how* organizations become competent in negotiating the challenges ahead.

References

Alderfer, C. P. (1982). Problems of changing white males' behavior and beliefs concerning race relations. In P. S. Goodman & Associates (Eds.), *Change in organizations: New perspectives on theory, research and practice* (pp. 122-165). San Francisco: Jossey-Bass.

Allport, G. W. (1954). *The nature of prejudice.* Reading, MA: Addison-Wesley.

Argyris, C. (1990). *Overcoming organizational defenses.* Boston: Allyn & Bacon.

Asch, S. E. (1951). Effects of group pressure upon the modification and distortion of judgment. In H. Guetzkow (Ed.), *Groups, leadership, and men* (pp. 177-190). Pittsburgh: Carnegie.

Bar-Tal, D., & Geva, N. (1986). A cognitive basis of international conflicts. In S. Worchel & W. G. Austin (Eds.), *Psychology of intergroup relations* (pp. 118-133). Chicago: Nelson-Hall.

Beer, M., Eisenstadt, R. M., & Spector, B. (1990, November-December). Why change programs don't produce change. *Harvard Business Review,* p. 158.

Brewer, M. B. (1979). In-group bias in the minimal intergroup situation: A cognitive-motivational analysis. *Psychological Bulletin, 86,* 307-324.

Cox, T. H., Lobel, S. A., & McLeod, P. L. (1991). Effects of ethnic group cultural differences on cooperative and competitive behavior on a group task. *Academy of Management Journal, 34,* 827-847.

Deutsch, M. (1973). *The resolution of conflict.* New Haven, CT: Yale University Press.

Fisher, R., & Ury, W. (1981). *Getting to yes: Negotiating agreement without giving in.* Boston: Houghton Mifflin.

Friedman, R. A., & Robinson, R. J. (1993). Justice for all? Union versus management response to unjust acts and social accounts. *International Journal of Conflict Management, 4,* 99-117.

Gergen, K. (1978). Toward generative theory. *Journal of Personality and Social Psychology, 36,* 1344-1360.

Gerstein, M. S. (1987). *The technology connection: Strategy and change in the information age.* Reading, MA: Addison-Wesley.

Greenhalgh, L. (1986). Managing conflict. *Sloan Management Review, 27,* 45-52.

Hackman, J. R. (Ed.). (1990). *Groups that work (and those that don't).* San Francisco: Jossey-Bass.

Handy, C. (1990). *The age of unreason.* Boston: Harvard Business School Press.

Hofstede, G. (1980). *Culture's consequences: International difference in work-related values.* Beverly Hills, CA: Sage.

Hughes, R. (1993). *Culture of complaint: The fraying of America.* New York: Oxford University Press.

Ibarra, H. (1992). Homophily and differential returns: Sex differences in network structure and access in an advertising firm. *Administrative Science Quarterly, 37,* 422-447.

Jackson, S. E., & Alvarez, E. B. (1992). Working through diversity as a strategic imperative. In S. E. Jackson & Associates (Eds.), *Diversity in the workplace: Human resources initiatives* (pp. 13-29). New York: Guilford.

Jervis, R. (1976). *Perception and misperception in international politics.* Princeton, NJ: Princeton University Press.

Kanter, R. M. (1989). *When giants learn to dance.* New York: Simon & Schuster.

Kanter, R. M. (1991, May-June). Transcending business boundaries: 12,000 world managers view change. *Harvard Business Review,* pp. 151-164.

Kelley, H: H., & Stahelski, A. J. (1970). Social interaction basis of cooperators' and competitors' beliefs about others. *Journal of Personality and Social Psychology, 16,* 66-91.

Kelman, H. C., & Cohen, S. P. (1986). Resolution of international conflict: An interactional approach. In S. Worchel & W. G. Austin (Eds.), *Psychology of intergroup relations.* Chicago: Nelson-Hall.

Keltner, D., & Robinson, R. J. (1993). The influence of disclosure on misconstrual in negotiations: An investigation of conflict escalation and resolution. *International Journal of Conflict Management, 4,* 249-262.

Kolb, D. M., & Putnam, L. L. (1992). The multiple faces of conflict in organizations. *Journal of Organizational Behavior, 13,* 311-324.

Kotter, J. (1982). *The general managers.* New York: Free Press.

Kotter, J. (1994). *Success.* New York: Free Press.

Lawrence, P. R., & Lorsch, J. (1967). *Organization and environment.* Boston: Harvard Business School Press.

Lax, D. A., & Sebenius, J. K. (1986). *The manager as negotiator.* New York: Free Press.

Levine, R. A., & Campbell, D. T. (1972). *Ethnocentrism: Theories of conflict, ethnic attitudes, and group behavior.* New York: John Wiley.

Nisbett, R. E., & Ross, L. (1980). *Human inference: Strategies and shortcomings of social judgment.* Englewood Cliffs, NJ: Prentice Hall.

Nkomo, S. M. (1992). The emperor has no clothes: Rewriting race in organizations. *Academy of Management Review, 17,* 487-513.

Pettigrew, T. F. (1979). The ultimate attribution error: Extending Allport's cognitive analysis of prejudice. *Personality and Social Psychology Bulletin, 5,* 461-476.

Pruitt, D. G., & Rubin, J. Z. (1986). *Social conflict: Escalation, stalemate, and settlement.* New York: Random House.

Robinson, R. J., & Friedman, R. A. (1994). *Mistrust and misconstrual in union-management relationships* (Working paper). Cambridge, MA: Harvard Business School.

Robinson, R. J., & Keltner, D. (1994). *The Western canon debate: A case study of perceived versus actual partisan extremism.* Unpublished manuscript.

Robinson, R. J., Keltner, D., Ward, A., & Ross, L. (in press). Actual versus assumed differences in construal: "Naive realism" in intergroup perception and conflict. *Journal of Personality and Social Psychology.*

Ross, L., Bierbrauer, G., & Hoffman, S. (1976). The role of attribution processes in conformity and dissent. *American Psychologist, 31,* 244-268.

Ross, L., Greene, D., & House, P. (1977). The false consensus effect: An egocentric bias in social perception and attribution processes. *Journal of Experimental Social Psychology, 13,* 279-301.

Ross, L., & Nisbett, R. E. (1991). *The person and the situation: Construing social reality.* New York: McGraw-Hill.

Schelling, T. (1960). *The strategy of conflict.* Cambridge, MA: Harvard University Press.

Selman, R. (1980). *The growth of interpersonal understanding.* New York: Academic Press.

Senge, P. M. (1990). *The fifth discipline: The art and practice of the learning organization.* New York: Doubleday-Currency.

Stillinger, C., Epelbaum, M., Keltner, D., & Ross, L. (1994). *The reactive devaluation barrier to conflict resolution.* Manuscript submitted for publication.

Sumner, W. G. (1906). *Folkways.* Lexington, MA: Ginn.

Susskind, L., & Cruikshank, J. (1987). *Breaking the impasse.* New York: Basic Books.

Thomas, D. A. (1993). Racial dynamics in cross-race developmental relationships. *Administrative Science Quarterly, 38,* 169-194.

Tjosvold, D. (1991). *The conflict positive organization: Stimulate diversity and create unity.* Reading, MA: Addison-Wesley.

White, R. K. (1977). Misperception in the Arab-Israeli conflict. *Journal of Social Issues, 33,* 190-221.

Zuboff, S. (1988). *In the age of the smart machine: The future of work and power.* New York: Basic Books.

Experimental
Explorations

The chapters in Part III report experimental investigations of the role of social context in negotiations. Humans are context-sensitive decision makers and problem solvers, and our perceptions, strategies, and interpretations of the world depend critically on the texture of the social environment. The interwoven themes developed in this section illustrate the richness and importance of social context. All of the chapter authors share the assumption that details of the social context influence the process of negotiation through their impact on people's preferences, interpretations, and ethical values.

In Chapter 10, Morris, Sim, and Girotto propose that the temporal sequence of decision making in a negotiation may influence the social heuristics that are evoked, and may, in that way, influence the nature of the decisions that are made. These authors discuss two such heuristics, which they call "ethical obligation" and "causal illusion." The latter refers to the cognitive illusion that one's actions may, in circumstances in which it is physically impossible, have a "mystical" impact on the actions of others. For instance, if one cooperates in a game of Prisoner's Dilemma, one may "magically" induce cooperation in the other player, even though the other will never have knowledge of one's choice. The heuristic of ethical obligation concerns reciprocity, the rule that dictates that like should bring like: Favors should be rewarded by favors, and harm should be punished. The hypothesis that Morris et al. propose is that these two heuristics will be differentially evoked as a function of whether the decision maker believes him- or herself to be making a choice before or after the other decision maker. One cannot "magically" influence another's choice unless one makes one's choice first; likewise, one cannot reciprocate another's cooperation unless one believes the other has made a choice before oneself.

Using a different negotiation task, Murnighan and Pillutla, in Chapter 11, explore the ethical dimensions of ultimatum bargaining. In this task, unlike the Prisoner's Dilemma task used by Morris et al., in which the players are structurally symmetric, the players have distinctly different roles. One player, the offerer or ultimator, proposes a division of a fixed amount of money to the receiver. The proposal specifies how much of the stake each of the two will receive. The receiver may accept the offer, in which case both receive the proposed amounts, or may reject it, in which case no one gets anything. This task has been used to examine the conflict between fairness (dividing the pot equally) and self-interest (giving the receiver only enough to keep him or her from rejecting the proposal). From the results of a series of experiments in which they varied the information the receiver had about the size of the pot being divided by the offerer, Murnighan and Pillutla conclude that the two different roles, offerer and receiver, evoke different moral frames (or heuristics) by means of which to evaluate the negotiation. They argue that the offerer tends to construe the negotiation as an economic opportunity for him- or herself. The offerer can use the knowledge of the receiver's state of ignorance strategically to increase the profit the offerer can make. The receiver, however, has a different perspective, one that emphasizes the importance of sharing the pot equally. The difference in these moral frames, strategic maximizing as opposed to fairness, creates a fertile ground on which hostility and misunderstanding can grow.

The importance of the construal of the negotiation is highlighted also by Larrick and Blount in Chapter 12. They point out that ultimatum bargaining games and certain types of n-person Prisoner's Dilemma-like games called resource dilemmas are structurally identical. There is a common pool of money (or some other resource) that is to be divided between two participants. However, there are many nuances that differentiate the two situations. In resource dilemmas there is the presumption of common ownership, whereas in ultimatum games, the offerer seems to "have" the resource. In resource dilemmas there is no explicit distinction between offerers and receivers; there are just two participants, one of whom must go first. These nuances color the social context in predictable ways, leading to measurable differences in behavior.

The importance of group membership is explicitly addressed in Chapter 13 by Kramer, Shah, and Woerner. These authors contrast two hypotheses about the role of group status in ultimatum games. The first, the out-group derogation hypothesis, proposes that out-group members are viewed as less trustworthy and more selfish than in-group members. Thus out-group members who make small, unfair offers will be seen as more unjust than will in-group members who make the same offers. The contrasting proposition, the in-group violation hypothesis, assumes that in-group members are expected to be supportive of other in-group members. If this expectation is violated—for instance, by an in-group member's making a low, unfair offer— in-group members will be judged more harshly than out-group members. The evidence from the experiments reported in this chapter tends to favor the out-group derogation hypothesis. The studies show conclusively that group membership plays an important role in how the ultimatum bargaining game is played and interpreted, a result that would not be expected from models of "rational" behavior that ignore the social texture of interaction. Like Larrick and Blount in Chapter 12, Kramer et al. demonstrate the importance of an aspect of the social context that has no role in economic theories. Their chapter and the final chapter in Part III both acknowledge the essentially social nature of humans and the role of human groups.

Negotiation is about something—rights, resources, property. As Larrick and Blount show, different ways of describing a negotiation setting may lead to different strategies, especially if the differences in description imply different entitlements to the resource. In Chapter 14, Carnevale addresses the problem of different construals of ownership from a cultural perspective. That is, rather than manipulating variables that could affect the perception of ownership, he selects subjects from cultures that view ownership either as an individual or as a collective concept. His question concerns the implications for negotiations of construing ownership as "mine" as opposed to "ours." One implication is that the barriers to negotiation that arise from the endowment effect, the tendency to overvalue a object that one owns because the pain of losing it exceeds the simple pain of not having it, may differ if ownership is culturally collective rather than individual. Carnevale presents data that indicate people from collectivistic backgrounds do not exhibit either the "mere ownership" effect or the endowment effect, but they do show an analogous effect for collectively owned possessions. Thus culture seems to be one of the many factors that influence the ways in which the social context of negotiations will be construed.

10

Time of Decision, Ethical Obligation, and Causal Illusion
Temporal Cues and Social Heuristics in the Prisoner's Dilemma

MICHAEL W. MORRIS
DAMIEN L. H. SIM
VITTORIO GIROTTO

Same Dilemma, Different Timing

Scenario 1

"You're facing a year in prison for this morning's holdup, but it'll be 10 years if I can prove that you and your partner Rod are the ones behind the string of holdups that have been terrorizing this city. So I'm gonna make you an offer—an offer you can't refuse." The lieutenant gives you the standard offer: Rat on Rod and the D.A. lets you off completely but locks up Rod for 10 years. He warns that Rod also gets the offer, and if both partners rat, then both get 4 years. Then he leaves you in the interrogation cell to think it over. You ponder— "I'm best off if I rat . . . yet together, as partners, we're best off if we cooperate with each other by not ratting . . . yet Rod would cooperate only if he assumed that I would too . . . " Your thoughts are interrupted when the door opens. The lieutenant enters and says, "It's time to make your decision now. I've already been to Rod's cell and heard his decision." What do you decide?

Scenario 2

Imagine Scenario 1, but with a slightly different ending: The lieutenant enters and says, "It's time to make your decision now. Afterwards, I'll go to Rod's cell and ask him make up his mind." What do you decide?

Social Context and Social Heuristics

To rat on your partner or to cooperate with him? How did you make your decision in the two scenarios? One prediction can be derived from the theory of games (Luce & Raiffa, 1957). According to game theory, the lieutenant is right—his offer is one you cannot refuse. In both scenarios, you choose the strategy that optimizes your individual outcome.[1] Ratting on Rod is the dominant strategy because you are better off ratting whether or not Rod rats on you. (And, of course, the theory also predicts that Rod would rat. It predicts an "equilibrium point" outcome that is the least favorable joint outcome for the partners in crime.)

We suspect, however, that for many readers this prediction is false; we suspect that you decided to cooperate in these Prisoner's Dilemma scenarios. Objections to game-theoretic predictions, in many cases, rest on the fact that real-world decision makers are embedded in rich social contexts and hence are influenced by relationships and norms in addition to economic payoffs. But in this case, our suspicions rest on findings that decision making departs from economic rationality even when people are taken out of rich social contexts and placed in the context of an experimental game. The Prisoner's Dilemma (PD) game was originally designed by Flood and Dresher for such an experiment, which found that cooperative outcomes were common and "equilibrium point" outcomes rare (Poundstone, 1992). In the hundreds of subsequent studies that have been conducted, both of repeated and of one-shot PD games, generally between one-third and one-half of subjects have cooperated (see Rapoport, 1988; Rapoport & Chammah, 1965; Rapoport, Guyer, & Gordon, 1976).

How can cooperation in PD games be explained? In repeated games, the players have an ongoing relationship, so the decision to cooperate may reflect an attempt to influence the other player—by cultivating a reputation, by inducing reciprocity, and so forth. Cooperation can be explained as a social influence strategy that serves a player's long-run self-interest. The conditions under which a cooperative strategy optimizes a player's outcome have been explored analytically (Kreps, Milgrom, Roberts, & Wilson, 1982; Kreps & Wilson, 1982) and empirically (Axelrod, 1984). In one-shot games, however, there is no ongoing relationship between players. Because social influence is impossible, cooperation is always suboptimal in terms of an individual's outcome. Nonetheless, subjects act as if social influence were possible: The rate of cooperation is as high as in repeated games (Sally, in press). The explanation may be that subjects take the same approach to one-shot games as to repeated games: They follow rules of thumb learned through their experiences of interdependent decision making in everyday social contexts. That is, decision makers simplify dilemmas by introducing tacit assumptions about social relations—they respond to uncertainty by automatically drawing on mental representations of typical social contexts. In short, the explanation may be that you can take the decision maker out of a social context, but you can't take the social context out of the decision maker.

A complete descriptive model of PD decision making must account for the mix of rational and nonrational decisions observed in studies. A model must go beyond a game-theoretic proposal in two respects: First, it must posit heuristic decision processes that underlie nonrational decisions; second, it must identify the cues that trigger each heuristic process. Previous research has identified several processes for interdependent decision making that can be called *social heuristics,* to distinguish them from more general *cognitive heuristics* for judgments under uncertainty (see Bazerman, Gibbons, Thompson, & Valley, 1994; Messick, 1991). One heuristic is to act as obligated by the ethical norm of reciprocity (Hofstadter, 1983/1985). Another heuristic is to act as if one could causally influence the decision (Shafir & Tversky, 1992). But little is known about when decision makers heuristically follow ethical obligations or causal illusions instead of basing decisions on a rational analysis of outcomes. In this chapter, we propose hypotheses about a parameter—the timing of decisions—that differentially affects these decision processes, and we report two experiments in support of these hypotheses.

Before introducing our hypotheses in detail, we can illustrate our proposal by explaining the decision processes (conscious or unconscious) we believe led readers to cooperate in the two scenarios above: We anticipated that in Scenario 1, where Rod's decision had occurred in the past, many of you would decide to cooperate because you assumed that Rod had, and that you were obligated to reciprocate. In Scenario 2, where Rod's decision was to occur in the future, we believe that fewer cooperated owing to an assumed ethical obligation, and more cooperated because of a tacit assumption that doing so would somehow influence the odds of Rod's cooperating.

Ethical Obligation

A decision to cooperate in the first scenario was likely based on the assumption that Rod had already cooperated. But given this assumption, why cooperate? Why not rat on Rod and let him rot in prison? You would walk free and would not have to worry about seeing Rod for 10 years. Perhaps the answer is that you would not be free, because you would face retribution for violating a more fundamental rule than the statute against armed robbery. This is the rule of reciprocity, that one is obligated to match the beneficence that another has extended in good faith. A violator would be punished both by his or her own emotions (e.g., guilt) and by society (e.g., Rod's friends would seek vengeance, others would lose trust in you).

Ethical principles vary greatly across individuals and cultures, but a few that serve basic social functions are widely shared. One of these, reciprocity, has been called a "cement of society" (Elster, 1989) because it leads to behaviors that hold together social organizations. Essentially, this norm obligates a person to match what another person has provided. It can be seen in interpersonal exchanges ranging from the explicit give-and-take of concessions in negotiation (Cialdini, 1993) to the implicit turn taking of self-disclosure in conversation (Altman & Taylor, 1973). A reciprocity norm benefits society by ensuring rewards for those who initiate exchanges of goods and services. It fosters trade, the formation of interpersonal interdependencies, and ultimately the establishment of stable social organizations.

It is not surprising, given the importance of reciprocity, that it is followed in many cultures studied by ethnographers (Gouldner, 1960; Mauss, 1954). In some cultures the rule has been formalized into gift-exchange rituals (Gouldner, 1960) or into explicit ethical philosophies. An early example, Confucius's (479 B.C./1938) counsel to "repay kindness with kindness and evil with justice," dictates responses when the other's behavior is known; more recent variants, such as Kant's (1788/1949) categorical imperative, concern when the behavior of others is unknown. There is evidence from cross-cultural experiments that those who violate the rule are punished through social disapproval (Gergen, Ellsworth, Maslach, & Seipel, 1975). Some have argued that humans are evolutionarily prepared for the cognitive task of detecting rule violators in social exchange (Cosmides, 1989).

Decision Heuristic

Given that reciprocity is important and universal in social relations, we might expect that people make decisions to reciprocate through cognitive shortcuts rather than through conscious, effortful analysis of outcomes. There is evidence that a heuristic process guides decision making when a person perceives an obligation. In an experiment by Regan (1971), subjects in a baseline condition were simply asked by a confederate to buy raffle tickets. The amounts of tickets purchased were generally low and were a function of the subjects' liking for the confederate. In another condition, subjects first received an unsolicited gift (a Coke) from the confederate and then were asked to buy tickets. The amounts purchased were twice as high as in the first condition and were no longer a function of liking for the confederate. Instead of weighing how much they valued the outcome of helping the confederate, subjects reflexively acted to match the confederate's beneficence.

A sign of heuristic processing is systematic error. In this context, an error is a decision to give that one later regrets. Evidence for this comes from field studies of how decision-making processes are exploited by salespeople and solicitors. Cialdini (1993) studied the Hare Krishna sect's technique of pinning a "gift" (e.g., a flower) on a pedestrian and subsequently requesting a donation. The typical reaction was visible annoyance at the benefactor but inability to override the obligation heuristic by deciding simply to walk away:

> With a nod of resignation, [the pedestrian] fishes in his pocket and comes up with a dollar or two that is graciously accepted. Now he can walk away freely, and he does, "gift" in hand, until he encounters a waste container—where he throws the flower, with force. (p. 30)

Temporal Cue

We propose that an important cue to obligation is that the other person in an exchange has already made his or her decision. It is the person who acts later in time on whom the obligation of reciprocity falls—on whom a mismatch in the exchange is blamed. Why is this? A crucial way in which the reciprocity norm fosters exchange is by reducing the natural reluctance to act first—to give a good or service to another that will not be repaid immediately (Tiger & Fox, 1971). Clearly, the norm would not serve this function unless the obligation falls on the person who acts later in time. Moreover, in most exchanges it is logical to place the obligation on the person who acts later in time, because that person is in a position to determine whether the outcome is a match or a mismatch. However, in some interdependence relationships, placing the obligation and the blame for a mismatch on the latter actor is not logical, because the latter actor has no greater power than the earlier actor to determine the outcome. In such contexts, timing is a "misleading cue" that triggers spurious perceptions of obligation and ultimately absurd patterns of blame assignment. A possible example comes from a study by Miller and Gunasegaram (1990) in which they described a $1,000 prize that was offered to a pair of individuals if the two tossed coins that came up matching. In response to the outcome "Jones goes first and tosses a head; Cooper goes next and tosses a tail," the vast majority of subjects predicted that Cooper (who acted later) would be blamed more by himself and by Jones. Following temporal cues, subjects placed the obligation to match the other's toss on Cooper, even though he had no greater control. We propose that subjects would also rely on temporal cues to obligation in a PD game with decisions separated in time. Although neither PD player can ensure a match of decisions, the player who acts later in time will more likely perceive him- or herself as ethically obligated to match the opponent than will a player who acts earlier in time. Hence:

- H1: A PD player who acts earlier in time than his or her opponent will be less likely to follow the ethical obligation heuristic.

Causal Illusion

In Scenario 2, a decision to cooperate was made with the knowledge that Rod had not yet made up his mind. You may have pictured Rod sitting on the fence of indecision, in a precarious balance, teetering one moment toward the side of cooperators and the next moment toward the side of rats. In most everyday contexts, an undecided person can be swayed toward one's wished-for decision by one's own behavior. Perhaps, out of a mental habit formed in these contexts, you cooperated in the hope of swaying Rod (even though you lacked a conscious theory about how your decision would causally influence Rod's decision).

There are many principles by which people organize and make sense of experience, but a few central ones are deeply ingrained and widely shared. Causality has been called a "cement of the universe" (Hume, 1739/1987) because it connects events occurring at different points in time. We rely on it to explain the present from the past and to predict the future from the present. Moreover, knowledge of cause-effect relations allows us to control or at least influence the course of events in our environment. Researchers of causal perception have found it useful to distinguish physical from social causality because the nexuses of cause and effect differ in these domains. Whereas one billiard ball causes another to move only by transferring force through physical contact, one billiards player can cause another player to move simply by transferring information (e.g., by saying aloud, "Move"). The conditions under which subjects perceive causality in these two domains reflect this actual difference in the working of causality. In the physical domain, spatial contiguity of objects is required: Michotte's (1952) subjects perceived causality in a display where an object A collided with a stationary object B and B moved off, but not in a minimally different display where there was a small spatial gap between the point where A's motion stopped and the point where B's began. By contrast, in the social domain, spatial contiguity is not required: Heider and Simmel's (1944) subjects perceived social influence between animate objects that did not come into contact but merely into proximity. Yet some conditions for causal perception hold in physical and social domains, such as temporal priority: A cause cannot come later in time than its effect. Einhorn and Hogarth (1986) include this among their proposed general cues to causation, and studies comparing analogous physical and social events have found that, in both domains, causal perceptions are evoked by temporal priority and spatial proximity (Morris, 1993).

Given the importance of causal inference, it is not surprising that reliance on basic cues to causation seems culturally universal, perhaps even innate. Cross-cultural comparisons have found that, though the locus of attribution for social events varies, cultures do not vary in the more basic phenomenon that temporal priority and spatial proximity of events evoke perceptions of causality (Morris, Nisbett, & Peng, 1994). Evidence that these basic tendencies in causal perception may be driven by an innate, evolved heuristic process comes from findings that infants make the same fine-grained distinctions in perceptions of causality as do adult subjects (Leslie, 1982; Leslie & Keeble, 1987). And just as errors owing to perceived obligation are exploited by solicitors, errors owing to heuristic causal processing are exploited by another profession. Kelley (1980) analyzed how the illusions of stage magicians depend on the audience's heuristic of inferring causality between events from spatiotemporal contiguity.

Decision Heuristic

Many attribution theorists assume that causal perception serves the function of distinguishing which events in the environment are controllable (Heider, 1958; Kelley, 1972). Decision making about controllable events differs fundamentally from decision making about other events, because instead of passively choosing between decision paths based on how the event will affect one, one can actively choose between paths in order to affect the event. Hence we suggest that perception of causal influence over an event triggers a decision heuristic of acting so as to influence the environment. Evidence that decisions follow such a heuristic comes from cases in which people act on causal perceptions that are illusory. Behavior based on causal illusions has long been studied as "magical thinking" in non-Western cultures by anthropologists (Malinowski, 1948) and in children by child development researchers (Piaget, 1929/1960). More recently sociological studies of gambling have described the same tendencies in Western adults. Craps players act as though they control the dice, for example, by throwing them softly to produce low numbers or throwing hard for high numbers (Henslin, 1967). Casino managers sometimes fire dealers who experience runs of bad luck (Goffman, 1967).

If illusions of control are errors that result from a decision heuristic, we would expect to observe them in contexts with "misleading cues" to the possibility of causal influence.[2] Experimental evidence supports this expectation. In games of chance, illusions of control over physical events are enhanced by cues to the relevance of skillful performance, such as "practice" before the actual game, "competition" against a confederate dressed like an inept schnook, or "choice" of lottery ticket numbers (Langer, 1975; Langer & Roth, 1975; Turnbull, 1981).[3] In social conflicts, illusions of control over another's behavior are engendered by cues to the relevance of bargaining skills. Illusions are demonstrated by experiments in which the subject faces a confederate whose decisions strictly follow a preprogrammed schedule. In distributive bargaining, subjects have an illusion of control over the opponent and over the final settlement in a condition where the opponent makes an extreme initial demand and then retreats to a moderate demand, but not in a condition where the opponent makes a moderate initial demand and refuses to retreat (Benton, Kelley, & Liebling, 1972). In a repeated PD game, subjects react more favorably to an opponent who shifts from a low to a high rate of cooperation (seeming to be influenced) than to an opponent who maintains a consistently high rate of cooperation (Oskamp, 1971).

Temporal Cue

An important (and somewhat obvious) cue to the controllability of an event is that it has not yet occurred. Timing is not a cue to the applicability of a particular influence skill, but a cue to the possibility of causation itself. Experiments manipulating the timing of physical and social events have found illusions of control to be affected. In dice-throwing experiments, subjects have been given a task either before or after the dice were tossed but before the outcome was disclosed. Before the dice were tossed, subjects bet more on the outcome (Strickland, Lewicki, & Katz, 1966) and were more confident in predicting the outcome (Rothbart & Snyder, 1970). Likewise, the timing of another person's behavior affects perceptions of the controllability and predictability of the behavior (Strickland, Gruder, & Kroupa, 1964). In short, although subjects act as if they could control outcomes to which they have no causal connection, but they apparently accept the limitation that an event in the past is a "sealed fate" that they cannot control.

There is some evidence that temporal cues engender illusions of control in the PD game. Swinth (1967) found that subjects developed more trust for a cooperative PD opponent in a condition where the opponent moved first than in a condition where the two players moved simultaneously. An interpretation is that a cooperative decision that is a "sealed fate" at the time of the subject's decision is attributed to the opponent's spontaneous goodwill, whereas one that is an "open fate" is illusorily attributed to the subject's influence. We propose that a PD player who acts before his or her opponent will be more likely to reason from an illusion of control than will a player who acts after the opponent.

- H2: A PD player who acts later in time than his or her opponent will be less likely to follow the causal illusion heuristic.

Consequentialism and Evidence for Heuristic Reasoning

So far, we have described two heuristic processes that lead to decisions to cooperate in the PD, but we have said nothing about how to distinguish them empirically. To do so, we will draw on a method developed by Shafir and Tversky (1992) for determining whether or not decisions to cooperate are consequentialist (in the sense that they follow from an analysis of outcomes or consequences). Decision making in uncertainty involves a disjunction of possible outcomes. For example, a player of the PD game shown in Figure 10.1 has to consider his or her payoff if the opponent competes and if the opponent cooperates, as diagrammed in Figure 10.2. Consequentialist choices must satisfy an axiom of decision making under uncertainty known as Savage's sure-thing principle (STP). The STP says that if you prefer x to y given all possible states of the world, then you should prefer x to y when uncertain about which state will occur (Savage, 1954). In the PD game, the STP implies that if you prefer to compete when the opponent has cooperated and you prefer to compete when the opponent has competed, then you should prefer to compete in uncertainty. A choice to cooperate in uncertainty, given your preference for competition in each possible state of the world, would be nonconsequentialist.

Shafir and Tversky (1992) had subjects play PD games in three conditions of information about their opponent: opponent's strategy known to be *cooperation,* opponent's strategy known to be *competition,* and opponent's strategy *unknown.* The researchers predicted that the nonconsequentialist pattern of decisions would be observed if some subjects are guided by a causal illusion:

> Once the player knows that the other has chosen either to compete or cooperate, it is clear that competition will be more advantageous to him than cooperation. But [in uncertainty] . . . although each player cannot affect the other's decision, he may be tempted to do his best (in this case, cooperate) to bring about the mutually desired state. (p. 453)

OTHER

cooperate   compete

	cooperate	compete
cooperate	You: 75 Other: 75	You: 25 Other: 85
compete	You: 85 Other: 25	You: 30 Other: 30

YOU

Figure 10.1. A Prisoner's Dilemma Payoff Matrix
NOTE: This matrix was used in the current experiments and in that of Shafir and Tversky (1992). The cell entries indicate the number of points that you and your opponent receive, contingent upon your choices.

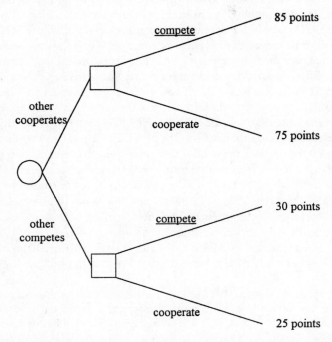

Figure 10.2. Tree Diagram of the Decision Faced in the Prisoner's Dilemma in Figure 10.1
NOTE: Your decisions in certainty are represented by squares; the uncertain event (the other's decision) is represented by a circle.

───── TABLE 10.1 ─────
Hypotheses About PD Strategy as a Function of the Timing
of the Other's Decision

Heuristic	Indicative Pattern		Predicted Rate	
	Knowledge of Other's Strategy	Decision	Timing of Other's Decision	
			Past	Future
Ethical obligation	unknown	C	high	low
	known			
	cooperation	C		
	defection	D		
Causal illusion	unknown	C	low	high
	known			
	cooperation	D		
	defection	D		

NOTE: The choice to compete is referred to as "defection" in descriptions of the design and results.

In support of this proposal, Shafir and Tversky found that one fourth of responses were characterized by the nonconsequentialist pattern (cooperate when the opponent's strategy is unknown but compete when it is known to be cooperation or known to be competition). Importantly, this pattern is not consistent with cooperation for ethical reasons. As Shafir and Tversky (1992) argue:

> These players followed a variant of Kant's Categorical Imperative: act in the way you wish others to act. They felt less compelled, however, to act in ways others have already acted. This pattern suggests that some of the cooperation observed in one-shot PD games may stem *not from a moral imperative* . . . but, rather, from a combination of wishful thinking and nonconsequential evaluation. (p. 459; emphasis added)

Ethical obligation does not predict a nonconsequentialist pattern; it predicts that a player will cooperate when the opponent's strategy is unknown, but also, of course, that the player will cooperate when the opponent's strategy is known to be cooperation. In other words, it predicts a pattern akin to the "tit-for-tat" strategy found in repeated PD games (Axelrod, 1984).[4] The patterns of responses indicative of ethical obligation and causal illusion heuristics are summarized in Table 10.1. We expect that both of these heuristics contribute to cooperative decisions in the PD, but that their relative frequency differs with the timing of the decision. Table 10.1 outlines how hypotheses about heuristics and timing response can be operationalized in terms of the patterns.

Experiment 1

Experiment 1 conceptually replicated the three within-subject conditions of Shafir and Tversky's (1992) design while also manipulating the timing of the opponent's decision as a between-subjects factor. The primary goal was to test hypotheses about temporal cues that trigger decision heuristics in the PD. A secondary goal was to bolster the evidence for cooperation due to a causal illusion by observing nonconsequentialist decision patterns with a different experimental procedure. Instead of playing PD games on a computer, which may have led Shafir and Tversky's subjects to imagine that their responses were somehow transmitted to their opponents, our subjects played on questionnaire forms. Instead of playing three distinct PD games in different conditions, which may have led Shafir and Tversky's subjects to think in terms of a repeated game, our subjects played only one game and then were asked two counterfactual questions about their decisions under the other conditions of information about the opponent's strategy.

Counterfactual questions also served a tertiary goal of exploring Shafir and Tversky's interpretation of why it is difficult to reason consistently in the PD. Behavior that violates a basic normative rule of decision making, such as STP, calls not only for a "positive analysis" of the heuristic that produces the observed response but also for a "negative analysis" of why the rational pattern is hard to produce (Kahneman & Tversky, 1982). Shafir and Tversky (1992) argue that it is difficult to evaluate two disjoint outcomes, two branches of the decision tree, simultaneously: "People may consider all the relevant outcomes but, due to the presence of uncertainty, may not see their own preferences very clearly. . . . Broadening the focus of attention results in a loss of acuity" (pp. 456-457). If so, then difficulty may arise in counterfactual simulations of preferences in uncertainty. A person may be better able to judge his or her own preference in a state of certainty ("If I had known that the opponent had cooperated, then I would have . . . ") than in a state of uncertainty ("If I had not known the opponent's decision, then I would have . . . "). In the first case, the person may be able to give an accurate answer—an answer matching what his or her preference would be in that state of certainty. In the second case, the person may fail to accurately simulate his or her preference in uncertainty and may be biased in the direction of his or her preference in the status quo state of certainty.[5] Hence, the following research question:

- Q1: Will a PD player be able to simulate his or her preference in a counterfactual state of uncertainty as accurately as in a counterfactual state of certainty? When simulating uncertainty, will the player be biased by the relatively greater availability of his or her preference in the actual state of certainty than in the opposite state?

Method

Overview of Design

Each subject made decisions about the Prisoner's Dilemma under three conditions of knowledge about the other person's strategy (*unknown* versus known *cooperation* versus known *defection*). Subjects actually played a PD game in one knowledge condition, and then were asked to reason counterfactually about each of the remaining two conditions. For example, subjects who played the PD game with the opponent's strategy unknown were subsequently asked what their decisions would have been had they known that the opponent's strategy was cooperation and had they known that it was defection. Subjects were randomly assigned to four between-subjects conditions that varied in the PD game played. In the first two conditions, subjects played against an opponent whose strategy was unknown—what varied was the timing of the opponent's decision. In Condition 1 the decision was *past* (occurred a week ago), and in Condition 2 it was *future* (to occur one week hence). The contrast between these conditions allowed tests of hypotheses about temporal cues and heuristic use (H1 and H2).

Condition 1 and 2 subjects encountered the three information conditions (unknown, cooperation, defection) in the same order as did Shafir and Tversky's (1992) subjects. Condition 3 and 4 subjects encountered them in different orders. Condition 3 subjects played a PD game with knowledge that the opponent's strategy was cooperation and then were asked for counterfactual decisions had they known it was defection and had it been unknown. Condition 4 subjects played with knowledge that the opponent's strategy was defection and then were asked for counterfactual decisions had they known it was cooperation and had it been unknown. Comparisons among Conditions 2, 3, and 4 allowed a test of the hypothesis about bias in counterfactual simulations of preference (Q1).[6]

Subjects

Participants in the experiment were 106 Stanford University undergraduates who were at the start of an hour-long session of unrelated studies. Sessions were held for groups of subjects in dormitory dining halls.

Procedure and Materials

Each subject was given a booklet with a cover sheet explaining that the session would involve completion of business decision-making problems. A prominent coding number appeared on the cover sheet, and subjects were instructed *not* to write their names on this "anonymous survey." The next page presented a game that was explained by analogy to "a small company deciding how 'competitively' to set its price for an item also sold by an 'opponent' company. It stands to benefit by 'cooperating' with the opponent (keeping its prices high) if that opponent also cooperates (keeps its price for the item high). But the company stands to lose by 'cooperating' if the opponent 'competes' (if the opponent undersells it and steals its customers). By 'competing' in this situation the other company would profit greatly." Instructions explained that these companies cannot communicate and face each other on only one occasion. Each subject was led to believe that he or she faced an opponent who was "a participant in this study at another university" with whom the subject was paired solely for this game and whose identity would not be learned. The payoffs were described with reference to the matrix shown in Figure 10.1. Subjects were strongly encouraged to play as if their payoffs in the game determined their payment for the session.

Below the matrix appeared the manipulation of knowledge about the opponent's strategy. In Condition 1, a subject read, "In this game you are paired with an opponent from a class that played this game last week." After this appeared the decision prompt, "Your move is?" The next page, titled "Hypotheticals," presented two "merely hypothetical questions about the game you just played." On the top half of the page the question, "What if you had known that your opponent's move was COOPERATE?" was followed by a counterfactual prompt: "Your move *would have been*?" On the bottom half appeared "What if you had known that your opponent's move was COMPETE?" followed by a second counterfactual prompt. In Condition 2, subjects were told, "In this game you are paired with an opponent from a class that will play this game next week" and were prompted for a decision. The hypotheticals that followed posited knowledge of this future decision: "What if you had known that your opponent's move will definitely be COOPERATE?" and "What if you had known that your opponent's move will definitely be COMPETE?" In Condition 3, subjects were told, "In this game you will find out what your opponent's move is before deciding on your move." Then subjects were told, "Your opponent's move is: COOPERATE," and were prompted for a decision. The hypotheticals that followed were "What if you had known that your opponent's move was COMPETE?" and "What if you had not known your opponent's move?" Condition 4 varied from this only in that subjects considered actual competition and counterfactual cooperation.

Results and Discussion

The responses of subjects in each condition to the three PD decisions are presented in Table 10.2. Decisions in actual games resembled those observed

———— **TABLE 10.2** ————
Rate of Cooperation in PD Games Across Conditions
(Experiment 1) (in percentages)

	Timing			
	Past	*Future*		
	Condition 1	Condition 2	Condition 3	Condition 4
Actual game	U	U	C	D
	39	**36**	44	8
Counterfactual games	C	C	D	C
	61	36	7	42
	D	D	U	U
	4	8	**52**	**23**
N	28	25	27	26

NOTE: U = unknown; C = known cooperation; D = known defection.

by Shafir and Tversky (1992), in that nearly 40% of subjects cooperated when the other's strategy was unknown (Conditions 1 and 2) and less than 10% cooperated when the other competed (Condition 4), yet results differed in that slightly more than 40% cooperated when the other cooperated (Condition 3). Our procedure differed from Shafir and Tversky's in a few ways that might account for this difference, such as that game payoffs did not actually determine payments to subjects. Such an effect would not interact with timing conditions and hence does not bias the results for or against the hypotheses; however, it might reduce the frequency of decision patterns and thereby limit statistical tests.

The pattern of decisions in counterfactual games supported the expectation of bias in simulated preferences under uncertainty (Q1). This was tested within the three conditions (2, 3, and 4) where the opponent's decision was an open fate. As can be seen by a comparison of the means in boldface in Table 10.2, the cooperation rate in actual uncertainty (36%) is not well approximated by that in simulations of uncertainty (52% and 23%; $\chi^2[2, 78] = 4.72$, $p < .01$). Counterfactual preferences differed from the benchmark of actual preferences in a pattern consistent with the proposed availability bias: Condition 3 subjects who had actually faced a cooperator overestimated (when compared with what others did in the corresponding condition, 52% versus 36%) and Condition 4 subjects who had actually faced a defector underestimated (23% versus 36%). These biases are particularly dramatic in light of the accuracy with which preferences in certainty were simulated. Actual cooperation rates in conditions of certainty are very well approximated by the corresponding counterfactual cooperation rates, both for known cooperation (44% versus 36% and 42%) and known defection (8% versus 7% and 8%).

——— TABLE 10.3 ———
PD Strategy Use as a Function of the Timing of the Other's Decision
(Experiment 1)

PD Strategy	Indicative Decision Triad		Observed Rate (%)	
	Knowledge of Other's Strategy	Decision	Timing of Other's Decision	
			Past	Future
Ethical obligation	unknown	C	32	16
	known			
	cooperation	C		
	defection	D		
Causal illusion	unknown	C	7	16
	known			
	cooperation	D		
	defection	D		
Other strategies			61	68
N			28	25

Hypotheses about decision heuristics and timing were tested in Conditions 1 and 2, which contrasted timing while holding constant the order of the three knowledge conditions. Decision heuristics can be analyzed in terms of decision patterns over the three within-subject conditions. Overall, the most frequent pattern was noncontingent defection, DDD (36%). Next came the patterns indicative of heuristics: ethical obligation, CCD (24%), and causal illusion, CDD (12%). Besides these two patterns of interest, the only other cooperators were a few who showed noncontingent cooperation, CCC (2%). The rate of the two patterns as a function of decision timing can be seen in Table 10.3. As predicted from H1, the CCD pattern indicative of decisions based on ethical obligation was less frequent when the opponent's decision was in the future, albeit nonsignificantly ($\chi^2[1, 53] = 1.86$). And, as predicted from H2, the CDD pattern indicative of decisions based on causal illusion was less frequent when the opponent's decision was in the past. Unfortunately, because of the low rate of this pattern and the low number of subjects, the planned statistical test of this trend could not be performed. In sum, the effects of decision timing (graphically depicted in Figure 10.3) were very consistent with our hypotheses, but a more powerful experiment will be necessary in order to reject the null hypotheses.

A discrepancy between the Experiment 1 results and those of Shafir and Tversky (1992) is that the pattern indicative of causal illusion was less frequent in our data. A few aspects of our procedure may have reduced cues to this

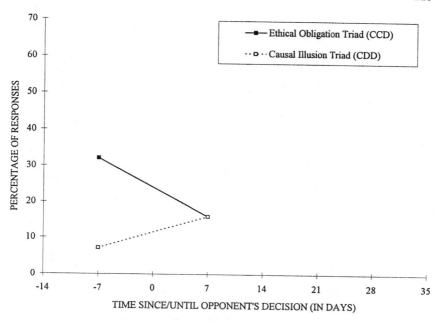

Figure 10.3. Frequency of Decision Patterns as a Function of Opponent Decision Timing in Experiment 1

NOTE: Ethical obligation-based reasoning was more frequent when the opponent's decision was in the past than when it was in the future. Causal illusion-based reasoning was more frequent when the opponent's decision was in the future than when it was in the past.

heuristic. First, our subjects faced the three PD decisions consecutively instead of facing them interspersed with unrelated problems. Studies have found that nonconsequentialist patterns of decisions are far less frequent when the juxtaposition of problems makes the logic of STP transparent (Tversky & Shafir, 1992). Second, our subjects may have been less prone to causal illusion because of the timing manipulation. We told them that the opponent's decision was either past or future in order to contrast clear cases of sealed fate and open fate, respectively. Shafir and Tversky's subjects were told that the opponent's decision was simultaneous or in the present. This is also an open-fate condition, and it may be more likely to evoke a causal illusion because of the temporal proximity of cause-and-effect events. Einhorn and Hogarth (1986) conclude from studies of causal judgment that it is difficult to perceive cause-effect relationships in absence of temporal contiguity. This may be true even in causal illusions: An event that lies in the remote future may seem "out of reach"—too far removed from one's own behavior to be causally influenced by it.

Experiment 2

The primary goal in Experiment 2, as in Experiment 1, was to test hypotheses about decision timing and heuristics in the PD. Relative to Experiment 1, the procedure was changed slightly in order to make the logic of STP less transparent, yet the subjects were drawn from a population more trained in rational decision making. A secondary goal was to investigate timing effects beyond those predicted by the sealed-fate versus open-fate distinction. To do so, we examined a more comprehensive range of timing conditions. Various times in the past and future were included, as well as the present. The present may be a condition in which cooperation is particularly likely, because both the ethical obligation and causal illusion heuristics would be triggered.

Method

Overview of Design

As in the first two conditions of Experiment 1, all subjects played the standard PD game (opponent's strategy unknown) and then simulated what their decisions would have been had they known that the opponent's strategy was cooperation and had they known that it was competition.

Subjects were randomly assigned to six between-subjects conditions that varied in the timing of the opponent's decision. The opponent's decision was described as taking place one week ago, yesterday, today, tomorrow, next week, or next month.

Subjects

Participants were 216 Stanford University M.B.A. students who were given a voluntary "decision-making problem set" in a class on organizational behavior. The pattern of responses to problems, including the PD game, was presented in subsequent class sessions to illustrate theories of judgment and decision making.

Procedure and Materials

Each student was randomly assigned one of six versions of the problem set. Part A was completed during a 20-minute session in class; part B was completed after class or outside of class. Subjects were instructed to write code names (e.g., Batman) instead of their real names on both parts. In Part A, after several problems requiring likelihood assessments and choices between gambles, the PD problem was presented on a page headed by participant code number. Instructions told the subject that, for this game, he or she was paired with an M.B.A. student at Northwestern who received the matching code number. Instructions explained: "Since you and your opponent will not be able to communicate, you will have to make your decisions without knowing the other's decision. . . . This is a one-time game where you have to decide whether to compete or to cooperate." Each subject was asked to imagine that he or she and the opponent would receive payoffs next month ranging from $25 to $85 according to the matrix shown in Figure 10.1. Below the matrix appeared the manipulation of the perceived timing of the opponent's decision. This sentence always began, "The one thing that we can tell you about your opponent is that they" and finished, in the six conditions respectively, as follows:

1. "made their decision when they were given this problem a week ago."
2. "made their decision when they were given this problem yesterday."
3. "are making their decision on this problem today."
4. "will make their decision when given this problem tomorrow."
5. "will make their decision when given this problem next week."
6. "will make their decision when given this problem next month."

Subjects were prompted for their decisions and then completed a number of other unrelated problems in Part A of the booklet. They were asked to complete Part B, which comprised two counterfactual PD questions among some unrelated problems, after class the same day. The counterfactual PD question began, "Remember the game in class where your opponent was a [Northwestern] student? You were told . . . " and repeated the entire text of the PD instructions and problem. Then it posed the scenario, "What if you had been given 'bonus information' that the other person's decision was: Cooperate," and asked, "Your decision *would have been?*" After several unrelated problems, another page appeared that was identical except that it posed the counterfactual question concerning an opponent known to compete.

Results and Discussion

The rate of cooperation across the six timing conditions can be seen in Table 10.4. In general, cooperation rates were high. Cooperation rates were highest when the other person's decision was simultaneous or very recent. Unfortunately, not all subjects handed in Part B, the after-class problem set that comprised the counterfactual PD games, but an adequate 72% response rate was achieved. Hypotheses about decision heuristics were tested on the

TABLE 10.4

Rate of Cooperation in PD Games Across Conditions
(Experiment 2) (in percentages)

	Knowledge Condition	Timing Condition					
		Week Ago	Yesterday	Today	Tomorrow	Next Week	Next Month
Actual game	unknown	42	78	74	57	66	51
N		31	36	34	37	41	37
		(55)	(82)	(78)	(58)	(62)	(54)
N		20	22	27	31	29	28
Counter-factual games	cooperation	55	77	52	48	38	50
	defection	10	9	0	16	10	18
N		20	22	27	31	29	28

NOTE: Rates in parentheses reflect the subset of subjects for whom complete data were available.

subsample of 157 subjects for whom we have responses in all three PD conditions. It is interesting to ask whether the subjects in this subsample (who cooperatively returned Part B) were more cooperative in the PD game than the others (who failed to return it). As can be inferred from Table 10.4, their cooperation rate was slightly higher, but not significantly so (64% versus 54%; $\chi^2[1, 216] = 1.85$, n.s.).

Subjects' responses were, once again, analyzed in terms of triadic patterns of decisions. Relative to Study 1, there was less noncontingent competition, DDD (23%). Most frequent was the pattern indicative of ethical obligation, CCD (37%), and also fairly frequent was the pattern indicative of causal illusion, CDD (19%). These two patterns accounted for all cooperative strategies except for a few instances of noncontingent cooperation, CCC (5%). Hypotheses about decision heuristics and timing were tested by comparing the rates of these patterns across conditions in which the other's decision is in the past, present, or future (as shown in Table 10.5). As predicted from H1, the CCD pattern indicative of decisions based on ethical obligation was less frequent when the opponent's decision was in the future than otherwise ($\chi^2[1, 157] = 10.04$, $p < .005$). And, as predicted from H2, the CDD pattern indicative of decisions based on causal illusion was less frequent when the opponent's decision was in the past than otherwise ($\chi^2[1, 157] = 5.87$, $p < .02$).

A secondary goal of Experiment 2 was to search for other timing effects by including more conditions than in Experiment 1. The results can be clearly

TABLE 10.5

PD Strategy Use as a Function of the Timing of the
Other's Decision (Experiment 2)

PD Strategy	Indicative Decision Triad		Observed Rate (%)		
	Knowledge of Other's Strategy	Decision	Timing of Other's Decision		
			Past	Present	Future
Ethical obligation	unknown	C	52	48	26[a]
	known				
	cooperation	C			
	defection	D			
Causal illusion	unknown	C	10[a]	30	21
	known				
	cooperation	D			
	defection	D			
Other strategies			38	19	53
N			42	27	88

a. Rate significantly different from those in the other two conditions.

seen by comparing the plot of pattern frequency across timing conditions
(Figure 10.4) with the analogous plot from Experiment 1 (Figure 10.3). In the
"last week" and "next week" conditions, Experiment 2 results mirror Experiment 1 results. However, in other conditions, results suggest a more complex
pattern. Although the frequency of CDD responses approximates the step
function predicted by the sealed-fate versus open-fate dichotomy, it is highest
for an opponent decision "today" and tapers off for decisions in the remote
future. A statistical test of this trend will have to await future experiments with
more conditions, but the finding suggests that the metaphor of sealed versus
open bonds of fate that has guided psychological discussion of control illusions may not fully capture timing effects. Another traditional metaphor, that
fate ripens like a fruit—that there is a fateful moment in which an event is
most "ripe" for change—may serve to describe the pattern in Figure 10.4. An
opponent's decision is most ripe to be influenced in the present or near future.
Decisions "today" and "tomorrow" were most likely to be met by cooperation
based on a causal illusion (they are ripe). Decisions in the more remote future
were not as tempting to try to influence (not yet ripe). Decisions in the past
were not tempting at all (no longer ripe). Ripeness may also serve to describe
the finding that the opponent's decisions in the recent past or in the present
evoke a stronger sense of obligation than those in the more remote past (no
longer ripe) or those to be made in the future (not yet ripe for reciprocation).

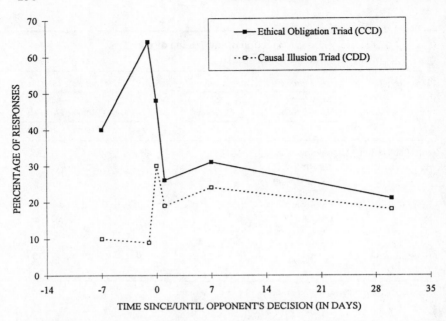

Figure 10.4. Frequency of Decision Patterns as a Function of Opponent Decision Timing in Experiment 2

NOTE: Ethical obligation-based reasoning was more frequent when the opponent's decision was in the past or present than when it was in the future. Causal illusion-based reasoning was more frequent when the opponent's decision was in the present or future than when it was in the past.

General Discussion

Contribution of Current Findings

Primarily, the two experiments presented above provide additional evidence for Shafir and Tversky's (1992) claim that some of the cooperation observed in the one-shot PD game reflects an illusory attempt to bring about cooperation from the other player. In the "today" condition of Experiment 2, which corresponds most closely to Shafir and Tversky's procedure, the frequency of nonconsequentialist decision patterns reached the level they observed. It is important to note that this was in a procedure that differed from theirs in two ways that rule out possible alternative explanations. First, there was no computer connection between players that could possibly raise a subject's suspicion that responses were transmitted to the opponent. Second, only one PD game was played, so it was not possible to perceive the procedure as a repeated game.

Moreover, findings about decision timing support Shafir and Tversky's positive analysis that nonconsequentialist choices in the PD reflect, in their terms, "wishful thinking" or "quasi-magical thinking" or, in our terms, a decision heuristic of attempting influence based on a causal illusion. Consistent with this proposal, the nonconsequentialist pattern was more frequent when the opponent's decision had not yet already happened (H2). The proposal that this motive for cooperation is distinct from previously noted ethical motives is supported by the finding that patterns indicative of ethical obligation were differentially affected by the time parameter—they were more frequent when the opponent's decision had already happened (H1). Also, Shafir and Tversky's negative analysis that nonconsequentialist choices occur because it is difficult to hold disjunctions of possible states in mind is supported by the finding that subjects can accurately simulate preferences in certainty but not preferences in uncertainty. Finally, the current results suggest that decision making may be affected not only by the temporal priority of events but by the temporal contiguity of events.

Temporal Contiguity and Decision Making

A general pattern in Experiment 2 was that subjects were more likely to decide to cooperate when the opponent's decision was temporally contiguous with their own decisions. Not only the overall rate of cooperation but also the frequency of patterns indicative of each heuristic peaked near the present (see Figure 10.4). Temporal contiguity was expected to foster causal illusion responses on the basis of findings that it is an important cue in causal judgment and perception, but the same pattern occurred more dramatically for ethical obligation responses. Why would temporal contiguity also foster the perception of obligation?

A general effect of temporal contiguity can be understood in light of a recent finding about mental accounting. Henderson and Peterson (1992) presented subjects with two variants of Tversky and Kahneman's (1981) "additional cost trap" problem, in which one has lost the ticket to a play and must decide whether or not to buy another. Of subjects who were told that the discovery of the ticket's being lost occurred "a few days before the play," 67% indicated that they would buy a new a ticket. But of those who were told the discovery occurred "as you enter the theater," only 42% would buy a new ticket. When the loss of the old ticket was made contiguous in time with the purchase of the new ticket, subjects were much more likely to include the cost of the lost ticket in the perceived cost of the play. An interpretation of this finding is that events are cognitively integrated when coded in terms of a common causal or transactional schema (Linville & Fischer, 1991), and temporal contiguity facilitates this coding.

The same interpretation can be applied to our findings about temporal contiguity and cooperation in the PD game. Heuristics for PD decision making require the coding of independent events (decisions of self and opponent) in terms of a common causal or obligation schema. (For an analysis of these schemata, see Morris & Nisbett, 1993.) Decisions that are temporally contiguous are more likely to be coded in terms of a schema and processed heuristically; decisions separated in time are more likely to be considered as independent.

The Evolution of Causal Illusion

The conditions under which decision making based on ethical obligation (tit-for-tat) leads to favorable outcomes have been investigated extensively in computer tournaments and studies of actual social conflicts (Axelrod, 1984; Bendor, Kramer, & Stout, 1991). It is interesting to speculate about conditions under which decision making based on causal illusion leads to favorable outcomes. Our aim is not to analyze how a causal illusion computer program would fare in a repeated PD game tournament (or even to describe what a causal illusion program would look like). Rather, our aim is to try to identify conditions in social conflicts where a causal illusion would bring better outcomes than would other available decision processes. One answer is that from the standpoint of collective outcomes, any process resulting in cooperation in a mixed-motive game is adaptive. And because ethical obligation may not be available as a line of reasoning to the player who moves first in a game, it would be more adaptive for this player to reason from a causal illusion than to reason from outcomes.

A somewhat more satisfying answer is that reasoning from a causal illusion is adaptive in some conditions when a decision maker's emotional needs are taken into account. A basic assumption of social psychologists (Heider, 1958), learning theorists (Bandura, 1977), and psychoanalytic theorists (Fenichel, 1945) has been that a sense of personal control is necessary to a healthy self-concept. A parallel argument has been made by anthropologists about magical thinking. Malinowski (1948) found that magical beliefs about fishing were absent in Trobriand villages on the inner lagoon, where fishing is predictable and safe, but present in villages on the open sea, where fishing is uncertain and hazardous; he concludes that magical beliefs serve to reduce anxiety in conditions where one cannot control the environment. Subsequent ethnographic evidence is mixed, but some systematic evidence comes from Hyman and Vogt's (1967) survey across a sample of U.S. counties of the prevalence of "water witches" (professional diviners of underground water who rely on the dipping motion of a cleft stick). Counties classified by the U.S. geological survey as having conditions that make it difficult to locate groundwater (by standard geological criteria) were higher in the number of practicing water witches. The magical belief seems to persist where it is most needed to reduce the anxiety of decision making in uncertainty. An analogy can be seen between this conclusion and recent psychological claims that illusions of control arise in the face of threat and serve to maintain a sense of well-being (Taylor & Brown, 1988).

However, it would be most interesting to find conditions where a causal illusion is adaptive in terms of a decision maker's individual economic outcome. Hyman and Vogt (1967) argue that witching as a decision procedure may, in fact, be adaptive not only in terms of a well driller's mental well-being but also in terms of his or her material outcome. This might be the case if a local witch has worked long enough for trial-and-error learning of the features of local terrain where drilling tends to be successful, and applies this knowledge (consciously or unconsciously) when wielding the divining stick. In counties where none of the methods of an outside geologist can produce above-chance predictions about the location of groundwater, the odds of success may be better with a witch. In short, this decision procedure may work in practice for reasons other than those in which its users believe. A similar argument has been presented by Moore (1957) about a decision procedure of a Labrador hunting society. When food has run out because of lack of success in hunting, the life-or-death decision of where to hunt next is made in the following way. A caribou shoulder bone is held over a fire until it cracks from the heat, and the random pattern of cracks is then read as a map that leads the hunters to their prey. If it did not bring good outcomes, this practice would not have survived (because its inventors would not have survived). But why does it work? Moore argues that, relative to the natural alternative of choosing to hunt where success has come in the past, the random process reduces the probability of returning to an overhunted area. Also, it eliminates the possibility of the caribou learning to anticipate where hunters will threaten next. Again, a decision procedure based on illusion may bring more favorable outcomes than alternative procedures.[7]

Can a similar story be told about the adaptiveness of decision making based on causal illusion in the PD game? A strategy that sustains mutual cooperation in a repeated game will bring better long-run outcomes than one that does not. A causal illusion is sustained in a repeated game against a cooperative opponent by the following process: After Trial 1, you attribute your opponent's cooperation in Trial 1 to your cooperation in Trial 1; your cooperation in Trial 1 has the actual effect of causing your opponent to cooperate in Trial 2; after Trial 2, you attribute your opponent's cooperation to your cooperation in Trial 2; and so forth. That is, the illusion of same-trial influence is sustained in part by the reality of subsequent-trial influence. But are there conditions in which decisions based on this illusion of same-trial influence lead to better outcomes than those based on veridical perception of subsequent-trial influence? One clear advantage of causal illusion is that it avoids destructive endgame dynamics. A player reasoning from causal reality has no reason to cooperate on the ultimate trial of the game, and anticipation of the opponent's recognizing this takes away the player's reason to cooperate on the penultimate trial, and so forth. The mutual cooperation between the player and his or her opponent will unravel before the end of the game. By contrast, a player reasoning from a causal illusion will cooperate on the penultimate trial (in an attempt to evoke cooperation on that trial) and, by doing so, will induce cooperation in the ultimate trial. Mutual cooperation will not unravel.

A sports analogy may clarify how a causal illusion may serve better than a veridical causal perception. Students of various sports find it adaptive to let their play be guided by illusions about the effects of "follow-through" after hitting a ball. A golfer, for example, who fails to hit the ball squarely will be instructed by the pro to keep her head down while completing the full motion of her swing. Because, in reality, a golf ball leaves the club in mid-swing, it is an illusion that the position of the golfer's head at the finish of the swing has any causal impact on the ball's trajectory. Nonetheless, this illusion is adaptive because focusing on the finish produces a better beginning than does focusing on the beginning. Likewise, in the PD game, focusing on illusory same-trial influence may sustain a beneficial pattern of subsequent-trial influence longer than does focusing on subsequent-trial influence. Sometimes the best way to bring about what you want is to try to do something else.[8]

Implications for Negotiation
and Conflict Management

A few recommendations can be drawn from the current findings. The first is addressed to negotiators or decision makers in mixed-motive conflicts. Often there is a choice of whether to move before or after your opponent. The current findings suggest that the choice ought to depend on whether you estimate the opponent to be strongly bound by ethical obligations. If yes, then you should announce that you have made a decision before the opponent does, so that he or she will feel obligated. If no, then you should announce that you will make a decision simultaneous with or just after the opponent's decision, so that he or she will have an illusion of control. (There may also be further ways to cultivate an illusion of control, such as sending misleading cues to the relevance of skill.)

A similar recommendation is addressed to mediators. Mediators often shuttle between two parties, because more concessions are revealed to the mediator than to the opposing party. A mediator must then choose strategically when to reveal information in order to create momentum in the exchange of concessions. For example, suppose you learned that Party A was willing to give concession x and would like concession y from Party B. There are two strategies for how to proceed with Party B. The recommendation, again, turns on whether you judge B to be strongly bound by ethical obligation. If yes, then you should announce that Party A has made concession x and afterward request concession y. If no, then you should describe Party A as undecided about whether to make concession x and as "ripe" for influence, and afterward suggest that concession y will greatly influence Party A.

A final recommendation is addressed to designers of conflict resolution procedures. A goal is to structure procedures in ways that facilitate the cooperative behavior necessary for reaching integrative solutions (see Brett, Goldberg, & Ury, 1990). Theorists have argued for attention to the timing of costs and benefits in potential contracts (Coleman, Heckathorn, & Maser, 1989). Also, the timing of information exchange has been discussed in the context of problematic voting strategies (see Raiffa, 1982). For example, in multiple-party negotiation an integrative agreement requires that all parties air their preferences by a series of votes on proposals. However, a party can gain power by misrepresenting his or her preferences after hearing the votes of others (i.e., the party can feign opposition to a point that others need and demand concessions in return for compromising on the point). To prevent strategic misrepresentation, some procedures require that votes be disclosed simultaneously through the use of ballots. A recommendation from the current findings is to go a step further in control over timing, and require simultaneous voting. Why? It is desirable that each party have the causal illusion that his or her cooperation will evoke cooperation from the other parties. This illusion (and cooperation based on it) will not occur when a party sees that the others have already marked their ballots. Hence causal illusions will be fostered by a structure in which votes of others are not only unknown but undetermined at the time of one's own vote (see Greene & Yolles, 1993).

Notes

1. Our statements refer to traditional game theory, not to recent attempts to incorporate social psychological variables into utility functions (e.g., Rabin, 1992).

2. We use the phrase *illusion of control,* as is customary, to refer to behaviors. It is not implied that subjects performing these behaviors necessarily have a conscious belief in their power to control the outcome.

3. Conversely, recent research (Koehler, Gibbs, & Hogarth, in press) has found that causal illusions are reduced when cues to the random nature of outcomes trigger reasoning from statistical heuristics (Fong, Krantz, & Nisbett, 1986; Nisbett, Krantz, Jepson, & Kunda, 1983).

4. This strategy is to cooperate in the first round and thereafter to match the opponent's move in the previous round.

5. In other words, a person at the fork of the decision tree (the circle in Figure 10.2) may be able to simulate his or her preference on a branch of the tree (a square in Figure 10.2), but a person on a branch of the tree may have difficulty simulating his or her preference at the fork of the tree. This person on a branch of the tree would likely be biased by the higher availability of the branch on which he or she sits.

6. The ability of a group of subjects to simulate preferences was evaluated only in comparison to the preferences expressed by others who actually experienced the state that the first subjects counterfactually simulated (e.g., Condition 2 subjects experienced the uncertainty that Condition 3 and Condition 4 subjects simulated). A reason for this between-subjects comparison is that within-subjects comparisons run into the problem of self-fulfilling predictions (see Kahneman & Snell, 1990).

7. This review draws on a discussion of superstition by Jahoda (1971).

8. This argument draws on a discussion of free will by Dennett (1984).

References

Altman, I., & Taylor, D. A. (1973). *Social penetration: The development of interpersonal relationships.* New York: Holt, Rinehart & Winston.

Axelrod, R. (1984). *The evolution of cooperation.* New York: Basic Books.

Bandura, A. (1977). *Social learning theory.* Engelwood Cliffs, NJ; Prentice Hall.

Bazerman, M., Gibbons, R., Thompson, L., & Valley, K. (1994). When and why do negotiators outperform game theory? In R. N. Stern & J. Halpern (Eds.), *Nonrational elements of organizational decision making.* Ithaca, NY: Industrial and Labor Relations Press.

Bendor, J., Kramer, R. M., & Stout, S. (1991). When in doubt: Cooperation in the noisy Prisoner's Dilemma. *Journal of Conflict Resolution, 35,* 691-719.

Benton, A. A., Kelley, H. H., & Liebling, R. M. (1972). Effects of extremity of offers and concession rates on the outcomes of bargaining. *Journal of Personality and Social Psychology, 24,* 409-415.

Brett, J. M., Goldberg, S. B., & Ury, W. L. (1990). Designing systems for resolving disputes in organizations. *American Psychologist, 45,* 162-70.

Cialdini, R. B. (1993). *Influence: Science and practice* (3rd ed.). New York: HarperCollins.

Coleman, J. L., Heckathorn, D. D., & Maser, S. M. (1989). A bargaining theory approach to default provisions and disclosure rules in contract law. *Harvard Journal of Law and Public Policy, 12,* 639-709.

Confucius. (1938). *The analects of Confucius* (A. Waley, Trans.). London: Allen & Unwin. (Original work published 479 B.C.)

Cosmides, L. (1989). The logic of social exchange: Has natural selection shaped how humans reason? Studies with the Wason selection task. *Cognition 31,* 187-276.

Dennett, D. C. (1984). *Elbow room: The varieties of free will worth wanting.* Cambridge: MIT Press.

Einhorn, H., & Hogarth, R. (1986). Judging probable cause. *Psychological Bulletin, 99,* 3-19.

Elster, J. (1989). *The cement of society: A study of the social order.* New York: Cambridge University Press.

Fenichel, O. (1945). *The psychoanalytic theory of neurosis.* New York: W. W. Norton.

Fong, G. T., Krantz, D. H., & Nisbett, R. E. (1986). The effects of statistical training on thinking about everyday problems. *Cognitive Psychology, 18,* 253-292.

Gergen, K., Ellsworth, P., Maslach, C., & Seipel, M. (1975). Obligation, donor resources, and reactions to aid in three cultures. *Journal of Personality and Social Psychology, 31,* 940-949.

Goffman, E. (1967). *Interaction ritual: Essays on face-to-face behavior.* Garden City, NY: Anchor.

Gouldner, A. W. (1960). The norm of reciprocity: A preliminary statement. *American Socio-logical Review, 25,* 161-178.

Greene, S. B., & Yolles, D. J. (1993). *Perceived determinacy of unknown outcomes.* Unpublished manuscript, Princeton University, Department of Psychology.

Heider, F. (1958). *The psychology of interpersonal relations.* New York: John Wiley.

Heider, F., & Simmel, M. (1944). An experimental study of apparent behavior. *American Journal of Psychology, 57,* 243-249.

Henderson, P., & Peterson, R. (1992). Mental accounting and categorization. *Organizational Behavior and Human Decision Processes, 51,* 92-117.

Henslin, J. M. (1967). Craps and magic. *American Journal of Sociology, 73,* 316-330.

Hofstadter, D. R. (1985). Dilemmas for superrational thinkers, leading up to a luring lottery. In D. R. Hofstadter, *Metamagical themas: Questing for the essence of mind and pattern.* New York: Basic Books. (Reprinted from *Scientific American,* June 1983)

Hume, D. (1987). *A treatise of human nature.* Oxford: Clarendon. (Original work published 1739)

Hyman, R., & Vogt, E. Z. (1967). Water witching: Magical ritual in contemporary United States. *Psychology Today,* pp. 35-42.

Jahoda, G. (1971). *The psychology of superstition.* Middlesex: Penguin.

Kahneman, D., & Snell, J. (1990). Predicting utility. In R. H. Hogarth (Ed.), *Insights in decision making: A tribute to H. J. Einhorn.* Chicago: University of Chicago Press.

Kahneman, D., & Tversky, A. (1982). On the study of statistical intuitions. *Cognition, 11,* 123-141.

Kant, I. (1949). *Critique of practical reason and other writings in moral philosophy.* Chicago: University of Chicago Press. (Original work published 1788)

Kelley, H. H. (1972). Attribution in social interaction. In E. E. Jones, D. E. Kanouse, H. H. Kelley, R. S. Nisbett, S. Valins, & B. Weiner (Eds.), *Attribution: Perceiving the causes of behavior.* Morristown, NJ: General Learning Press.

Kelley, H. H. (1980). Magic tricks: The management of causal attributions. In D. Gorlitz (Ed.), *Perspectives on attribution research and theory: The Bielefeld Symposium.* Cambridge, MA: Ballinger.

Koehler, J. J., Gibbs, B. J., & Hogarth, R. M. (in press). Shattering the illusion of control: Multi-shot versus single-shot gambles. *Journal of Behavioral Decision Making.*

Kreps, D., & Wilson, R. (1982). Reputation and imperfect information. *Journal of Economic Theory, 27,* 253-279.

Kreps, D. M., Milgrom, P., Roberts, J., & Wilson, R. (1982). Rational cooperation in the finitely repeated Prisoner's Dilemma. *Journal of Economic Theory, 27,* 245-252.

Langer, E. J. (1975). The illusion of control. *Journal of Personality and Social Psychology, 32,* 311-328.

Langer, E. J., & Roth, J. (1975). Heads I win, tails it's chance: The illusion of control as a function of the sequence of outcomes in a purely chance task. *Journal of Personality and Social Psychology, 32,* 951-955.

Leslie, A. M. (1982). The perception of causality in infants. *Perception, 11,* 173-186.

Leslie, A. M., & Keeble, S. (1987). Do six-month-old infants perceive causality? *Cognition, 25,* 265-287.

Linville, P. W., & Fischer, G. W. (1991). Preferences for separating or combining events. *Journal of Personality and Social Psychology, 60,* 5-23.

Luce, R. D., & Raiffa, H. (1957). *Games and decisions.* New York: John Wiley.

Malinowski, B. (1948). *Magic, science, and religion.* Garden City, NY: Doubleday.

Mauss, M. (1954). *The gift* (I. G. Cunnison, Trans.). London: Cohen & West.

Messick, D. M. (1991). Equality as a decision heuristic. In B. Mellers (Ed.), *Psychological issues in distributive justice.* New York: Cambridge University Press.

Michotte, A. E. (1952). *The perception of causality.* New York: Basic Books.

Miller, D. T., & Gunasegaram, S. (1990). Temporal order and the perceived mutability of events: Implications for blame assignment. *Journal of Personality and Social Psychology, 59,* 1111-1118.

Moore, O. K. (1957). Divination: A new perspective. *American Anthropologist, 59,* 69-74.

Morris, M. W. (1993). *Culture and cause: American and Chinese understandings of physical and social causality.* Unpublished doctoral dissertation, University of Michigan, Psychology Department.

Morris, M. W., & Nisbett, R. E. (1993). Tools of the trade: Deductive schemas taught in psychology and philosophy. In R. E. Nisbett (Ed.), *Rules for reasoning.* Hillsdale, NJ: Lawrence Erlbaum.

Morris, M. W., Nisbett, R. E., & Peng, K. (1994). Causal attribution across domains and cultures. In G. Lewis, D. Premack, & D. Sperber (Eds.), *Causal cognition.* New York: Oxford University Press.

Nisbett, R. E., Krantz, D. H., Jepson, C., & Kunda, Z. (1983). The use of statistical heuristics in everyday inductive reasoning. *Psychological Review, 90,* 339-363.

Oskamp, S. (1971). Effects of programmed strategies on cooperation in the Prisoner's Dilemma and other mixed-motive games. In L. Wrightsman (Ed.), *Cooperation and exploitation in mixed-motive games.* New York: Brooks/Cole.

Piaget, J. (1960). *The child's conception of the world.* London: Kegan Paul. (Original work published 1929)

Poundstone, W. (1992). *Prisoner's Dilemma.* Garden City, NY: Doubleday.

Rabin, M. (1992). *Incorporating fairness into game theory* (Working Paper No. 92-198). Berkeley: University of California, Department of Economics.

Raiffa, H. (1982). *The art and science of negotiation.* Cambridge, MA: Harvard University Press.

Rapoport, A. (1988). Experiments with n-person social traps I: Prisoner's Dilemma, weak Prisoner's Dilemma, Volunteer's Dilemma, and Largest Number. *Journal of Conflict Resolution, 32,* 457-472.

Rapoport, A., & Chammah, A. (1965). *Prisoner's Dilemma.* Ann Arbor: University of Michigan Press.

Rapoport, A., Guyer, M. J., & Gordon, D. G. (1976). *The 2×2 game.* Ann Arbor: University of Michigan Press.

Regan, R. T. (1971). Effects of a favor and liking on compliance. *Journal of Experimental Social Psychology, 67,* 599-609.

Rothbart, M., & Snyder, M. (1970). Confidence in the prediction and postdiction of an uncertain event. *Canadian Journal of Behavioural Science, 2,* 38-43.

Sally, D. (in press). Conversation and cooperation in social dilemmas: Experimental evidence from 1958 to 1992. *Rationality and Society.*

Savage, L. J. (1954). *The foundations of statistics.* New York: John Wiley.

Shafir, E., & Tversky, A. (1992). Thinking through uncertainty: Nonconsequential reasoning and choice. *Cognitive Psychology, 24,* 449-474.

Strickland, L. H., Gruder, C. L., & Kroupa, K. W. (1964). Response time as a cue in person perception. *Psychological Reports, 15,* 827-837.

Strickland, L. H., Lewicki, R. J., & Katz, A. M. (1966). Temporal orientation and perceived control as determinants of risk-taking. *Journal of Experimental Social Psychology, 2,* 143-151.

Swinth, R. L. (1967). The establishment of the trust relationship. *Journal of Conflict Resolution, 11,* 335-344.

Taylor, S. E., & Brown, J. D. (1988). Illusion and well-being: A social psychological perspective on mental health. *Psychological Bulletin, 103,* 193-210.

Tiger, L., & Fox, R. (1971). *The imperial animal.* New York: Holt, Rinehart & Winston.

Turnbull, W. (1981). Naive conceptions of free will and the deterministic paradox. *Canadian Journal of Behavioural Science, 13,* 1-13.

Tversky, A., & Kahneman, D. (1981). The framing of decisions and the rationality of choice. *Science, 211,* 453-458.

Tversky, A., & Shafir, E. (1992). The disjunction effect in choice under uncertainty. *Psychological Science, 3,* 305-309.

11

Fairness Versus Self-Interest
Asymmetric Moral Imperatives
in Ultimatum Bargaining

J. KEITH MURNIGHAN
MADAN M. PILLUTLA

This chapter is about ultimatum bargaining. Before we describe our recent research, however, we want to present a rather lengthy but pertinent story about a week-long negotiation workshop in Europe, where, among many other exercises, 36 executives participated in an ultimatum game (Murnighan, 1991). The game is quite simple. Half of the group (designated respondents) left the room while we presented the instructions to the other half, who would have the role of offerers. Their task was sequential: For the first round, each offerer needed to find a nonofferer partner (a respondent) and make him or her a monetary offer that was some portion of $100. The offerer could choose how large the offer would be: It could range from one penny to the entire $100. The respondent would accept or reject this offer and, after all of the interactions were revealed and discussed, a second round would follow. The rules for the second round were the same as the first, except that everyone needed a new, different partner, and this time offerer and respondent would be dividing $1 million. The total amounts ($100 and $1 million) were the offerers' private information and would not be revealed to the respondents until after they had

AUTHORS' NOTE: This chapter benefited considerably from our interactions with seminar groups at Cornell, Northwestern, and Simon Fraser Universities and the University of British Columbia, as well as from the reactions of the participants at the Stanford Conference on the Social Context of Negotiation (March 1994) and the constructive comments of the editors.

accepted or rejected their offers. After we outlined the rules for the offerers, respondents returned to the room and were also told the rules. Everyone had the same information, except for the amounts to be divided (known only to the offerers).

Offerers wandered around the room holding one finger in the air, looking for partners; respondents held two fingers up. Anyone could say anything they wanted at any time. However, once an offerer delivered an offer, frequently in writing, it could not be changed, the offerer could not seek a different partner (or the respondent a different offer), and the respondent could only accept or reject the offer he or she had just received. If the respondent accepted, he or she received the (imaginary) amount and the offerer received whatever was left. If the respondent rejected the offer, both received nothing. An acceptance or rejection ended the negotiation.

When everyone was finished making, accepting, or rejecting their first offers (dividing $100), the results were posted for all to see, and the interactions were discussed. Then the exercise was repeated, with the rules remaining the same. Offerers were asked to find new partners for the second round, and, again, the amount was not revealed to respondents. This time it was $1 million.

The first round results are shown in Table 11.1; these were also displayed for the group. Offers ranged from $1.95 to $60; most offers were accepted, but five offers of various sizes were rejected. The discussion flowed freely and, at one point, focused on the smallest offer, $1.95. The recording of this offer on the board, along with its acceptance, had led to considerable laughter from the group. So we asked the respondent, a businessman named Ulf, why he had accepted it. He said that it was easy. It took him about 20 seconds to accept the offer. Prorating the amount over an hour meant that he was being paid about $400 an hour, and that wasn't bad. The group obviously appreciated this analysis. He went on to say that he would accept any offer made to him because it made him better off financially, but that he would judge the person by the size of the offer he or she had made. This quieted everyone's laughter, and after the discussion wound down, the group went on to the next round.

In the meantime, one of the offerers had left to take a long-distance phone call. To keep the numbers of offerers and respondents equal, one of the authors (the coordinator of the exercise) acted as an offerer. After people had milled around for awhile, Ulf came to the front of the room and said that he had been sitting quietly in the back, and no one had approached him to make an offer. This was noteworthy in itself. Then he said that we would have to make him an offer. We said that we knew what he was going to do: He was going to accept our offer and judge us personally by how large it was. He agreed. We hesitated, and ultimately exercised the instructor's prerogative: We never did make an offer to Ulf, but presented the decision to the rest of the group and asked them what they would offer him.

—— TABLE 11.1 ——
Ultimatum Games Played by European Executives

$100 Payoffs for			$1 Million Payoffs for		
Offerer	Respondent	Response	Offerer	Respondent	Response
98.05	1.95	accept	999,990	10	accept
95	5	accept	999,900	100	accept
95	5	reject	999,775	225	accept
90	10	accept	999,750	250	accept
89.75	10.25	accept	999,400	600	accept
85	15	accept	999,250	750	accept
84	16	accept	996,500	3,500	accept
75	25	accept	995,000	5,000	accept
75	25	accept	975,000	25,000	accept
75	25	reject	975,000	25,000	accept
70	30	accept	950,000	50,000	accept
70	30	reject	949,950	50,050	accept
55	45	accept	900,000	100,000	accept
50	50	accept	770,000	230,000	accept
50	50	accept	750,000	250,000	accept
50	50	reject	750,000	250,000	accept
50	50	reject	750,000	250,000	accept
40	60	accept			

NOTE: Offerers divided $100 and then $1 million. Respondents did not know how much was being divided until after each round.

The original offers dividing $1 million are shown in Table 11.1: They ranged from a low of $10 to a high of $250,000 (25% of the total); all were accepted. In percentage terms, offerers offered less than when they were dividing $100. (Some of this was strategic; offerers had used one offer to set up the other.)

The offers to Ulf are shown in Table 11.2. Here the range was much broader: Two people offered $1; eight offered half a million. People essentially used the entire feasible range of offers.

These offers were not treated as everyday, straightforward negotiation exercises; rather, people seemed to take them quite seriously. This exercise, and Ulf's reactions to it, then, highlight the fact that the ultimatum game is not just a simple bargaining exercise, with no moral consequences. Instead, it provides the basis for potentially serious personal judgments. As a result, when we have conducted our empirical research on ultimatums, we have paid attention to the quantitative and personal outcomes. This uncontrolled exercise altered our otherwise rational outlook on these interactions. In particular, Ulf's portion of the exercise (which we have repeated with several other groups, with similar

———— TABLE 11.2 ————
Offers to Ulf, Who Will Accept the Offer and Judge
the Offerer by the Amount Offered

Offers ($)	Frequency
1	2
1.95	1
50	2
100	1
250	1
400	1
500	2
750	1
1,000	4
10,000	1
30,000	1
50,000	1
50,050	1
100,000	1
250,000	3
300,000	2
320,000	1
400,000	1
500,000	8

NOTE: Offerer divided $1 million; Ulf did not know how much was being divided until afterward.

results) contributes to our conclusions about asymmetric moral imperatives in ultimatum bargaining.

In essence, we have found that offerers and respondents take very different approaches to this task. Because the offers are real ultimatums (i.e., they cannot be negotiated), offerers have considerable power. They usually realize this and tend to act strategically, often formulating their offers to give themselves the best chance at maximizing their monetary outcomes. In contrast, respondents, who seem to realize their relatively weak position and tend not to be happy about it, look for offerers to present them with offers that they feel are fair. These differing approaches to the task represent asymmetric moral imperatives. We devote the rest of this chapter to presenting how we have come to these conclusions, and to discussing their potential consequences in other contexts.

Ultimatums

Bargaining typically includes elements of both cooperation and competition. Cooperation is necessary to secure an agreement; competition surfaces around agreement terms. The competitive aspects of a negotiation can often wind down to an endgame where one party makes a "take it or leave it" offer (e.g., Roth, Murnighan, & Schoumaker, 1988). Examples are numerous. The most obvious may be in collective bargaining, where parties negotiate until the eleventh hour before one side or the other makes or concedes to an ultimatum. Interactions with children ("Do this or else"), mail-order flyers ("You must respond by May 23"), and the pricing policies of retail merchants can also be conceptualized as ultimatums. In fact, most retail purchases depend on a seller setting the price and a buyer paying that price. Surprisingly, empirical research on ultimatums had not appeared in the literature until 1982, when the *Journal of Economic Behavior and Organization* published Guth, Schmittberger, and Schwarze's article on ultimatum bargaining. These researchers used the simple experimental procedure that we duplicated in our exercise (and in our ultimatum studies). The important difference in our approach, however, is that we have always looked at two conditions: complete information, in which offerers and respondents both know how much is being divided and this information is common knowledge (i.e., both know that both know, and so on); and partial information, in which respondents do not know how much is being divided (as exemplified in our workshop exercise).

Game theory's models of subgame perfect equilibrium (Selten, 1965) analyze both conditions, and ultimatum games in general, from the respondent's perspective, at the end of the game, and work backwards to the beginning. Because something is better than nothing, the respondent should accept almost any offer, even if it is very small. In turn, offerers should make extremely small ultimatum offers—and these should be accepted. This prediction reflects the fact that the offerer has tremendous control: Once an offer has been made, it cannot be changed, and the respondent can only accept or reject it.

Empirical findings on complete-information ultimatum games indicate, however, that such outcomes are rare (e.g., Guth et al., 1982; Guth & Tietz, 1990). In particular, average offers typically approach 50/50 divisions of the payoff, and, as the value of offers drops, rejections become more frequent. Even when the games are expanded to two or more periods, with offers alternating between the players, there is a strong pull toward 50/50 offers (e.g., Ochs & Roth, 1989). As a result, several authors have suggested that fairness drives the results of these experiments and, by extension, other ultimatum interactions (Guth & Tietz, 1990).

In this chapter we summarize a series of experiments directed toward testing whether fairness norms can explain the unpredicted but systematic behaviors observed in ultimatum game research. Two studies focused directly on whether concerns for fairness affect the size of ultimatum offers (which are consistently larger than predicted), one study focused directly on whether fairness is the central concern of respondents who reject ultimatum offers (also counter to prediction), and two studies attempted to establish the conditions in which (a) game-theoretic predictions are supported and (b) fairness concerns are strongest.

Fairness Concerns

In their early research, Guth et al. (1982) asked 21 offerers each to make a one-shot offer to 21 respondents. Total payoffs ranged from 4 to 10 deutsche marks. Seven people proposed 50/50 agreements; the average was 65/35; two offers were rejected. The same participants (now assumed to be experienced) made offers and responses the next week as well, resulting in three 50/50 offers, an average offer of 69/31, and six rejections. The authors conclude that "subjects often rely on what they consider to be a fair result."

Subsequent findings continued to yield larger-than-expected offers and anywhere from 15% to 20% rejections (for a summary, replication, and extension of previous work, see Ochs & Roth, 1989). Although these findings may reflect a desire to appear fair, the strongest evidence for fairness comes from a study by Kahneman, Knetsch, and Thaler (1986) in which people reported a willingness to sacrifice some of their own outcome to punish someone who had offered an unequal division to another player in a previous game.

In related research, Forsythe, Horowitz, Savin, and Sefton (1989) studied ultimatum and dictator games in which respondents could have no influence on outcome distributions: They could accept or reject their offers, but their actions did not affect the dictator's self-determined outcome. None of the ultimatum offerers demanded the whole payoff—and most dictators did not either. Instead, they still offered part of the total (albeit a small portion) to the other party. Related research by Hoffman, McCabe, Shachat, and Smith (1994) and Bolton, Katok, and Zwick (in press) found that dictators offered even less. And in ultimatum games, Kravitz and Gunto's (1992) offerers reported that they would make small offers that were close to game-theoretic predictions if they knew that respondents would accept any offer. These studies indicate that when others (respondents or the experimenter) can evaluate offers, people are more likely to make larger offers. As power and anonymity increase (with limits—see Bolton et al., in press), people reduce their offers. This suggests that the equality heuristic (one prominent measure of fairness—see Allison & Messick, 1990) is sensitive to conditions. In sum, questions about offerers' fairness concerns are still open. Our first experiment addressed this issue directly.

Straub and Murnighan (in press)

Straub and Murnighan (in press) conducted two experiments; many of their methods were included in subsequent studies and are briefly summarized here. Offerers made a series of offers, knowing that only one of them might be put into effect. Respondents also accepted or rejected a series of offers, ostensibly from different offerers, knowing that only one of them might determine their monetary winnings. Respondents could accept or reject all, none, or some of the offers they received. Offerers and respondents never had any information about the identities of their counterparts. Their payoffs always depended on the potential selection of one of their offers or responses in a lottery following all of their choices. Payoffs were not made to all offerers and respondents, but to at least one person in each experimental group. Individual payoffs ranged from a matter of cents to as much as $97 for a task that took less than an hour. The expected return, however, tended to be quite small.

The major addition to ultimatum research methods in this study was the inclusion of a partial-information condition, in which respondents did not know how much offerers were dividing. Providing people with information that allows them to calculate the other person's outcomes is unusual in normal, everyday negotiations. Although bargainers may have some idea about their counterparts' potential profits, this information is rarely certain. Thus, by investigating conditions in which respondents did not know how much offerers were dividing, the researchers expanded the range of ultimatums under investigation and may have approached a more typical negotiation situation.

The use of partial and complete information conditions also allowed Straub and Murnighan to propose an operational definition for fairness (unlike almost all previous research). Following the strong social consensus displayed by people in the Kahneman et al. (1986) study, they defined offerers who made identical offers in the partial and complete information conditions as *truly fair* and those who made consistent 50/50 offers as *perfectly fair*. Offerers who increased their offers when respondents knew how much they were dividing were operationally defined as *strategic*. In Greenberg's (1990) terms, their complete-information offers were larger than partial-information offers so that they could appear fair. In more economic terms, they used their asymmetric information advantage strategically.

The first experiment put people into the role of (a) respondents to partial- and complete-information offers and (b) offerers of partial- and complete-information offers, in that order. The major results indicated that respondents accepted significantly smaller offers in partial-information compared with complete-information conditions. A majority of respondents indicated, when

———— TABLE 11.3 ————

Frequency of Respondents Who Accepted Any Offer, and Mean
and Median Lowest Acceptable Offers in Complete- and
Partial-Information Conditions

Condition	Accepting Any Offer		Mean Lowest Acceptable Offer ($)	Median Lowest Acceptable Offer ($)
	n	%		
Partial information	29/45	64	1.04	0.01
Complete information				
$10	11/46	24	1.92	1.00
$30	13/49	27	6.36	4.00
$50	13/49	27	10.38	7.50
$60	13/49	27	12.94	9.00
$80	12/49	24	17.43	12.00
$100	12/49	24	20.21	15.00
$1,000	10/49	20	166.68	100.00
$1,000,000	10/49	20	104,866.50	5,000.00

SOURCE: Straub and Murnighan (in press, Experiment 1).

they did not know how much was being divided, that they would accept any offer (even $.01); on average, however, their lowest acceptable offer was still significantly greater than $.01 (see Table 11.3). On the offer side, complete-information offers were significantly larger than partial-information offers, indicating that most offerers were strategic rather than truly fair.

Straub and Murnighan's results and those of Harrison and McCabe (1992) also showed that 50/50 offers were actually more effective (in an expected value sense, given our samples of respondents) than small offers and, in many cases, provided offerers with their best possible returns (see Table 11.4). Thus it appears that expectations of rejection and simple attempts to maximize outcomes can explain the incidence of large ultimatum offers rather than norms of fairness.

The second of Straub and Murnighan's two experiments studied only respondents (no offerers) and added a no-strings-attached condition, where no one was involved as offerer and "free" money was simply offered to people. This study broke the task down to its most elemental form. If people rejected small amounts of no-strings money, then the underlying assumption that anything is better than nothing, and that more is better than less, would not be strictly supported. It also provided a test of whether the earlier results in the partial-information findings actually did support the subgame perfect equilibrium predictions.

—— TABLE 11.4 ——
Expected Payoffs to Offerers in the Complete-Information Conditions ($)

Amount to Be Divided	Optimal Offer	Expected Payoff From $.01 Offer	Expected Payoff From Median Offer	Expected Payoff From 50% Offer	Expected Payoff From Optimal Offer
10	3	2.39	5.00	5.00	5.33
30	5	7.96	11.76	14.69	15.31
50	10	13.26	24.49	24.49	25.31
60	20, 30	15.92	29.39	29.39	29.39
80	40	19.59	38.37	38.37	38.37
100	20	24.49	43.78	48.98	50.61

SOURCE: Straub and Murnighan (in press, Experiment 1).

The results indicated that people often did reject small amounts of "free" money, in almost exactly the same proportion as they rejected partial-information offers (see Table 11.5). Some people commented that anything less than 25 cents was not worth anything to them because it would not fit in a parking meter. Others rejected anything less than 50 cents because it was not enough to buy a soda. Both the no-strings and partial-information offers differed significantly from complete-information offers (the third set of offers seen by these respondents; see Table 11.5). Thus, although people did not always accept the smallest of offers in the partial-information condition, they tended to accept offers as small as they would if they were offered free money. This suggests that the subgame perfect equilibrium predictions are clearly supported in this condition. These experiments also indicate that offerers appear to be strategic rather than fair.

In a postexperimental questionnaire, respondents who were asked to explain why they rejected offers typically invoked the concept of fairness. But these same people acted strategically when they were ultimatum offerers, leading to questions of their consistency, if not their honesty. Citing concerns for fairness may be a socially acceptable and convenient way to reject small monetary offers. Straub and Murnighan hypothesized that the often observed emotional reaction that followed small offers reflected more than unfairness reactions. They proposed that a more complete explanation for the rejection of small ultimatum offers may be wounded pride, and that people invoke fairness as a post hoc, socially acceptable rationalization of their essentially spiteful behavior.

The next study focused more explicitly on the fairness explanation for ultimatum offerers. In particular, it is the only experiment we are aware of that has induced fairness norms prior to ultimatum offers and responses. As such, it used the experimental method to test this explanation directly for large ultimatum offers. It also provided the first test of the wounded pride/spite hypothesis.

——— TABLE 11.5 ———
Lowest Acceptable Offers in the No-Strings-Attached,
Partial-Information, and Complete-Information Conditions

Condition	Accepting Any Offer		Mean Lowest Acceptable Offer ($)	Median Lowest Acceptable Offer ($)
	n	%		
No strings attached	36/90	40	0.42	0.05
Partial information	35/91	38	0.40	0.09
Complete information, $10	20/88	23	1.04	1.04

SOURCE: Straub and Murnighan (in press, Experiment 2).

Pillutla and Murnighan (in press)

The two experiments in this investigation attempted to activate fairness norms by providing offerers or independent third parties with the opportunity to add fairness labels to large and small offers prior to presenting them to respondents. Thus respondents knew ahead of time that some of their offers would have fairness labels, and offerers knew that they or others (third parties) might attach "This is fair" labels to some of their offers.

The first experiment dealt only with respondents; they received four partial-information offers, then four complete-information offers where they knew that the offerer was dividing $10. For each set of offers, two were relatively large (between $3 and $4.25) and two small (between $.40 and $.60); two had labels (fair or unfair) and two did not. The source of the labels was either the offerer or an independent third party, and respondents knew who had labeled the offer.

We expected that third-party labels would have straightforward effects: Unfair labels would lead to more rejections than no labels, which would lead to more rejections than fair labels. Social comparison theory (Festinger, 1954) also suggests that, in the partial-information conditions, where respondents know only the absolute but not the relative size of the offer, these effects should be magnified: People will use any available information—especially the evaluation of an independent third party—to help inform their choices.

Offers that are labeled by offerers, on the other hand, evoke the economic concept of "cheap talk" (Farrell & Gibbons, 1989), which refers to any unverifiable information that self-interested negotiators present to their counterparts without incurring costs. Cheap talk formalizes the idea that people should not believe everything they hear. Thus economic models suggest that offerers' fairness claims should have no effect. With no other information (i.e., the partial-information conditions), however, such labels may be persuasive.

TABLE 11.6

Frequencies of Respondents' Acceptances in Experiment 1

	Offerers' Labels								
	Fair				No Label				
	Partial Information		Complete Information		Partial Information		Complete Information		n
Offers	n	%	n	%	n	%	n	%	
Large	31	100	28	90	29	94	30	97	31
Small	25	81	17	55	23	74	18	58	

| | Third Party's Labels | | | | | | | | |
	Fair				No Label				
Large	22	96	21	91	17	74	21	91	23
Small	20	87	14	61	11	48	11	48	

| | Third Party's Labels | | | | | | | | |
	Unfair				No Label				
Large	24	83	22	76	29	100	26	90	29
Small	11	38	7	24	18	62	12	41	

When respondents have complete information about the amount being divided, they can evaluate the quality of the offer without paying attention to fairness labels (see Bazerman, Loewenstein, & White, 1992). A small offer labeled fair by an offerer, then, may provoke stronger negative emotions than unlabeled offers. This condition tests our wounded pride/spite hypothesis, using a more subtle manipulation than the "power statement" used by Kravitz and Gunto (1992) (i.e., "I know you'd like more, but that's the way it goes. Take it or leave it!"), which led to a drop in acceptance rates.

The results indicate that large offers were generally accepted, in all of the conditions (see Table 11.6). Apparently, offers of more than $3 were too enticing to pass up, even when a third party had labeled them as unfair. Thus it appears that people accept offers if they are large enough, irrespective of fairness.

Small offers in the partial-information conditions were most affected by a third party's fairness labels. Although fair labels by offerers had little impact, fair labels by third parties led to an 87% acceptance rate, about as high as for large offers. When a third party labeled offers unfair, few were accepted (32-36%). Most of the effects for small offers, then, supported the logic of social comparison theory.

Offerers' labels were essentially ignored. Thus the wounded pride/spite prediction was not supported. Instead, respondents reacted as if an offerer's labels were cheap talk. The results did suggest that fairness concerns were important in accepting or rejecting offers. When people could not evaluate an offer, they accepted or rejected offers based on a neutral third party's evaluation.

A second experiment was designed to indicate whether offerers were motivated to be truly fair, to appear fair, or to be blatantly strategic. We used the same definition as Straub and Murnighan (in press) and expanded on it: Offerers whose complete-information offers exceeded their partial-information offers were defined as wanting to appear fair; offerers whose offers were identical, regardless of the respondents' information, were defined as truly fair, as in Straub and Murnighan (in press). Further, fair offerers should have also been unaffected by the presence of third parties. Offerers wanting to appear fair, on the other hand, should have increased the offers that a third party would evaluate to avoid the rejection of an offer labeled unfair. In addition, the opportunity to label one's offers provided strategic offerers with an opportunity to be even more strategic, by decreasing their offers when they could add fairness labels to their partial-information offers. In so doing, they could take advantage of information asymmetries and a potentially persuasive message. This strategy is the antithesis of fairness. In summary, then, we defined offerers as fair if they were not bothered by third-party or respondent evaluations of the size of their offers; strategic offerers were those who guarded against such evaluations by increasing their offers when they knew that others would know how much they were dividing; and blatantly strategic offerers were those who also took advantage of fairness labels by reducing their offers even further.

In the offerer label condition, offerers added a "This is fair" label to a specified half of their offers: They knew which offers would carry the fairness label and which would not. In the third-party conditions, offerers were told that an independent third party would evaluate half of their offers and would attach a fair or unfair label or no label before a respondent received it; the other half of their offers would not be evaluated and would have no labels. Everyone made four offers (complete or partial information × label/no label) for each of seven amounts—$10, $30, $50, and $70 (for real) and $100, $1,000, and $1 million (hypothetically) in ascending order—in either the offerer or the third-party condition.

At the end of the experiment, the lotteries were conducted, real offers were made (and accepted), and two offerers and two volunteer respondents were paid. Respondents accepted offers of $5 and $20, both in partial-information conditions; offerers received $65 and $50.

The means for the information, label, and source conditions are shown for each of the amounts in Table 11.7. The data were consistent for each of the amounts: Offerers made relatively large offers in the complete-information and third-party label conditions; they made smaller offers in the no-label, partial-information conditions; and they made the smallest offers in the

TABLE 11.7

Mean Offers and Percentage of the Total to Be Divided
(in real dollars) for the Information and Fairness Label Conditions

Amount Divided ($)	Information	No Label		Cheap Talk Fair Label		Third Party Fair Label	
		M	%	M	%	M	%
10	partial	3.54	35	2.61	26	4.67	47
	complete	4.66	47	4.27	43	4.85	48
30	partial	7.50	25	5.97	20	13.00	43
	complete	12.77	43	12.41	41	13.50	45
50	partial	10.84	22	8.77	17	21.80	44
	complete	21.56	43	20.36	41	22.20	44
70	partial	14.75	21	12.10	17	29.90	43
	complete	28.85	41	28.76	41	31.00	44
100	partial	19.05	19	14.53	15	41.20	41
	complete	40.65	41	37.97	38	44.50	44
1,000	partial	175.72	18	82.20	8	634.80	63
	complete	498.17	50	353.64	35	652.20	65
1 million	partial	63,413	6	61,052	6	240,443	24
	complete	303,573	30	309,935	30	300,227	30

SOURCE: Pillutla and Murnighan (in press, Experiment 2).
NOTE: $n = 66$ in the no-labels conditions and 33 in each of the labels conditions.

partial-information conditions when "This is fair" was attached to their offers and attributed to them. The same pattern of results surfaced for a frequency count of 50/50 offers.

Categorizing people as truly fair, wanting to appear fair, and/or strategic on the basis of their offers indicates that few offerers were truly fair. Only 2 of 66 offerers were truly fair; that is, they made the same offers in the information and the third-party conditions. When a third party was going to evaluate the offers, almost all offerers increased their offers, especially in the partial-information conditions. When they added their own fairness labels, most offerers took advantage of both the information conditions and the addition of fairness labels: They were about as strategic as they could possibly be.

Unlike respondents, offerers did not treat fairness labels as if they were cheap talk. They acted as if their own fairness labels would lead respondents to accept smaller offers, even in the complete-information condition. One explanation for this result is that people's greed overwhelmed their ability to predict their respondents' reactions. This is in line with Bazerman and Carroll's (1987) and Lawler's (1986) argument that negotiators rarely put themselves in their counterparts' shoes.

These results support those of other studies (e.g., Kahn & Murnighan, 1993; Straub & Murnighan, in press) in suggesting little support for ultimatum offerers' taking fairness into consideration in their offering behavior. In fact, this study goes considerably further, providing almost no basis for thinking that ultimatum offerers are trying to be fair when they make their offers. Instead, they seem to be blatantly strategic. Thus these results call into question conclusions suggesting that a substantial minority of the population is consistently altruistic, regardless of the context (e.g., Rapoport, 1988).

These results bring the research on ultimatum bargaining full circle. Early research (e.g., Guth et al., 1982) was based on a theoretical model of economic rationality and self-interested behavior—a model that has formed the basis of considerable theorizing about human behavior. Repeated observation of departures from the model's predictions led to a shift of theoretical emphasis, with notions of fairness predominating. These results make a strong case for the fact that these previous results only presented an illusion that people were acting fairly. Instead, it appears that ultimatum offerers try to look fair to serve their own self-interests. Rather than being truly fair, they are strategic: they offer more only to avoid rejection or to avoid having their offers labeled "unfair."

This strategic behavior may well include competitive motives much like those at work in "might over morality" findings (Liebrand, Jansen, Rijken, & Suhre, 1986), which suggest that competitive bargainers view negotiations as a choice between weak and strong behavior (might), whereas more cooperatively oriented bargainers view the negotiation choice as one between good and bad (morality). It is easily conceivable that offerers might view 50/50 offers as weak and increasingly self-beneficial offers as strong. However, such an interpretation also works well as a rationalization for self-interested behavior. Our conceptualization of "strategic behavior" encompasses the competitive aspects of these reactions.

The importance of fairness concerns for respondents, and whether their evaluation of an offer as unfair is sufficient to explain the frequent rejections of ultimatum offers, remains an open question. Our next study addressed more directly whether the wounded pride/spite hypothesis might explain reactions better than simple concerns for fairness.

Pillutla and Murnighan (1994)

The wounded pride/spite hypothesis states that a respondent will look for an offer that he or she feels is fair; if the offer is smaller than expected, the respondent's reaction will be personal (wounded pride and even anger) and he or she will take personal action (spite), causing the offerer (and the respondent) to get nothing. The study discussed in the preceding section tested this hypothesis by combining small offers with a statement (purportedly from the offerer) that the offer was fair, even though it was a small fraction of the amount being divided (50 cents out of $10). But rejections did not increase; instead, respondents consistently ignored offerers' claims of fairness, apparently treating them as "cheap talk."

In this new study, we varied the methods of previous studies by boosting the amount that offerers were dividing, by continuing to give respondents small offers, and by giving them outside options as a basis for making outcome comparisons. In addition, by providing respondents with information about whether offerers knew that they had small outside options, we provided conditions where anger might accentuate respondents' reactions, beyond their perceptions that the small offer was unfair.

The presence of a fixed outside option provided respondents with a stronger basis for evaluating the worth of the offers they received. Respondents without an outside option but with information about how much was being divided could use the offerers' outcomes as a basis for comparison with their own. (This is how judgments of fairness are assumed to be made.) Perceptions of unfairness, however, can arise even when respondents are unaware of the amounts the offerers are dividing. Croson (1993), for instance, reports that a lack of information leads to widely varying expectations: Many use the value of the offer to arrive at self-serving but incorrect conclusions about the amount being divided. Although respondents without outside options might use zero as a reference point to evaluate their offers, previous respondents have reported that they formulated their own (unfounded) expectations about how much they might gain. A specific outside option (0, $1, or $2 in this study) can replace these uncertain expectations and provide respondents with a stronger basis for evaluating their offer.

In this experiment (a) all offers were either $1 or $2; (b) outside options were $0, $1, or $2; (c) respondents either knew or did not know that offerers were dividing $20 (the complete- and partial-information conditions); and (d) in the common-knowledge condition, respondents knew that the offerers knew the value of their outside options prior to making the offers, and in the not-common-knowledge condition, they knew that the offerers did not have this knowledge.

Two control conditions were also included, with the $1 and $2 offers now representing 50% of the amount being divided ($2 and $4). These controls checked whether people might reject small offers that were nevertheless fair (i.e., 50%). Rejections would indicate that people were using some basis other than fairness to reject offers. We expected that people would generally accept these offers, even when they had equivalent outside options.

Our analyses focused primarily on conditions where an offer was identical to a respondent's outside option. These are the circumstances where respondents may be most affected by their knowledge of what the offerers knew before making their offers. When offerers do not know the value of the outside option (the not-common-knowledge condition), there is room to forgive an offerer for making small offers. This room disappears when the offerer has knowledge about the outside option: Respondents can then attribute malicious greed to offerers and may find it easier to respond spitefully.

We designed this experiment to boost the frequency of rejections to see whether they resulted from feelings of unfairness and/or the stronger reaction of spite. Partial information and not common knowledge should have led most people to accept any offer that was at least as large as their outside options. When respondents had no information but did know that offerers knew the value of their outside options, rejections were particularly (and generally) spiteful, because the respondents had no information about how much of the payoff they were denying the offerers. (Offerers could be dividing a small amount fairly and respondents would be denying them a chance of a positive outcome.) By contrast, the complete-information/common-knowledge condition should have generated the most spite. Here, all the blame for the low offer can be leveled at the offerer, and respondents can take low offers personally. Thus increased rejections from the not-common-knowledge to the common-knowledge conditions were taken as support for the spite hypothesis. Here, the offers do not change, but information attributed to the offerer does: These attributions should lead to more anger than any of the other conditions—and the most spiteful rejections.

Table 11.8 displays the frequencies and percentages of offers accepted. More than 80% of the respondents accepted the control condition offers, suggesting that most of the other rejections depended to a great degree on concerns for fairness. Compared with controls, acceptances in comparable experimental conditions ($1 offers with outside options of $1; $2 offers with outside options of $2) dropped to 44% and 22% with partial and complete information, respectively. We attribute this increase in rejections to concerns for fairness and spite.

Respondents without outside options understandably accepted almost all $2 offers in the partial-information condition; they rejected only a few $1 offers (accepting 92.4%). In the complete-information condition, where they knew that $20 was being divided, rejections increased slightly: 83.7% of the $2 and 73.9% of the $1 offers were accepted, with fewer acceptances when respondents knew that the offerers knew their outside options (see Table 11.8).

Overall, partial-information offers with no common knowledge led to 77% (204 of 265) acceptances (excluding $1 offers with outside options of $2). Adding complete information reduced acceptances to 63% (167 of 265). This drop is attributable to both fairness concerns and spite. Adding common knowledge reduced acceptances even further, to 47.2% (91 of 193). This larger drop is directly attributable to spite. Also, none of these rejections is predicted by subgame perfect equilibrium models. In every condition, people accepted more partial-information than complete-information offers. They also accepted

TABLE 11.8
Frequencies of Acceptances (rejections in parentheses)

Amount Being Divided ($)	Outside Options ($)	The Offer ($)	Partial Information				Complete Information			
			Not Common		Common		Not Common		Common	
			n	%	n	%	n	%	n	%
20	0	1	50 (3)	94.3	35 (4)	89.7	45 (8)	84.9	23 (16)	59
		2	52 (1)	98.1	39 (0)	100	48 (5)	90.6	29 (10)	74
	1	1	26 (27)	49.1	16 (23)	41	15 (38)	28.3	8 (31)	20.5
		2	48 (5)	90.6	35 (4)	89.7	42 (11)	79.2	24 (15)	61.5
	2	1	0 (53)	0	0 (39)	0	0 (53)	0	0 (39)	0
		2	28 (25)	52.8	18 (21)	46.2	17 (36)	32.1	9 (30)	23.1
2	1	1					44 (9)	83	34 (5)	87.2
4	2	2					42 (11)	79.2	35 (4)	89.7

SOURCE: Pillutla and Murnighan (1994).

NOTE: This table excludes participants (a) who accepted an offer of $1 when they had an outside option of $2 and (b) who said that they did not understand the exercise in the postexperimental questionnaire.

more not-common-knowledge than common-knowledge offers, especially with complete information.

Logit analyses revealed significant effects for offer size, outside options, knowledge, and information. The beta weights were positive for offer size and negative for the other factors, indicating that acceptances increased with offer size but decreased with increasing outside options, common knowledge, or complete information. Additional analyses indicated that the offer size by outside option and the knowledge by information interactions were also significant. These findings indicate that people were more likely to reject offers that were equal to or less than their outside options and to accept offers that exceeded their outside options, and that the effects of common knowledge were strongest in the complete-information condition; that is, drops in acceptance rates were most severe in the common-knowledge/complete-information conditions. This also supports the wounded pride/spite hypothesis.

The results suggest that the common-knowledge effect, although more pronounced in the complete-information condition, was also significant in the partial-information conditions. This could happen only if respondents made attributions of unfairness to the offerers and also reacted with anger when their information about the offerers' knowledge increased. A simple unfairness hypothesis can explain the significant effect for information; that is, people who know that the offerer is dividing $20 and can easily determine that offerers will do much better than they do if they accept their small offers reject offers that they perceive as unfair. But a simple fairness hypothesis cannot explain the significant knowledge effect: People reject more offers when they know that offerers know their outside options. This knowledge allows respondents to surmise that the offerers are taking advantage of them.

Our results suggest that fairness concerns are a necessary but incomplete explanation of why people reject small ultimatum offers. A more complete explanation is that people reject offers when they are hurt or angered by the offers and, concomitantly, the offerers. The frequency of rejections increases markedly when respondents react with spite.

Note that in the control condition, knowledge had no effect on acceptance rates. This strengthens our conclusions that unfair offers are necessary before people make attributions and get angry. In the control condition, there was no reason for respondents to attribute unfairness to offerers, and acceptances actually increased (not significantly) rather than decreased with common knowledge.

Previous studies have reported consistent results that did not match the strong game-theoretic predictions (e.g., Croson, 1993; Ochs & Roth, 1989). This study added economic variables (information, common knowledge, and outside options) to psychological concepts (wounded pride, anger, and spite) in an attempt to explain ultimatum rejections. As in previous studies, significantly more offers were rejected when respondents could determine that the offers were essentially unfair (giving them much less than the offerers would receive if the offers were accepted) *and* the offerers knew respondents' alternative outcomes. Adding anger to unfairness seemed to cause spiteful reactions that increased rejections. Unfairness alone led to many rejections; spite led to more.

In conjunction with the findings on offerers (e.g., Pillutla & Murnighan, in press), the picture of the two sides of ultimatum bargaining now looks like this: Offerers in strict ultimatum games like these are handed considerable power. They are the first movers and have considerable discretion in the offers they can make. They seem to recognize their strength, and their apparently automatic reaction is to be strategic and look for ways to increase their own outcomes. They take advantage of fairness labels when they can, and they guard against unfairness labels (and the greater chance of a rejection) when faced with either a third party's or a respondent's knowing how much they are dividing.

In contrast, respondents are in a much weaker position: They can only accept or reject the offers they receive. They cannot negotiate a better deal in any meaningful way. With any experience, they realize their lack of power. At the same time, they seem to hope for and sometimes expect offers that are reasonable and fair (not necessarily 50/50). When they receive offers that are not large enough, they may react with spite and reject offers that are otherwise beneficial.

The asymmetry of the two parties' outlooks is particularly striking. The powerful party—the offerer—is strategic: If the offerer gets too greedy (in the respondent's eyes), the offer is rejected—spitefully. If the offerer calculates well, however, the offer is accepted, and the offerer gets at least half of the total. The offerer is concerned about the fairness perceptions of the respondent, but only as far as these affect the offerer's own outcomes. The offerer shows little, if any, concern for the fairness of the outcome the respondent actually receives. We would tentatively predict (and plan to test) that this asymmetry is present in the same individuals: People who shift between being offerers and respondents will shift their outlooks as well, without considering the inconsistency of their actions.

These findings provide a fairly complete explanation of ultimatum behavior as we have observed it in our studies. They leave out one element, however, that has been neglected in bargaining research in general: the development of bargaining strategies. Why do offerers respond to the opportunity to make an ultimatum strategically? And why do concerns for fairness and feelings of wounded pride, anger, and spite characterize respondents?

In research with Michael Saxon, we decided to use ultimatums—a very simple form of negotiation—to investigate how children bargain. In particular, we gave kindergartners, third, sixth, and ninth graders, and college students the opportunity to make and respond to a series of ultimatum offers, with complete and partial information, for money and M&Ms, to determine whether there is any easily identifiable pattern to the development of bargaining reactions.

Murnighan and Saxon (1994)

Recently, a number of researchers have emphasized the importance of creating a "developmental economic psychology" that will illuminate how children are socialized into and react to the economic world (Leiser, Roland-Levy, & Sevon, 1990; Webley & Lea, 1993). In our experiments we tried to understand the economic behavior of children by giving them tasks that they would understand and enjoy.

Much of the previous work on ultimatums has used elements of socialization and cultural determinacy, such as concerns for fairness, to explain findings. If these concerns are learned, then studying people with different life experiences (in this case, groups that differ in age and gender) and in different socialization stages should provide important information about the underlying foundations of the behaviors we have observed. This project was designed to gather information about children's ultimatum bargaining behavior and the development of concerns for fairness. As a first step, we combined models of distributive justice in children (e.g., Damon, 1980) with economic theories of rational choice to generate hypotheses about children's ultimatums.

Anecdotal evidence suggests that young children commonly experience ultimatums and other threats (Murnighan, 1991). Parents' attempts at discipline (e.g., "Stop that, or else . . . ") often give children take-it-or-leave-it choices. And during the more complicated give-and-take that is required in the gradual, reciprocal concession making of normal negotiations, younger children may simplify and view the situation in the black-and-white terms that characterize ultimatums. As a result, young children may react to negotiations with strong, tenacious stands that lead either to successful outcomes or to disagreement.

Older children, on the other hand, may not only be able to handle more complex negotiations, but may tend to lose the younger child's dogmatic tenacity, possibly because of increasing self-consciousness (Elkind, 1980). So far, the research related to children's bargaining has focused almost exclusively on children's allocation norms (e.g., Streater & Chertkoff, 1976) or their competitiveness in a matrix game (e.g., Toda, Shinotsuka, McClintock, & Stech, 1978).

The research literature on children's expressions of self-interest and fairness has used one basic procedure. First, two children perform a task. Then, one of the two is asked to divide a reward. Most designs incorporate false feedback to establish that one child's performance is equal to, better, or worse than the other's. Allocations are then categorized as reflecting norms of equality, equity (i.e., outcomes that are proportional to performance differences), or some combination of the two (e.g., ordinal equity, where the better performer gets more, but not proportionally more, than the poorer performer).

Findings consistently show that younger children are own-gain oriented (e.g., Keil, 1986; McClintock, Moskowitz, & McClintock, 1977). Wide disparities in performance have often led to allocations based on ordinal equity (Keil & McClintock, 1983). In addition, fair allocations (proportional or ordinal equity or equality) by self-interested allocators increase with age (e.g., Avermaet & McClintock, 1988). Handlon and Gross (1959), for instance, found that kindergartners were much more likely to keep a majority of the prize than were fourth, fifth, and sixth graders, who were most likely to split it equally. Damon's (1980) model of social reasoning reflects these findings, with children (a) being primarily self-interested prior to 5 years of age, (b) focusing on equality as a way to prevent conflict in the 5-7 age group, and (c) beginning to think in terms of equity thereafter. Hook and Cook's (1979) review, in particular, suggests that increases in proportional equity match the increase in children's ability to calculate and apply proportionality. Taken together, these results expand Piaget's (1932/1965) early observations: Not only do concerns for equality seem to increase with age, but so do concerns for and the ability to calculate equity.

At the same time, research on generosity suggests that children become more generous as they get older (e.g., Zarbatany, Hartmann, & Gelfand, 1985) and that girls are more generous than boys. But research on children's competitiveness also shows that children become increasingly competitive with age across several cultural groups (e.g., Kagan & Madsen, 1972; Toda et al., 1978). An extrapolation of these results to ultimatum bargaining suggests that younger children will be more selfish, less generous, less fair, but less competitive than older children, and that girls will be more generous than boys.

Ironically, the less complicated cognitive abilities of younger children and their stronger self-interested motivations may make them a particularly sensitive sample for testing economic theory's extreme predictions in ultimatum games. In particular, previous research on generosity suggests that younger children may be especially likely to make very small offers. At the same time, their inability to delay gratification suggests that they may also be more likely to accept small offers. Thus not only does the study of younger children provide an opportunity to map the development of bargaining strategies and behaviors, but younger children may also be a population that can provide subgame perfect equilibrium predictions with their strongest support.

Murnighan and Saxon's (1993) experiment used two procedures: a paper-and-pencil format for older children (sixth and ninth graders) and college students, to ensure that their responses were comparable to those from previous research; and a face-to-face procedure, to ensure that the younger children (kindergartners and third and sixth graders) understood the task. Sixth graders completed either the face-to-face procedure or the question-naire, allowing a direct comparison of the effects of the two procedures.

In the face-to-face procedure, the children made take-it-or-leave-it offers of money and M&Ms to anonymous others; they also responded to a series of offers constructed by the experimenters, but ostensibly originating with another child. As respondents, children were told to imagine another child was offering them money (dividing an unspecified total or $1) or M&Ms (dividing an unspecified total or 10). Restrictions by the children's school administration made actual payoffs impossible.

Respondents received offers of 1, 2, 3, 5, 10, 25, and 50 cents, in that order, or from 1 to 10 M&Ms, one at a time, on the table in front of them until they had accepted three consecutively. (Because many of the kindergartners did not know the difference between a nickel and a quarter, their monetary responses were not analyzed.)

As offerers in the face-to-face procedure, children made partial-information offers, dividing $1, before dividing 4, 5, 10, and 11 M&Ms (small and large amounts of an even and an odd number of M&Ms), before making complete-information offers using the same amounts. During the experiment, the complete- or partial-information nature of the situation was frequently reem-phasized. We also asked children why they had chosen particular actions. All interactions were tape-recorded.

The results provide a considerable body of information about the hypothe-ses and about children's ultimatum bargaining behaviors. We will move through the data, starting with the younger children first.

Kindergartners exhibited no guile whatsoever: They displayed no general inclination toward strategic behavior. As offerers, they usually separated the coins into two roughly equal piles and pushed one of the two piles across the desk as their offer to the other child. As respondents, they rarely refused the offer of one penny; they refused the offer of one M&M even less often. The most striking result for the kindergartners was that 12% of them gave the other child all of the coins and all of the M&Ms. We did not see this behavior in any other group.

Unlike some kindergartners, third graders understood the value of money. They also showed the first signs of strategic behavior. In particular, many of the boys shaded their partial-information offers.

The most noteworthy results for third graders centered on how they dealt with the issue of equality. When they were asked to make an offer dividing 5 (or 11) M&Ms, many asked whether they could cut one in half. When told that they could not, girls tended to offer more than half (3 and 6), keeping less than half for themselves, whereas boys did the reverse. At the same time, more

—————— TABLE 11.9 ——————
Monetary Offers (in percentages of the amount divided)
for the Gender and Information Conditions

| | Female | | Male | |
| | Partial Information | Complete Information | Partial Information | Complete Information |
Grades				
Third-sixth				
M	40.4	42.3	34.3	42.2
median	50	50	42.5	50
Sixth/ninth/college				
M	38.3	42.4	31.3	42.6
median	42.3	50	32.9	49.1

SOURCE: Murnighan and Saxon (1993).
NOTE: Third- and sixth-grade offerers were dividing $1 in each case, face-to-face; sixth-grade, ninth-grade, and college offerers were dividing amounts ranging from $1 to $1 million using the questionnaire procedure.

than half of the third graders offered 2, 3, 5, and 6 M&Ms (or some slight variation of this pattern) when they were dividing 4, 5, 10, and 11, in both the complete- and partial-information conditions.

More important, when they responded to M&M offers from another child and knew that 10 M&Ms were being divided (the complete-information condition), 13 of 40 third graders (7 girls and 6 boys) rejected 1, 2, 3, and 4, accepted 5, and rejected 6, 7, 8, 9, and 10. A lack of equality, for them or for the other child, was the reason given for the rejections. These third graders exhibited what we have labeled "extreme fairness."

Overall, younger children offered more but accepted less than older children (see Tables 11.9 and 11.10). Girls' offers were equal to or larger than those of boys, over all age groups. Girls were also less strategic than boys: They shaded their offers as often as boys, but less severely (see Table 11.9). This dichotomy in the sexes appeared among third graders and continued for all older ages in this sample.

Finally, we observed qualitative differences between money and M&Ms: For every age group, more children accepted offers of one M&M than accepted one cent, in both the complete- and partial-information conditions. Of 241 respondents, 98 (41%) accepted one cent in the partial-information conditions; 134 (56%) accepted one M&M. For complete information, 62 (26%) accepted one cent; 104 (43%) accepted one M&M.

Also, the only adults in this sample, college students, offered less and were willing to accept even less than younger respondents. This observation—that is, that college students moved closer to matching the predictions of economic theory—suggests a distinct relaxation of the stringent fairness criteria exer-

TABLE 11.10

Respondents' Lowest Acceptable Offers (in cents for the
face-to-face procedure and dollars for the questionnaire procedure)

Grade	No Strings	Partial Information	Complete Information
Face-to-face procedure			
kindergarten			
mean		2.82	4.05
median		1.0	1.0
n		45	43
third			
mean		3.50	10.65
median		2.0	3.0
n		40	40
sixth			
mean		5.81	10.64
median		1.5	5.0
n		36	36
Questionnaire procedure			
sixth			
mean	.37	.18	1.53
median	.04	.10	.50
n	59	55	56
ninth			
mean	.395	.48	1.665
median	.01	.05	1.00
n	58	52	55
college			
mean	.42	.51	1.12
median	.05	.05	1.00
n	90	140	138

SOURCE: Murnighan and Saxon (1993).
NOTE: For the face-to-face procedure, offerers divided $1; for the questionnaire procedure, offerers divided $10.

cised by younger children. With increasing age, people may be willing to accept much less than half, especially as the amount to be divided increases. And even these numbers may be inflated, given that people's ability to reject real amounts of money of considerable magnitude (e.g., sixth graders who would actually reject $300 or more when $1,000 is being divided) is clearly open to question.

Alternative explanations for the shift in behavior of the college students include the possibility that they may be less affected by and less prone to quick emotional reactions than the children in the study. Recent research by Frank, Gilovich, and Regan (1993) suggests another explanation: that college students have had the chance to study economics and, as a result, have become more consistent in their bargaining strategies. These possibilities open doors for future research.

Relevance to Economic Models

Straub and Murnighan (in press) found that small amounts of money (e.g., less than 25 or 50 cents) were almost meaningless to many respondents. Some children also refused very small amounts of money (e.g., a penny or two). As one third-grade boy who rejected the offer of a penny put it: "You can't buy anything with a penny. It's not going to do you a lot of good, unless you save up your pennies, which could take a very long time, because it takes 25 to equal a quarter." He rejected 2, 3, 4, and 5 cents as well, but accepted 10, saying, "You can buy a piece of candy with 10 cents." Thus, even when people did reject small amounts of money, it may have been because they judged the amounts to be subjectively (rather than objectively) meaningless.

Economic models rarely address the behavior of children (see Webley & Lea, 1993). By replicating previous support for theoretical predictions for respondents in the partial-information conditions, these data expand the domain of the predictions to very young respondents. As children get older, as they know how much is being divided, or if they are making rather than responding to ultimatum offers, they provide much less support for theoretical predictions.

Like adults, children rejected small, complete-information offers and offered more than small amounts. Again, the third-grade boy quoted above explained why. When he made a partial-information offer dividing $1, he offered 50 cents, because "then it would be 50/50. Both of us would have 50 cents." When he was asked to make a similar offer in the complete-information condition, he said, "Twenty-five cents. No, 60 cents, because sometimes I like to give people some more than I got. Sometimes I let them have all of it, and I just keep what I have. Sometimes money doesn't matter; it depends on what I feel." These quotes suggest that children understand some of the psychological concepts that might be effectively incorporated into economic models. (For a notable example in a related arena, see Roth & Erev, 1993.)

Conclusion

Previous ultimatum bargaining researchers tended to conclude that unforeseen effects resulted from fairness concerns. Thus we operationally defined fairness and tested the conditions where it appeared. The collection of data from our projects documents quite clearly that concerns for fairness provide little explanatory value for offerers, and only part of the explanation for respondents' rejections: The simple cognitive reactions associated with fairness concerns may explain some idiosyncratic rejections; additional, emotional reactions make wounded pride and spite compelling explanations for even more of these originally unexpected rejections.

Thus, although fairness concerns are certainly relevant, they now appear to be too simple an explanation for why game theory's strong predictions for ultimatum games are so rarely supported. Self-interested offerers do not support game theory's predictions because they want to avoid rejections and because unpredicted, nonequilibrium behavior is more valuable and effective than equilibrium behavior (Prasnikar & Roth, 1992). Respondents, on the other hand, do not support the theoretical predictions for essentially psychological reasons. In particular, we observe that offerers and respondents are motivated by asymmetric moral imperatives. Most offerers define the situation as an opportunity for monetary gain; they tend to be blatantly strategic. Many respondents, on the other hand, owing to their relatively powerless position, define the situation morally. (A small minority of respondents view the situation as an economically rational actor would, and are willing to accept any amount that is offered.) This asymmetry can lead to disagreement and unhappiness for both parties—for the offerer, following a rejection, or for the respondent, in accepting an offer that he or she feels is unfair. From a strictly utilitarian perspective, these reactions can lead to considerable inefficiencies. From a social perspective, they can sour negotiations and make future interactions particularly problematic.

References

Allison, S. T., & Messick, D. M. (1990). Social decision heuristics and the use of shared resources. *Journal of Behavioral Decision Making, 3,* 195-204.

Avermaet, E. van, & McClintock, C. G. (1988). Intergroup fairness and bias in children. *European Journal of Social Psychology, 18,* 407-428.

Bazerman, M. H., & Carroll, J. S. (1987). Negotiator cognition. In B. M. Staw & L. L. Cummings (Eds.), *Research in organizational behavior* (Vol. 9, pp. 247-288). Greenwich CT: JAI.

Bazerman, M. H., Loewenstein, G. F., & White, S. B. 1992. Reversals of preference in allocation decisions: Judging an alternative versus choosing among alternatives. *Administrative Science Quarterly, 37,* 220-240.

Bolton, G. E., Katok, E., & Zwick, R. (in press). Dictator game giving: Rules of fairness versus acts of kindness. *International Journal of Game Theory.*

Croson, R. (1993). *Information in ultimatum games: An experimental study.* Unpublished manuscript, Harvard University.

Damon, W. (1980). Patterns of change in children's social reasoning: A two-year longitudinal study. *Child Development, 51,* 1010-1017.

Elkind, D. (1980). Strategic interactions in early adolescence. In J. Adelson (Ed.), *Handbook of adolescent psychology.* New York: John Wiley.

Farrell, J., & Gibbons, R. (1989). Cheap talk with two audiences. *American Economic Review, 79,* 1214-1223.

Festinger, L. (1954). A theory of social comparison processes. *Human Relations, 7,* 117-140.

Forsythe, R., Horowitz, J. L., Savin, N. E., & Sefton, M. (1989). The statistical analysis of experiments with simple bargaining games. *Games and Economic Behavior, 6,* 347-369.

Frank, R. H., Gilovich, T., & Regan, D. T. (1993). Does studying economics inhibit cooperation? *Journal of Economic Perspectives, 7,* 159-171.

Greenberg, J. (1990). Looking fair vs. being fair: Managing impressions of organizational justice. In B. M. Staw & L. L. Cummings (Eds.), *Research in organizational behavior* (Vol. 12). Greenwich, CT: JAI.

Guth, W., Schmittberger, R., & Schwarze, B. (1982). An experimental analysis of ultimatum bargaining. *Journal of Economic Behavior and Organization, 3,* 367-388.

Guth, W., & Tietz, R. (1990). Ultimatum bargaining behavior: A survey and comparison of experimental results. *Journal of Economic Psychology, 11,* 417-449.

Handlon, B. J., & Gross, P. (1959). The development of sharing behavior. *Journal of Abnormal and Social Psychology, 59,* 425-428.

Harrison, G. W., & McCabe, K. A. (1992, March). *Expectations and fairness in a simple bargaining experiment.* Paper presented at the annual meeting of the Public Choice Society, New Orleans.

Hoffman, E., McCabe, K., Shachat, K., & Smith, V. (1994). Preferences, property rights and anonymity in bargaining games. *Games and Economic Behavior, 7,* 346-380.

Hook, J., & Cook, T. D. (1979). Equity theory and the cognitive ability of children. *Psychological Bulletin, 86,* 429-445.

Kagan, S., & Madsen, M. (1972). Rivalry in Anglo-American and Mexican children of two ages. *Journal of Personality and Social Psychology, 24,* 214-220.

Kahn, L. M., & Murnighan, J. K. (1993). A general experiment on bargaining in demand games with outside options. *American Economic Review, 83,* 1260-1280.

Kahneman, D., Knetsch, J., & Thaler, H. (1986). Fairness and the assumption of economics. *Journal of Business, 59,* S285-S300.

Keil, L. J. (1986). Rules, reciprocity, and rewards: A developmental study of resource allocation in social interaction. *Journal of Experimental Social Psychology, 22,* 419-435.

Keil, L. J., & McClintock, C. G. (1983). A developmental perspective on distributive justice. In D. Messick & K. Cook (Eds.), *Theories of equity: Psychological and sociological perspectives.* New York: Praeger.

Kravitz, D., & Gunto, S. (1992). Decisions and recipients in ultimatum bargaining games. *Journal of Socio-Economics, 21,* 65-84.

Lawler, E. J. (1986). Bilateral deterrence and conflict spiral: A theoretical analysis. In E. J. Lawler & B. Markovsky (Eds.), *Advances in group processes* (Vol. 3, pp. 107-130). Greenwich, CT: JAI.

Leiser, D., Roland-Levy, C., & Sevon, G. (1990). Introduction. In D. Leiser, C. Roland-Levy, & G. Sevon (Eds.), Economic socialization [Special issue]. *Journal of Economic Psychology, 11,* 467-468.

Liebrand, W. B., Jansen, R., Rijken, V., & Suhre, C. (1986). Might over morality: Social values and the perception of other players in experimental games. *Journal of Experimental Social Psychology, 24,* 203-215.

McClintock, C. G., Moskowitz, J. M., & McClintock, E. (1977). Variations in preferences for individualistic, competitive, and cooperative outcomes as a function of age, game, class, and task in nursery school children. *Child Development, 48,* 1080-1085.

Murnighan, J. K. (1991). *The dynamics of bargaining games.* Englewood Cliffs, NJ: Prentice Hall.
Murnighan, J. K., & Saxon, M. S. (1994). *Ultimatum bargaining by children and adults.* Manuscript submitted for publication.
Ochs, J., & Roth, A. E. (1989). An experimental study of sequential bargaining. *American Economic Review, 79,* 355-384.
Piaget, J. (1965). *The moral judgment of the child.* New York: Free Press. (Original work published 1932)
Pillutla, M. M., & Murnighan, J. K. (1994). *Adding anger to perceptions of unfairness: Spiteful rejections of ultimatum offers.* Unpublished manuscript, University of British Columbia.
Pillutla, M. M., & Murnighan, J. K. (in press). Being fair or appearing fair: Strategic behavior in ultimatum bargaining. *Academy of Management Journal.*
Prasnikar, V., & Roth, A. E. (1992). Considerations of fairness and strategy: Experimental data from sequential games. *Quarterly Journal of Economics, 107,* 865-888.
Rapoport, A. (1988). Findings from a series of experimental games. *Journal of Conflict Resolution, 32,* 457-472.
Roth, A. E., & Erev, I. (1993, June 18-20). *Learning in extensive-form games: Experimental data and simple dynamic models in the intermediate term.* Paper presented at the Nobel Symposium on Game Theory, Bjokborn, Sweden.
Roth, A. E., Murnighan, J. K., & Schoumaker, F. (1988). The deadline effect in bargaining: Some experimental evidence. *American Economic Review, 78,* 806-823.
Selten, R. (1965). Spieltheoretische Behandlung eines Oligopol Modells mit Nach-fragetragheit. *Zeitschrift für Gesamte Staatswissenschaft, 121,* 301-324.
Straub, P. G., & Murnighan, J. K. (in press). An experimental investigation of ultimatums: Complete information, fairness, expectations, and lowest acceptable offers. *Journal of Economic Behavior and Organization.*
Streater, A. L., & Chertkoff, J. M. (1976). Distribution of rewards in a triad: A developmental test of equity theory. *Child Development, 47,* 800-805.
Toda, M., Shinotsuka, H., McClintock, C. G., & Stech, F. J. (1978). Development of competitive behavior as a function of culture, age, and social comparison. *Journal of Personality and Social Psychology, 36,* 825-839.
Webley, P., & Lea, S. E. G. (1993). Towards a more realistic psychology of economic socialization. *Journal of Economic Psychology, 14,* 461-472.
Zarbatany, L., Hartmann, D. P., & Gelfand, D. M. (1985). Why does children's generosity increase with age: Susceptibility to experimenter influence or altruism? *Child Development, 56,* 746-756.

12

Social Context in Tacit Bargaining Games

Consequences for Perceptions
of Affinity and Cooperative Behavior

RICHARD P. LARRICK
SALLY BLOUNT

Affinity and Cooperation

In his classic essay on tacit bargaining games, Schelling (1960) presented subjects with the following question:

> You and your partner are to be given $100 if you can agree on how to divide it without communicating. Each of you is to write the amount of his claim on a sheet of paper; and if the two claims add to no more than $100, each gets exactly what he claimed. If the two claims exceed $100, neither of you gets anything. How much do you claim?

Schelling found an overwhelming preference for claiming an equal share ($50). He then presented a second decision task, similar to the first, except that the money to be divided was lost by one party and found by the other, and a mediator had suggested that a 2/1 division in favor of the original owner was appropriate. Both losers and finders were unanimous in making claims consistent with the proposed 2/1 division. Schelling contended that the two questions are "logically the same," but that social context produces divergent responses. Although the assertion of logical equivalence is questionable, Schelling's concern with social context anticipates the central theme of this volume: Social relationships must be incorporated into the formal study of bargaining.

In this chapter, we examine the role of social context by taking Schelling's method seriously. We demonstrate how differences in behavior observed across tacit bargaining games that are "logically the same" can illuminate our understanding of the social cognitive processes that underlie negotiation behavior. Specifically, we emphasize the role that the negotiator's perceptions of relationships play in mediating the effect of social context on behavior. We focus on the traditional dichotomy between cooperative behavior and competitive behavior, which we define, respectively, as actions that maximize the total of both parties' payoffs and actions that maximize one party's payoff relative to the other.

We begin by briefly reviewing three prominent social psychological theories of relationships as we develop a model of how social context affects negotiation behavior. In this model, we assert that a critical mediating variable between social context and cooperative behavior is the degree to which a party perceives him- or herself to have an affinity with another interested party. We use the model to interpret two lines of recent research and observe that perceptions of affinity and, consequently, cooperative behavior are highly labile. Subtle differences in how behavior is elicited within a specific social context can dramatically change behavior. This lability has clear implications for how the influence of social context on behavior should be examined in future research.

Social Psychological Models of Negotiation

One characteristic that distinguishes social psychological approaches to negotiation from other approaches is an interest in how perceptions of relationships mediate the effect of social context on behavior (Deutsch, 1985; Pruitt & Rubin, 1986; Rubin, Pruitt, & Kim, 1994). Both Pruitt and Rubin's (1986) "dual concern model" and Deutsch's (1985) analysis of "perceptions of interdependence and psychological orientation" emphasize that differences in social context create different interpretations of an interaction. These differences, in turn, underlie a negotiator's decision to behave cooperatively or competitively.

Pruitt and Rubin (1986; Rubin et al., 1994) argued that negotiators will behave cooperatively or competitively depending on their perceptions of two dimensions of relationship: concern for their own outcome and concern for the other party's outcome. Pruitt and Rubin asserted that the key dimension that distinguishes cooperative from competitive behaviors is concern for the other party's welfare. When concern for the other party is high, a negotiator is more motivated to cooperate with the other party, either by yielding to the other party or by collaborating with the other party. Competitive behavior, which Pruitt and Rubin termed *contending*, occurs when concern for the other party is low.

According to Pruitt and Rubin (1986), many contextual factors increase a sense of concern for another party. In exploring these factors, they distinguished between factors that give rise to genuine concern and factors that give rise to instrumental concern (i.e., helping another with the expectation that it will improve one's own outcome). Among the factors likely to increase genuine concern are proximity (Festinger, Schachter, & Back, 1950), similarity (Byrne, 1971; Newcomb, 1961), and common group identity (Brewer & Kramer, 1985), which can arise from categorization (Brewer & Silver, 1978; Tajfel, 1982) or from facing a common fate or common goal (Sherif, 1966). All of these factors tend to produce favorable attitudes toward another party, including feelings of affiliation, liking, and concern for the party's welfare. Among the factors that increase instrumental concern are interdependence and future interaction.

In a similar vein, Deutsch (1982, 1985) argued that perceptions of social relations produce specific psychological orientations toward another party. He defined psychological orientation as an internally consistent cluster of cognitive processes, motivational tendencies, and moral dispositions that correspond to specific types of relations between two parties. Two of the principal dimensions of social relations Deutsch examined are cooperation-competition and power. *Cooperation-competition* entails liking (e.g., "positive-negative interpersonal disposition"), affiliation (e.g., "association-disassociation"), and outcome structure (e.g., zero-sum versus variable sum). The corresponding cognitive schema judges whether "we are 'for' each other or we are 'against' each other." *Power* entails relative position (e.g., "superordination-subordination") and relative control of outcomes (e.g., "equal versus unequal"). The corresponding cognitive schema judges the relative power of the participants in a relationship to benefit or harm the other.

Deutsch described how the two dimensions of cooperation-competition and power combine to create different psychological orientations. In a relationship with equal power and cooperative partners, each party expects to be treated equally and strives to treat the other equally. By contrast, in an equal, competitive relationship, the expectation is that each party will strive to gain superiority. When relationships are unequal, orientations once again diverge, depending on whether the parties are cooperative or competitive. In a relationship with unequal but cooperative partners, the expectation is that the more powerful party is obligated to employ its power to benefit the less powerful one, not just itself, and that the weaker party is obligated to submit to and respect the more powerful party. In a relationship with unequal and competitive partners, the expectation is that the stronger party will exploit the weaker party, who may accept the exploitation or resist it.

Deutsch's model and Pruitt and Rubin's model share many similarities, and each has some comparative strengths and weaknesses. The dimension that Deutsch described as cooperation-competition has many points in common with Pruitt and Rubin's concept of concern for the other party. Both capture the fundamental notion that one party's interest in another party underlies cooperative and competitive behaviors. However, Pruitt and Rubin avoided the common misconception—to which Deutsch seemed to subscribe—that cooperation and competition lie at opposite ends of a single dimension. Further, Deutsch was not systematic in drawing an explicit link between psychological orientations and behavior. As an example, his cooperation-competition dimension encompassed both perceptions (e.g., being associated with the other party) and behavior (e.g., cooperating with the other party). Yet Pruitt and Rubin's model overlooks a dimension of social motivation that Deutsch addressed and that many theorists consider crucial: the interpersonal comparison of outcomes (McClintock, 1972; Messick & Sentis, 1985; Loewenstein, Thompson, & Bazerman, 1989). Thus, in describing the dimensions of relationships, Pruitt and Rubin's elegant model omits important comparative processes, whereas Deutsch's complex model describes many important processes, but with inadequate precision.

In our effort to develop a social cognitive model integrating the strengths of these earlier models, we were very influenced by Brown's (1965) model of social relationships. Brown, a psycholinguist by training, derived his model based on his analysis of the historical evolution of European pronouns of address. From this analysis, he proposed that interpersonal relationships can be characterized along two basic dimensions: solidarity and status. He observed that relationships marked by feelings of solidarity tend to encourage the use of familiar pronouns, such as *du* or *tu,* whereas relationships marked by differences in status often require the use of formal pronouns, such as *vos, vous,* or *Sie.* Of solidarity, Brown noted:

> In every human society there is some conception of differential solidarity. Men everywhere understand what is meant by such a question as: "Who are the people whose welfare is of great importance to you and who are the people for whom you are less concerned?" If status is the vertical of social relationship, solidarity is the horizontal. Solidarity is often talked about in terms of being close or remote, near or far, the in-group versus the out-group. The grounds for solidarity are varied: kinship, identities of age, sex, nationality, similarities of education and occupation, a shared fate, and simply prolonged contact. (p. 57)

Of status, Brown wrote:

> In every human society there seems to be some conception of differential social value. . . . Social status accrues to a person in the degree that he possesses

characteristics valued by his society. In this general abstract sense status has the
same meaning everywhere. However, there is much latitude for cultural variation in the characteristics which are taken as the basis for status. These can be
physical strength and skill, position in the kinship system, sex, lineage, occupa-
tion, wealth, roles in an organization like the army or the church. (p. 55)

According to Brown, perceptions of status and solidarity are influenced by
relationship factors that are perceived as either symmetrical or asymmetrical
in nature. Solidarity tends to emerge in relationships marked by symmetries,
such as similarity and proximity, whereas differential status tends to emerge
in relationships marked by asymmetries, such as differences in position and
power. Logically, perceptions of solidarity and differential status can coexist
in the same relationship, because two parties can have a symmetrical relationship on one feature (e.g., group membership) and an asymmetrical relationship
on another (e.g., leader and follower). For example, it is easy to imagine that
a caring employer and loyal employee would perceive both solidarity and
differential status in their relationship. Likewise, both can be absent from a
"relationship," as in the case of two strangers. Nevertheless, Brown observed
that there is an "essential antagonism between solidarity and differential status"
(p. 84). Brown argued that liking and superiority cannot easily be experienced
simultaneously, because liking tends to be based on a symmetrical relationship, whereas superiority tends to be based on an asymmetrical relationship.
Liking and inferiority cannot easily be experienced simultaneously for the
same reasons.

We find Brown's constructs of solidarity and status insightful, and they have
been useful to us in our attempts to understand behaviors we have observed in
previous studies of negotiation. Furthermore, we find Brown's classification
of basic relationship features in terms of symmetries and asymmetries elegant.
Although the model is necessarily simplistic, it offers a means for organizing
a large catalog of relationship factors studied by social psychologists, such as
similarity and proximity, into a coherent framework. It also provides an
intriguing psychological explanation for how these factors affect interpersonal behavior.

Drawing on these three models, our model identifies two perceptual dimensions of relationships critical to interpreting negotiation behavior. First,
as both Deutsch (1982, 1985) and Pruitt and Rubin (1986) noted, social context affects the concern one party feels for another. However, as Brown (1965)
noted, this concern is typically accompanied by some sense of identification
with the other party. In our model, we call this dimension *perceptions of
affinity*, to connote both identifying with the other party as well as feeling

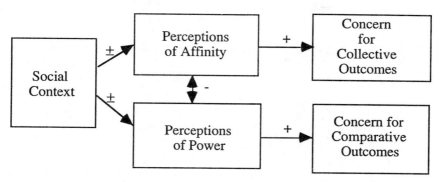

Figure 12.1. The Effect of Social Context on Negotiation Behavior

concern for the other party. The social context that produces perceptions of affinity is one in which two parties share symmetrical relations, such as common group membership, similar characteristics, and proximity. The behavioral consequence of affinity is to increase concern for collective outcomes.

The second perceptual dimension of social context that we identify is *perceptions of power*. It is drawn from Deutsch's (1985) power construct and Brown's (1965) status construct. The social context that produces differential power is one in which two parties share asymmetrical relations, such as differences in the control of resources or the control of decisions. The behavioral consequence of differential power is to draw attention to comparative outcomes. As Deutsch suggested, the evaluation of comparative outcomes depends on expectations about the appropriate use of power. In general, when power differences match expectations, they will be perceived as legitimate and the weaker party will be more willing to tolerate disparity. However, when power differences deviate from expectations, they will be perceived as illegitimate and the weaker party will be concerned with minimizing unfavorable comparative outcomes.

A summary of our model is depicted in Figure 12.1, which shows that social context influences two critical perceptual dimensions: perceptions of affinity and perceptions of power. These perceptions are influenced, in part, by the extent to which the social context is marked by symmetrical versus asymmetrical relational elements. Although a relationship can be characterized by both affinity and power differences, the model reflects the inherent antagonism that Brown observed between status and solidarity. Perceptions of affinity are then directly related to the tendency to value collective outcomes and to behave cooperatively. Perceptions of power are directly related to the tendency to value comparative outcomes and to behave competitively.

Review of Recent Empirical Findings

In this section, we apply our model to two lines of research on tacit bargaining games in which social context has been found to affect cooperative behavior. The first line of research examines the tendency for decision makers to behave more cooperatively in social dilemmas than in ultimatum bargaining games. We review two studies that demonstrate that structurally equivalent versions of the two tasks produce differences in cooperative behavior. The studies also provide evidence that these differences in cooperation are caused by differences in perceptions of affinity. The second line of research examines the tendency for decision makers to behave more cooperatively when they attribute the cause of an unfavorable allocation to the environment rather than to another human. We review two studies that are consistent with the interpretation that perceptions of affinity underlie cooperative behavior.

Social Dilemmas Versus Ultimatum Bargaining Games

Inspired by Hardin's (1968) "tragedy of the commons," social dilemma studies seek to simulate situations in which a group shares a scarce resource, such as water, grazing land, or petroleum (Dawes, 1980). To maintain the shared resource, everyone must cooperate and not overconsume; however, cooperation conflicts with the individual's desire to maximize personal outcomes. Social dilemmas are simulated in the laboratory by having three to six subjects draw resources from a joint, replenishable pool. Subjects are told in advance what the average individual consumption level is that will maintain the pool over the length of the exercise. They are also given a rough idea of the length of the exercise and told that they will be compensated based upon their total individual consumption. Individual choices are not directly observable or personally identifiable, and feedback about depletion is received collectively and often delayed. Cooperation is measured as the degree to which individuals reduce their own consumption to increase the common resource. Research on social dilemmas shows that the group usually extinguishes the scarce resource prematurely.

Ultimatum games are a more recent research paradigm, first explored by Guth, Schmittberger, and Schwarze (1982). In the ultimatum game, two subjects are asked to divide a fixed amount of money. One subject is given the role of proposing a division, and the other is given the role of accepting or rejecting the proposal. We will refer to these two roles as Player 1 and Player 2, respectively. If Player 2 accepts the division, both subjects get the proposed amount; if Player 2 rejects it, neither gets anything. Research using this game has consistently shown that individuals do not behave in the way that economic models would predict. According to game theory, Player 1 should offer Player 2 the smallest possible positive amount and keep the remainder. Furthermore, Player 2 should accept this offer because it is greater than zero. In reality, because of fairness concerns, subjects in the Player 1 position frequently offer the other subject more than a trivial amount, frequently favoring an equal division. And subjects in the Player 2 position who receive highly unfavorable offers often reject them, preferring to get nothing at all.

The studies reviewed here (Larrick & Blount, 1995) were motivated by the observation that, within these two well-established research traditions, structurally equivalent versions of each game were being studied with strikingly different results. Budescu, Rappaport, and Suleiman (1992; Budescu, Suleiman, & Rappaport, 1993) studied a class of social dilemmas in which two-person groups were asked to share a common resource pool. Each member made a request from the resource pool, and, if the total request did not exceed the pool, all members were granted their requests; otherwise, each received nothing. In some conditions, requests were made sequentially, such that Player 2 made a request knowing Player 1's request. From a game-theoretic perspective, this version of a social dilemma is structurally equivalent to the traditional ultimatum game—Player 1 makes a division, and Player 2 can "accept" it by requesting an amount less than or equal to the remainder or "reject" it by claiming more than the remainder. Consistent with ultimatum results, Budescu et al. (1992) found that the first player tended to request more than the second. However, their results suggest a much higher tolerance for unequal payoffs on the part of Player 2 than is typically observed in ultimatum studies.

A high tolerance for unequal payoffs was also found by Messick and Allison (1987) in a study of six-player, sequential social dilemmas. Subjects were asked to make requests from a pool of 24 points (in which each point was potentially worth \$.50). An equal distribution of the points would be 4 to each player. Although the dilemma was presented as a six-player game, all subjects were assigned the role of Player 6 and presented with "unfair" requests by the first five players that left them with 3, 2, 1, or zero points. Even so, 90% of all subjects requested amounts equal to or less than the remaining points, thereby letting all players receive their requested amounts. Most dramatically, 73% of the subjects who were left zero requested zero! Player 2 subjects in ultimatum bargaining games rarely, if ever, are willing to accept zero.

The studies we will review here were designed to compare two-party versions of each task to test whether these observed differences in cooperative behavior could be replicated in a controlled experiment (Larrick & Blount, 1995). The model developed in this chapter suggests several explanations for why the social context of a two-party social dilemma might elicit higher perceptions of affinity for Player 1 and, consequently, more cooperative behavior by Player 2. The first explanation is that the tasks establish *different beliefs about ownership of the resource pool.* In social dilemma experiments, subjects are typically told that they jointly own a shared resource pool. In ultimatum games, ownership is usually not made explicit. The result may be that the symmetry of sharing a common fate (Campbell, 1958) evokes stronger perceptions of affinity for Player 1 in the social dilemma task relative to the ultimatum bargaining task. Consequently, cooperation is more prevalent. We tested the importance of this explanation in the first study by holding ownership constant across the two tasks (Larrick & Blount, 1995).

A second explanation is that *differences in Player 1's actions* across the two tasks may evoke different perceptions of Player 1's power and change Player 2's perceptions of affinity for Player 1. In the ultimatum bargaining task, Player 1 is given control over specifying both Player 1's and Player 2's outcomes. In the social dilemma task, Player 1 specifies only Player 1's outcome—specifying Player 2's outcome is left to Player 2. Player 1's enhanced role in the ultimatum bargaining task may lead Player 2 to be more concerned with potential exploitation than in the social dilemma task. Player 2's perceptions of power or status differences will be stronger, thereby decreasing perceptions of affinity. We tested the importance of this explanation in our second study (Larrick & Blount, 1995) by holding Player 1's actions constant across the two tasks.

A third explanation is that *differences in Player 2's actions* across the two tasks may evoke different perceptions of affinity. In both tasks, Player 2 has the power to make or break the outcome. In the ultimatum bargaining task, Player 2's alternatives take the form of accepting or rejecting Player 1's action. In the social dilemma task where Player 2 makes a counterclaim, Player 2's alternatives are enriched (i.e., a broader range of actions is possible) and symmetrical in form to Player 1's. To the extent that Player 2 perceives him- or herself as having equal voice (Folger, 1977, 1986) or equal control over the procedure (Lind & Tyler, 1988), Player 2 may feel greater affinity for Player 1 and be more inclined to cooperate.

We tested these explanations in two studies (Larrick & Blount, 1995). In the first, 105 M.B.A. students completed a resource allocation questionnaire that was phrased in terms of either a social dilemma or an ultimatum bargaining game. The instructions stated that subjects would be randomly paired with a student in another section to participate in a resource allocation task. A potential pool of $7 would be made available by the experimenter. Each student in the pair would be randomly assigned to the role of either Player 1 or Player 2.

The descriptions of Player 1's and Player 2's actions varied by condition. In the ultimatum condition, subjects were told:

> Player 1 will be asked to propose a division of $7.00 between the two players, such as $X for Player 1 and $7 − X for Player 2. Then, Player 2 will be asked whether he/she accepts or rejects this proposal. If Player 2 accepts the proposal, each

player will get the amount Player 1 proposed. If Player 2 rejects the proposal, neither student will receive any money.

In the social dilemma condition, subjects were told:

> Player 1 will be asked to state a claim for some portion of $7.00, such as $X. Then, knowing $X, Player 2 will be asked to state his or her claim for some portion of $7.00, let's say $Y. If the total of the two claims ($X + $Y) is equal to or less than $7.00, each player will get the amount he or she claimed. If the total is more than $7.00, neither student will receive any money.

After reading the instructions, subjects were presented with two sets of questions. One set asked for the decisions they would make if they were randomly assigned to the Player 1 role; the other set asked about their decisions if they were randomly assigned to the Player 2 role. Subjects' decisions as Player 2 were elicited by presenting them with every possible Player 1/Player 2 division, starting at a $7/$0 and decreasing by $.50 increments to $0/$7. In the ultimatum game condition, the first division was phrased, "If Player 1 proposes: $7.00 for Player 1, $0.00 for Player 2," to which subjects responded by checking "accept" or "reject." In the social dilemma condition, the first division was phrased, "If Player 1 claims: $7.00 for Player 1, which leaves $0.00," to which subjects responded by stating how much they would claim for themselves. To analyze the Player 2 variable, we coded each subject's responses as a single value—the lowest amount that the subject accepted as Player 2. In ultimatum games, this amount was the smallest offer for which the subject marked "accept." In social dilemmas, this amount was the smallest remainder left by Player 1 for which the subject did not "break the bank" (i.e., claim more than the remainder).

The most notable finding from Study 1 was that, even though ownership of the pool was held constant across conditions, subjects in the social dilemma condition were significantly more likely to accept the $7/$0 division than were subjects in the ultimatum bargaining game condition. Of 54 subjects in the social dilemma condition, 16 (30%) claimed $0 when presented with a $7/$0 division, compared with only 1 subject in the ultimatum game condition ($p < .001$). The size of this effect is quite striking, considering how subtle the differences were between the two tasks. It is also striking because, although the effect was not as large as the one obtained by Messick and Allison (1987), it occurred in a two-party rather than a six-party social dilemma. With six parties, there may be mitigating factors that enhance Player 6's cooperation, such as difficulty in identifying a blameworthy party and exacting revenge without harming "innocent" participants. In the two-party social dilemma, there is no ambiguity about attributions of blame, and revenge can be targeted with precision.

───── **TABLE 12.1** ─────
Explanations for Rejecting the $7/$0 Division by Condition

───

Ultimatum game condition

"I decided to exercise my power to not let the other player benefit through exclusion of me, even though I wouldn't benefit either way."

"Too unbalanced; both participants required for either to make any money. Therefore, neither should claim entire amount."

"I don't receive anything. Player 1 would be $7 richer if I accepted; however, since I don't even know who Player 1 is, I have no motive to help them."

"Player 1 is too greedy. I must get at least .50 for my efforts of filling out this form."

"Player 1 gets everything, I get nothing. I have no incentive to give Player 1 everything."

"Player 1 understood the rules and should have been willing to share. Player 1's presumption that they might try to get all $7 I viewed as arrogant and did not wish them to benefit unilaterally."

Social dilemma condition

"If I'm not getting any money, than neither is Player 1." ($7.00)

"Player 1's choice leaves nothing for me so I will not allow Player 1 to receive anything either." ($7.00)

"I want to force Player 1 to minimize his gain and maximize my gain, therefore I am going to eliminate him from receiving any compensation above a 50%/50% split." ($7.00)

"I decided either way, I would get zero, so to be fair, I may as well make it so Player 1 gets zero, too." ($1.00)

"Player 1, being selfish, should not be rewarded." ($7.00)

"I penalize 1 for being greedy, assuming Player 1 understood the rules." ($7.00)

───

NOTE: Amounts in parentheses are the amounts the subjects claimed as Player 2.

We then designed a second study to control for differences in Player 1's actions across the two tasks. Specifically, Player 1's actions were described in both conditions using only social dilemma terms (i.e., "Player 1 will be asked to state a claim for some portion of the $7.00, such as $X"). When Player 2's decision was elicited, social dilemma terms were also used to describe Player 1's actions (e.g., "If Player 1 claims: $7.00 for Player 1, which leaves $0.00"). Only the response format for Player 2 varied between the two conditions. Subjects in the ultimatum game condition responded to each proposed division by marking "accept" or "reject"; subjects in the social dilemma condition responded by stating a counterclaim.

The results replicated those found in Study 1 and demonstrated that controlling for Player 1's action did not remove the significant difference in cooperation observed across the two tasks. The $7/$0 division was accepted significantly more often in the social dilemma condition (17 of 46) than in the ultimatum game condition (6 of 50) ($p < .01$). Although subjects in the ultimatum game condition were more willing to accept a $7/$0 division in Study 2 (6 of 50) than in Study 1 (1 of 51), this increase was not significant.

———— **TABLE 12.2** ————
Explanations for Accepting the $7/$0 Division by Condition

Ultimatum game condition

"Whatever my decision is, I do not get any money, but my decision to accept leaves Player 1 rich. I made a new friend!"

"I accepted all the propositions, although, if I had done it more carefully, I would have rejected $7 vs. $0."

Social dilemma condition

"Joint welfare was maximized."

"Maximizing utility between the two of us—regardless of whether or not I know the person. If I would have chosen a nonzero number, we both would get 0. $7 is shifted from U of C to a student's pocket."

"Maximizing the total utility; this may seem far too rational, but at least I know that as a team, we are taking the GSB for all we can."

"Better Player 1 gets money than neither of us."

"Better that someone gets $7 than no one getting any money."

"I get nothing if I claim more than 0. Might as well let Player 1 get all the money."

"Did not want amount to exceed $7. Wanted to be rewarded."

"It has to be a total less than $7 so that at least one of us gets the money."

NOTE: Only two subjects in the ultimatum condition accepted the $7-$0 division. Both of their responses appear here.

Together, the findings of Studies 1 and 2 demonstrate that simply altering *how Player 2's actions are expressed* (but not the effect of those actions—in each task, Player 2 is choosing whether to make or break the deal) significantly increases the rate of cooperation. Thus, as we noted earlier, subtle differences in how behavior is elicited within a specific context can change behavior dramatically. The effect of these differences can be traced through their influence on perceptions of affinity. Consider the open-ended responses we elicited in Study 2 (Larrick & Blount, 1995). We asked half of the subjects to give their reasons for their decisions about the $7/$0 division; their responses are summarized in Tables 12.1 and 12.2. In Table 12.1, among the subjects who rejected allowing Player 1 to get $7, it is interesting to see that in both conditions similar responses were given. The themes that run through these responses reflect concern with perceived status or power differences, including avoiding exploitation, maintaining a fair balance between the players, and retaliating for not being given any benefit. In contrast, as Table 12.2 shows, subjects who accepted the $7/$0 division gave responses reflecting very different goals. The themes that run through their responses reflect strong perceptions of affinity, including a high concern for the other party, maximizing joint outcome, exploiting a common enemy, benefiting at least one party, and not wasting the resource.

Environmental Versus Social Causes
of Outcome Allocations

We turn our attention now to a set of findings that show how causal attributions affect decision making in tacit bargaining tasks. To put this work in context, consider the observations reported by Talarowski (1982; cited in Rutte, Wilke, & Messick, 1987) regarding the 1976-1977 drought in California. He found that people who used more water than they were allocated tended to believe that the drought had been caused by people, whereas those who stayed at or below their allocations tended to believe that the drought was environmentally induced. Similarly, as part of a broader lab study, Rutte et al. (1987) found that subjects in a social dilemma who believed that resource shortages were environmentally induced behaved more cooperatively and consumed less of the scarce resource than subjects who believed that resource shortages were the result of fellow group members' actions. These findings suggest that how people behave in social allocation contexts may be, in part, dependent upon their attributions regarding the causes of allocations. They care not only about the objective attributes of social allocations, but also about how these allocations come to be (Ross & Fletcher, 1985).

Motivated by this observation, Blount White (1992/1993) conducted several tacit bargaining game experiments to examine explicitly how, given the same allocation, environmental attributions might evoke more cooperative behavior than social attributions. In line with the model developed in this chapter, Blount White reasoned that these attributions would have varying effects on perceptions of affinity (which she refers to as "affiliation"). Under environmental attributions, she argued, "the focal individual will cognitively perceive him/herself as affiliated with the other interested party(ies). This assertion combines the role of common fate (Campbell, 1958) with the role of external threats (Sherif, 1966) on perceived group identity and cohesion." In contrast, regarding social attributions, she wrote, "the other party, who has an interest in what outcome results and is able to affect that outcome, is less likely to be perceived as affiliated by the focal individual. Instead, a comparative attitude is more likely to be adopted (Judd & Park, 1988)" (p. 49).

To examine this distinction, Blount White (1992/1993) conducted two ultimatum bargaining game experiments in which she manipulated whether Player 2 believed that a proposal was attributable to a human source (Player 1) or to an environmental source (a computer-simulated roulette wheel). The materials and procedures were similar to those we employed in the Larrick and Blount (1995) study. In Study 1, subjects in the human-source condition were told:

Each student in the pair will be randomly assigned to the role of either proposer or decider. The proposer will propose a division of $10.00, such as $X for the proposer and $10 − X for the decider. The decider will then decide whether to accept or reject the proposed division.

In the environmental-source condition, it was explained:

Each student in the pair will be randomly assigned to the role of either other student or decider. A computer-simulated roulette wheel, which allocated equal probability to each possible outcome, will be spun to determine a proposed split of the $10 between the other student and the decider, such as $X for the other student and $10 − X for the decider. The decider will then decide whether to accept or reject this proposed division.

This initial study yielded a significant difference in the degree of cooperation between these two conditions. None of the Player 2 subjects in the human-source condition stated a willingness to accept zero if Player 1 were to receive $10. However, 33% of subjects in the environmental-source condition were willing to accept such a proposal ($p < .001$).

In Study 2, through deception, Blount White (1992/1993) explicitly controlled for differences between the two conditions in expectations about the likely distribution of potential offers. Specifically, all subjects were assigned to the Player 2 position and shown one of two possible distributions of so-called actual proposals. They were then told that the proposal they would receive would be drawn from this distribution. The expectations and attribution conditions were fully crossed. The results replicated those found in Study 1 and demonstrated no effect for differences in expectations. Again, the $10/$0 division was accepted significantly more often in the environmental-source condition (33% of subjects) than in the human-source condition (8% of subjects).

Together, these findings demonstrate that differing attributions regarding the causes of allocations, independent of the allocations themselves, affect the propensity to cooperate. Based on our model, this difference can be explained through contextual effects on perceptions of affinity. When attributions are environmentally based, perceptions of affinity with other interested parties are high. People experience themselves as subject to a common fate over which none of the interested parties has control. When attributions are made to an interested party, concern for comparative outcomes and perceptions of potential power differences are salient. People experience concern about being exploited because of their disadvantageous position, thereby decreasing perceptions of affinity and the incidence of cooperative behavior.

Concluding Comments

In this chapter we have briefly reviewed three theories of relationships (Brown, 1965; Deutsch, 1985; Pruitt & Rubin, 1986) to develop a model of how social context affects negotiation behavior through perceptions of relationship. We then applied this model to recent research that found differences in cooperation between structurally equivalent bargaining tasks. This research shows that subtle changes in how social context is described affect the rate of cooperative behavior. The first line of research shows that the form of a player's decision in a tacit bargaining game, and the concomitant feelings of equality or inequality, affects perceptions of affinity and the tendency to cooperate. The second line of research shows that the perceived source of an allocation affects cooperation. When allocations are attributed to an interested party, subjects in the Player 2 role experience unequal power and a concern for comparative outcomes. When allocations are attributed to the environment, these subjects perceive having power equal to (or greater than) Player 1, and are more concerned with collective outcomes. Both sets of findings contradict traditional economic predictions regarding the evaluation of outcomes. However, using our model, these results can be interpreted in terms of perceptions of power and perceptions of affinity.

The finding that minimal changes in social context alter perceptions of affinity bears a strong resemblance to the minimal group effect studied by Tajfel, Turner, and colleagues (Tajfel, 1982). However, unlike the traditional intergroup manipulations, in the studies we have reported, people were not actually assigned to groups. Instead, the structure of the task determined whether subjects perceived a minimal group consisting of themselves and the other player. As is the case with many minimal group findings, the results reported in our earlier work (Larrick & Blount, 1995) and by Blount White (1992/1993) are surprisingly strong and robust given the subtlety of the manipulation and the nonsocial nature of the pen-and-paper exercise. What is striking is that Player 2's perception of a minimal group seemed to be triggered at least in part by the description of each role's relative power. In conditions that replicated the traditional ultimatum game, perceptions of unequal power led subjects to draw the group boundary inward to include only the self. However, in the social dilemma conditions of the Larrick and Blount (1995) study, in which Player 2 was allowed to make a counterclaim, perceptions of equal power led subjects to expand the group boundary to include the other party. Similarly, in the environmental-source condition in Blount White's (1992/1993) study, in which a common fate was introduced, perceptions of equal (or greater) power also led subjects to move the group boundary outward.

As we look forward, we are struck by the complexity of the task faced by our research community in unraveling the link between social context and negotiation behavior. The tacit bargaining studies reported here provide clear evidence that people's perceptions of relationships, and consequently their tendency to behave cooperatively, are highly labile. Our purpose in this chapter has been to encourage other researchers to consider how even minimal differences in social context can affect behavior through perceptions of relationships.

References

Blount White, S. (1993). The role of causal attributions in social decision making (Doctoral dissertation, Northwestern University, 1992). *Dissertation Abstracts International, 53,* 6044.

Brewer, M. B., & Kramer, R. M. (1985). The psychology of intergroup attitudes and behavior. *Annual Review of Psychology, 36,* 219-243.

Brewer, M. B., & Silver, M. (1978). In-group bias as a function of task characteristics. *European Journal of Social Psychology, 8,* 393-400.

Brown, R. (1965). *Social psychology.* New York: Free Press.

Budescu, D. V., Rappaport, A., & Suleiman, R. (1992). Simultaneous vs. sequential requests in resource dilemmas with incomplete information. *Acta Psychologica, 80,* 297-310.

Budescu, D. V., Suleiman, R., & Rappaport, A. (1993). *Positional order and group size effects in resource dilemmas with uncertain resources.* Unpublished manuscript, University of Illinois.

Byrne, D. (1971). *The attraction paradigm.* New York: Academic Press.

Campbell, D. T. (1958). Common fate, similarity, and other indices of the status of aggregates of persons as social entities. *Behavioral Science, 3,* 14-25.

Dawes, R. M. (1980). Social dilemmas. *Annual Review of Psychology, 31,* 169-193.

Deutsch, M. (1982). Interdependence and psychological orientation. In V. Derlega & J. L. Grzelak (Eds.), *Cooperation and helping behavior: Theories and research.* Orlando, FL: Academic Press.

Deutsch, M. (1985). *Distributive justice: A social psychological perspective.* New Haven, CT: Yale University Press.

Festinger, L., Schachter, S., & Back, K. (1950). *Social pressures in informal groups: A study of human factors in housing.* New York: Harper & Brothers.

Folger, R. (1977). Distributive and procedural justice: Combined impact of "voice" and improvement of experienced inequity. *Journal of Personality and Social Psychology, 35,* 108-119.

Folger, R. (1986). Mediation, arbitration, and the psychology of procedural justice. *Research on Negotiation in Organizations, 1,* 57-79.

Guth, W., Schmittberger, R., & Schwarze, B. (1982). An experimental analysis of ultimatum bargaining. *Journal of Economic Behavior and Organization, 3,* 367-388.

Hardin, G. J. (1968). The tragedy of the commons. *Science, 162,* 1243-1248.

Judd, C. M., & Park, B. (1988). Outgroup homogeneity: Judgments of variability at the individual and group levels. *Journal of Personality and Social Psychology, 46,* 1193-1207.

Larrick, R. P. & Blount, S. (1995). *Claiming versus accepting: Decisions in social dilemmas and ultimatum games.* Unpublished manuscript, University of Chicago.

Lind, E. A., & Tyler, T. R. (1988). *The social psychology of procedural justice.* New York: Plenum.

Loewenstein, G., Thompson, L., & Bazerman, M. H. (1989). Social utility and decision making in interpersonal contexts. *Journal of Personality and Social Psychology, 57,* 426-441.

McClintock, C. G. (1972). Social motivation: A set of propositions. *Behavioral Science, 17,* 438-454.

Messick, D. M., & Allison, S. T. (1987). Accepting unfairness: Outcomes and attributions. *Representative Research in Social Psychology, 17,* 39-50.

Messick, D. M., & Sentis, K. P. (1985). Estimating social and nonsocial utility functions from ordinal data. *European Journal of Social Psychology, 15,* 389-399.

Newcomb, T. M. (1961). *The acquaintance process.* New York: Holt, Rinehart & Winston.

Pruitt, D. G., & Rubin, J. Z. (1986). *Social conflict: Escalation, stalemate, and settlement.* New York: McGraw-Hill.

Ross, M., & Fletcher, G. J. O. (1985). Attribution and social perception. In G. Lindzey & E. Aronson (Eds.), *Handbook of social psychology* (pp. 73-122). New York: Random House.

Rubin, J. Z., Pruitt, D. G., & Kim, S. H. (1994). *Social conflict: Escalation, stalemate, and settlement* (2nd ed.). New York: McGraw-Hill.

Rutte, C., Wilke, H., & Messick, D. M. (1987). Scarcity and abundance caused by people or the environment as determinants of behavior in a resource dilemma. *Journal of Experimental Social Psychology, 23,* 208-216.

Schelling, T. C. (1960). *The strategy of conflict.* Cambridge, MA: Harvard University Press.

Sherif, M. (1966). *In common predicament: Social psychology of intergroup conflict and cooperation.* Boston: Houghton Mifflin.

Tajfel, H. (1982). Social psychology of intergroup relations. *Annual Review of Psychology, 33,* 1-39.

Talarowski, F. S. (1982). *Attitudes toward and perception of water conservation in a Southern California community.* Unpublished doctoral dissertation, University of California, Santa Barbara.

13

Why Ultimatums Fail

Social Identity and Moralistic Aggression in Coercive Bargaining

RODERICK M. KRAMER
PRI PRADHAN SHAH
STEPHANIE L. WOERNER

> Human beings are consistent in their codes of honor, but endlessly fickle with reference to whom the codes apply.
>
> *E. O. Wilson (1978, p. 170)*

An ultimatum is a form of coercive bargaining strategy that is used to induce compliance or force concessions from a presumably recalcitrant opponent. The importance of ultimatums is suggested by the prominent role they have played in contemporary conflicts over the past few decades, including international conflicts, such as the Berlin crisis, the Cuban missile crisis, the Falklands War, and the Persian Gulf War (see, e.g., Beschloss, 1991; Blight & Welch, 1989; George, 1993; Janis, 1983; Jervis, Lebow, & Stein, 1986), as well as organizational conflicts, such as the battle for Eastern Airlines (Bernstein, 1990), the air traffic controllers' strike (Shostak & Skocik, 1986), and the making of the film *Heaven's Gate* (Bach, 1984).

The logical structure of an ultimatum is quite simple, consisting of three essential components (George, 1993): (a) a demand made of an opponent, (b)

AUTHORS' NOTE: We are grateful to Max Bazerman, Margaret Neale, and Joel Podolny for providing opportunities for data collection. We also thank Dave Baron, Jon Bendor, Marilynn Brewer, Linda Ginzel, Dave Kreps, Keith Murnighan, Michael Morris, Lee Ross, Alvin Roth, and Tom Tyler for their helpful inputs at various stages of this research.

a sense of urgency communicated that compliance with the demand is required, and (c) a threat of punishment offered as a consequence for failure to comply. For an ultimatum to be efficacious, the threat must be "credible to the opponent and sufficiently potent to impress upon him that compliance is preferable" (George, 1993, p. 7). An ultimatum thus presents its intended target with a disjunctive choice between two relatively unattractive imperatives of the form, Take it or leave it, or, Do it or else.

Despite their logical simplicity, ultimatums are very complex and interesting psychological phenomena. One indication of this complexity is the fact that ultimatums have played a conspicuous role in both the resolution and the escalation of major conflicts over the past century. For example, during the Cuban missile crisis, President John F. Kennedy issued a series of ultimatums to Chairman Khrushchev regarding the removal of Soviet ballistic missiles from Cuba. Ultimately, Khrushchev complied with this demand, leading to a successful resolution of the conflict—at least from the perspective of the United States.[1]

In the protracted and acrimonious contract negotiations between air traffic controllers and the federal government in the 1980s, in contrast, the use of ultimatums fared less well (Shostak & Skocik, 1986). U.S. air traffic controllers, frustrated over their working conditions and benefits, threatened to bring the nation's air travel to a crippling standstill by going on strike unless their demands for higher salaries and improved working conditions were met. Although the controllers were confident that they would prevail, their strategy unraveled dramatically when President Reagan countered with an ultimatum of his own: Return to work within 48 hours or be fired. The controllers failed to comply and were immediately replaced; a threat that the controllers had mistakenly judged to be noncredible was indeed carried out.

As these examples make clear, ultimatums sometimes fail to achieve their aims, especially when the target of an ultimatum does not respond in the fashion hoped for by the decision maker posing the ultimatum. They also illustrate the important role misperception and miscalculation play in such situations.

Such examples invite consideration of the factors that influence the efficacy of an ultimatum. Why do decision makers in some instances comply with ultimatums and in other cases resist them? What factors predict capitulation versus defiance? This is the primary question addressed by our research. In approaching it, we focus on how the efficacy of an ultimatum is affected by the social context in which an ultimatum is embedded. Specifically, we investigate how the in-group or out-group status of the decision maker delivering an ultimatum influences the target's or recipient's judgment about an ultimatum and his or her behavioral response to it (i.e., whether the recipient ultimately chooses to comply with or reject it). Our analysis is motivated by recent theory and research on the effects of social identity on conflict behavior (for a recent discussion, see Kramer, Pommerenke, & Newton, 1993). According to this research, individuals evaluate and respond to bargaining strategies quite differently depending upon whether the person using them is a member of the individuals' own social group or from another social group.

To develop the argument that social identity plays an important role in judgment and decision making about ultimatums, we organize the chapter as follows. First, we provide a brief overview of theory and research on ultimatum bargaining. Next, we suggest how the social identity of an ultimator influences a recipient's response to the ultimatum. We then offer some results from three recent experiments that support our conceptual analysis. Finally, we conclude by discussing implications and contributions of the research.

Reactions to Ultimatums:
An Overview of Previous Research

Given their importance, it is not surprising that the study of ultimatums has attracted a considerable amount of attention from scholars representing a variety of disciplines, including economics, political science, and social psychology (George, 1991; Guth & Tietz, 1990; Jervis et al., 1986; Schelling, 1958; Stein, 1993). Several distinct theoretical traditions and methodological approaches characterize this research. One approach has been to focus on historical case studies of conflicts involving ultimatums, in order to extract useful insights and lessons about the conditions under which they are likely to succeed or fail (George, 1991, 1993; Janis, 1983; Jervis et al., 1986; Kahn & Kramer, 1990; Stein, 1993). These studies have generally focused on several issues, including how psychological processes such as misperception and miscalculation contribute to ultimatum failures, the impact of dysfunctional group dynamics and decision processes on risk taking or risk avoidance in such situations, and the role of organizational routines and institutional inertia in ultimatum failures.

An alternative approach to studying ultimatums has been to use laboratory analogues to test predictions derived from game-theoretic models of ultimatum behavior (e.g., Binmore, Shaked, & Sutton, 1985; Guth, Schmittberger, & Schwarze, 1982). To date, the most widely used experimental analogue for this purpose has been the ultimatum bargaining game. In the prototypical version of this game, two decision makers must divide some fixed number of resources. One decision maker is assigned the role of resource allocator (ultimator) and the other is assigned the role of recipient. The ultimator is allowed to make an offer to the recipient as to how the contested resources should be divided. The recipient then has an opportunity to decide whether to accept or reject this offer. If the offer is accepted, the resources are divided accordingly and the game is over. If the offer is rejected, both decision makers receive nothing and the game is terminated. This simple but elegant game captures many of the essential structural and psychological features of ultimatum bargaining situations. Much like research using the Prisoner's Dilemma, the ultimatum bargaining game has generated a rich and often provocative set of empirical findings (see, e.g., Binmore et al., 1985; Guth et al., 1982; Guth & Tietz, 1990; Thaler, 1988).

Noncooperative game theory has been the major theoretical engine driving much of the early empiricism in this stream of research. This theory is attractive, at least in part, because of the clean predictions it makes about ultimatum bargaining behavior: The theory posits that decision makers making an ultimatum will offer the smallest positive amount to another party, on the assumption that, being rational, the other party should prefer any positive offer, no matter how small, over the prospect of ending up with nothing. Similarly, the other party should accept such an offer on the same grounds: Something dominates nothing. From the standpoint of a purely economic or utilitarian perspective, the logic of noncooperative game theory is compelling and unassailable.

Unfortunately, the results of many empirical studies using the ultimatum bargaining game have documented the poverty of this prediction: It has repeatedly been found that recipients of ultimatums reject a wide range of positive offers. In fact, they frequently reject offers that deviate much from an equal division of the resources (see e.g., Binmore et al., 1985; Guth et al., 1982; Kahneman, Knetsch, & Thaler, 1986a, 1986b; Ochs & Roth, 1989).

In trying to resolve the discrepancy between the crisp theoretical predictions of noncooperative game theory and the soggy empirical results that theory has spawned, a number of researchers have advanced the argument that fairness considerations may influence how recipients react to ultimatums (see discussions by Bazerman, 1991; Kahneman et al., 1986a, 1986b; Neale & Bazerman, 1991; Ochs & Roth, 1989). According to this argument, ultimatums fail (are rejected) when recipients view them as unfair or exploitative. The notion that decision makers have a positive utility for fairness (which produces a resistance to unfairness) is consistent, of course, with a substantial body of earlier research suggesting that decision makers find accepting the so-called sucker's payoff psychologically aversive—people dislike being taken advantage of, and are often willing to incur personal losses in order to spite an offending party. It is suggested also by research on interactional justice and relational models of procedural justice (e.g., Bies & Moag, 1986; Lind & Tyler, 1988).

One way of thinking about these findings is in terms of what Cialdini and his associates have termed *injunctive norms* (Cialdini, Reno, & Kallgren, 1990; Reno, Cialdini, & Kallgren, 1993). Injunctive norms represent "rules or beliefs as to what constitutes morally approved and disapproved conduct" (Cialdini et al., 1990, p. 1015). As such, they prescribe how various kinds of conflicts, including those pertaining to the allocation of scarce resources between the parties to a conflict, ought to be resolved. As Cialdini et al. note, injunctive norms are different from descriptive norms, which merely summarize how people typically or "normally" behave in social situations.

The importance of this distinction becomes clear when one considers how differently people react to violations of injunctive versus descriptive norms. When descriptive norms are breached, people are likely to react by thinking that the offender's behavior is odd or, quite literally, *ab*normal. However, little psychological reactance is engendered, in part because the costs of such a breach to the observer are generally trivial. When injunctive norms are violated, in contrast, psychological reactions are likely to be much stronger, sometimes even culminating in feelings of moral outrage (see Bies, 1987).

These arguments suggest, then, that one reason ultimatums are rejected is that recipients construe a demand that they accept less than half of a divisible resource as a violation of an important fairness norm. General support for this idea is provided by recent research by Messick and his colleagues on the potency of the equality heuristic in social decision making (Messick, 1993; Messick & Schell, 1992).

The term *moral aggression* has been used to refer to the intense negative reactions individuals sometimes experience when confronted with evidence that injunctive norms have been violated, especially norms regarding just, fair, or trustworthy behavior (see, e.g., Brewer, 1981; Campbell, 1975; Trivers, 1971). The notion of moralistic outrage and aggression draws attention to a very basic social phenomenology: People often have a very limited tolerance for other people who are cheating on the social contract, especially when they are doing their own part to uphold or to conform to such norms (Schelling, 1958; Wilson, 1978).

As we argue more fully in the next section, however, not all such norm violations are perceived by recipients as equally egregious. In particular, we consider how the social identity of an ultimator affects the judgment and decision-making processes of the targets of those ultimatums.

Asymmetries in Responding to Ultimatums: A Social Identity Perspective

In setting the stage for this argument, it may be helpful for us first to offer a few preliminary remarks about social identity theory. Social identity theory seeks to explain how membership in social groups influences interpersonal and intergroup cognitions and behaviors (for overviews, see Hogg & Abrams, 1988; Tajfel & Turner, 1986). *Social identity* is defined as "that part of an individual's self-concept which derives from his knowledge of membership in a social group (or groups), together with the value and emotional significance attached to that membership" (Tajfel, 1978, p. 63). One of the most robust findings to emerge from several decades of research on social identity theory is that the same actions by a member of one's own group are evaluated quite differently from the same actions by a member of another social group (for reviews, see Brewer, 1979; Brewer & Kramer, 1985).

Social identity theory and research suggests, however, two distinct but equally plausible predictions regarding the direction of this influence (i.e., how the in-group versus out-group status of an ultimator affects recipients' reactions to an ultimatum). Although both predictions are motivated by the notion of moralistic aggression, they appeal to different intuitions about how decision makers react to unfair demands.

The first possibility, which we term the *out-group derogation hypothesis,* posits that decision makers will react more strongly to an unfair ultimatum when the ultimator is an out-group member. This hypothesis is suggested by research on in-group bias, which has demonstrated that out-group members are typically viewed as less honest, less fair, and less trustworthy than in-group members (Brewer, 1979; Levine & Campbell, 1972). This same research has shown that causal attributions for socially disapproved behaviors tend to be more negative and extreme when an actor is an out-group member than when he or she is an in-group member (for overviews, see Brewer & Kramer, 1985; Hewstone, 1992). As a result, socially unattractive behaviors from out-group members are likely to be construed as particularly diagnostic of these individuals' lack of character, or their evil or malevolent intentions (see Janis, 1983). Such research suggests that moral transgressions by out-group members are likely to generate more intense and extreme reactions than comparable transgressions by in-group members. According to this out-group derogation logic, then, recipients should judge an unfair ultimatum more negatively when it is made by an out-group member than when it is made by an in-group member.

There is, however, a competing in-group-centered hypothesis, which we term the *expectancy violation hypothesis.* According to this hypothesis, individuals will react more strongly and more severely to unfair ultimatums when they come from in-group members. After all, in-group members are expected to behave in a trustworthy and fair fashion in their exchanges and transactions with other members of their group. This hypothesis is further suggested by the fact that individuals' expectations about compliance with social norms often conform closely to social group boundaries (Hogg & Abrams, 1988): In-group members presume that other members of their social group share similar values, are constrained by similar codes of conduct, and embrace the same social norms and values.

Consequently, even though people may expect negative behavior from out-group members, such behavior is not expected (or tolerated) from other in-group members. This line of reasoning suggests that people are likely to find transgressions committed by members of their own social group to be particularly offensive. This in-group-centered version of the moral aggression argument has been articulated most forcefully by Campbell (1975) and Brewer (1981). Accordingly, a rival proposition to the out-group derogation argument is that recipients will judge unfair ultimatums made by in-group members more negatively than comparable ultimatums made by out-group members.

Our arguments thus far have focused on recipients' judgmental or evaluative reactions to unfair ultimatums. However, the out-group derogation and in-group violation arguments also lead to different predictions about recipients' behavioral responses to such ultimatums. The out-group derogation hypothesis suggests that retaliatory behavior predicated on moralistic aggression should be most severe when directed against out-group members. Thus, based on this reasoning, one would predict that recipients will be more likely to refuse or reject unfair demands from out-group members than from in-group members. The in-group violation hypothesis suggests, in contrast, the opposite prediction: that recipients will be more likely to reject unfair demands from in-group members than unfair demands that are made by out-group members.

Although obvious, it may be worth noting that economic and game-theoretic models of ultimatum bargaining behavior essentially argue the null hypothesis (i.e., that the in-group/out-group status of an ultimator has no effect on judgment or behavior). According to these models, reaction to an ultimatum should be dictated purely by the impact of the ultimator's demand on the recipient's economic self-interest or well-being. Thus the social context of an ultimatum should have no discernible impact on the recipient's choice behavior. In short, a recipient should be *indifferent* to the in-group versus out-group status of an unfair ultimator.

Study 1

To investigate these competing hypotheses, we conducted an experiment in which we manipulated an ultimator's social identity and the fairness of the ultimatum. Study 1 thus employed a 2 × 2 (Group Identity × Fairness of Ultimatum) between-subjects factorial design. We manipulated social identity by varying whether the person making the ultimatum was an in-group or an out-group member, and we manipulated the fairness of the ultimatum by varying whether recipients were offered an equal or unequal share of the resources available for allocation.

Overview of Procedures

The participants in our study were 110 M.B.A. students enrolled in a conflict course who participated in the study in exchange for course credit and an opportunity to earn money. Participants were told at the start of the experiment that they would be paired with one other individual and would participate in a bargaining task.

Participants were informed there were two roles in the bargaining task: offer maker and recipient. One of them would be randomly assigned to the offer maker role and the other would be assigned to the recipient role. Both offer makers and recipients were told the task involved deciding how to divide $25.00 between them. Offer makers would have an opportunity first to decide how much of the $25.00 they wanted to offer the other person with whom they would subsequently be paired and how much they wanted to keep for themselves. Offer makers were assigned code numbers so that their offers could be made anonymously. Those assigned to the offer maker role would make their decisions and record them on pieces of paper along with their code numbers. These decisions would be collected by the experimenter and randomly distributed either to another member of the offer maker's own class or to a member of another class.

Those assigned to the recipient role were told that they would receive offers either from other members of their own class or from members of another class. While they were awaiting their offers, recipients completed a preallocation questionnaire that asked them to make predictions about the offers they expected and what they thought would be the most rational offer.

Social Identity Manipulation

Individuals in the *in-group identity condition* were informed that they would receive offers from other members of their own class. Individuals in the *out-group identity condition* were informed that they would receive offers from members of another class.

Fairness of the Ultimatum

Although individuals were led to believe that they were actually interacting with other persons, in actuality we predetermined the offers in order to manipulate their perceived fairness. Individuals assigned to the *fair demand condition* received offers of $12.50 (half of the amount available to the offer makers). Individuals assigned to the *unfair demand condition* received offers of $7.50. To strengthen the manipulation, and increase the psychological immediacy of the other, we also included with each offer a brief written note, presumably from the ultimator. In the fair demand condition, the note said, "I am offering $12.50 because splitting the money is the fairest thing to do." Those in the unfair demand condition received a note saying, "I am offering $7.50 because something is better than nothing."[2]

Recipients then made their decisions as to whether to accept or reject the offers. They wrote their answers on slips of paper that ostensibly were to be relayed back to the offer makers. They also completed postdecision questionnaires that included a series of questions regarding their judgments about the offers they had received and the person with whom they had interacted.

During debriefing, we probed individuals for any suspicion about the reality of the offers. Three participants in the study expressed mild skepticism regarding the offers. To be conservative, we dropped their data from subsequent analyses, leaving data for 107 participants (it should be noted, however, that separate analyses including all of the data showed no substantive differences in the results).

Results and Discussion

Our discussion focuses on the two primary categories of dependent variables most relevant to the hypotheses: recipients' judgments and evaluative reactions about the ultimatums they received, and their behavioral responses to those ultimatums.

Judgments About Ultimatums

We argued earlier that a primary way in which the effects of social identity should manifest themselves is in terms of asymmetries in the judgmental or evaluative reactions of recipients to their offers as a function of the in-group versus out-group status of an ultimator. To investigate these asymmetries, we included a number of measures in our study. Among other things, we asked recipients to indicate how rational, selfish, fair, and exploitative they thought the demands they received from the ultimators had been. We also asked them to indicate how irritated and how happy they were with the offers that had been made to them.

Analyses of variance of these measures revealed the following results (the cell means for all of these results are displayed in Table 13.1; levels of significance for the effects are reported in parentheses in the text). First, and not surprisingly, unfair demands were viewed as less rational than fair demands ($p < .001$). They were also viewed as more selfish ($p < .001$), more exploitative ($p < .001$), and less fair ($p < .001$). Recipients also expressed greater irritation

―――― TABLE 13.1 ――――
Judgmental Reactions to Ultimatums as a Function
of Ultimator's Social Identity and Fairness of Ultimatum (Study 1)

	Social Identity of Ultimator			
	In-Group		Out-Group	
	Fairness of Ultimatum			
	Fair	Unfair	Fair	Unfair
Rationality of ultimatum	6.58	4.48	6.43	3.98
Selfishness of ultimatum	1.46	4.81	1.69	5.60
Exploitativeness of ultimatum	1.13	4.44	1.50	5.57
Fairness of ultimatum	6.88	3.59	6.98	2.33
Happy with offer	6.79	4.59	6.76	2.88
Irritated by offer	1.13	3.19	1.67	4.54

NOTE: Ratings are on a 7-point scale, where 1 = *not at all* and 7 = *very*.

with unfair demands ($p < .001$) and indicated they were less happy with the offers they had received ($p < .001$). Thus, overall, recipients' responses to unfair demands were quite strong and negative.

The social identity manipulation also produced a number of main effects. As can be seen in Table 13.1, demands were viewed as more exploitative ($p < .02$), less fair ($p < .01$), and marginally more selfish ($p < .08$) when they came from out-group members. Recipients were also significantly less happy ($p < .001$) and more irritated ($p < .01$) by the offers from out-group members. These main effects are consistent, of course, with a simple in-group bias. However, the moral aggression hypothesis implies further that there should be a greater extremity of reaction specifically to the unequal offers as a function of the in-group versus out-group status of the ultimator. This would emerge in the form of two-way interactions between the social identity of the ultimator and the fairness of his or her demand. There were three interactions displaying this pattern. First, unequal offers from out-group members were viewed as more unfair ($M = 2.33$) compared with the same unequal offers from in-group members ($M = 3.59$) ($p < .002$). Second, recipients were clearly less happy with the offers from out-group members ($M = 2.88$) than they were with the same offers from in-group members ($M = 4.59$) ($p < .001$). Finally, they were more irritated with unequal offers when they came from out-group members ($M = 1.67$) than when they came from in-group members ($M = 3.19$) ($p < .02$).

To summarize, the pattern of interactions observed in our data is consistent with the out-group derogation hypothesis, and lends little support to the in-group violation hypothesis.

Behavioral Response to Ultimatums

Recall that, according to the out-group derogation hypothesis, recipients should be more likely to reject unequal offers from out-group members than from in-group members, whereas the in-group violation hypothesis predicts that recipients will be more likely to reject unequal offers when they come from in-group members. A chi-square analysis revealed that acceptance rates did vary significantly as a function of experimental condition ($p < .001$). First, and perhaps not altogether surprisingly, equal offers tended to be accepted regardless of the in-group/out-group status of the ultimator. In fact, no offer entailing an equal split was rejected. In the case of unequal offers, however, the group status of the ultimator had a pronounced effect on acceptance rates. Recipients accepted only 43% of the offers from out-group members. In contrast, the acceptance rate was 75% for comparable offers when they were believed to have been made by in-group members. Consistent with the judgmental data, these results favor the out-group derogation hypothesis.

Study 2

The results of our first study demonstrate quite clearly that the social identity of the ultimator making an unfair demand influences how recipients respond to that demand. To explore this relationship further, we conducted a second study in which we examined how strategic uncertainty in the decision-making environment influences this relationship. Political scientists and social psychologists have long recognized the important role strategic uncertainty plays in conflict situations (see, e.g., general discussions by Jervis, 1976; Jervis et al., 1986; Kramer, 1989; Kramer, Meyerson, & Davis, 1991). Uncertainty about the motives and intentions of an adversary, they have noted, considerably complicates the process of responding to the adversary's actions. In such situations, miscommunications and misperceptions add to the fog of battle and impede judgment and decision-making processes.

Although approaching the problem from a different theoretical starting point, recent theory and research on cooperation in Prisoner's Dilemma situations point to a similar conclusion (Axelrod, 1984; Bendor, 1987; Bendor, Kramer, & Stout, 1991). These studies have shown that one important strategic implication of "noise" (uncertainty about others' intentions) is that it reduces the efficacy of a number of strategies for eliciting cooperation. For example, noise causes reciprocity-based strategies such as tit-for-tat to be too provokable: By failing to give the partner the benefit of the doubt, such strategies set off cycles of mutual recrimination, leading to retaliatory "action-reaction" spirals (Axelrod, 1984; Bendor et al., 1991).

Extrapolating from this research, we designed our second study to explore several hypotheses regarding how social identity affects expectations in ultimatum bargaining contexts. We hypothesized that individuals in ultimatum situations would expect more reasonable demands (operationalized as higher offers) from in-group members than from out-group members. Second, we hypothesized that individuals would be more likely to attribute unreasonable demands (low offers) to out-group members than to in-group members. Third, and relatedly, we expected that individuals would be more likely to attribute reasonable demands (generous offers) to in-group members than to out-group members. And finally, we expected that individuals would be more likely to accept low offers when they thought they were being made by in-group members than when they thought they were coming from out-group members.

On the basis of previous research on social identity and attributional processes, we also explored a number of hypotheses regarding how the social identity of ultimators would affect the attributions recipients make about offers after uncertainty about the ultimator's identity is resolved. Specifically, we hypothesized that individuals would be more likely to attribute unequal offers from in-group members to external factors (i.e., a bad draw on the noise term) rather than to internal factors (i.e., intentionally making an unequal offer). Relatedly, we hypothesized that individuals would be more likely to attribute equal offers from in-group members to internal factors (i.e., they had actually intended to make an equal offer) than to external factors (i.e., a positive draw on the noise term).

We also hypothesized that individuals would be more likely to attribute unequal offers from out-group members to internal factors (i.e., they had originally intended to make an unequal offer) than to external factors (i.e., the draw on the noise term was unfavorable). Finally, we hypothesized that individuals would be more likely to attribute equal offers from out-group members to external factors (i.e., a positive draw on the noise term) than to internal factors (i.e., they had actually intended to make an equal offer).

Overview of Procedures

To test these hypotheses, we conducted an experiment that paralleled Study 1 in most regards. As in Study 1, the social identity of the ultimator (in-group or out-group member) varied, as did the fairness of the ultimatum (demands entailed ostensibly an unfair/unequal division or equal/fair division of resources). Participants were given a general introduction to the ultimatum bargaining game and information regarding the roles of offer maker and recipient. Although participants were led to believe that they were actually interacting with real persons, the offers they received were predetermined prior to the experiment. Thus all participants were assigned to the recipient role. Offers were obtained from the classes involved in the study prior to the ultimatum exercise to create the illusion that participants were supplying offers for the in-group condition during the exercise. Participants were told that the out-group offers they received were sent by express courier prior to the session. A Federal Express envelope sent from the rival institution and opened in the session was used to enhance the credibility of the manipulation and to suggest that the offers were genuine.

After these general remarks, participants were told that, after the offer makers had decided how much they wanted to offer the recipients with whom they had been paired, the experimenter would randomly add or subtract 0 to 100% of that amount from the offer. The experimenter would draw a slip of paper from a bowl containing 201 slips of paper, each of which had a number ranging from −100% to 0 to +100%. Thus the offer that recipients ultimately received contained two components: (a) the amount the offer maker had originally intended to offer and (b) a noise term. If the noise term drawn was positive, the recipient would receive more money than the offer maker had originally intended. Conversely, if the noise term was negative, the recipient would receive less money than the offer maker had intended. Because participants would see only the aggregated numbers (actual offers with noise), they would not know how much the offer makers had actually intended for them to receive.

Participants were told that the offer makers were aware of the fact that a noise component would be added to or subtracted from their offers prior to their being relayed to the recipients. Thus the primary difference between Study 1 and Study 2 was that noise in the communication channel was introduced, so that some ambiguity was present regarding the offer maker's demand.

The introduction of noise raises several interesting strategic possibilities. First, it obviously provides an opportunity for offer makers to exploit, if they wish, the attributional ambiguity created by this noise by cheating or trying to "sneak under" the noise. On the other hand, for the offer maker who wishes to be fair, it complicates the process of demonstrating intended fairness, because a bad draw on the noise term might degrade the generosity of the offer. Recipients recognize these dilemmas as well, so noise makes the social inference process complicated from the recipient's perspective, because it makes judgments regarding the intentions of the ultimator and the fairness of the offer received more difficult (for further discussion and some empirical evidence regarding how decision makers resolve these trade-offs, see Bendor, 1987; Bendor et al., 1991; Kramer, 1989; Kramer et al., 1991).

To test the first set of hypotheses, it was necessary to obtain some judgmental data prior to individuals' receiving their offers and/or any information pertaining to the social identity of the offer maker. Accordingly, we asked participants to complete a questionnaire regarding their expectations about the upcoming bargaining session. Participants then received envelopes containing their offers. Specifically, they were asked to indicate whether they thought the offers they had received were from in-group or out-group members, and also to make various attributional judgments. Thus, up to this point, the social identities of the ultimators were not disclosed.

After completing this questionnaire, each recipient was given another envelope revealing the purported identity of his or her offer maker, made a decision to either accept or reject the offer, and then was asked to fill out a questionnaire regarding his or her perceptions of the actual offer and the noise component involved in the offer. These data were used to evaluate the second set of hypotheses regarding the effects of social identity on attributions about intentions.

Social Identity Manipulation

As in Study 1, we manipulated the social identity of the ultimators by varying their in-group versus out-group status. Individuals assigned to the in-group identity condition were informed that they were interacting with fellow classmates in the M.B.A. program (i.e., an offer made in the previous class session by another member of the class). Individuals assigned to the out-group identity condition were informed that their offers were from students at a rival business school.

Fairness of the Ultimatum

As in Study 1, we manipulated the fairness of the ultimatum by varying whether the offer involved an equal or unequal division of the available resources. Individuals assigned to the fair demand condition received offers between $12.63 and $11.81. Individuals assigned to the unfair demand condition received offers between $6.63 and $5.81. (The mean range of numbers used in the false feedback was comparable to that used in Study 1. However, in order to strengthen the credibility of the noise manipulation, we used a range of nonwhole numbers to suggest that noise was being added to or subtracted from the original offer.)

Results and Discussion

To assess individuals' expectations prior to receiving their ultimatums, we asked them to indicate what they thought (a) was the most sensible offer for an ultimator to make and (b) was the most likely offer that the ultimator would make. Individuals were also asked the minimum amounts they would accept from the ultimators. The primary behavioral measure was simply whether recipients accepted or rejected the ultimatums they received.

―――― **TABLE 13.2** ――――
Recipients' Prebargaining Offer Expectations
as a Function of Ultimator's Social Identity (Study 2)

Variable	In-Group	Out-Group
Most sensible offer	10.54	10.01
	(4.17)	(4.62)
Predicted actual offer	10.33	9.58
	(3.72)	(3.26)
Minimum acceptable offer	7.30	7.30
	(4.88)	(4.91)

We were also interested, of course, in how information about an ultimatum affected individuals' inferences about the identity of the ultimator. We assessed this in two ways. First, we asked recipients to indicate how likely they thought it was that the offers they had received had come from in-group versus out-group members. Second, we asked them to provide measures of confidence regarding their attributions about the identities of the ultimators. We asked them also to provide estimates of both of the components that affected the offers they ultimately received (i.e., the size of the actual offers the ultimator had intended and the amount of noise that had been added to or subtracted from those initial offers). Finally, we asked the participants several questions regarding their overall perceptions of the ultimators and their reactions to the offers.

Prebargaining Expectations

To determine how, if at all, the social identities of the ultimators affected recipients' expectations, we examined first the prebargaining expectations data. In strong support of the first hypothesis, significant differences were obtained with respect to individuals' perceptions of the most sensible offers for offer makers to make as a function of whether they were in-group versus out-group members. As Table 13.2 shows, individuals thought that the most sensible offer for an in-group member to make was significantly higher than that of an out-group member ($p < .05$). There were also significant differences in the amount that individuals thought offer makers would actually offer as a function of the ultimator's social identity. Specifically, individuals thought in-group members would actually offer significantly more than would out-group members ($p < .01$). Perhaps surprisingly, in light of the strong ex post decision data from Study 1, however, recipients thought ex ante that the social identities of the ultimators had no effect on the minimum amounts the recipients would accept from offer makers ($p > .05$).

—— TABLE 13.3 ——————————————————————————

Probability Estimates and Attributions as a Function
of Ultimator's Social Identity and Fairness of Ultimatum (Study 2)

	Size of Offer	
	Low	High
Probability that offer received was from out-group member	.54	.46
Probability that offer received was from in-group member	.47	.55
Attributional confidence that offer came from out-group member	.64	.14
Attributional confidence that offer came from in-group member	.36	.86

Postbargaining Inferences and Attributions

Analyses of the data pertaining to recipients' judgments after having received their offers reveal a number of interesting patterns. First, with respect to the question of whether they thought that their fair versus unfair offers had been made by in-group versus out-group members, the results indicate strong support for the second and third hypotheses. In particular, there were significant differences in individuals' estimates of the probability that their offers had come from in-group or out-group members. As can be seen in Table 13.3, recipients who had received very unfair (low) offers estimated the probability that the offers had been made by out-group members significantly higher than when they had received high offers ($p < .01$). When participants were asked to estimate the probability that very fair (high) offers were made by in-group members, in contrast, the opposite pattern was observed: Individuals who had received high offers estimated significantly higher probabilities that their offers had come from in-group members compared with those who had received low offers ($p < .01$).

Based upon the offers they had received, individuals were also asked to make attributions about the identities of the offer makers (i.e., indicate their confidence in thinking these persons were in-group or out-group members). Group membership was dummy coded, 1 = in-group offer maker and 0 = out-group offer maker. The results indicate robust support for the second and third hypotheses. As can be seen in Table 13.3, individuals were more likely to attribute equal offers to in-group members (mean = .86; $SD = .35$) and unequal offers to out-group members (mean = .38; $SD = .50$; $t = 3.83$, $p < .001$). In addition, a chi-square test, conducted to determine if there was a significant interaction between the type of offer received and individuals' beliefs regarding the identities of the offer makers, provided further support for the hypotheses. As is evident in the table, a greater percentage of participants receiving unfair or low offers thought their offers had come from out-group members rather than in-group members, but the opposite pattern was found with respect to fair (high) offers ($p < .0001$).

Overall, these results provide further evidence of the robust effects of social identity on behavior in ultimatum situations. In comparing the results of Studies 1 and 2, it is important to note that in Study 2, as another way of investigating how social identity relations affect judgment and decision-making processes, we reversed the logic of hypothesis testing that we used in Study 1. In other words, rather than providing unambiguous information about the social identity of the ultimator and investigating how that affected their reactions to demands that were fair or unfair, in Study 2 we presented recipients with demands and then asked them to make inferences about the social identities of the ultimators based upon the ultimators' purported behavior.[3]

Study 3

The primary aim of Study 3 was to investigate more systematically how noise affects recipients' responses to out-group ultimators' offers when they possess complete information about the ultimators' original intentions. From a purely economic standpoint, information about intentions should not influence recipients' judgments about the fairness or unfairness of the offers themselves—only absolute payoffs or outcomes matter. However, if moralistic aggression is a potent force in such situations, then information about intentions should matter a great deal. In other words, from an attributional standpoint, knowing how an ultimator responded to noise strategically (in particular, whether he or she had used the noise to try to take advantage of the opportunity it created) is diagnostic. We reasoned that attributions about the intentions of ultimators should influence recipients' behavior above and beyond information about objective economic outcomes alone. Specifically, we hypothesized that information that is diagnostic of intended fairness—that is, the intention to divide resources equally—would matter more than the outcome itself.

Overview of Procedures

The general procedures were similar to those employed in the previous two studies, with the following exceptions. First, to test the major hypothesis, we need to compare behavior in a noisy versus a noiseless ultimatum situation. Thus, although noise was constant across conditions in Study 2, in Study 3 we manipulated it as an independent variable. Accordingly, Study 3 employed a 2 × 2 (Fairness of Ultimatum × Level of Uncertainty) between-subjects factorial design. Fairness of the ultimatum (fair versus unfair offer) was crossed with two levels of uncertainty (no noise versus noise). Also, because we were interested mainly in how information about intentions would affect reaction to out-group members' ultimatums, in this study all participants were told that the offers they had received were from out-group members (i.e., M.B.A. students at a rival business school). Participants were also informed that the offer makers knew whether their offers were to be subject to the uncertainty component.

Participants were then given envelopes containing cards with the amounts offered to them by the other parties. In the no-noise condition, of course, the amount actually offered was simply the amount originally intended by the ultimator. In the noise condition, in contrast, the amount originally intended by the ultimator was stated, along with precise information about the amount of noise added to or subtracted from that offer. Participants were then asked to indicate whether they wanted to accept the final offers (intended offer plus or minus noise) or reject them.

Uncertainty Manipulation

We manipulated uncertainty by varying whether recipients received offers that were altered by a noise (noise condition) component or were the actual offers originally intended for them by the offer makers (no-noise condition). Participants in the noise condition were told that the amounts offered by the offer makers would be altered by a random noise component of +100% to −100%. Thus the offers originally intended for them by the offer makers could be drastically altered in a positive or negative way (increased or decreased, depending upon the noise). Participants in the no-noise condition were told that their offers were the actual amounts offered by the offer makers, with no noise disturbance.

Fairness Manipulation

We manipulated the fairness of the ultimatum by varying whether the final offers recipients received entailed a relatively equal versus unequal share of the resources. Fair versus unfair offers in the noise condition were structured such that the fair (equal) versus unfair (unequal) final offers were caused by large positive versus large negative noise terms, respectively. In the unfair offer condition with noise, the amount originally offered by the offer maker was $12.50, and the noise component was −48%. Thus the actual offer to the recipient was $6.50. Although this actual offer falls into the unfair category in terms of absolute amount, recipients knew that the offer makers had originally intended a fair (equal) division of resources. In the fair offer with noise condition, in contrast, the amount originally offered by the offer maker was $6.50, and the noise component was +92%. Thus the actual offer to the recipient was

--------- TABLE 13.4 ---------
Compliance Rates as Function of Fairness
and Noise (Study 3) (in percentages)

	Uncertainty	
Fairness of Ultimatum	*No Noise*	*Noise*
Unfair	67	100
Fair	83	77

$12.50. Although this offer is very fair in terms of objective payoffs, the recipients knew that the offer makers had originally intended for the recipients to receive a very unequal share of the resources. If moralistic aggression is driving behavior, this additional knowledge should matter.

Results and Discussion

Recall that the interesting feature of this study is that, although noise was present in the communication channel between ultimator and recipient, recipients nonetheless had complete, "inside" information about the demands (i.e., knew the size of the original offers and the noise components that had been added or subtracted from those offers). Thus there was no attributional ambiguity regarding the ultimator's intentions.

A chi-square test was used to determine if acceptance rates were affected by the level of uncertainty about intentions in conjunction with the actual fairness of the ultimatum itself. The results support the hypothesis. As can be seen in Table 13.4, when noise was not present, recipients were more likely to reject unequal offers compared with equal offers. However, this finding was reversed in the noise condition: Participants receiving unequal offers that were the result of bad luck with respect to the draw from noise distribution were more likely to accept offers (100%) than were those who received equal offers (77%).

The results obtained in the noisy communication condition indicate quite clearly the importance of information about intentions. When recipients knew that ultimators had intended an equal division of resources, they were perfectly willing to accept highly unequal offers. It was, after all, merely bad luck that the offers had been degraded by external factors beyond the ultimators' control. In contrast, quite a few recipients were willing to reject an equal share of the resources when they knew that the ultimators had intended to keep more for themselves. These results are consistent with a moralistic aggression hypothesis: The only reason to reject these offers was to spite the ultimators (deny them resources and, possibly, teach them a lesson). Note that, because this was a one-shot game, the lesson could not benefit the recipient (i.e., there is no reputational or "demonstration effect").[4]

Although the findings of the no-noise condition are generally similar to previous findings showing that recipients are likely to reject unequal offers even though they result in positive economic gain, the fact that 17% of the individuals in the noiseless condition were willing to reject equal offers is somewhat puzzling—it is hard to imagine why anyone would reject an equal offer. However, given that all of the ultimators were out-group members from another business school, out-group derogation may have played a role here.

Construed broadly, our results are consistent with those of several other recent studies that have investigated the impact of uncertainty on ultimatum bargaining behavior (Croson, 1993; Kagel, Kim, & Moser, 1993; Straub & Murnighan, 1993). Straub and Murnighan (1993) found that recipients accepted significantly lower offers when they were not aware of the amounts being divided (partial information) than when they had full knowledge (complete information) about the amounts. Kagel et al. (1993) found similar results, although they operationalized uncertainty differently. In their study, rather than allocating money, ultimators were asked to divide chips, which were to be turned in at the end of the experiment. The chips had different rates of exchange for the offer makers and for recipients. Under conditions of uncertainty, players knew their own rates of exchange but were unaware of their opponents'. Kagel et al. found that recipients were more forgiving about unequal splits when the offer makers lacked complete information.

We should note a difference in our operationalization of strategic uncertainty, however. In our study, uncertainty was operationalized as an environmental form of noisy communication—as if static in the channel were present. This was intended to reflect the idea of imperfect communication, miscommunication, and misunderstanding. In other studies, uncertainty has been operationalized as asymmetries in the knowledge available to the offer makers and recipients regarding the amount of resources to be divided.

One slightly disturbing implication of our finding is that ultimators may be able to increase compliance if they can successfully manipulate recipients' attributions about the reasons for an ultimatum even when, in terms of its face value, it is perceived to be unfair.

Implications and Conclusions

The results of the experiments reported in this chapter demonstrate quite clearly the impact of social context on how decision makers construe coercive bargaining attempts. Using three different approaches, we documented a similar pattern of judgmental and behavioral asymmetry in recipients' response to ultimatums that was linked to the social identities of the actors presenting the ultimatums. Overall, this pattern supports the out-group derogation hypothesis over the in-group violation hypothesis. In some respects, these results were a disappointment to us. When designing this research, we viewed the in-group violation hypothesis—the possibility that individuals would construe unfair demands as more offensive and egregious violations of a social contract when they emanated from members of the individuals' own social group—as the more interesting and provocative conjecture.

However, even apart from our stubborn enthusiasm for this hypothesis, there are reasons we are reluctant to abandon it. First, the fact that we found a lack of support for this in-group version of the moralistic aggression hypothesis does not necessarily mean the hypothesis itself is invalid. There is, after all, a basic limitation of the paradigm used in the present research—at least from the standpoint of its external validity. Although the ultimatum bargaining game is a good laboratory analogue for studying coercive bargaining behavior in some respects, it has limitations and drawbacks. Most obviously, the violations of fairness it entails are relatively trivial: At most, participants in the present experiments stood to lose a few dollars when playing these games; indeed, their pride more than their pocketbooks were at stake. In real-world settings, however, where the costs and consequences of such violations are more substantial, the level of moral aggression observed within groups might be considerably stronger. For example, an ultimatum delivered by a colleague in one's department on an important issue might produce a much more intense moral reaction than the same threat delivered by a faculty member from another department: The out-group member's selfishness is, after all, anticipated and to be expected. One way of thinking about such real-world situations is that the implicit psychological contract among individuals is quite strong, in contrast to the minimal social situations and trivial consequences associated with those captured in the lab (see Robinson & Rousseau, 1994; Rousseau & Parks, 1993). Of course, ex post and in our defense, we should emphasize that the aim of our experiments was to demonstrate the lower bounds of what we had ex ante hoped would be a rather robust effect. Thus use of a minimal paradigm seemed warranted. A future experiment to capture our elusive result should, therefore, rely on strong manipulations and contexts.

In closing, we should emphasize also that the present research was stimulated largely by an interest in understanding better why ultimatums fail. As noted earlier, there is already considerable research suggesting why ultimatums fail from the standpoint of deficiencies in the judgment and decision-making processes of ultimators. We know, for example, that negotiators are often overconfident and suffer from illusions of control (see, e.g., Kramer et al., 1993; Neale & Bazerman, 1991). However, we know relatively less about how the targets of coercive bargaining attempts construe such behavior. Accordingly, we decided to focus in these studies primarily on target reactions to ultimatums. It is interesting, however, to view our findings in conjunction with previous work that has examined the other side of the coin. Rothbart and Hallmark (1988), for example, investigated the perceived efficacy of various kinds of influence attempts as a function of the in-group versus out-group status of the target. They found that individuals tended to view coercive strategies as more efficacious than conciliatory strategies when dealing with out-group versus in-group members. Viewed together, these results suggest why conflicts involving ultimatums so often escalate through a series of destructive action-reaction spirals: Each side views the other as more susceptible to coercive strategies, while at the same time resenting the use of those same strategies against themselves. If, on top of such perceptual asymmetries, we add individuals' tendency to be preoffended by the offers they receive from out-group members, the escalatory potential in such situations becomes even more stark.

Notes

1. Interpretation of the efficacy of Kennedy's ultimatums remains, however, a subject of considerable debate, because they were part of a complex bargaining mix that included other inducements and a great deal of tacit signaling.
2. To enhance the internal validity of this manipulation, we first conducted a pilot study in which we asked M.B.A. students enrolled in an evening program to rate the fairness/unfairness of various magnitudes of unequal offers. We found that participants rated an equal offer to divide $25.00 into two equal parts as very fair ($M = 6.81$) but rated an offer of a $17.50/$7.50 split as very unfair ($M = 2.10$) on a 7-point scale ($1 = $ *not at all fair* to $7 = $ *very fair*).
3. None of the attributional hypotheses was supported.
4. Note the added twist that accepting the unequal offer provided the recipient with a means of "spiting" the offer maker, who ended up with less than he or she had originally intended. On the other hand, recipients who ended up with equal offers because of the noise term were perfectly willing to forgo half of the monetary prize in order to punish offer makers who had intended unfair offers, consistent with the idea of moralistic aggression.

References

Axelrod, R. (1984). *The evolution of cooperation.* New York: Basic Books.
Bach, S. (1984). *Final cut: Dreams and disaster in the making of* Heaven's Gate. Beverly Hills, CA: Morrow.
Bazerman, M. H. (1991). Fairness, social comparison, and irrationality. In J. K. Murnighan (Ed.), *Social psychology in organizations: Advances in theory and practice.* Englewood Cliffs, NJ: Prentice Hall.
Bendor, J. (1987). In good times and bad: Reciprocity in an uncertain world. *American Journal of Political Science, 31,* 531-558.

Bendor, J., Kramer, R. M., & Stout, S. (1991). When in doubt: Cooperation in a noisy Prisoner's Dilemma. *Journal of Conflict Resolution, 35,* 691-719.

Bernstein, A. (1990). *Grounded: Frank Lorenzo and the destruction of Eastern Airlines.* New York: Simon & Schuster.

Beschloss, M. R. (1991). *The crisis years: Kennedy and Khrushchev, 1960-1963.* New York: HarperCollins.

Bies, R. J. (1987). The predicament of injustice: The management of moral outrage. In L. L. Cummings & B. M. Staw (Eds.), *Research in organizational behavior* (Vol. 9, pp. 289-319). Greenwich, CT: JAI.

Bies, R. J., & Moag, J. (1986). Interactional justice. In R. J. Lewicki, B. H. Sheppard, & M. H. Bazerman (Eds.), *Research on negotiation in organizations.* Greenwich, CT: JAI.

Binmore, K., Shaked, A., & Sutton, J. (1985). Testing noncooperative bargaining theory: A preliminary study. *American Economic Review, 75,* 1178-1180.

Blight, J. G., & Welch, D. A. (1989). *On the brink: Americans and Soviets reexamine the Cuban missile crisis.* New York: Hill & Wang.

Brewer, M. B. (1979). Ingroup bias in the minimal intergroup situation: A cognitive-motivational analysis. *Psychological Bulletin, 86,* 307-324.

Brewer, M. B. (1981). Ethnocentrism and its role in interpersonal trust. In M. B. Brewer & B. E. Collins (Eds.), *Scientific inquiry in the social sciences.* San Francisco: Jossey-Bass.

Brewer, M. B., & Kramer, R. M. (1985). The psychology of intergroup attitudes and behavior. *Annual Review of Psychology, 36,* 219-243.

Campbell, D. T. (1975). On the conflict between biological and social evolution and between psychology and moral tradition. *American Psychologist, 30,* 1103-1126.

Cialdini, R. B., Reno, R. R., & Kallgren, C. A. (1990). A focus theory of normative conduct: Recycling the concept of norms to reduce littering in public places. *Journal of Personality and Social Psychology, 58,* 1015-1026.

Croson, R. T. (1993). *Information in ultimatum games: An experimental study.* Unpublished manuscript.

George, A. L. (1991). *Forceful persuasion: Coercive diplomacy as an alternative to war.* Washington, DC: U.S. Institute of Peace Press.

George, A. L. (1993). *Bridging the gap: Theory and practice in foreign policy.* Washington, DC: U.S. Institute of Peace Press.

Guth, W., Schmittberger, R., & Schwarze, B. (1982). An experimental analysis of ultimatum bargaining. *Journal of Economic Behavior and Organization, 3,* 367-388.

Guth, W., & Tietz, R. (1990). Ultimatum bargaining behavior: A survey and comparison of experimental results. *Journal of Economic Psychology, 11,* 417-449.

Hewstone, M. (1992). The "ultimate attribution error"? A review of the literature on intergroup causal attribution. *European Journal of Social Psychology, 20,* 311-335.

Hogg, M. A., & Abrams, D. (1988). *Social identifications: A social psychology of intergroup relations and group processes.* London: Routledge.

Janis, I. L. (1983). *Groupthink* (2nd ed.). Boston: Houghton Mifflin.

Jervis, R. (1976). *Perception and misperception in international politics.* Princeton, NJ: Princeton University Press.

Jervis, R., Lebow, N., & Stein, J. (1986). *Psychology and deterrence.* Baltimore: Johns Hopkins University Press.

Kagel, J. H., Kim, C., & Moser, D. (1993). *"Fairness" in ultimatum games with asymmetric information and asymmetric payoffs.* Unpublished manuscript.

Kahn, R. L., & Kramer, R. M. (1990). Untying the knot: De-escalatory processes in international conflict. In R. L. Kahn & M. N. Zald (Eds.), *Organizations and nation-states: New perspectives on conflict and cooperation.* San Francisco: Jossey-Bass.

Kahneman, D., Knetsch, J. L., & Thaler, R. H. (1986a). Fairness and the assumptions of economics. *Journal of Business, 4*(part 2), S285-S300.

Kahneman, D., Knetsch, J. L., & Thaler, R. H. (1986b). Fairness as a constraint on profit
seeking: Entitlements in the marketplace. *American Economic Review, 76,* 728-741.

Kramer, R. M. (1989). Windows of vulnerability or cognitive illusions? Cognitive processes
and the nuclear arms race. *Journal of Experimental Social Psychology, 25,* 79-100.

Kramer, R. M., Meyerson, D., & Davis, G. (1991). How much is enough? *Journal of Personality
and Social Psychology, 58,* 984-993.

Kramer, R. M., Pommerenke, P. L., & Newton, E. (1993). The social context of negotiation:
Effects of social identity and interpersonal accountability on negotiator judgment and
decision making. *Journal of Conflict Resolution, 37,* 633-656.

Levine, R. A., & Campbell, D. T. (1972). *Ethnocentrism: Theories of conflict, ethnic attitudes,
and group behavior.* New York: John Wiley.

Lind, A., & Tyler, T. (1988). *The social psychology of procedural justice.* New York: Plenum.

Messick, D. M. (1993). Equality as a decision heuristic. In B. Mellers (Ed.), *Psychological issues
in distributive justice.* New York: Springer-Verlag.

Messick, D. M., & Schell, T. (1992). Evidence for an equality heuristic in social decision
making. *Acta Psychologica, 80,* 311-323.

Neale, M. A., & Bazerman, M. H. (1991). *Cognition and negotiator rationality.* New York: Free
Press.

Ochs, J., & Roth, A. E. (1989). An experimental study of sequential bargaining. *American
Economic Review, 79,* 335-385.

Reno, R. R., Cialdini, R. B., & Kallgren, C. A. (1993). The transsituational influence of social
norms. *Journal of Personality and Social Psychology, 64,* 104-112.

Robinson, S. L., & Rousseau, D. M. (1994). Violating the psychological contract: Not the
exception but the rule. *Journal of Organizational Behavior, 15,* 245-259.

Rothbart, M., & Hallmark, W. (1988). In-group–out-group differences in perceived efficacy
of coercion and conciliation in resolving social conflict. *Journal of Personality and Social
Psychology, 55,* 248-257.

Rousseau, D. M., & Parks, J. M. (1993). The contracts of individuals and organizations. In L. L.
Cummings & B. M. Staw (Eds.), *Research in organizational behavior* (Vol. 15, pp. 1-43).
Greenwich, CT: JAI.

Schelling, T. C. (1958). The strategy of conflict: Prospectus for a reorientation of game theory.
Journal of Conflict Resolution, 2, 203-264.

Shostak. A. B., & Skocik, D. (1986). *The air traffic controllers' controversy: Lessons from the
PATCO strike.* New York: Human Sciences Press.

Stein, J. (1993). Threat-based strategies of conflict management: Why did they fail in the Gulf?
In S. Renshon (Ed.), *The political psychology of the Gulf War: Leaders, publics, and the
process of conflict.* Pittsburgh: University of Pittsburgh Press.

Straub, P. G., & Murnighan, J. K. (1993). *An experimental investigation of ultimatums:
Complete information, fairness, expectations, and lowest acceptable offers.* Evanston, IL:
Northwestern University, Dispute Resolution Research Center.

Tajfel, H. (1978). Social categorization, social identity, and social comparison. In H. Tajfel
(Ed.), *Differentiation between social groups* (pp. 61-76). London: Academic Press.

Tajfel, H., & Turner, J. C. (1986). The social identity theory of intergroup behavior. In S.
Worchel & W. G. Austin (Eds.), *Psychology of intergroup relations.* Chicago: Nelson-Hall.

Thaler, R. H. (1988). Anomalies: The ultimatum game. *Journal of Economic Perspective, 2,*
195-206.

Trivers, R. L. (1971). The evolution of reciprocal altruism. *Quarterly Review of Biology, 46,* 35-57.

Wilson, E. O. (1978). *On human nature.* New York: Bantam.

14

Property, Culture, and Negotiation

PETER J. CARNEVALE

Ownership of property is often the basis for negotiation. "This is our land" and "That was my idea" are common statements that often define the issues in conflict. The terms *our* and *my* in statements of ownership indicate an important element of property: that ownership is tied closely to social identity and the sense of self.

Instances of ownership conflict are numerous. Kuhn (1962) has written about the sometimes bitter disputes between scientists who seek to validate ownership of a scientific concept. Negotiations about the environment often entail access to resources on public lands and issues of use payments and preservation (e.g., Cushman, 1994). In international affairs, conflicts of ownership often involve the booty of imperial wars and plundered art objects (e.g., Riding, 1993). Workplace conflicts are often cast in terms of workers' property rights in their jobs (Gould, 1986), with Webb and Webb (1914) stating that protecting a job from encroachment "appears as fundamental a basis of the social order as it does to owners of land" (p. 566).

The idea that there is a close relationship between ownership and self-concept is not new in psychology. More than a century ago, William James (1890) provided interesting thoughts on the matter: "An instructive impulse drives us to collect property; and the collections thus made become, with different

AUTHOR'S NOTE: I am grateful to Rod Kramer for very helpful comments on this chapter. This material is based upon work supported by the National Science Foundation under Grant BNS-8809263 to Peter Carnevale and Grant SBR-9210536 to Peter Carnevale and Harry Triandis.

degrees of intimacy, part of our empirical selves" (p. 293). James went on to note that it is often difficult to distinguish between what is described as "me" and what is described as "mine." Heider (1958) suggests that ownership entails a "unit relation" between person and object.

In this chapter, I examine negotiation over ownership of property. In line with the general theme of this volume, I focus on property negotiation in its cultural context, which is perhaps the broadest social context within which negotiation can occur. To limit the discussion, I consider only one cultural concept, collectivism/individualism, and consider how it can influence the behavior of individuals and groups in relatively simple, bilateral negotiation.

My general thesis is that culture can influence negotiation over property through its influence on self-concept. This thesis stems from two key propositions:

1. The sense of ownership of property is closely tied to self-concept.
2. Collectivism and individualism are closely tied, at the level of the individual, to self-concept and the extent to which the self incorporates elements of the group to which the individual belongs (see Markus & Kitayama, 1991).

I will argue that collectivism and individualism can influence the preference formulation process in negotiation, particularly when the issues to be negotiated involve property and whether the property is owned by the individual or by the group.

To lay the foundation for this thesis, in the following sections I review literature on conflict and culture, on collectivism and individualism, and on ownership. I then present recent, preliminary data from several experiments that suggest that the three concepts of property, culture, and negotiation do have something to do with one another. Finally, I conclude with an argument that the general paradigm that guides behavioral work on negotiation should be expanded to incorporate culture as a parameter.

Culture and Negotiation

One goal of cultural analyses of negotiation is to discover etic (universal) rules and emic (culture-specific) rules. The anthropologist Gulliver (1988) stated it nicely:

Conceptualize the pattern of a basic universal process applicable to all kinds of negotiations at whatever societal level (from interpersonal to international), in whatever socio-cultural context and irrespective of the issues in contention. . . . [This is] useful to the extent it can facilitate cross-cultural comparison and the identification of fundamental features and processual interactions. (p. 253)

We want to know what the common elements are in order to facilitate cultural comparisons.

Anthropological studies of conflict and culture often depict conflicts over property. Billings (1991), for example, wrote about the Tikana of Northern New Ireland and the Lavongai of New Hanover, neighbors on adjacent islands in the Bismarck Archipelago north of Papua New Guinea, each with a population of about 7,000. According to Billings, these groups have much in common, but they settle disputes differently, in manners consistent with their "styles" of culture. The Tikana are group oriented, whereas the Lavongai are individualistic. Billings described a conflict in Tikana: "Two old women . . . each thought a baby pig was her own. . . . It developed into a dispute about where the boundary was between their two houses . . . [and] led to great interest in the community for resolving the conflict. . . . Eventually, the property in question became group property" (p. 252). This contrasts sharply with disputes among the Lavongai, which are resolved privately, in often violent face-to-face conflict, without group involvement.

There is some evidence for cultural variation in negotiation behavior. Kelley et al. (1970) have shown that regions of the world, and regions of the United States, differ in terms of the degree to which subjects will define a negotiation task as cooperative or competitive. More recently, Roth, Prasnikar, Okuno-Fujiwara, and Zamir (1991) examined cultural differences in an ultimatum bargaining game. In ultimatum bargaining, one subject proposes a division of a resource and the other subject either accepts or rejects the division. If the other accepts it, both subjects receive the proposed allocation. However, if the other rejects it, both subjects get nothing. Roth et al. found no differences across samples (United States, Yugoslavia, Japan, Israel) in acceptance rates, which is an index of general market behavior. However, they found large differences in the amounts subjects were willing to accept, with Japanese and Israeli subjects willing to accept lower amounts. These differences in amounts accepted cannot be attributed to language, currencies, or experimental confounds, because the market-level negotiation variables did not differ; rather, the differences can be explained in terms of cultural differences in perceived fairness.

Perhaps the strongest approach to understanding cultural variation in negotiation behavior is to tie such cultural comparisons to established theory of culture. Carnevale and Triandis (1993) offer several testable propositions about negotiation behavior as a function of one relatively well-known dimension of culture: collectivism/individualism.

Collectivism and Individualism

The constructs of individualism and collectivism have been discussed in many contexts in the social sciences (Lukes, 1973). In the areas of values, social systems, morality, religion, cognitive differentiation, economic development, the structure of constitutions, and others, the concepts used have all been closely related to individualism and collectivism constructs (Triandis, 1994).

Hofstede (1980) identified dimensions of work behavior in analyses of data from subdivisions of the IBM Corporation in many countries. One of those dimensions was collectivism versus individualism: "Individualism pertains to societies in which the ties between individuals are loose. . . . Collectivism as its opposite pertains to societies in which people from birth onwards are integrated into strong, cohesive ingroups, which throughout people's lifetime continue to protect in exchange for unquestioning loyalty" (Hofstede, 1991, p. 5). Individualism is very high in the United States, and generally in most English-speaking countries (Hofstede, 1980). Collectivism can be found in parts of Europe (e.g., southern Italy, rural Greece) and much of Africa, Asia, and Latin America.

Whence collectivism? Triandis (1994) suggested that affluence is an important correlate, as is the number of groups that a person can be a member of. The more complex the social structure, the more such groups there are. Individuals can then join them or leave them, according to whether the groups satisfy their personal needs. Individualism is a consequence of (a) the number of available groups (e.g., urban environment), (b) affluence (one does not need groups as much if one is affluent), (c) social mobility, and (d) geographic mobility (one can change groups more easily; groups cannot influence individuals as much). The American frontier, migration, and affluence may have been the major determinants of American individualism.

Corresponding to the individualism and collectivism concepts at the cultural level are processes at the psychological level: idiocentrism and allocentrism. There are numerous defining attributes of allocentrics and idiocentrics (Triandis, 1994). For allocentrics, the group is the basic unit of social perception, the self is defined in terms of in-group relationships, in-group goals have primacy over or overlap with personal goals, in-group harmony is a value, and social behavior tends to be very different with other in-group members versus with out-group members. For idiocentrics, the individual is the basic unit of social perception, the self is an independent entity, personal goals have primacy over in-group goals, in-group confrontation is acceptable, and social behavior with other in-group members is not very different from that with out-group members.

In individualistic cultures, the organizing theme is the centrality of the autonomous individual, with members whose selves include more private elements (e.g., I am kind; my strengths are many). In collectivist cultures the organizing theme is the centrality of the collective—family, tribe, ethnic group—and the self has more collectivist elements (e.g., my family expects me to be kind; my coworkers believe that I have many strengths). Members of individualistic cultures also have public selves with more individualistic elements (e.g., people in general expect me to be kind) whereas those in collectivist cultures have public selves with more collectivist elements (e.g., people in general expect me to be a good family man).

The most important cognition for individualists is *I, me, mine*; for collectivists, it is *us, we, ours* versus *they* and *them* (Triandis, 1994). Because there are more elements in the private, collective, or public selves in some cultures than in others, the probability that different types of elements will be sampled differs in different cultures (Trafimow, Triandis, & Goto, 1991).

One measure of collectivism is the I-AM Scale. Subjects are simply asked to fill in the blank in the phrase "I am _." The subject's responses are analyzed for content that reflects individual aspects of the self ("a hard worker") versus collective or social aspects of the self ("a caring son").

Other measures of collectivism include attitudes, determined with questionnaire items that ask the subject, for example, to indicate the degree of agreement with statements such as the following: "I would rather struggle through a personal problem by myself than discuss it with friends"; "Aging parents should live at home with their children." Agreement with the former item is indicative of idiocentrism, whereas agreement with the latter is indicative of allocentrism.

Collectivism, Individualism, and Negotiation

Evidence has been gathered that supports aspects of the hypothesized relationships between collectivism/individualism and negotiation behavior. Chan, Triandis, Carnevale, Tam, and Bond (1994) tested the hypothesis that collectivists are more sensitive to the nature of the relationship with the person they face in negotiation. They used samples of subjects in the United States and Hong Kong, and also measured allocentrism and idiocentrism. Subjects in each culture were asked to negotiate with either a friend or a stranger. A 2 × 2 factorial design involved culture (Hong Kong, Champaign) and relationship (friend versus stranger). The laboratory task was a computer version of the standard integrative bargaining paradigm popularized by Pruitt (1981). Each subject sat at a computer that he or she thought was connected to another computer, and was led to believe that he or she would communicate via a computer network with the other negotiator. The other negotiator's behavior was, in fact, simulated by a computer program. The name of the other negotiator (either the name of the subject's friend or the name of a stranger) appeared on each screen as the negotiation progressed.

Table 14.1 presents data from the Chan et al. study on total concessions made in the negotiation as a function of culture and relationship. As can be

—— TABLE 14.1 ————————————————————————————

Total Concessions Made in Negotiation as a Function of Collectivism and
Individualism (U.S. Versus Hong Kong Subjects), and Relationship With
the Opposing Negotiator

	U.S. Subjects	Hong Kong Subjects
Stranger	7.18	6.66
Friend	7.82	8.28

SOURCE: Data from Chan et al. (1994).

seen, the data support the in-group/out-group aspect of the theory of collectivism. The effect of relationship (the difference between negotiating with a
friend and negotiating with a stranger) was greater in the Hong Kong sample
than in the U.S. sample.

The Hong Kong subjects showed greater cooperation with a friend, and less
cooperation with a stranger, than did the U.S. subjects. (It should be noted
that the subjects in the Hong Kong sample scored as more allocentric than the
U.S. subjects on the measures of allocentrism/idiocentrism. It should also be
noted that the subjects in Hong Kong did not rate their friends to be better
friends than did subjects in the United States, which otherwise would have
indicated a confound.)

The data in Table 14.1 suggest that collectivists find it more difficult to
separate relationships from negotiation behavior. The data also are consistent
with the ideas that collectivists are more concerned with preserving harmony
in the group and that they are less willing to risk losing the relationship. Analysis
of the character of the messages sent by subjects in the Chan et al. study
indicated that the negotiators in Hong Kong were more likely to send cooperative messages to their friends than were negotiators in the United States.

A relevant and interesting anecdote comes from Barbara Huie (1987), who
describes a case of mediation of a conflict between a collectivist group and an
individualistic group. The conflict occurred along the Texas Gulf Coast. The
mediation was conducted by a conciliator who worked for the Community
Relations Service, a U.S. government agency. The context for the conflict was
provided by the many Southeast Asians living in Texas, many earning their
livings by fishing and shrimping in the Gulf of Mexico.

Different perceptions characterized each side of this conflict. On one side,
"white shrimpers along the Texas Gulf Coast were angered that groups of
Vietnamese shrimpers would work their nets in the same area, overfishing the
waters." And on the other side, "when a white shrimper discovered a good
harvesting spot, other white shrimpers would pass, leaving the lucky individual alone to reap the rewards of his labor. Vietnamese shrimpers on the other

hand, upon discovering a good spot, would invite others to the area to share in the good fortune" (Huie, 1987, p. 8). The two groups apparently valued the resource differently, in the sense that they differed in their willingness to share the resource with others in the group.

Ownership

In a recent study, Jim Beggan (1992) defined the concept of "mere owner-ship" and demonstrated that subjects come to value an object as a direct function of their having it in their possession (see also Nuttin, 1985, 1987). In the paradigm that Beggan developed, subjects sit at a table and evaluate small objects, such as a plastic key holder, some chocolate, some peanut brittle, a bar of soap, a key ring, a small stapler, plastic combs, and a cold drink insulator, ostensibly as part of a study of consumer preferences. Subjects are told, prior to their evaluations, "Keep one as a gift for participating." The subjects then rate the objects on attractiveness, value, quality, and design, using 7-point scales. In Beggan's study, subjects evaluated the objects they owned as higher on all these dimensions ($M = 5.55$) than the objects they did not own ($M = 4.50$). Adequate control conditions helped eliminate mood and attention as alterna-tive explanations.

Beggan (1992) offers an argument akin to that given by William James (1890), mentioned at the outset of this chapter. That is, he argues for a self-extension perspective, where objects owned are incorporated into the self-concept and thus are susceptible to a self-enhancement bias. In other words, ownership increases fondness for a good, which may be seen as an egocentric bias in possessions (see Allison, Messick, & Goethals, 1989).

Culture and Ownership

The central question is, Can culture influence the sense of ownership and therefore the preference formulation process in negotiation? Carnevale and Radhakrishnan (1994, Experiment 1) conducted a study to test the idea that the mere ownership effect identified by Beggan varies with culture and varies with whether or not the object owned is owned by the individual (as in Beggan's study) or owned by the group. The key ideas were to separate a *mere individual ownership* effect from a *mere group ownership* effect and to see if these effects vary for allocentric and idiocentric subjects.

Subjects came to the laboratory with a friend or alone, to participate in a study of "consumer preferences." About half of the subjects were U.S. citizens and native English speakers, whereas the others, mostly students from Korea,

————— TABLE 14.2 ——————————————————————————
Relative Willingness to Pay as a Function of Individual
and Group Ownership, and Collectivism and Individualism
(Target Object – Mean of Other Objects)

	Group Owns	No Owner	Self Owns
Collectivists	9.58	.37	−.15
Individualists	1.47	3.27	13.43

SOURCE: Partial data from Carnevale and Radhakrishnan (1994, Experiment 1).

were nonnative English speakers. The method was identical to that used by
Beggan (1992). First, however, subjects completed a 16-item idiocentrism and
allocentrism attitude scale (Triandis, 1994).

The subjects were told to look at and evaluate six candy products being
considered for use as free promotional gifts by an advertiser. There was one
target item, a 50-cent bag of M&Ms. There were several ownership conditions,
defined as what happened with regard to ownership just prior to the ratings.
The ownership conditions included the following:

1. "You and your friend get the target item."
2. No ownership: simply evaluate the target and the other items.
3. "You get the target item."
4. "Some other subject gets the target item" (the subject will get one of the other
   items, but it has not yet been determined which one).

The subjects were asked, "How much would you be willing to pay for this
item?" The response format was in U.S. dollars and cents. Table 14.2 shows
data on the prices given for the target item (the M&Ms) minus the average
price of all of the other items that subjects saw on the table.

As can be seen in Table 14.2, a mere ownership effect was found, but only for
idiocentric subjects. There was no self-own effect for allocentric subjects. As
expected, the pattern was the opposite for the allocentric subjects. There was
a group ownership effect for allocentric subjects, but not for idiocentric subjects.
(The two groups were determined by a median split on the allocentrism attitude
scale.)

Also, consistent with the theory of collectivism outlined earlier, the ownership that was held by some "other," who was a stranger, had a greater negative
effect for collectivists than for individualists. Knowing that another person
owns an object is not uncommon, as when one sees a "sold" sign on a house or
on an item in a store, such as an audio system.

Endowment Effect

Another perspective on ownership is provided by Kahneman, Knetsch, and Thaler (1990): an "endowment effect." These authors argue that an individual who is assigned the property right to a good will be more likely to retain it in bargaining. Here, the effect of ownership is to induce a dislike for giving up the object owned. This effect can be contrasted with that described by Beggan (1992), where the effect of ownership is defined in terms of an increase in fondness for a good as a result of possession.

Kahneman et al. used an induced-value bargaining paradigm in which objects, such as chocolate bars, were distributed to half the members of a class. Those who received the bars were asked the minimum price they would accept to sell them, and those without the bars were asked the maximum price they would pay to acquire them. In one study, the sellers set a price of $3.98; buyers set a price of $1.25.

In another study, Kahneman et al. (1990) placed subjects in one of three groups: (a) "sellers," who were given coffee mugs and asked to indicate whether or not they would sell the mugs at a series of prices ranging from $0 to $9.25 (the data: $7.12 valuation); (b) "buyers," who indicated they were willing to buy mugs at each of these prices (the data: $2.87 valuation); and (c) "choosers," who were asked to choose, for each of the possible prices, between mugs like the ones they could see and cash (the data: $3.12 valuation). It is important to note that for both the sellers and the choosers, the objective wealth position was identical. This ruled out possible income effects as an explanation of the greater valuations that were given by the sellers.

Kahneman et al. (1990) argue that the allocation of a mug to a seller induced a sense of endowment that the choosers did not share, inducing a dislike for giving it up. In their words, an "instant endowment effect: the value that an individual assigns to such objects as mugs, pens, . . . chocolate bars appears to increase substantially as soon as that individual is given the object . . . [and is] due to a reference point shift and consequent value change induced by giving a person possession of a good" (p. 1342).

Loewenstein and Issacharoff (1994), in addition to providing evidence that mood is not an explanation of the effect, further show that the manner in which ownership is achieved affects the valuation of objects. These researchers found an endowment effect when subjects attributed ownership to their own performance rather than when ownership was attributed to chance; also, an endowment effect was obtained when ownership was attributed to performance that was exemplary, but not when performance was poor.

Group Endowment Effect

Carnevale and Radhakrishnan (1994, Experiment 2) conducted a study to test the idea that the endowment effect identified by Kahneman et al. varies with culture and with whether or not the object owned is owned by the individual (as in Kahneman et al.'s study) or by the group. The key ideas were to separate an individual endowment effect from a group endowment effect and to see if these effects vary for allocentric and idiocentric subjects. Can culture influence the effect of reference positions on preferences?

Subjects came to the laboratory with a friend or alone, to participate in a study of "consumer preferences." About half of the subjects were U.S. citizens and native English speakers, whereas the others, mostly students from Korea, were nonnative English speakers. The method was similar to that used by Kahneman et al. (1990, Experiment 8).

Subjects in the seller role were told:

You now own the object in your possession that is on the table in front of you. You have the option of selling it if a price, which will be determined later, is acceptable to you. For each of the possible prices below indicate whether you wish to: (1) Sell your object and receive this price or (2) keep your object and take it home with you. For each price indicate your decision by marking an X in the appropriate column.

Subjects in the buyer role were told:

You do not own the object that you see on the table in front of you. You have the option of buying one if a price, which will be determined later, is acceptable to you. For each of the possible prices below indicate whether you wish to: (1) Pay this price and receive an object to take home with you or (2) not buy an object at this price. For each price indicate your decision by marking an X in the appropriate column.

The group versus individual endowment conditions were crossed with the buyer/seller roles. In the group case, two subjects, who were friends, were asked to answer the questions together. In the individual case, the procedure was identical to that used by Kahneman et al., except that the subject was in a room alone and not in a large classroom with other subjects.

The subjects were told to look at a pen on the table in front of them and make their judgments; then they were shown a bag of M&Ms and asked to make the judgments again (the order of the ratings of the two items was counterbalanced). The response format was a modified form of the one that was used in the Kahneman et al. (1980) study:

——— TABLE 14.3 ———
Buying and Selling Prices as a Function of Individual
and Group Ownership, and Collectivism and Individualism

| | Collectivist | | Individualist | |
	Sell	Buy	Sell	Buy
Individual	1.18	.90	1.05	.40
Group	1.38	.86	.99	.84

SOURCE: Partial data from Carnevale and Radhakrishnan (1994, Experiment 2).

At a price of $8.75 I will buy _ I will not buy _
At a price of $8.25 I will buy _ I will not buy _

and so on, or

At a price of $8.75 WE will sell _ WE will not sell _
At a price of $8.25 WE will sell _ WE will not sell _

and so on.

Table 14.3 shows data on a measure of buying and selling prices set by groups and individuals for the pen. As can be seen, an individual endowment effect that replicated the Kahneman et al. (1990) data was obtained, but this effect was present only for idiocentric subjects. There was no significant individual endowment effect for the allocentric subjects. Also, there was a group endowment effect for allocentric subjects, but not for idiocentric subjects. (These groups were defined through median split on the attitude measure, as in Experiment 1.) The data in Table 14.3 suggest that for allocentrics, loss aversion is greater for groups than for individuals; for idiocentrics, loss aversion is greater for individuals than it is for groups.

Additional analyses suggest that the divisibility of the object owned was an important moderator variable, with the idiocentric subjects showing a group endowment effect for the package of M&Ms, which, of course, could be opened and shared.

Conclusions

Culture may be important at all phases of negotiation, including concession making and the likelihood of agreement (Chan et al., 1994). The studies reported in this chapter emphasize its importance in the preference formulation process. Different cultural groups—individualists and collectivists—may value objects to be negotiated differently depending on whether the objects are defined as group property or individual property.

A key question is, How is property construed? How people view property may differ across cultural contexts (see Rudman, 1988, 1991). For example, land in collectivist cultures often has meanings associated with ancestors and sacredness, whereas in individualist cultures people buy and sell land freely. Veblen (1899) tells us that individual ownership is a dominant feature of economic systems, and that primitive societies that lack systems of individual ownership are among the most peaceable (p. 24). Hui and Triandis (1986) have shown that collectivism clusters on seven categories that include "sharing of material and nonmaterial resources." The results of Carnevale and Radhakrishnan's (1994) work suggest that property is valued in the context of person and culture characteristics, and this can influence negotiation behavior.

The traditional dominant theoretical paradigm that underlies behavioral approaches to theory and research on negotiation should be expanded (Carnevale & Pruitt, 1992; Pruitt & Carnevale, 1993). In the traditional paradigm, the parties, whether individuals or groups, are treated as unitary decision makers with preferences that are guided by self-interest. This paradigm is shown schematically in Figure 14.1A. Conditions that prevail at the time of negotiation are assumed to have an impact on psychological states, such as motives, perceptions, and cognitions (path A in Figure 14.1A). These states, in turn, have either a direct impact on outcomes (path B) or an impact that is mediated by the strategies and tactics chosen by the parties (paths C and D).

The traditional paradigm has been a good starting point for the development of theory and research, but it is overly simplistic. It does not come to grips with the social context of negotiation. It overlooks important phenomena such as social norms, relationships between negotiators, group decision processes, and the behavior of third parties (Pruitt & Carnevale, 1993). And it ignores cultural variables and the preference formulation process concerning the issues at hand—for example, whether they involve property that is owned by the group or by the individual.

It is important to develop a theory of negotiation that allows for cultural variation. A mature theory should also help us to understand what happens in negotiations between representatives of different cultures and how to overcome the problems in such negotiations (Dupont & Faure, 1991). A modified model, the *culture negotiation paradigm,* is presented in Figure 14.1B. Conditions that prevail at the time of negotiation are assumed to have impacts on both psychological states (path A1 in Figure 14.1B) and cultural variables that may activate and be relevant. These psychological states and cultural variables may interact, and each may, in turn, have either a direct impact on outcomes (path B1 or B2) or an impact that is mediated by the strategies and tactics chosen by the parties (paths C1, C2, and D). For example, one condition that may

A. The common negotiation paradigm:

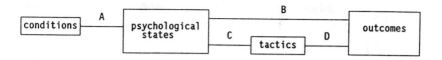

B. The culture negotiation paradigm:

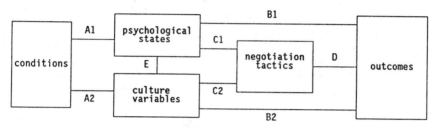

Figure 14.1. The General Negotiation Paradigm

prevail at the time of negotiation is whether the negotiation entails individually owned property or group-owned property. This may activate a culturally relevant variable such as group-based self-concept, which may affect loss aversion, a psychological state, and thus affect positions taken in the negotiation.

In this sense, culture is defined as a mediating variable, not a moderator variable. This is predicated on the notion that cultural analyses of negotiation are particularly useful to the extent that they can implicate processes that have explanatory power. Too often, efforts to understand culture in negotiation have involved efforts to characterize the negotiation styles found in various nations, in the absence of explanation. The point is, it is not so meaningful to say that people in country X do "this" and people in country Y do "that." Rather, we should specify the underlying theoretical processes that distinguish the two groups on the relevant measure. It is these processes that we want to generalize.

References

Allison, S. T., Messick, D. M., & Goethals, G. R. (1989). On being better but not smarter than others: The Muhammad Ali effect. *Social Cognition, 7,* 275-296.

Beggan, J. K. (1992). On the social nature of nonsocial perception: The mere ownership effect. *Journal of Personality and Social Psychology, 62,* 229-237.

Billings, D. K. (1991). Cultural style and solutions to conflict. *Journal of Peace Research, 28,* 249-262.

Carnevale, P. J., & Pruitt, D. G. (1992). Negotiation and mediation. *Annual Review of Psychology, 43,* 531-582.

Carnevale, P. J., & Radhakrishnan, P. (1994). *Group endowment and the theory of collectivism.* Unpublished manuscript, University of Illinois at Urbana-Champaign, Department of Psychology.

Carnevale, P. J., & Triandis, H. C. (1993). *Culture and negotiation behavior* (National Science Foundation Grant No. SBR-9210536). Urbana: University of Illinois, Department of Psychology.

Chan, D. K.-S., Triandis, H. C., Carnevale, P. J., Tam, A., & Bond, M. H. (1994). *Comparing negotiation across cultures: Effects of collectivism, relationship between negotiators, and concession pattern on negotiation behavior.* Unpublished manuscript, University of Illinois at Urbana-Champaign, Department of Psychology.

Cushman, J. H. (1994, September 30). Congress ends bid for a mining tax. *New York Times,* p. A1.

Dupont, C., & Faure, G. (1991). The negotiation process. In V. A. Kremenyuk (Ed.), *International negotiation: Analysis, approaches, issues* (pp. 40-57). San Francisco: Jossey-Bass.

Gould, W. B., IV. (1986). The idea of the job as property in contemporary America: The legal and collective bargaining framework. *Brigham Young Law Review, 1986,* 885-918.

Gulliver, P. H. (1988). Anthropological contributions to the study of negotiations. *Negotiation Journal, 4,* 247-255.

Heider, F. (1958). *The psychology of interpersonal relations.* New York: John Wiley.

Hofstede, G. (1980). *Culture's consequences: International differences in work-related values.* Beverly Hills, CA: Sage.

Hofstede, G. (1991). *Culture and organizations: Software of the mind.* London: McGraw-Hill.

Hui, C. H., & Triandis, H. C. (1986). Individualism and collectivism: A study of cross-cultural researchers. *Journal of Cross-Cultural Psychology, 17,* 225-248.

Huie, B. (1987, September). Cross-cultural conflict on the Texas Gulf Coast. *Dispute Resolution Forum,* p. 8.

James, W. (1890). *The principles of psychology* (Vol. 1). New York: Henry Holt.

Kahneman, D., Knetsch, J., & Thaler, R. (1990). Experimental tests of the endowment effect and the Coase theorem. *Journal of Political Economy, 98,* 1325-1348.

Kelley, H. H., Sure, G. H., Deutsch, M., Faucheux, C., Lanzetta, J. T., Moscovici, S., Nuttin, J. M., & Rabbie, J. M. (1970). A comparative study of negotiation behavior. *Journal of Personality and Social Psychology, 16,* 411-438.

Kuhn, T. S. (1962). *The structure of scientific revolutions.* Chicago: University of Chicago Press.

Loewenstein, G., & Issacharoff, S. (1994). *Source-dependence in the valuation of objects.* Unpublished manuscript, Carnegie Mellon University, Department of Social and Decision Sciences.

Lukes, S. (1973). *Individualism.* Oxford: Basil Blackwell.

Markus, H., & Kitayama, S. (1991). Culture and self: Implications for cognition, emotion, and motivation. *Psychological Review, 98,* 224-253.

Nuttin, J. M., Jr. (1985). Narcissism beyond gestalt and awareness: The name letter effect. *European Journal of Social Psychology, 15,* 353-361.

Nuttin, J. M., Jr. (1987). Affective consequences of mere ownership: The name letter effect in twelve European languages. *European Journal of Social Psychology, 17,* 381-402.

Pruitt, D. G. (1981). *Negotiation behavior.* New York: Academic Press.

Pruitt, D. G., & Carnevale, P. J. (1993). *Negotiation in social conflict*. Pacific Grove, CA: Brooks/Cole.

Riding, A. (1993, September 29). Return of booty protested in France. *New York Times*, p. B3.

Roth, A. E., Prasnikar, V., Okuno-Fujiwara, M., & Zamir, S. (1991). Bargaining and market behavior in Jerusalem, Ljubljana, Pittsburgh, and Tokyo: An experimental study. *American Economic Review, 81*, 1068-1095.

Rudman, F. W. (1988). Dominance, social control, and ownership: A history and a cross-cultural study of motivations for private property. *Behavioral Science Research, 22*, 130-160.

Rudman, F. W. (Ed.). (1991). To have possessions: A handbook on ownership and property [Special issue]. *Journal of Social Behavior and Personality, 6*(2).

Trafimow, D., Triandis, H. C., & Goto, S. (1991). Some tests of the distinction between the private and the collective self. *Journal of Personality and Social Psychology, 60*, 649-655.

Triandis, H. C. (1994). *Culture and social behavior*. New York: McGraw-Hill.

Veblen, T. (1899). *The theory of the leisure class: An economic study of institutions*. New York: Macmillan.

Webb, S., & Webb, B. (1914). *Industrial democracy*. London: Longman.

Author Index

Subject Index

About the Contributors

Max H. Bazerman (B.S.E., University of Pennsylvania; M.S., Ph.D., Carnegie-Mellon University) is J. Jay Gerber Distinguished Professor of Dispute Resolution and Organizations at the J. L. Kellogg Graduate School of Management at Northwestern University. His research focuses on decision making, negotiation, fairness, social comparison processes, and environmental decision making and dispute resolution. He is author or coauthor of more than 90 research articles, and author, coauthor, or coeditor of seven books, including *Judgment in Managerial Decision Making* (3rd ed., 1994), *Cognition and Rationality in Negotiation* (with M. A. Neale, 1991), and *Negotiating Rationally* (with M. A. Neale, 1992). His former doctoral students have taken professorial positions at leading business schools throughout the United States, including Northwestern, Duke, Cornell, Harvard, and the University of Chicago.

Sally Blount is Assistant Professor of Behavioral Science at the University of Chicago's Graduate School of Business. Her research focus is in the areas of negotiations and social decision making. Her work has included the study of negotiation behavior in dyadic fixed-sum bargaining tasks and social dilemmas, the study of individual behavior under social versus environmental attributions, and the effect of social comparison processes on choice. She received her Ph.D. in 1992 from the J. L. Kellogg Graduate School of Management at Northwestern University.

Peter J. Carnevale is Associate Professor in the Department of Psychology, University of Illinois, Urbana—Champaign. His current work focuses on culture in negotiation, cooperation in resource dilemmas, computer simulation of negotiation behavior, grievance behavior in organizations, and mediation of social conflict. He is coauthor, with Dean Pruitt, of *Negotiation in Social Conflict* (1993), and of the article "Negotiation and Mediation" in the 1992 *Annual Review of Psychology*.

Deborah I. Chapman is Associate Director of the School Leadership Project at Dartmouth College. Prior to this role she held positions at the Amos Tuck School of Business Administration at Dartmouth College and at the Stanford Graduate School of Business. She has degrees from Skidmore College and Pennsylvania State University. She has spent several years researching the relationship between negotiators from a broad, interdisciplinary perspective and has coauthored five papers presented at the Academy of Management's annual meetings. Her other area of scholarly interest is in the role of collaborative learning in organizational change.

Vittorio Girotto is a Researcher at the University of Trieste, where he studies deductive reasoning, counterfactual thinking, and decision making. He received a master's degree at Padua University and a Ph.D. at Bologna University (1987). He was a postdoctoral researcher at the University of Aix-en-Provence and a Researcher at the Institute of Psychology of the National Research Council in Rome from 1988 to 1992. He is the author of a monograph (in Italian), *Reasoning* (1994), and coeditor of the volume *Psychology of Thinking* (in press), in collaboration with P. Legrenzi. He has been a visiting fellow at CREA at the Ecole Polytecnique in Paris and at the Department of Psychology of Princeton University.

Leonard Greenhalgh is Professor of Management at the Amos Tuck School of Business Administration at Dartmouth College. He comes from a practitioner background, having worked as a manager in a multinational corporation, founded and run two small corporations, and worked full-time as a management consultant. He was born and raised in Great Britain and completed his education in the United States. He received a Ph.D. from Cornell University, building on an undergraduate education in engineering and science and an M.B.A. He has been at the Amos Tuck School since 1978 and has also taught at Stanford and Cornell. His teaching and research have concentrated on managing strategic relationships, particularly when these are strained by conflict. He has published articles on this topic in the *Academy of Management Journal, Journal of Conflict Resolution, Management Science, Group Decision and Negotiation,* and several other journals and edited books.

J. Richard Harrison is Associate Professor in the School of Management at the University of Texas at Dallas. He received his Ph.D. in organizational behavior from Stanford University. His research interests include organizational decision making, corporate governance and control, and computer simulation of organizational processes.

Roderick M. Kramer is Associate Professor of Organizational Behavior at the Graduate School of Business, Stanford University, where he teaches courses in negotiation, group dynamics, and power and politics, as well as an introductory course on organizational behavior. Previously, he worked for several years as Program Director of the USC Norris Cancer Center's Cancer Information Service, and as Program Director of the UCLA Jonsson Cancer Center's Public and Patient Education Programs. He earned his Ph.D. in social psychology from UCLA. His research focuses primarily on decision making in various kinds of conflict situations, such as social dilemmas, negotiations, and international conflicts. Most recently, his research has focused on the role of cognitive illusions in negotiation, small group conflicts, and resource management dilemmas in organizations. He has written more than 40 scholarly articles that have appeared in such journals as the *Journal of Personality and Social Psychology, Journal of Experimental Social Psychology, Journal of Conflict Resolution,* and *Organizational Behavior and Human Decision Processes.*

Laura Kray is currently working toward her doctoral degree in social psychology at the University of Washington. She received her bachelor of arts degree at the University of Michigan in 1993, concentrating on the study of organizational behavior. Her research interests include the study of group judgment and decision processes, negotiation, and procedural justice in organizations. She has presented her research at the meetings of the International Association for Conflict Management.

Richard P. Larrick is Assistant Professor of Behavioral Science at the University of Chicago's Graduate School of Business. He received a Ph.D. in social psychology from the University of Michigan in 1991, and was a Visiting Assistant Professor and postdoctoral fellow at Northwestern University's J. L. Kellogg Graduate School of Management from 1991 to 1993. His principal areas of research interest are negotiation and judgment and decision making. In his previous research he has examined social and motivational aspects of decision making, such as avoidance of regret, and rationality in judgment and choice, such as people's use of cost-benefit reasoning in everyday decisions.

Edward J. Lawler is Professor of Organizational Behavior in the School of Industrial and Labor Relations at Cornell University. He received his Ph.D. in sociology at the University of Wisconsin—Madison in 1972 and was a faculty member in the Department of Sociology at the University of Iowa for more than 20 years before moving to Cornell in 1994. He is the current editor of

Social Psychology Quarterly and the series editor of *Advances in Group Processes.* He is coauthor, with Samuel B. Bacharach, of *Power and Politics in Organizations* (1980) and *Bargaining* (1981). In addition to continuing work on commitment in exchange (with Jeongkoo Yoon), he is completing a project on the effectiveness of unilateral initiatives as tactics for resolving impasses in explicit bargaining.

Elizabeth A. Mannix is Associate Professor of Behavioral Science in the Center for Decision Research at the Graduate School of Business of the University of Chicago. She holds a Ph.D. from the Committee on Social and Organizational Psychology at the University of Chicago. Her research interests focus on dyadic and multiparty negotiation, power and coalition formation, social dilemmas in organizations, and the effects of time on negotiation and decision making. She has published articles in *Organizational Behavior and Human Decision Processes, Journal of Personality and Social Psychology, Journal of Applied Psychology,* and the *Journal of Experimental Social Psychology.*

David M. Messick is the Morris and Alice Kaplan Professor of Ethics and Decision in Management in the J. L. Kellogg Graduate School of Management of Northwestern University. He received his B.A. degree in psychology from the University of Delaware and his M.A. and Ph.D. degrees in psychology from the University of North Carolina, Chapel Hill. He served on the faculty of the University of California, Santa Barbara, for more than 25 years before joining the Northwestern faculty in 1992. He is an experimental social psychologist who has published extensively on a variety of problems having to do with decision making in social environments. He has served as associate editor and editor of the *Journal of Experimental Social Psychology.* He has been awarded two Fulbright grants for research and teaching in the Netherlands, as well as an East-West Exchange Fellowship from the National Academy of Science for research in Budapest in 1990. In 1986, he was selected as the Distinguished Alumnus of the Department of Psychology of the University of North Carolina. His current research and teaching involves the application of psychological theory and methods to the study of ethical aspects of business decision making.

Michael W. Morris is Assistant Professor of Organizational Behavior at the Stanford University Graduate School of Business. He obtained a B.A. in English literature and cognitive science from Brown University. As a doctoral student in cognitive and social psychology at the University of Michigan, he conducted research on the cognitive processing of events and causal relationships. His dissertation, which investigated cultural differences in causal attribution, received the 1993 Award from the Society for Experimental Social Psychology.

His current research addresses a cluster of related topics, including causal cognition in social conflict, cultural differences in perception of organizational conflict and injustice, the role of interpersonal rapport in conflict resolution, and the role of counterfactual reasoning in learning.

J. Keith Murnighan is the W. J. Van Dusen Chair of Management and Professor in the Faculty of Commerce at the University of British Columbia in Vancouver. He received his Ph.D. in social psychology from Purdue University in 1974, and taught at the University of Illinois for 19 years before moving to UBC. His research focuses on negotiation and interpersonal interaction, and currently addresses altruism, ethics, fairness, cooperation, self-interest, repentance, and the competitive urge. He has published articles in more than 20 different journals, primarily in the fields of organizational behavior, social psychology, and economics. His recent books include *Bargaining Games: A New Approach to Strategic Thinking in Negotiations* (1992) and an edited volume, *Social Psychology in Organizations: Advances in Theory and Research* (1993). He currently serves as associate editor of *Administrative Science Quarterly*.

Margaret A. Neale is the J. L. and Helen Kellogg Distinguished Professor of Dispute Resolution and Organizations at the J. L. Kellogg Graduate School of Management at Northwestern University. Her major research interests include bargaining and negotiation, the allocation of burdens and benefits, behavioral decision theory, the collaborative process, and the impact of relationships on organizational decision makers. She is the author of more than 60 articles on these topics, and is coauthor of three books: *Organizational Behavior: A Management Challenge* (with G. B. Northcraft; 2nd ed., 1994), *Cognition and Rationality in Negotiation* (with M. H. Bazerman; 1991), and *Negotiating Rationally* (with M. H. Bazerman; 1992).

Erika Peterson is a doctoral student in social psychology at the University of Washington; she plans to receive her degree in 1996. She received her undergraduate degree with high honors in psychology from the University of Michigan. She has collaborated on research on team negotiations, on relationships in negotiation, and on personal evaluations of life events, and has presented papers at meetings of the Academy of Management, the International Association for Conflict Management, and Judgment and Decision Making.

Madan M. Pillutla will complete his Ph.D. in organizational behavior at the University of British Columbia in 1995. He holds an M.S. in organizational behavior, a master's degree in human resources management, and a B.E. in mechanical engineering. His research interests focus on negotiation, institutional theory, and subtle forms of organizational communication. His dissertation addresses the interplay of power, fairness, justice, and normative constraints within ultimatum bargaining. Some of his work will soon appear in the *Academy of Management Journal*.

Jeffrey T. Polzer is Assistant Professor of Management in the Graduate School of Business at the University of Texas at Austin. He received his Ph.D. from the J. L. Kellogg Graduate School of Management at Northwestern University. His current research interests include group identification, intergroup relations, conflict resolution and negotiation, and decision making in social dilemma contexts.

Dean G. Pruitt is Distinguished Professor in the Department of Psychology at the State University of New York at Buffalo. He received his Ph.D. from Yale University. He is author or coauthor of *Negotiation Behavior; Social Conflict: Escalation, Stalemate, and Settlement*; and *Negotiation in Social Conflict*. He is editor or coeditor of *Theory and Research on the Causes of War* and *Mediation Research: The Process and Effectiveness of Third-Party Intervention*. He is a Fellow of the American Psychological Association and the American Psychological Society. In 1992, he received the Harold D. Lasswell Award for Distinguished Scientific Contribution to Political Psychology from the International Society of Political Psychology, and in 1994 he received the Award for Significant Contribution to Conflict Management Literature from the *International Journal of Conflict Management*. He has been President of the International Association for Conflict Management and Vice President of the International Society of Political Psychology.

Robert J. Robinson is a faculty member of the Harvard Business School, where he teaches negotiation skills and decision analysis, and the author of numerous academic and business articles. He grew up in South Africa, where he completed a B.Com., B.A., and M.A. He worked as an internal consultant facilitator, emphasizing job redesign, quality programs, and cultural change, before completing a Ph.D. in social psychology in 1991 at Stanford University, specializing in group conflict. His various research projects center on issues of conflict, negotiation, and ideology. He has also published on workplace legal and health issues. His current focus is a long-term study called "The Conflict-Competent Organization," which is concerned with looking at forces that will place growing stress on traditional organizational management skills and that will increase workplace conflict, leading to the need for specific conflict competencies, particularly negotiation skills.

Charles D. Samuelson is Associate Professor in Industrial and Organizational Psychology at Texas A&M University. He received his B.S. degree in psychology from Tufts University and M.A. and Ph.D. degrees from the University of California at Santa Barbara. His research interests center on the broad topic of social interdependence and decision making, including social dilemmas, resource allocation, group processes, and resource conservation. His current work investigates both cognitive and normative influences on the sharing rules used by groups to allocate common resources.

Pri Pradhan Shah is Assistant Professor at the Carlson School of Management, University of Minnesota. She received her doctoral degree in organizational behavior from the J. L. Kellogg Graduate School of Management at Northwestern University. Her research interests include negotiation, decision making, and relationships.

Damien L. H. Sim is currently a doctoral student at the Stanford University Graduate School of Business. He graduated from the University of California at Los Angeles in 1992 with a B.A. in psychology and business economics. Prior to attending UCLA, he served as an officer in the Singapore Armed Forces. At Stanford, he has been researching counterfactual thinking processes and decision-making processes. He is currently investigating the role of cognitive reference points in consumer decisions about prices.

Leigh Thompson (Ph.D., Northwestern University, 1988) is Associate Professor of Psychology at the University of Washington. Her current research, funded by the National Science Foundation, examines social judgment processes in negotiation, social relationships in group decision making, and information and communication in competitive decision making. In 1991, she received an NSF Presidential Young Investigator Award; she is currently a fellow at the Center for Advanced Study in the Behavioral Sciences. She has published articles in such journals as *Psychological Bulletin, Journal of Personality and Social Psychology,* and *Organizational Behavior and Human Decision Processes,* and she is working on a book titled *Social Psychological Principles in Negotiation.*

Stephanie L. Woerner received her M.B.A. from the University of Texas at Austin and recently received her Ph.D. in organizational behavior from the Graduate School of Business at Stanford University. She is currently pursuing independent research in the Boston area. Her research interests include social comparisons in organizations, effects of identity-enhancing and identity-threatening information on the individual, influences on cooperation between individuals, and structural influences and social categorization processes in organizations. Her dissertation research examined the effects of unmet and

NEGOTIATION AS A SOCIAL PROCESS

exceeded performance expectations on social comparisons and the role of dispositional variables such as positive affect and self-esteem in comparisons.

Jeongkoo Yoon is a postdoctoral research associate in the Department of Organizational Behavior of the School of Industrial and Labor Relations at Cornell University. He received his Ph.D. in sociology from the University of Iowa in May 1994. His research interests are in the areas of social exchange, commitment to organizations, power processes, and social dilemmas. He is working with Edward Lawler on the development and testing of a theory based on the research reported in their chapter in this volume. He has published papers in *American Sociological Review* (with Edward J. Lawler), *Advances in Group Processes* (with Edward J. Lawler, Mouraine Baker, and Michael Large), and *Human Relations* (with Mouraine Baker and Jong-Wook Ko).